Basic Computer Engineering

Basic Computer Engineering

Dr. N. K. Tiwari, Scientist

Principal

Bansal College of Engineering, Bhopal

Dr. D. K. Swami

Director

VNS, Group of Institutions, Bhopal

BSP BS Publications

A unit of **BSP Books Pvt. Ltd.**

4-4-309/316, Giriraj Lane, Sultan Bazar,

Hyderabad - 500 095 - TG

Phone : 040 - 23445605, 23445688

Published by

 **BS Publications**

A unit of **BSP Books Pvt. Ltd.**

4-4-309/316, Giriraj Lane, Sultan Bazar,

Hyderabad - 500 095 – TG, INDIA

Phone : 040 - 23445605, 23445688

e-mail : info@bspbooks.net

www.bspbooks.net

ISBN: 978-93-85433-59-7 (HB)

Preface

Use of computers has become seemingly ubiquitous. Advancements in computer technology are making all efforts to make software so user friendly, that even a layman should utilize its potential to the fullest. Yet, to appreciate the technology truly one should know the fundamentals of computer engineering. Hence, the subject has been rightly included in initial years of engineering education by many universities. Fundamentals of computer engineering are equally important in other disciplines too, so that they use computers effectively in their own domains.

Growth of computer hardware and software technology has been tremendous since the inception of this versatile gadget. Study of computer science and engineering is very logical. Once building blocks of computer technology are introduced, then only one can learn the advance concepts.

This book covers all the essential fundamentals. With an introduction to basic hardware needed for input-output, storage and processing, it also covers operating systems concepts. Software types, MS office, fundamentals of programming, data structures and concepts of object oriented programming have been covered up to adequate details. Database is core to any modern application software; Data Base Management System has been covered concisely. Computer networks is breaking all barriers today, from wired networking in advance computer labs, it has reached up to the levels of common handy gizmos. With information technology flourishing and touching the lives of people, security hazards have also been surfacing. This book covers essentials of networking and basic security issues. On one hand book presents historical development of computers, on the other it touches Cloud computing, the latest paradigm related to internet based development and services.

Authors have tried to leverage their teaching experience to keep the language and tone in tune with learning the subject as a first course in computer science.

-Author

Contents

Chapter 1
An Introduction to Computers

Chapter 2

History of Computer

Chapter 3

Classification of Computers

Chapter 4

The System Concept

Chapter 5

Fundamentals of Operating System

Chapter 6

Microsoft Office

Chapter 7

Programming Concepts

Chapter 8

Programming Languages

Chapter 9

Program Design

Chapter 10

Fundamentals of Programming in C++

Chapter 11

Object Oriented Programming in C++

Chapter 12

Data Structures

Chapter 13

Computer Networks

Chapter 14

Computer Security

Chapter 15

Data Base Management System

Chapter 16
Cloud Computing

CHAPTER 1

An Introduction to Computers

1.1 Introduction

Today computers have an important and widespread influence on our society. Every educated person should study the basic disciplines of computer operation and its application. A student must study the basics of fundamental. Wherever there are phenomena of interest to man, there can be a science to describe and explain those phenomena. Computer Science is therefore the study of computer and the phenomena requesting from their use. We can give a more specific definition of computer science after we describe a computer.

A Computer is a device capable of accepting information or data, processing the information, and providing the results as an output, more specifically, a computer can be described as follows:

Computer is a data processor machine that can perform substantial computation, including numerous arithmetic or logic operations, without intervention by a human operator during the processor. It may be defined as a device capable of solving problems by accepting data, performing described operations on the data, and supplying the results of these operations or

Computer is a programmable, multiuse machine that accept data – raw facts and figures and process, or manipulates, it into information we can use, such as summaries or totals.

A visual representation or schematic diagram (Fig. 1.1) shows how the computer processes the information.

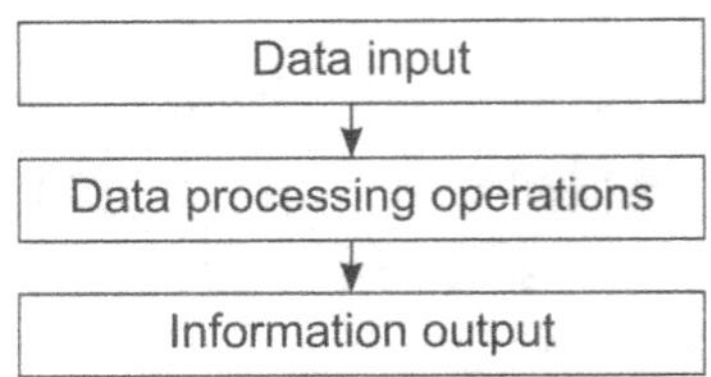

Fig. 1.1

1

1.2   Information Technology

Data communication, network and computer have brought a new technology, the information technology (IT). IT is the most powerful synthesis of computers and communications. Any information is useful only if it is accurate, relevant, precise and timely provide to the users. This would be possible, only when stored information is instantaneously retrievable at the time of need. Data receive from various sources and processing with the data, convert into information and forward it to other person or workstation. This is a networking environment.

Computer has become an indispensable tool, helping to shape the society it serves. The banking industry is an integrated part of the society, which has grown phenomenally since last three decades with manifold rise in its transactions and area of activities. Thus the role and utility of the computer and Information Technology cannot be over emphasized.

1.3   Comparison of Computer with Human Being

Computer and Human

- Have Memory
- Read Capability
- Perform arithmetic and logical calculation
- Manipulate symbols
- Make Comparisons

Human

- Make processing based on current situation
- Remember or read data from file
- Remember instructions for processing
- Write or speak out the output

Computer

- Hold program instruction in internal storage.
- Read data in machine readable form and store in the storage device.
- Make processing by choosing instruction based on comparison or an examination result at a point.
- Retrieve data from internal memory or secondary storage device.
- Output the results on an output device.

Comparison between Human and Computer

Character	Human	Computer
Speed of execution	Slow	Extremely fast
Continuous work	Poor	Excellent
Memory Retrieval	Inaccurate	Accurate
Accuracy	Make errors	No errors
Follow instructions	Perfect / Imperfect	Consistently
Ability to innovate	Good	Lacking

1.4   Characteristics of Computers

The vital characteristics of the computers are as follows:

Speed

Computer works on electrical pulses, which travel at incredible speeds and because the computer is an electronic device, its internal speed is instantaneous. An arithmetic calculation can be performed in a thousandth, millionth, billon thing even in a trillionth seconds. It is capable of executing over ten thousand instructions in a second.

Milli Sec. (ms)	-	1/1000 of second
Micro Sec (ms)	-	1/1000000 of second
Nano sec (ms)	-	1/1000000000 of second
Pico sec (ps)	-	1/1000,000,000,000

Storage

This is very important character of the computer, which separates it from other machine. The basic unit of storage is bit (acronyms of binary digit). The speed, at which computers perform, i.e. to input data and the instructions for processing, is humanly impossible. The storage space available in the central processing unit, being limited, large quantity of data and entire instructions of all the required programs cannot be stored in it. These are stored outside and read into the memory of CPU at the time of processing.

Bit	-	Smallest unit of storage
Nibble	-	4 Bits
Byte	-	8 Bits
KB	-	1024 bytes
MB	-	1024 KB
GB	-	1024 MB

Accuracy

Accuracy of the computers is consistently high. Errors in computing are due to machine failure, imprecise programming logic, inaccurate data, poorly designed systems. Precision is the degree of accuracy to which the computer gives the result. The precision of computers is phenomenal.

Versatility

Computers seem capable of performing almost any task, provided the task can be reduced to series of logical steps. It performs numeric and non-numeric tasks equally well. An algorithm, a step-by-step procedure, which applied to the problem, leads to solution. Programming is to convert this computer language to solve the problem.

Automation

Once a program is in the computer's memory, CPU allows the instructions until it meets the last instruction. Once the process had begun it would continue without human intervention until completion.

Diligence

Being a machine, a computer does not suffer from the human tracts of tiredness and lack of concentration. If millions of calculation are to be performed, computer performs all these calculations with the same speed and accuracy.

1.5   Limitations of Computers

The computer also has certain limitations, the computer works at very high speed and extremely accurate, this very characteristic becomes its limitation when a mistake over, because when a wrong instruction is issued, it excuses it with the same speed and accuracy that it would have executed with a right instruction. As a result, these are hardly any scope or time to recover.

The computers understand only instructions and cannot distinguish between suspicious and genuine customers. It does not posses and degree of intelligence and cannot take up even a simple action unless instructed to do so. It does not possess any morals, and therefore can be easily misused in the hands of a wrong individual. However, the computers never make any mistake or error. Errors whenever found are the computer based processing, due to human errors.

1.6   Information Processing and the Electronic Digital Computer

The electronic computer allows man to increase his productivity and permits him to do tasks he would be enabling to complete without computer. As we discussed above, the computer is a machine capable of

- Accepting data
- Performing described operations on the data
- Providing the results of these operations.

Thus computer also permits man to improve his output permit of time, or productivity. We can say that the computer's two most important contributions as a tool are to increase.

I – Speed of the operation

II – Accuracy of the results.

Of course, when we consider these two factors, we realise that the computer enables us to accomplish tasks that we would probably never even attempt manually. For example, if the number of input data is greater than several million and the time necessary to accomplish a task is more than fifty years. We would probably never attempt it, yet it is just tasks that we can ask the computer to accomplish. The term electronic implies that the computer is powered by electrical and electronics devices rather than by mechanical ones or those affected by heat or air pressure. Here digital refers to discrete non-continues quantities, as contrasted with continuous quantities.

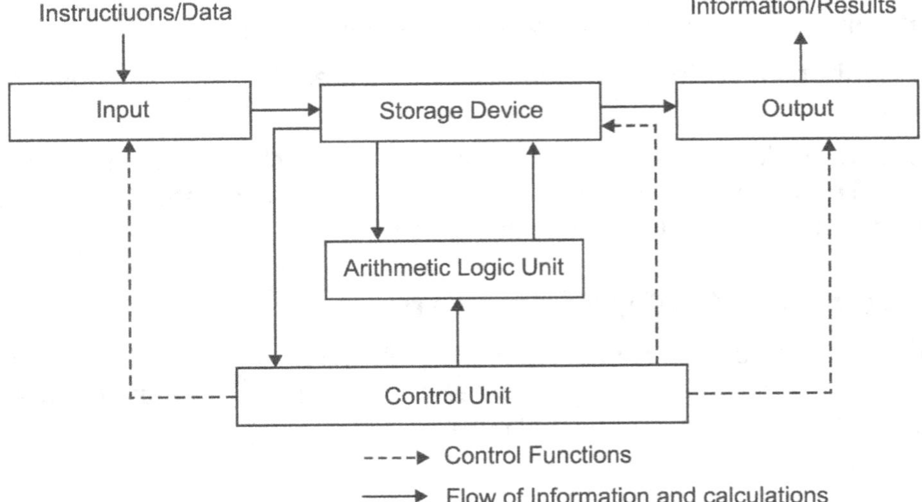

Fig. 1.2 Information Processing in Electronic Digital Computer

Electronic Digital computer is an information-processing device that accepts and processes data represented by discrete symbols. It is constructed primarily of electric or electronic devices.

We can use the computer to process the input data by sorting them, or by series of planned actions and operations open input taken may be illustrated by a common data processing operation which a person usually accomplishes manually, but which is increasingly accomplished automatically by data processing service companies. These processing works required:

- Data input
- Storage and retrieval of data
- Arithmetic Steps
- Output of result
- Control of all steps.

A Computer follows a similar process. It is composed of five basic units (Fig. 1.2).

Input unit: input data and instructions.

Storage or Memory unit: In which computer instructions and data as well as intermediate results are stored.

Arithmetic logic unit: In which mathematical operation can be performed and compare the numbers, results.

Output unit: provides the desired result in a suitable form.

Control unit: controls the data communication, operations and supervise overall operations of the computer.

The several devices are may accomplish the function of input, output and storages. The arithmetic and control functions are accomplished by the central processing unit located with storage in the pattern.

1.7   Components of the Computers

Computer is an electronic data processing machine. It is made up at various devices, which help you to enter date, process it and output the result. A computer system has three essential parts:

- Keyboard
- Central Processing Unit (CPU)
- Monitor

Block Diagram of a Computer

As shown in the block diagram (Fig. 1.3), the computer converts of three parts: Input device, CPU and output device. Keyboard, which is the input device, is connected to the central processing unit. Central processing unit consists of three sections memory, control unit and arithmetic logic unit

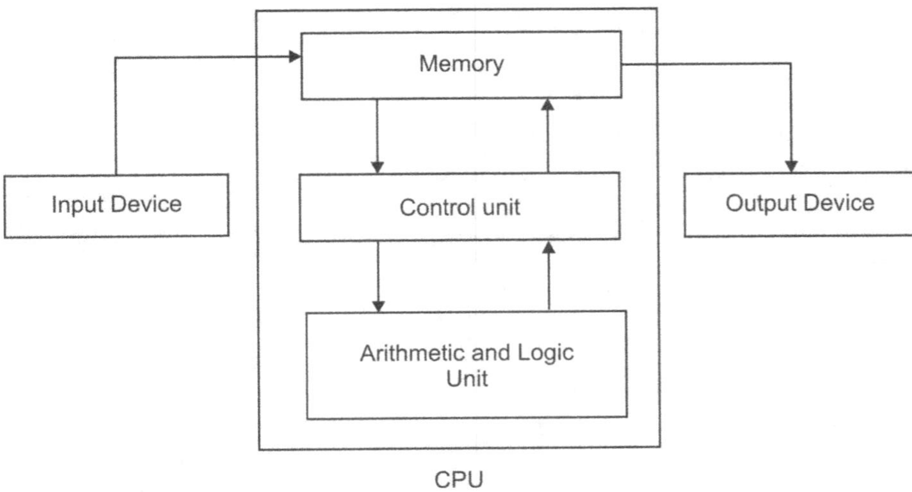

Fig. 1.3 Block diagram of computer

KEY BOARD: A common input device

Programs and data are entered into a computer through a keyboard, which is attached to a microcomputer or the terminal of a mini or large computer. A keyboard is similar to the keyboard of a type writer. It contains alphabets, digits, special characters and some control keys. When a key is pressed, an electronic signal is produced which is detected by an electronic circuit called keyboard encoder. A keyboard encoder may be special IC or a single chip microcomputer used as encoder. The function of an encoder is to detect which key has been pressed and send a binary code.

Central Processing Unit (CPU)

This is also called System unit, which is a technically known as Microprocessor (Fig. 1.4). CPU is the brain of computer.

It is made of three units:

1. Control unit   2. Arithmetic logic unit   3. Memory

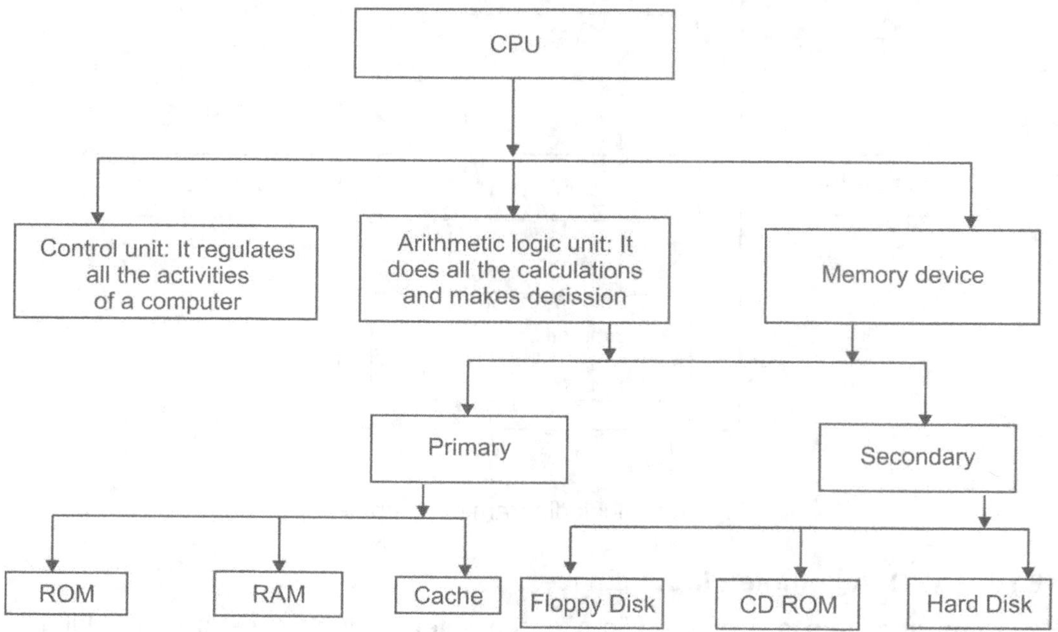

Fig. 1.4 Central Processing Unit with different Devices

- **Control unit:** The control section of the CPU maintains and directs the operations of the entire system. It acts like the central nervous system for all the components; though it does not process any data.

- **Arithmetic and logic unit (ALU):** The ALU processes the data entered all types of processing, mathematical calculation, comparison, decision making and processing of nonnumeric information takes place in ALU and data is once again moved to RAM

- **Memory:** Memory refers to the storage space in computer. Memory stores the data entered as well as the results given by the computer. Memory works on the application of binary system. The unit of memory is byte. Memory units can be divided into two sub-parts

    (a)   Primary storage   (b)   Secondary storage

Monitor: A common output device

Monitor also called video display units or CRTs, are output devices, shown programming instructions and data as they are input and after it is processed. Sometime a monitor is also referred to a video display terminal (VDT).

1.8   Registers

The register is the smallest high-speed storage area in the CPU. All data must be represented in a register before it can be processed.

1.9   Bus Architecture

Bus is a communication system that transfers data between different internal components of the computer, or between computers. This expression covers all related hardware components (wire, optical fiber, etc.) and software, including communication protocol.

Early computer buses were parallel electrical wires with multiple connections, Modern computer buses can use both parallel and serial connections. In serial bus, only one bit data transferred at a time amongst the various components while in parallel bus, several bits data transferred at a time amongst the various components. Bus can be wired in either a electrical parallel or daisy chain topology, or connected by switched hubs. The speed of bus measured in terms of number of bits transferred per second between two hardware components.

Bus can be divided into three types:

1. Control bus
2. Address bus
3. Data bus

1. **Control bus:** A control bus is a computer bus that is used by the CPU to communicate with devices that are contained within the computer. This occurs through physical connections such as cables or printed circuits.

   The CPU transmits a variety of control signals to components and devices to transmit control signals to the CPU using the control bus. One of the main objectives of a bus is to minimize the lines that are needed for communication. An individual bus permits communication between devices using one data channel. The control bus is bidirectional and assists the CPU in synchronizing control signals to internal devices and external components. It is comprised of interrupt lines, byte enable lines, read/write signals and status lines

2. **Data bus:** Data bus is used for transfer data amongst the different internal components. In recent computers 32 bit data buses available means buses can transfer 32 bits data at a time.

3. **Address bus:** An address bus is used to specify a physical address. When a processor or DMA-enabled device needs to read or write to a memory location, it specifies that memory location on the address bus (the value to be read or written is sent on the data bus). The width of the address bus determines the amount of memory a system can address. For example, a system with a 32-bit address bus can address 2^{32} (4,294,967,296) memory locations. If each memory address holds one byte, the addressable memory space is 4 GB. It is also known as memory bus.

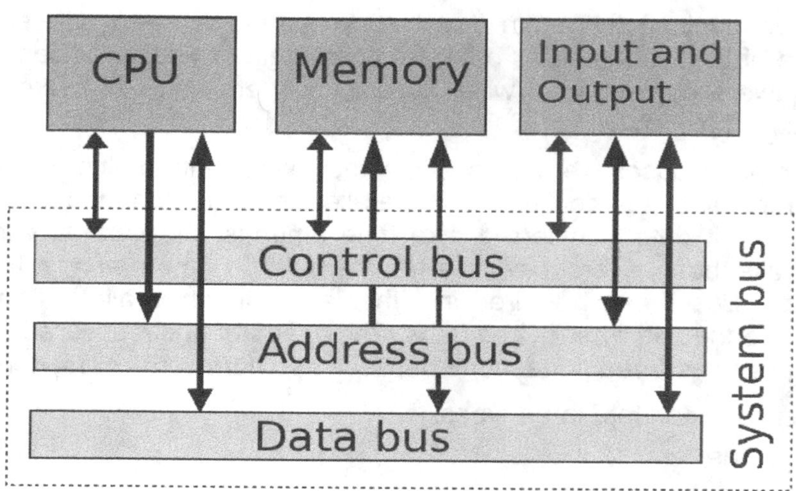

1.10　Instruction Set

Instruction set is a group of instruction that processor execute to perform various operation.

1.10.1 Classification of Instruction Set

A complex instruction set computer (CISC) has many specialised instructions, which may only be rarely used in practical programs. A reduced instruction set computer (RISC) simplifies the processor by only implementing instructions that are frequently used in programs; unusual operations are implemented as subroutines, where the extra processor execution time is offset by their rare use. Theoretically, important types are the minimal instruction set computer and the one instruction set computer, but these are not implemented in commercial processors. Another variation is the very long instruction word (VLIW) where the processor receives many instructions encoded and retrieved in one instruction word.

Complex instructions (CISC)

CISC processors include complex instructions in their instruction set. A single complex instruction does something that may take many instructions on other computers. Such instructions are typed by instructions that take multiple steps, control multiple functional units, or otherwise appear on a larger scale than the bulk of simple instructions implemented by the given processor. Some examples of complex instructions include:

- saving many registers on the stack at once
- moving large blocks of memory
- complex and/or floating-point arithmetic
- performing an automatic test-and-set instruction
- instructions that combine ALU with an operand from memory rather than a register

A complex instruction type that has become particularly popular recently is the SIMD or Single-Instruction Stream Multiple-Data Stream operation or vector instruction that is an operation that performs the same arithmetic operation on multiple pieces of data at the same time. SIMD have the ability of manipulating large vectors and matrices in minimal time. SIMD instructions allow easy parallelisation of algorithms commonly involved in sound, image, and video processing.

Reduced instruction set (RISC)

RISC is opposed to complex instructions can provide higher performance if this simplicity enables much faster execution of each instruction.

The general concept is that of a system uses a small, highly-optimized set of instructions, rather than a more specialsed set of instructions often found in other types of architectures. Another common trait is that RISC systems use the load/store architecture where memory is normally accessed only through specific instructions, rather than accessed as part of other instructions like.

The RSIC contains very few instructions from 0-100. It consists only frequently used instruction by the processor for the completion of program. The execution of these instructions is simple.

1.11 Computer Applications

The first digital computer was very costly and large sized and was used in military applications of calculating the speed of the ballistic missile. As computers have become less expensive, they are being used extensively in various areas of our lives. Computers have become ubiquitous in modern life. Computer can be used to get information about the location of a place in the map, reservation of tickets, books in a library, electronic mailing, banking, insurance, financial & weather forecasting, and entertainment, to name a few. Over the years, methods have been developed to allow computers to do things previously regarded as the exclusive domain of humans, for instance, read handwriting, play chess, or perform symbolic integration. The computer's characteristic as high speed of calculation, diligence, accuracy, reliability, and versatility has made it an integrated part in all business organizations. Some of the application areas of computers are discussed below.

- Computer Gaming
- Multimedia and Animation
- E-business
- Health Care
- Remote Sensing and Geographic Information System (GIS)
- Bio-Informatics
- Meteorology and Climatology

1.11.1 Computer Gaming

Computer gaming is one of the major important areas of Computer Applications. When computers were in its primitive stage, in the decade of 1950s, Tic-tac-toe and Tennis–for–two games were written by the programmers. It was envisioned very early that computers can be a great source of entertainment. Computer gaming today has shaped up as a multibillion dollar industry. In initial days games were designed and programmed by individual programmers. Slowly, with the advancement of hardware, computer gaming became popular and it became a huge commercial activity. Today a computer game project involves a big team, huge money and months or even years to complete it.

Computer games are being widely used for education and learning. Domain specific games are there for learning. There are games which can improve our typing skills, language skills, mathematical skills, general awareness and management skills etc. But as a matter of fact major commerce has been drawn by games for entertainment and fun.

Besides entertaining, computer games have been observed to be helpful in other areas too. Some hospitals have tried to subject their patients to computer games while dressing their wounds. Such patients felt less pain. Multi user online games, family games and LAN games have increased social activity. It is also claimed that computer gaming can improve visual skills for tasks like driving. Nowadays advanced games can track body movements of the player. Such games allow players to play games by using physical movements and help them to keep fit. Of course games are natural trainers; hence they are excellent education aid.

Major hazards of excessive computer gaming are; time wasters, being addicted to computer games, obesity, damage of ligament or nerves in the thumbs or fingers, sag in spine due to bad postures, immune to violent scenes, hooking to cyber world etc.

In present era, computer games entertain every age group of both male and female gender. Computer game players are broadly classified as casual players, professional or hardcore player and social game players.

Computer technology and computer games

Growth of the computer hardware such as processor speed, memory, graphics cards, display devices and interactive devices have significantly contributed to the advancement of computer games. Ultimately every computer game is software, essentially. Contemporary computer vendors had more or less similar hardware at any point of time but it is the developed game software and innovations that has given them edge over the others.

Computer gaming was started with devices with limited processing power, memory in Kilo Bytes, and ordinary graphics. Modern gaming is using 3D graphics, powerful multi-core processors, vast memories, multi button joysticks and movement measuring controlling devices. We are eyeing on utilizing cloud capabilities for easy resource sharing.

Initial computer games were solely developed by individual programmers. Modern computer gaming projects require teams comprising of programmers, story-writers, graphics and animation experts, sound specialists etc.

Personal Computer (PC) based Computer Games:

PC is a versatile machine with an easy upgradeability. PC has considerable advantage over consoles, such as:

- PCs are powerful machines with high processing speed and better graphics resolution.
- More memory and storage capacity
- Availability of mouse and keyboard
- Easy online connectivity.
- Being multi-utility device, PCs are widely available
- PC based games have taken lead on LAN gaming and online gaming. Its popular domain is MMORPG (Many Massive Multi-players Online Role Playing Games). Farmville is a popular game played together by millions on Face book, a social networking website.

Despite various advantages PCs pose serious challenges for game developers such as:

- Different PCs, may have different hardware configuration and operate on various platforms.
- It is a biggest challenge to hold on piracy of games.

Computer games are played on various devices. Game developer has to develop games for specific devices. Devices differ on various parameters. Be it played on any device with any name, ultimately it is software developed for that device. Video Games are also Computer Games. All devices on which computer games are played are also computers with some other forms. Other forms of computer games are presented below.

Arcade Machine Games

When computer games achieved initial commercial success, games were played on arcade machines. In market place there are specific machines on which computer games were played. As game parlour owners charge money on usage basis, games are required to be brief, easy to play and exciting. Player should always feel that next time, they can perform better. Such games are still very popular among kids and commonly available in Malls and Shopping arcades. The program developers have to consider all these factors for designing games for arcade machines.

Console Based Games: Console based games started their journey by gaming devices which are attached to the home TV, and cartridge containing various games were sold to be inserted into gaming device. Today, console based games have become very popular. These are dedicated gaming devices with state of the art configuration. These devices share maximum market share of computer gaming for following reasons.

- Game designers have to design games for specific machines with fixed hardware configuration, unlike Personal Computer games, where platform vary too much.
- It is easy to stop piracy of games, hence profitability is more.

Examples of recent console gaming devices are Play Station 3 by SONY, xBOX 360 by Microsoft and Nintendo's Wii etc.

Smart Phones, Tablets based computer gaming: Smart phones have brought revolution in games with their wide touch screens and online connectivity. Various independent developers offer downloadable game apps for smart phones like Apple's iPhone, android based and window based phones, that users can down load for free or on a nominal price. Computer games compatible to these devices even contribute to the sale of these devices. Modern tabs offer bigger screen and more powerful processors over smart phones and many a times share common games

Hand held Device based games: These are dedicated hand held devices for computer gaming. These are convenient to carry but lack power and display area size. Game designers also have the challenge to create exciting games with these limitations. Play Station Portable (PSP) is an example of device in this category. Hand held devised games have less market share.

1.11.2 Multimedia and Animation

Multimedia applications are most fascinating applications of computers. A Multimedia application is an application which uses a collection of multimedia. Multimedia is the field concerned with the computerized integration of text, graphics, drawings, images, video, animation, audio, and any other media where every type of information can be represented, stored, transmitted and processed digitally.

The mutimedia data is usually large as it involves audio and video. Processing mutimedia applications pose high overheads of storage, transfer bandwidth and processing. Exponential growth of computer technolgy have been able to support ever inceasing demands of multimedia applications. Softwre techniques like Data compression techniques have also greatly increased portability of mutimedia. Multimedia applications have brought revolution in the fields of Entertainment, Education, Corporate communications and refernce contents. Following are some typical multimedia applications that need computer and IT resources.

- World Wide Web
- Video conferencing
- Video-on-demand
- Interactive TV
- Games
- Virtual reality
- Digital video editing and production systems

Animations word relates to animating, that is giving life to objects. Animation is possible because an object seen by the human eye remains chemically mapped on the eye's retina for a brief time after viewing. Utilizing this fact animation is created by a series of slightly changed images shown in sequence within small time frames. Everybody knows Mickey Mouse, 50 years ago Walt Disney gave it life through animation. Animation requires high imagination acumen and it involved extreme hard work to achive in the absense of computers.

Computers have given great support to animation. Nowadays, computer animation is an independent field of study and has got great commercial activity. Animated cartoons, films have given life to imaginary characters using state of the art computers and technology. Jurassic Park, Beauty and the Beast, Toy Story, Shrek and Avtaar are popular animation films that have used computers to the fullest.

A still image from Avtaar animation Movie

There are many softwares like Flash, Director, Animator, Studio Max, SuperCard and that provide multimedia authoring and animation capabilites. Animation is a component of Multimedia technology. Computres have given momentum to the art and science of animation.

1.11.3 E-Business

E-Business or Electronic Business is the mode of business using information and communication technology. This includes the buying and selling of goods and services, along with providing technical or customer support through the Internet. E-commerce (electronic commerce) and M-Commerce (Mobile commerce) are the components of e-business. With the proliferation of internet technologies and expanding internet support infrastructure, e-business has got significant momentum in the past few years.

E-Business is known for online trading of products and services via world wide web or internet. On-line shopping is the core application of e-business.

On-line shopping advantages

E-shopping or on-line shopping reduces the channel of intermediate vendors. On-line shops run on computers using web technologies and do not require maintaining inventories of products. The products are usually supplied from distributor outlets. On-line shopping drastically reduces manpower cost as most of the tasks involved are taken care of by computer software. Some of the salient features of e-commerce through on-line shopping are presented below

- 24 x 7 shopping facility
- On-line updated catalogues
- No queues and crowds
- No requirement of carrying cash, on-line payment is facilitated
- Wide product range
- High availability of products
- Due to reduction of costs, on-line shops frequently offer discounts which shop owners are unable to match due to overheads

As the computer and internet is reaching to the masses, the e-shopping business is growing leaps and bounds. Some popular on-line shops are e-bay, flipkart, Amazon, homeshop18, naaptol and numerous others.

On-line Services Business

Computer users prefer to avail services as these saves their precious time. Banking, insurance, stock market updates, on-line bill payments are only a few amongst a plethora of services being offered on the internet.

E-advertising is a mode that is dominating prevalent modes of advertising. Google, everybody's essential tool, is the biggest service provider. Google has not charged a penny from its common end users and raised mammoth profits by e-advertisements.

With the popularity of cloud computing us of on-line services is expected to increase manifolds.

Other business support functions

In addition to providing on-line products and services there are many business activities where computers have significantly contributed. ERP solutions support the whole organization in functioning. ERP systems include modules to support all business functions. Even small business organizations need some back office support where computers have helped enormously. Some of them are listed below.

Marketing: Marketing is an essential component of a business comprising 4 Ps of Products, Promotions, Place and Price. Computer based marketing applications help managers to develop strategies that combine the four major elements of marketing.

Financial Accounting: Excellent benchmarked softwares are available to support timely finance and account management. Tally is a commonly used account software.

Forecasting: Computers have facilitated storing large amount of internal and external business data for the analysis and forecasting. Forecasting accuracy has increased with the use of specialized software. Sales forecasting is an important forecasting activity in business, among others.

Office Support: Modern offices are equipped with computer technologies to perform various tasks in an office system such as for document management system, message communication system, and office support systems.

1.11.4 Health Care

Computers and IT services have proved to be a boon for health care industry. The important applications of computers in health care are listed below.

Medical Records: In the past, organising, storing, and retrieval of medical records of patients were crucial tasks. Nowadays computers are efficiently used in health care to keep patient's records. These records can be patient files along with digital scans and X-rays. Computer databases provide an easy, low-space storage option for keeping a huge amount of information easily accessible to the medical staff members.

Computer Assisted Diagnosis: Sonography machines, CT Scanners and other technologically advanced scanners, function with the help of a computer. These automated machines assist doctors to diagnose obscure ailments with high degree of accuracy.

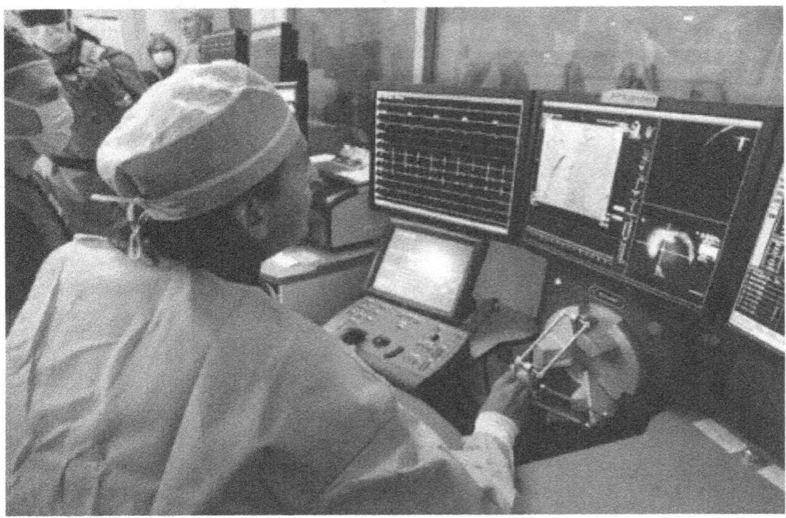

Minimally Invasive Surgery Tools: Nowadays minimally invasive surgeries with the help of computers are gaining advancement. These surgeries cut a small incision, and then place a small surgical tool with an attached camera inside the patient's body. This relieves the patient from a large surgical wound, and it helps in minimizing damage done to the body. Most of these minimally invasive tools use computers to drive the tools, and to relay images from inside the patient's body to provide a view to the doctors.

Internet Surgery: Internet Surgery makes use of fast Ethernet connections and robotic tools to perform the actual surgery. The surgeon does not have to be present in the room for this surgery to take place. The surgeon can be in any corner of the world and still feel exactly what he is doing, and looks at any tests he wants. With this technology, the surgeon can even practice the surgery before the actual surgery takes place.

Telemedicine: Telemedicine can be thought of as a specialised medical application which is concerned with providing medical care via remote communication links.

Medical Transcription: Medical transcription is a very rapidly growing IT enabled service industry. Medical transcription saves valuable time of busy doctors so that doctors can serve more patients. Medical transcriptionists help doctors from remote locations, by transcribing (typing) of doctor's reports from dictated audio files. The transcripts are maintained as patients visit details.

1.11.5 Use of computers in Remote Sensing & Geographic Information System

Remote sensing

Remote sensing is an extension of aerial photography which was prevailed for earth resources mapping and monitoring up to late seventies. The computers application facilitated the development of satellite borne systems and sensors for earth resources monitoring and promoted the technology of remote sensing for collection of information about the earth resources from space. Hence the remote sensing refers to technology and art of gathering the information (sensing) of earth resources from the large distance (Remote distance) and generally known as remote sensing technology.

Nowadays, remote sensing is widely utilized for mapping and monitoring of various earth resources like water (ocean, rivers and reservoirs etc), groundwater exploration and management, soil mapping, agriculture acreage assessment and crop health monitoring, Forest mapping and monitoring, Minerals exploration and mines mapping, Geological mapping, topographic and Geomorphologic mapping & applications, climatic and atmospheric monitoring and predictions, sea surface temperature mapping and tsunami prediction and early warning, Urban planning and sprawl mapping etc.

Computer technology and applications are essential at every stage of remote sensing technology:

1. **Satellite and sensor design, command and control:** The sensor design involves the computer application for optimization of sensors to discriminate various earth features and objects. The computers are extremely useful for sending commands to control the in-orbit satellite in space.

2. **Satellite borne data recording and storage:** Onboard Computers plays important roles in data recording in digital format and storage of data onboard.

3. **Satellite data transfer to earth stations:** Computer assisted communication enables the recorded data to send back to earth stations for further processing and use.

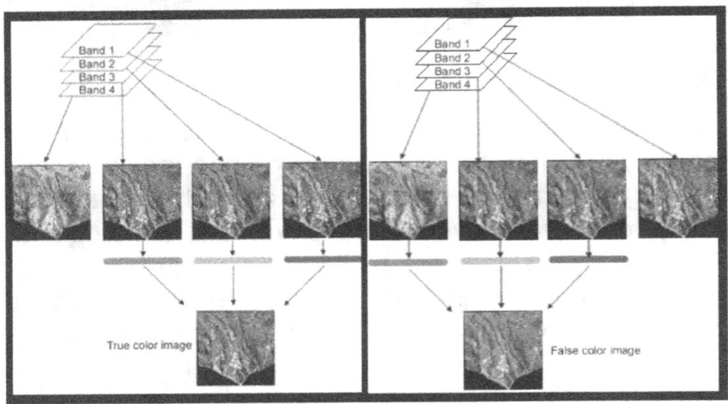

4. **Data processing for corrections and generations of final data in the form of imagery for end users:** The recoded raw data need some correction for compensations to atmospheric affects, and geometric irregularities in order to match the imagery data with real earth surface.

5. Computer based data/Image visualization and development and printing of photographic products. The satellite data available in digital format contains huge pixel data and with the help of Image processing software these can be seen on computer screen. The photographic image are also generated for further visual interpretation.

6. Computer aided data enhancement using various mathematical models in order to enhance the level of interpretation by maximizing differentiation among various earth objects/features.

7. Computer assisted identification of earth features and classification of various earth features like water, soil, vegetation, land use, human settlements, civil infrastructures planning, and mining, and navigation etc.

8. Generation of thematic mapping, a theme based map portraying informational database and useful for decision makers and monitoring and administrative agencies.

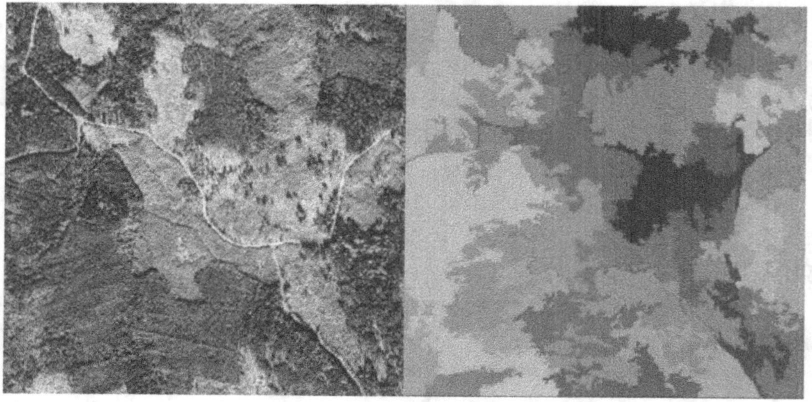

Geographic Information System (GIS)

Geographic Information System **(GIS)** is a computer system for performing geographical analysis. GIS has four interactive components: an input subsystem for converting into digital form (digitizing) maps and other spatial data; a storage and retrieval subsystem; an analysis subsystem; and an output subsystem for producing maps, tables, and answers to geographic queries. GIS is frequently used by environmental and urban planners, marketing researchers, retail site analysts, water resource specialists, and other professionals whose work relies on maps.

GIS has evolved, in part, from the work of cartographers, who produce two types of maps: general-purpose maps, which contain many different themes, and thematic maps, that focus on a single theme such as soil, vegetation, zoning, population density, or roads. These thematic maps are the backbone of the GIS because they provide a method of storing large quantities of fairly specific thematic content that can later be compared. This relatively simple yet versatile technique allowed cartographers to create and simultaneously view several thematic maps of a single geographical area. This system of overlays is a crucial element of GIS, which uses digital map layers rather than the transparent plastic sheets.

The arrival of the computer in the 1950s brought another essential component of GIS. By 1959 the American geographer Waldo Tobler had developed a simple model to harness the computer for cartography. His MIMO ("map in–map out") system made it possible to convert maps into a computer-usable form, manipulate the files, and produce a new map as the output. This innovation and its earliest descendants are generally classified as computerized cartography, but they set the stage for GIS.

In 1963 the English-born Canadian geographer Roger Tomlinson began developing what would eventually become the first true GIS in order to assist the Canadian government with monitoring and managing country's natural resources (Because of the importance of his contribution, Tomlinson became known as the "Father of GIS."). Tomlinson and others produced the first cartographic digital input device (digitizer) and the computer code necessary to perform data retrieval and analysis. They also developed the concept of explicitly linking geographic data (entities) and descriptions (attributes).

The two most common computer graphic formats are vector and raster, both of which are used to store graphic map elements. Vector-based GIS represents the locations of point entities as coordinate pairs in geographic space, lines as multiple points, and areas as multiple lines. Topographic surfaces are frequently represented in vector format as a series of non overlapping triangles, each representing a uniform slope. This representation is known as Triangulated Irregular Network (TIN). Map descriptions are stored as tabular data with pointers back to the entities. This allows the GIS to store more than one set of descriptions for each graphic map object.

1.11.6 Bioinformatics

Each living organism is formed from cells which is the basic structural and functional unit of life. Every cell has a complete set of instructions about making cells and their components. This set of instructions is known as genome. Thus, a genome can be thought of as the entire set of hereditary instructions required for building, running, and maintaining an organism, and passing life on to the next generation. The genome is made of a chemical called deoxyribonucleic acid or DNA. DNA's code is written using only four letters, A, C, G and T. As a sequence of alphabets makes a word, similarly, the meaning of DNA's code lies in the way the letters A, C, G, and T are arranged.

AGTCCGCGAATACAGGCTCGGT

Cells read the DNA sequence to make chemicals that a body needs. The genomic code breaks down into thousands of individual genes. Information from genes is given to cells to make the functional molecules called *proteins*, which have a unique chemical property. Proteins interact with each other to carry out thousands of functions, from digesting your dinner to synthesizing the small molecules that form a barrier between the inside of your cells and the outside world.

Computer Applications in Bioinformatics

Biologists want to collect all information about every gene in every genome, and from that information construct models of how genes work together to build up and maintain a living body. Availability of huge amount of biological data for experiments has become possible because of data has been made available on computers through Web. Analyzing this data to develop new models of how biological systems function, and for finding patterns to analyze new data sets is the work of bioinformatics. Bioinformaticians use many areas of computer science and engineering to process biological data. Complex machines are used to read in biological data at a much faster rate than before. Databases and information systems are used to store and organize biological data. Analyzing biological data may involve algorithms in artificial intelligence, soft computing, data mining, image processing, and simulation.

Major areas of applications of computer science and engineering in bioinformatics are as follows.

- **Signal Collection and Processing:** Signals collected from devices such as, DNA sequencers, CCD devices, spectrophotometers etc. are fed to computers (via an analog to digital converter) for further processing.
- **Analysis of DNA Sequence:** In bioinformatics, sequence analysis refers to the process of analysis of a DNA sequence to understand its features, function, structure, or evolution. Computers help in extracting patterns and rules from large data collections to characterize and predict features in new data. Nowadays, many computerized techniques and tools such as BLAST are available that provide sequence comparison (sequence alignment) with some known functions and analyze the alignment product to understand its biology.

- **Genome Annotation:** Within a genome, all of the nucleotides are not a part of genes. Large parts of the DNA do not serve any obvious purpose and hence is called junk-DNA. Annotation is another aspect of bioinformatics in sequence analysis and is the process of marking the genes and other biological features in a DNA sequence. Automatic computational methods such as GeneMark program assign functional meaning to uncharacterized data.

- **Evolutionary Biology:** Biological evolution is defined as any genetic change in a population that is inherited over several generations. It helps researchers to trace the evolution of organisms by measuring changes in their DNA and study of events such as gene duplication and horizontal gene transfer. Some computational softwares available to solve the above mentioned purpose are BEAST, CERVUS and MCALIGN.

- **Analysis of Mutations:** Genomes change between generations or over a lifetime. These changes are called mutations. Mutations come in many different shapes and sizes: a single letter may be changed, a whole segment of DNA sequence may be flipped over and reverse itself, or huge sections of the genome could be duplicated or deleted. A few of these changes can be seen under a high-powered microscope but must require techniques that can compare the sequence or activity of specific DNA segments. Software such as *Pyromaker* can detect genetic mutations and can aid in the diagnosis and selection of treatment for cancer mutation.

- **Modeling and Simulation:** For better understanding of biological processes, it is necessary to prepare a model and simulate it. It helps bioinformaticians in visualization of the complex biological networking. VANESA is powerful and easy to use modeling software through which scientists can automatically reconstruct important biomedical systems using the information available from databases.

1.11.7 Meteorology and Climatology

Meteorology is associated with routine weather prediction. The three basic aspects of meteorology are observation, understanding and prediction of weather. Modern computers and supercomputers facilitate weather prediction and forecasts. Numerical weather prediction uses complex computer programs known as forecasts models that run on super computers to provide predictions on atmospheric variables such as temperature, pressure, wind and rain fall.

Modern meteorologists have improved prediction accuracy by **numerical forecasting**, which uses mathematical equations to predict the weather. Such forecasting requires powerful computers and lots of observational data collected from land, sea and air. Collectively, all of these observations are huge. A normal computer would not be able to process this vast data. Meteorologists, nowadays, process this enormous data on supercomputers, millions of calculations per second. Thus computers have significant applications on meteorology.

Indian super computer PARAM YUVAII

Climatology is study of climate; this study is based on average values of weather records collected for a sufficiently longer duration. Climatologists use climate simulation models for simulation of past, present and future climates. This simulation again requires powerful computers.

Metrology and climatology differ in the sense that former predicts weather on daily or short term basis whereas latter predicts general trend of weather of a region over longer period of times.

CHAPTER 2

History of Computer

This chapter presents the history of the computers and how this machine evolved over the years. The beginning of computers started from the development of a counting system. Therefore we start with the very early ages.

2.1 Early Methods of Calculation

Today we do all calculation using computers; how were calculations done in olden days? The simplest calculating device was the finger. Even today we begin to learn calculations with the fingers but it has many limitations. You can only do simple additions and subtraction.

2.2 Abacus

In olden days, people learnt to do calculations by marking lines on the walls. This slowly developed into a device called the abacus.

The abacus was probably the first calculating device. It was invented over 3000 BC years ago and still read in some countries including India. An abacus consists of a row of wires held in wooden frame, which have balls or beds strong on them. Calculations are done on an abacus by sliding the beads along the wires. An abacus in skilled hand can work almost as fast as an electronic calculator. There are three different kinds of abacus.

2.2.1 The Russian Abacus

It has ten beads on each wire. Beds on the first wire present single units, beads on the seconds wire 10s beds on the third wire 100s and so on. Calculations are done by sliding the beads along the wires.

The Russian Abacus is shown in the Fig 2.1 represents the number **1,24,00,23,070**

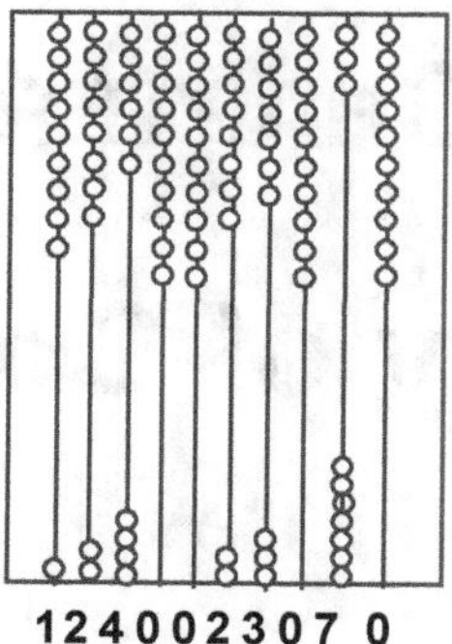

Fig. 2.1 Russian abacus

2.2.2 The Chinese Abacus

In a Chinese abacus, a beam divided into two regions, known as heaven and earth, divides the frame. There are two beads on one side of the beam and five on the other. A bead in heaven was considered whose value of five and a bead in earth a value of one.

Moving the beads away from or towards the beam did calculations. The bead has numerical value only when it is adjacent to the beam. The figure 2.2 shows a Chinese abacus presenting the number **1215235020**

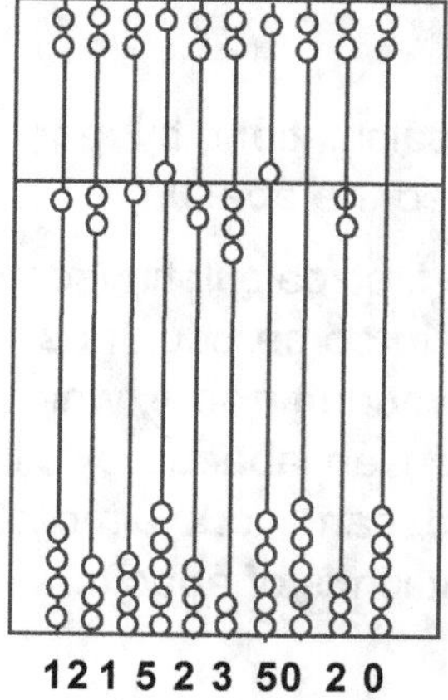

Fig. 2.2 Chinese abacus

2.2.3 The Japanese Abacus

In a Japanese abacus, one bead is in the heaven side and 4 beads in the earth are placed for calculations. The value of the beads is heaven was considered to have a value of five and a bead is the earth, a value of one this abacus are called SOROBAN. The Figure 2.3 shows a Japanese abacus presenting the number **1115235025**

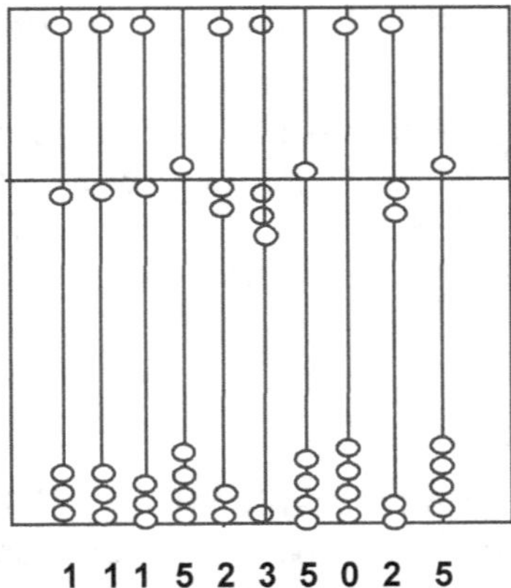

Fig. 2.3 Japanese Abacus

2.3   Napier's Bones

In the seventeenth century, John Napier, a mathematician from Scotland, did a considerable amount of work on calculations. He advised a set of even roods each hearing for faces, which were used as multiplication trolls. These rods were carved from bones so they called Napier's bones.

The road have number marked an them in such a way that, by placing them side, products and quotients of large numbers can be obtained.

2.4   Pascal's Mechanical Calculating Machine

In 1642, Blaire Pascal, a French mathematician, invented the machine; dialing a series of numbered wheels entered numbers. A series of toothed wheels transferred the movements to a deal, which showed the results. This machine also had limitation. It could be used for addition and subtraction only.

2.5   Leibnitz's Machine

1671, Goff pride Ven Leibnitz, a German Mathematician, invented a calculating machine which could perform multiplications and divisions; too. This machine was an improved version of Pascal's machine.

2.6   Babbage Analytical Engine

In 1821, Charles Babbage designed a machine called the difference engine. It was capable to calculate and print mathematical tables. Again in 1833-34 Babage designed his analytical engine which was program mechanical calculator.

The Analytical Engine had many features similar to modern computers. But it was too complicated to be built at that time. But for these ideas Charles Babbage is rightfully known as the FATHER OF COMPUTERS. Lady Ada Augusta-developed ideas for Babbage's machine. She is considered to be first programmer.

2.7   Hollerith's Card Machine

Herman Hollerith, an American Statistician in 1887-1890 developed a punch card reading machine. He used punch cards as input and output devices. This machine was used for tabulating and calculating data.

This machine was also known as Tabulating machine. It was used in 1890 as census process and proved to be very successful. Till recently punch cards were used in some computers.

2.8   The Analytical Engine by Babbage

It was a general purpose-computing device, which could be used for performing any mathematical operation automatically. It consisted of the following components.

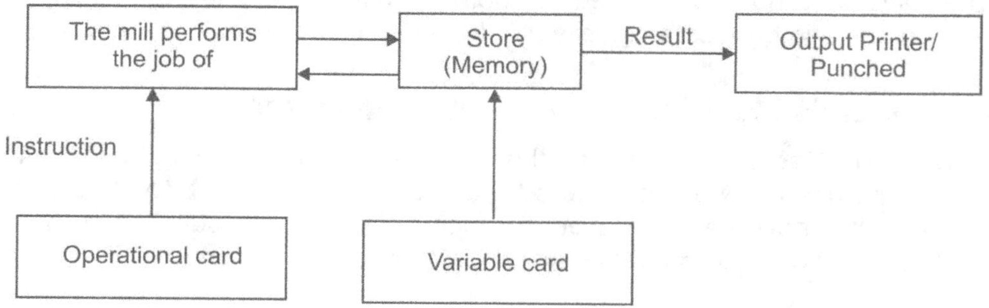

Fig. 2.4 Logical structure of Babbage's analytical engine

The Store: A mechanical Memory unit consisting of sets of center wheels.

The Mill: An arithmetic unit which is capable of performing the four basic arithmetic operations.

Cards: There are basically two types of cards.

    (a) Operation Cards: Selects one of for arithmetic operations by activating the mill to perform the selected function.

    (b) Variable Cards: Selects the memory locations to be used by the mill for a particular operation.

    (c) Output: Could be directed to a printer or a card-punch device.

Basic Features of Analytical Engine

- It was a general-purpose programmable machine.
- It had the provision of automatic sequence control, thus enabling programs to alter its sequence of operations.
- The Prussian of sign checking of result assessed.
- Mechanism for a changing or reversing of control card was permitted thus enabling execution of any desired instruction.

The Babbage machine is fundamentally the same as a modern computer. Unfortunately Babbage work could not completed, however as a tribute to Charles Babbage his analytical engine was completed in the last decade and it now on display at the science museum at London.

2.9　First Electro Mechanical Computer

A Harvard professor Howard Aiken, with the help of some IBM engineers, developed the first electro mechanical computer "MARKET". This Computer used Hollerith's punch cards. The principles of Charles Babbage were first time used practically in this computer.

This was huge machine, which occupied a large space. The inside of the machine had several miles of electrical wires, many electro-mechanical relays and mechanical counters for arithmetic calculations with all these circuits the machine look like a monster.

2.10　First Electronic Computer: ENIAC

ENIAC was the first general-purpose electronic computer, produced around 1943 for the US Army. It used 18,000 vacuum tubes, weighted 30 tons and occupied about 5000 square feet of space. It could perform 300 multiplications per second and it was fastest machine at the time of its development. In this machine, instructions were given by external Plug boards or switches.

2.11 EDSAC

Research work continued to make computers faster and smaller. John Van Nuemam a mathematician suggested that Computers could be used not only for storing data calculations but could be used in development of program. In 1949, the first Electronic Delay Storage Automatic Calculator (EDSAC) was made and used at Cambridge University, London.

2.12 EDVAC

In 1949, Eckert and Mauchly of More school developed the first stored program electronic computer and named it EDVAC. EDVAC stands for electronic discreet variable automatic computer. This was the first commercial data processing machine used to store data and program instructions in its memory through the binary number system.

2.13 UNIVAC

Eckert and Mauchly developed universal Automatic Computer in 1951 in their own company. In 1954 UNIVAC I was developed which was the computer used for business applications.

2.14 IBM 650

In the year 1955, Thomas Walton Jr son of IBM's founder was introduced this computer. This computer had a memory capacity of 2000 words. IBM 650 computer was widely accepted and become very popular which led IBM becoming the leader in computer production. The other computers produced by IBM were IBM 1401 and RAMAC 350.

2.15 First Generation of Computer

The computers produced and used between 1940-1955 were called first generation of computers.

The first generation computers were characterised by vacuum tube (Valve) circuitry. Hence they were very large, they were placed in large air-conditioned rooms. They had small internal storage and relatively very slow. The first generation machines used punched paper tape, punched card, magnetic wire, magnetic tape and printers as input/output devices.

The trends, which were encountered during the era of first generations computers, were

- The first generation computer's control was centralized in a single CPU, and all the operations required a direct intervention of the CPU.
- Use of finite-care main memory was start during this time.
- Concerts such as use of virtual memory and endure register started.
- Punched cards were used as input device.
- Magnetic tapes and magnetic drums were used as secondary memory.
- Binary coder or machine language was used as secondary memory.
- Towards the end, the use of symbolic language, which is now called assembly language started.
- Assembler a program that translates assembly language program to machine language was made.
- Computer was accessible to only programmer at time.
- Advent of von Neumann architecture.

2.16 Second Generation of Computer

The computer produced after 1955 are called second generation of computers. They had faster access and were more reliable than first generation of computers. Transistors replaced vacuum tubes of first generation in this period. By this time a wide range of input/output device such as higher performance magnetic tapes, magnetic drums and early magnetic disks were available. During the second generation, computer language such as FORTRAN and ALGOL were introduced. The second generation of computers started with the advent of transistorized computers.

The generation of computers is basically differentiated by a fundamental hardware technology. Each new generation of computer is characterized by greater speed, large memory capacity and smaller size than the previous generation. Thus, second generation computers were more advanced in terms of arithmetic and logic unit and control unit than their counter parts of first generation. Another feature of second generation was that by this time high-level language were beginning to be used and the transmission for system software were starting.

The first of the IBM 7090 was delivered in 1959, which was followed by the CDC 1604, Philco 2000 and Remington Rand's UNIVAC LARC. Other widely used second generation Computers were IBM 1620, IBM 1401 and IBM 7094.

2.17   Third Generation of Computer

IBM announced the third generation of computers in 1964 with its 360 line of computers. These used integrated circuits in the hardware. It also had the provision of facilities for time-sharing and multi programming. The speed and storage capacity of their computers were much higher than the previous generation computers and the size was much reduced.

In the third generation of computer, more than one user could work with the computer at the same time, whereas the first and second generation of computer worked on a one to one basis. Almost all computers introduced after 1960 were said to be third generation computers. Most of the mainframe computers used in India till the early 1980's were third generation computers only.

In integrated circuits the components such as transistors, resistors and conductors are fabricated on a semi conductor material such as silicon. Thus, a desired circuit can be fabricated in a tiny piece of silicon rather than assembling several discrete components into the same circuit, hundreds or even thousands of transistors could be fabricated on a single wafer of silicon. In addition, these fabricated transistors can be connected with a process of metallisation from logic circuits on the same chip they have been produced.

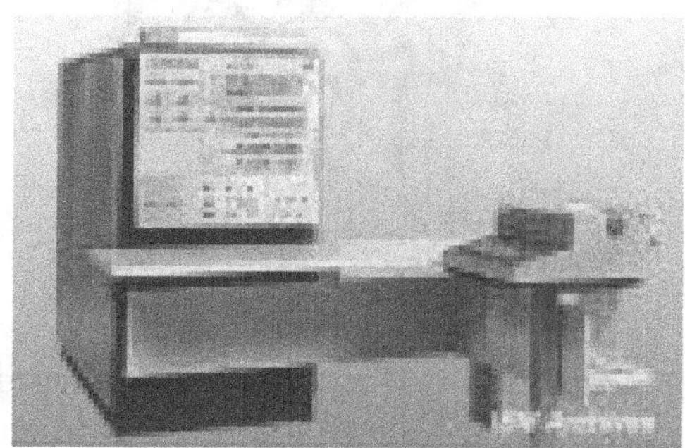

Integrated circuit is constructed on a thin wafer of silicon which is divided into a matrix of small area, an identical circuit pattern is fabricated on each of their areas and the wafer is then broken into chips. Each of these chips consists several gates, which are made using transistors only, and a number of input and output connection points. Each of these chips then can be packaged separately in a housing to protect it. In addition, this housing provides a number of Pins for connecting these chips with other circuits. The pins of these packages can be provided in two ways.

In two parallel rows with 0.1 inch spacing between two adjacent pins is each row. This package is called dual in line package (DIP) (Fig.2.6(a))

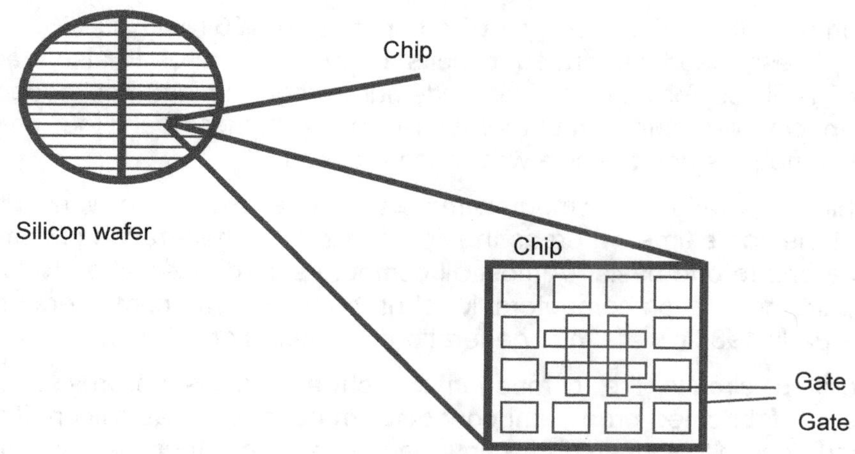

In case, more than hundred pins are required then pin grid away (WGA), where pins are arranged in arrays of rows and columns, with spacing between two adjacent pins of 0.1 inch (Fig. 2.6(b)).

Different circuits can be constructed on different wafers, all these packaged circuits chips then can be inter connected on a printed circuit board to produce several complier electronic circuits such as computers.

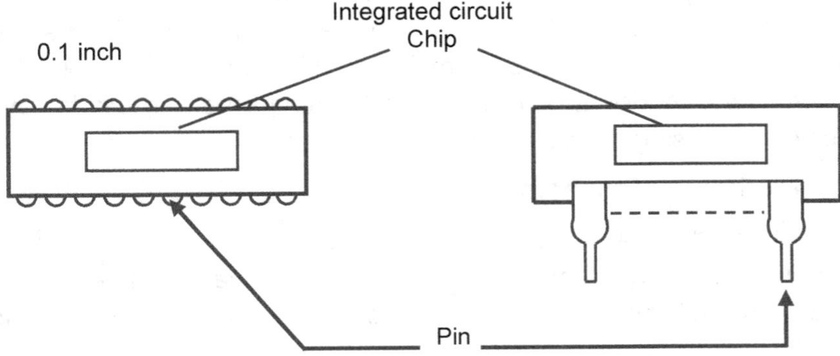

Fig. 2.6(a)   A 24 pin dual in line package (DIP)

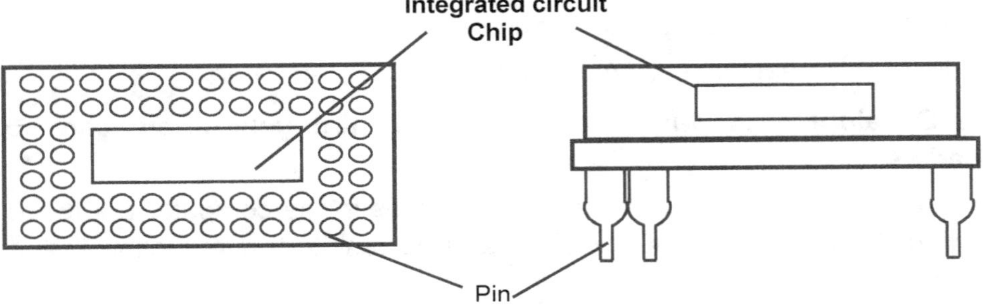

Fig. 2.6(b) 144 Pin-grid array (P4A) package

Densely packed Inspected circuit having following advantage

- **Low cost:** The cost of a chip has remained almost constant while the chip density is ever increasing. It implies that the cost of computer logic and memory circuitry reducing rapidly.
- **Fast Speed:** The more is density, the closer are the logic or memory elements, which implies shorter electrical paths and hence the higher operating speed.

- Size smaller
- Better portability
- Reduction in power and cooling requirements
- Reliability

Some of the examples of third generations computers are IBM system 360 family and DEC PDPI System. The third generation computers mainly used SSI chips. A family of computer consist of several models each model is assigned a model number, for example, the IBM system 360 family model 30, 40, 50, 65 and 75. As we go from lower model number to higher model number in this family, the memory capacity, processing speed and cost increases.

The main characteristics of the family

- The instructions set on a family are of similar type.
- The operating system used in family members is the same. In certain cases same features can be added in the operating system for the higher members.
- The speed of execution of instruction increases from low-end family members to upper end family members.
- The member of I/o ports interfaces increases.
- Memory size increases as we move towards higher members.

The Major Developments, which took place in third generation, can be summarised as

- IC circuits were starting to find their applications in the computer hardware replacing the discrete transistor circuits. This resulted in reduction in the cost and physical size of the computer.
- Semi conductor memories were starting to augment finite core memory is main memory.
- The CPU design was made simple and more flexible using a technique called microprogramming.
- Certain new techniques were introduced to increase the effective speed of program execution. These techniques were pipelining and multi processing.
- The operating systems of computers were incorporated with the efficient method of sharing the facilities or resources such as processor and memory space, automatically.

2.18 From Vacuum Tube to Microprocessor

Computers used to be made from vacuum tubes. Then the small transistor came followed by integrated circuit (IC), circuits made from the common mineral silicon and followed by the micro processor.

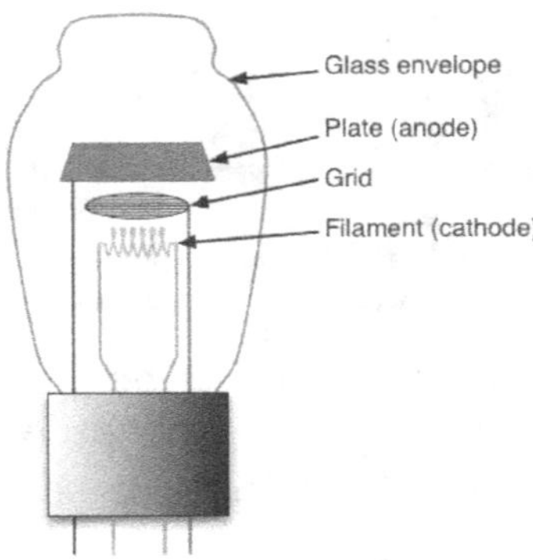

2.19 Fourth Generation of Computer

The fourth generations of computers were produced after 1970. The term fourth generation computer is used to designate microcomputers which use large-scale integrated circuits (LSI) and very large integrated. They had greater input/output capacity and system reliability.

Fourth generation computers

The most important criterion that can be used to separate them from third generation computers is that they have been designed work efficiently with the current generation of high-level languages.

Other developments that took place during 1975-1980 include: Package programs, word processing, voice response units and microprocessors. A microprocessor is a single "Chip" which by itself can perform the control, arithmetic and logical functions of a computer. A microcomputer is a collection of a small number of memory chips and some input/output devices.

Semiconductor Memories

Initially the IC technology was used for constructing processor, but soon it was realised that same technology can be used for construction of memory. The first memory chip was constructed in 1970 and could hold 256 bits. The cost of this chip is high, but gradually the cost of semi conductor memory is going down. The memory capacity per chip has increased as 1K, 4K, 16K, 64K, 256K, and 1M bits.

2.20 Microprocessors

Keeping pace with electronics as more and more component were fabricated on a single chip, fewer chips were needed to construct a single processor. Intel in 1971 got the break though of putting all the components on a single chip. The single chip processors are known as microprocessor. The Intel 4004 was the first microprocessor, it was a primitive microprocessor designed for a specific application. Intel 8080, which came in 1974, was the first general-purpose microprocessor. It was an 8-bit microprocessor. Motorola is another manufacturer in this field. At present 32, 64-, 128-bit general-purpose microprocessors are available in the market. Fig. 2.7 shows the families of INTEL & MOTOROLA microprocessor.

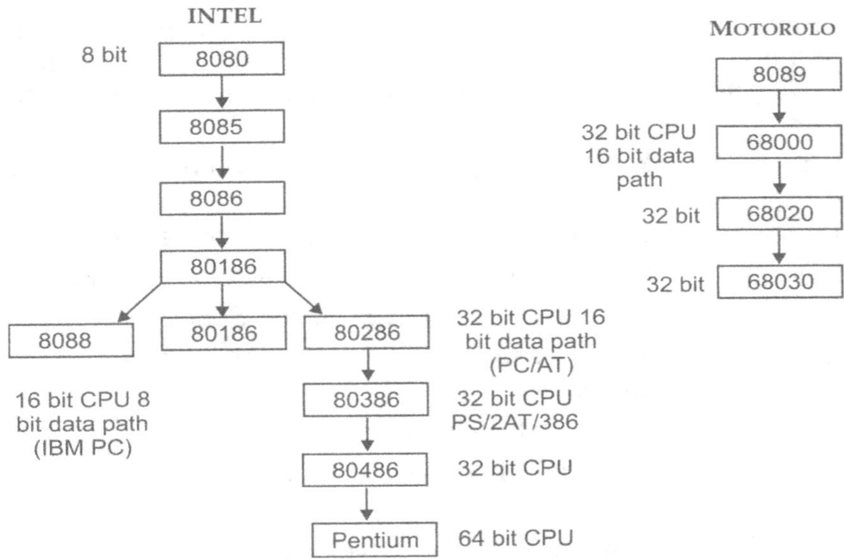

Fig. 2.6 Families of INTEL and MOTOROLA Microprocessor

2.21 Fifth Generation of Computer

In October 1981, a conference of 300 computer scientists and engineers from fourteen countries was held in Japan to discuss the features of the fifth generation computers.

These machines will incorporate Artificial intelligence, which will not be far different from that of human intelligence. They will use stored reservoirs of knowledge to make expert judgment and decisions. They will process non-numerical information such as pictures and graphs.

In these machines, intelligence will be greatly improved and the man machine interface will be closes to the human systems. Progress on these has not been as fast as originally planned although some significant advances have been made.

Let us have a look at the major milestone, which led to present day computers.

3000 B.C.	-	The abacus- first computing device developed
1600	-	Hindu-Arbic math become popular in Europe.
1617	-	John Napier introduced Napier Bones
1642	-	Blaise Pascal developed 'Pascaline' the first mechanical computer.
1673	-	Hebniz calculator developed
1801	-	Jacquard's punched card looms developed
1822	-	Charles Babbage invented difference engine
1832	-	Charles Babbage develops the principles of analytical engine. This was a first world programmable computer.
1843	-	Lady Augsta Ada, The world first Programmer suggested the use of Binary data in computers.
1847	-	George book publish his paper on book algebra – The basis of modern computation theory.
1890	-	Herman Hollerith developed punched card based machine -Tabulator.
1925	-	Vannevar Bush develop the first analog computer to solve differential equations.
1941	-	Korard Zecc of Germany Completes the world's first fully programmable digital computer named "Z-3"
1945	-	Korard Zecc develops 'Plankalkul' the first high-level language.
1946	-	Jhan Presper Eskert and John W. Mucheley developed ENIAC, the world's first fully electronic general purpose programmable digital computer.
1951	-	EDVAC, the first stored program computer developed.
1955	-	IBM introduces its first transistor-based calculator.
1956	-	FORTRAN the first scientific computer programming language developed.

1965	-	John G. Kameny developed BASIC language at Dartmouth College.
1968	-	The Intel Corp. was founded.
1971	-	The first microprocessor introduced.
1977	-	Steven Jobs and Stephen Wozniak design and build the apple computer.
1981	-	The first personal computer (PC) Introduced by IBM.

CHAPTER 3

Classification of Computers

3.1 Analog, Digital and Hybrid Computers

Computers, which are use today, are digital computers, they manipulate numbers. They operate on binary digits 0 and 1. They understand information composed of only Is and Is. In the case of alphabetic information, the alphabets are coded in binary digits. Computers do not operate on analog quantities directly. If any analog quantity is to be processed, it must be converted into digital quantity before processing. The output of a computer is converted into analog quantity. The components, which convert alphanumeric characters to binary format and binary output to alphanumeric characters, are the essential parts of a digital computer.

Digital computer

But the electronic components which convert analog quantity to a digital quantity and analog quantity are connected to digital computer as peripherals where needed, processing of analog quantity is usually encountered in industrial control and instrumentation, not in general propose computation, text manipulation or information storage retrieval or transmission.

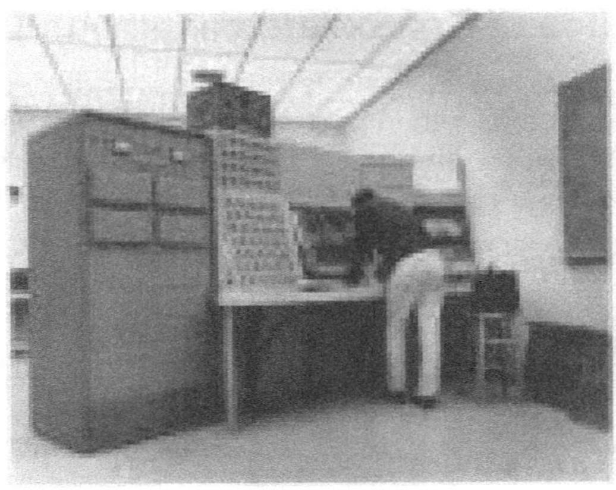

Analog computers

The computer, which can process analog quantities, is called analog computers; today analogy computers are rarely used. Earlier analog computers were used to simulate certain systems. They were used to solve differential equations.

Hybrid computers are combination of digital and analog. Hybrid computer is mainly used in medical field.

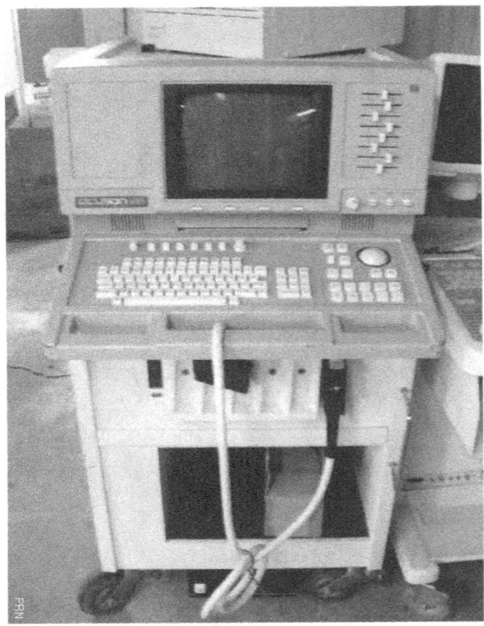

Hybrid computers

3.2   Classification of Computers based on Size

Computers can be classified in various ways depending upon its size, memory capacity, processing speed etc. Here we were going to discuss the broadly accepted classification of computer. The criteria of this classification is as discussed above. Computers are classified into four categories.

1. Main frame computers
2. Mini Computers
3. Micro Computers
4. Super Computers

3.2.1 Mainframe Computers

Mainframe computers are generally 32 bit machines or on the higher side. There are suited for organization, to manage high volume applications. Few of popular mainframe series are MEDHA, Sperry, DEC, IBM, HP, ICL etc. Mainframes are categorised just below super computers. In some ways mainframes are more powerful than super computers because they support more simultaneous programs while supercomputers can execute a single program faster than mainframe.

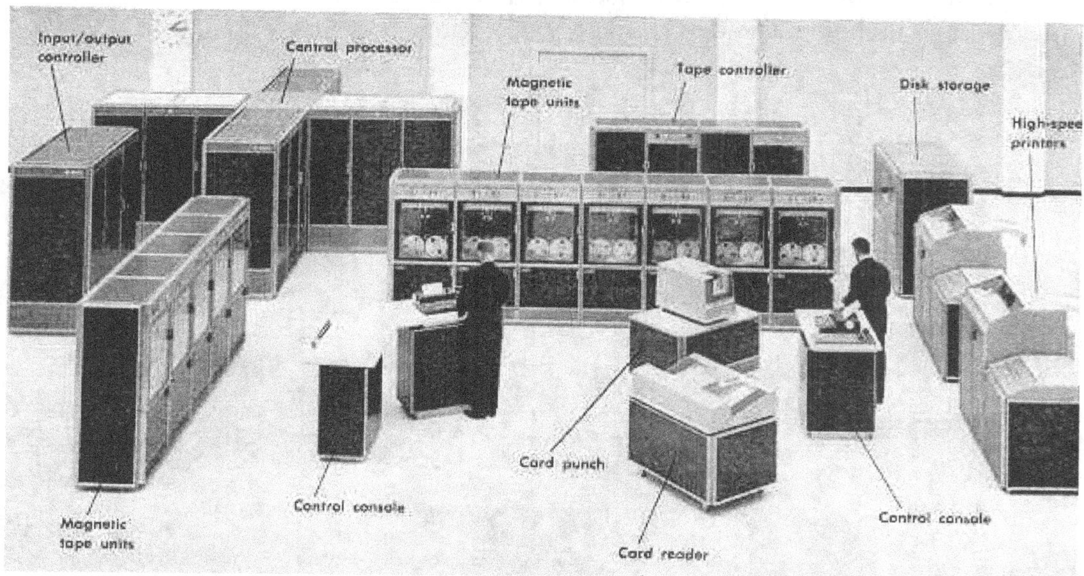

The Important features of mainframe are

*   They are big computer systems sensitive to temperature, humidity, dust etc.

- Qualified trained operators are required to operate them.
- They have wide range of peripherals attached.
- They have wide storage capacity
- They can use wide variety of software
- They are not user friendly
- They can be used for more mathematical calculations
- They are installed in large commercial places or government organization.

3.2.2 Mini Frame

The term minicomputer originated in 1960 when it was realised that many computing task do not required an expensive contemporary computers but can be solved by a small, inexpensive computer. Initial mini computers were 8 bit and 12 bit machines but by 1970's almost all mini computers were 16 bit machines.

The 16 bit minicomputer has the advantage of large instruction set and address field, and efficient storage to handling of text in comparison to lower bit machines. Thus, 16-bit minicomputer was more powerful machine, which could be used in variety of applications and could support business applications, along with the scientific application.

Mini frame

With the advancement in technology the speed, memory size and other characteristics developed and the minicomputer was then used for various stand alone or dedicated applications. The mini computer was also used as a multi-user system, which can be used by various users at the same time. Gradually the architectural requirement of mini computers grows and a 32 bit mini computer, which was called super mini, introduced. The super mini had more peripheral devices, larger memory and could support more users working simultaneously on the computer in comparison to previous mini computers. A mini computer has a multiprocessing system capable of supporting 4 to about 200 users simultaneously.

Traditionally, mini computers have been used to some of the need of medium sized companies or of departments within large companies, open for accounting or design and manufacturing (CAD / CAM). Mini computers are also becoming more important as 'servers'. A server is a computer on a network that manages network resources. The entire network is called client server network.

Characteristics of mini computer are

- They have less memory and storage capacity.
- They offer limited range of peripherals
- They can use limited range of software.
- End users can directly use it.
- They are not very sensitive to the external environment and hence are more generalized.
- They are used for data processing.

3.2.3 Micro Computers

A microcomputer's CPU has a microprocessor. The microcomputer originated in late 1970's. The first microcomputers were built around 8 bit microprocessor chips. 8 bit chip means that the chip can retrieves instruction/data from storage, manipulate, and process an 8 bit data at a time or we can say that the chip has a built in 8 bit data transfer path.

Micro Computer

An improvement on 8 bit chip technology was seen in early 1980's when a series of 16 bit chips namely 8086 and 8088 were introduced by Intel corporation, each one with an advancement over the other.

8088 is an 8116-bit chip i.e. an 8 primary storage, but processing is done within the chip using a 16-bit path at a time. 8086 is a 16116-bit chip i.e. the internal and external paths both are 16 bits wide both these chips can support a primary storage capacity of up to 1 mega byte. Intel 80286 is 16/32-bit chip and it can support up to 16 MB of primary storage.

Similar to Intel chip series, exists another popular chip series of Motorola. The first 16-bit microprocessor of this series is MC 68000. It is a 16/32 bit chip and can support up to 16 MB of primary storage. An advancement over 16/32 bit chips and the 32/32 chips some of the popular 32 bit chips are Intel's 80386 and MC 68020 Chip.

A small, relatively inexpensive computer designed for a few thousand rupees to over fifty thousand rupees. Personal computers first appeared in the late 1970. One of the most popular and first personal computers was the Apple II, Introduced in 1977 by Apple computer during the late 1970's and early 1980s; new models and competing operating system seemed to appear daily. Then, in 1981, IBM entered the pray with its first processor computer, Known as the IBM PC. The IBM PC, quickly become the personal computer of choice. In general, microcomputers are considered to be of two types:

(a) Personal computer

(b) Work Stations.

(a) **Personal Computer (PC):** The first personal computer produced by IBM was called IBMPC, and increasing the term PC come to mean IBM or IBM – Compatible personal computer, to the exclusion of other types of personal computers, such as Macintoshes. Microcomputers or PC comes in various sizes.

Desktop models: A computer designed to fit comfortably on top of a desk, typically with the monitor sitting on top of the computer. Desktop model computers are broad and flat, whereas tower model computers are norms and tall. Based on their shape, desktop model computers are generally limited to three internal mass storage devices. Desktop model designed to be very small are sometimes referred to as slim line models.

Portable or luggable: Portable means small and lightweight portable computer is a computer small enough to carry. Portable computers include notebook and sub notebook computers, hand held computers, palmtops and PDAS.

Laptop computers: A small, portable computer, small enough that can be sit on your lap. Now-a-days, laptop computers are more frequently called notebook computers. It is extremely lightweight personal computer. Notebook computers typically weight less then 6 ponds and are small enough to fit easily in a briefcase. Aside from size, the principal difference between a notebook computer and a personal computer is the display screen. Notebook computers use a variety of techniques, known as flat panel technologies, to produce a lightweight and non-bulky display screen. Notebook computers come with battery packs that enable you to run them without plugging them in electric socket. However, the batteries need to be recharged every few hours. The most common substances used in computer battery packs nickel cadmiums, Nickel metal hydride (NiMH) and Lithium gun.

Pocket or hand-held computer: A portable computer that is small enough to be held in one's hand. Although extremely convenient to carry, handheld computers have not replaced notebook computers because of their small keyboards and screens. Some manufacturers are trying to solve the small keyboard problems by replacing the keyboard with an electronic pen. However, these pen based devices rely on hand writing recognition technologies, which are still in their infancy.

Pocket computers may be classified into as three types

1. **Electronic Organizers:** Electronic Organizers or electronic diary are specialized pocket computers that mainly store appointments address, and ' to-do' lists.

2. **Palmtop:** A small computer that literally fits in palm is called palmtop. Composed to full size computers, palmtops are severely limited, but they are practical for certain functions such as phone books and calendars. Palmtops that use a pen rather than a keyboard for input are often called hand held computer or PDA's.

3. **PDA:** PDA stands for Personal Digital Assistant, a handheld device that combined computing, telephone, face and networking features. A typical PDA can function as cellular phone, fare sender and personal organizer. PDAs is pen based, using a stylus rather than a keyboard for input. Some PDA's can also react voice input by using voice recognition technologies.

(b) Workstation: Workstation are those computers which are used for engineering application, desktop publishing, software development and other type applications that require a moderate amount of computing power and relatively high quality graphics capabilities.

Workstations generally come with a large, high-resolution graphics screen, at least 64 MB of RAM, built in network support, and a graphical user interface. Most workstation also have a mass storage device as a disk drive, but a special type of workstation, called a diskless workstation comes without a disk drive. The most common operating systems for workstation are UNIX, LINUX and windows 2000, The leading manufacturing of workstations are SUN, Micro systems, Hewlett packets, Silicon Graphics Incorporated and Compaq.

Features of Micro Computers are

- They brought revolution in the history of computers.
- They are also known as personal computers.
- They are cheap and user friendly.
- This type of computer used wide range of software.

3.2.4 Super Computer

The fastest type of computer is called super computer. Super computer are very expensive and employed for specialized applications require immense amounts of mathematical calculations.

Super Computer

Weather forecasting requires a super computer; other uses of super computer include Space Technology, Animated Graphics, Fluid Dynamic Calculations, Nuclear Energy, Neno Technology research, Petroleum Exploration, Image Processing, biomedical applications.

The main difference between a super computer and a mainframe is that a Super computer channels all its power into executive a few programs as fast as possible, where as a mainframe uses its power to execute many programs concurrently.

Super Computer are designed in two ways

Vector Processor: The traditional design of super computers, now 50 years old, is vector processing. In vector processing, a relatively few large, highly specialised processor run calculations by a single large processor are by one, crating potential bottlenecks. In addition, the processors are costly to build, and they run so hot they need elaborate cooling systems.

Parallel processors: The newer design is based on parallel processors, which spreads calculations over hundreds or even thousand of standard, inexpensive microprocessors used in PCs. Tasks are Parceled out to a great many processor, which work simultaneously.

Features of super computer are

- They are huge computers installed in Space Centre, Nuclear Power stations etc.
- They are performing complete mathematical calculations.
- Only Scientists and mathematicians can operate them.
- They have huge memories & tremendous processing speed.

They used for whether Foresting, Image Processing, Remote Sensing, Animation Graphics etc.

CHAPTER 4

The System Concept

4.1 Introduction

You might have observed by now that we have been referring to a computer as a system (computer system). To know the answer let us first consider the definition of a system.

A system is group of integrated parts that have common purpose of achieving some objective(s). So, the following three characteristics are key of a system

1. A system has more than one element.
2. All the elements of a system are logically related.
3. All the elements of a system are controlled in such a way that the system goal is achieved.

Since a computer is made up of integrated components (input and output devices, storage, CPU) that work together to process the data when the program is executed, it is a system. The input or output units cannot function until they receive signals from the CPU. Similarly, the storage unit or the CPU alone is of no use. So the usefulness of each unit depends on other units and can be realised only when all units are put together (integrated) to from a system.

A computer system consists of:

1. Hardware
2. Software

4.2 Hardware

Hardware is a general term used to represent the physical components of the computer itself i.e. those components, which can be seen, touched. In computer system the hardware includes devices, like Keyboards, Monitor, Printer and the Central Processing unit:

1. Input devices
2. Output devices

3. Central Processing unit

4. Memory devices

5. Communication Devices

The electronic circuits consist of resistors, capacitors; ICs etc. inside a computer's cabinet are all examples of computer hardware. All input and output devices connected to computer are collectively known as peripherals. We can define peripheral as "A peripheral devices is any piece of hardware that is connected to a computer." examples are the keyboards, mouse, monitor and disk drives.

4.3   Software

Software is defined as sets of instructions stored as programs that govern the operation of a computer system and make the hardware run. "Software or computer programs are the step by step instructions that tell the computer what to do. In general software can be classified as "System Software" and "Application Software".

4.3.1 System Software

The user of a computer has at his disposal a large amount of software provided by the manufacturer. Most of this software contribute to the control and manage its internal resources and give optimum performance from the system.

A more detailed subdivision of such software is as follows:

Operating systems and control programs

Translators

Utilities and service programs

4.3.2 Application Software

Application software is defined as software that can be used to perform a general purpose or specific task, word processing software is used to create a text document or database software is used to create a database for a specific purpose, DTP software is used to create a document for electronic publishing. Application software may be either customised or packaged.

Customised software is that software which is designed for a particular customer for particular use. Packaged software is the kind of program developed for sale for general-purpose applications. This software is more commonly used in organisation & business applications.

4.4   Input Devices

Data and instruction are entered into a computer through input devices. An input device converts input data and instructions into a suitable binary form accepted by the computer. The most commonly used input device is a keyboard. A number of other input devices have also been developed which do not require typing for inputting information. For Examples: mouse, light pen, graphic tablet, joystick, track ball, touch screen etc. Each of these devices permits the user to select something on CRT screen by pointing to it. Therefore, these devices are called pointing devices. Voice input systems have also been developed. A microphone is used as a voice input device.

Input devices are categorised as keyboard entry and direct entry devices: In keyboard entry we use keyboard to enter the information into the computer readable form. Direct entry refers to many forms of data entry devices that are not keyboard. Such devices create machine-readable data. These include pointing devices, scanning devices, smart and optical cards, voice recognition devices etc.

Often keyboard and direct entry devices are combined in a single computer system. A Desk Top Publishing (DTP) system for example uses a keyboard, a mouse and a image scanner.

4.4.1 Keyboard

Programs and data are entered into a computer through a keyboard, which is attached to a microcomputer , mini or large computer. A keyboard is similar to the keyboard of a typewriter. It contains alphabets, digits, special characters and some control keys. When a key is pressed, an electronic signal is produced which is detected by an electronic circuit called keyboard encoder. A keyboard encoder may be a special IC or a single-chip microcomputer used as encoder. The function of an encoder is to detect which key has been pressed and send a binary code (corresponding to the pressed key) to the computer. The binary code may be an ASCII, EBCDIC or HEX code.

Conventional computer keyboards have all the keys that typewriter keyboards have plus others keys unique to computers. Actually, computer keyboards are easier to use than most typewriter keyboards because you can easily rectify your typing mistakes.

Standard typewriter keys: Typewriter keys are the same familiar QWERTY arrangement of letter, number, and punctuation keys found on any typewriter. QWERTY refers to the order of alphabet keys in the top left row on a standard typewriter keyboard.

The space bar, Shift, Tab, and Caps Lock Keys do the same things on the computer that they do on a typewriter. (When you press the Caps Lock Key, a light on your keyboards shows you are typing ALL CAPITAL LETTERS until you press the Caps Lock key again.)

An exception is the Enter (bent left arrow) key, which occupies the place where a carriage-return key would be on a typewriter. The Enter key, sometimes called the Return key, is used to enter commands into the computer.

Cursor-movement keys: The cursor is the symbol on the display screen that shows where data may be entered next. The cursor-movement keys, or arrow keys, are used to move the cursor around the text on the screen. These keys move the cursor left, right, up or down.

The keys labeled PgUp stands for page up and the key labeled PgDn stands for page down. These keys move the cursor one page or one screen at a time up (backward) or down (forward). Some software lets you use the Home key to move the cursor to the top of the document and the End key to move to the bottom of the document.

Numeric Keys: A separate set of keys, 0 - 9, known as the numeric keypad, is laid out like the keys on a calculator. The numeric keypad has two purposes.

Whenever the Num Lock key is off, the numeric keys may be used as arrow keys for cursor movement.

When the Num Lock key is on, the keys may be used for typing numbers, as on a calculator. A light is illuminated on the keyboard when the Num Lock key is pressed once and goes off when the Num Lock key is pressed again.

For space reasons, portable computers often lack a separate numeric keypad or the numeric keys may be superimposed on the typewriter letter keys and are activated by the Num Lock key.

Function Keys: Function keys are the keys labeled with an F and a number, such as F1 and F2 that are used for tasks that occur frequently. Desktop microcomputers usually have 12 function keys.

The software you are using defines the purpose of each function key. For example, pressing F2 may print your document in one program but save your work to disk in another. Special-purpose keys include Backspace, Del, Ins, Esc, Ctrl, and Alt. The uses of these special purpose keys are as follows:

Backspace (indicated by a left pointing arrow) erases as your move left over the preceding text you have typed.

Del (Delete) erases text to the right (on Macintoshes, to the left).

Ins (insert) allows you to type over (or push right) existing text, inserting new next.

Esc (Escape) may be used to cancel whatever task you are currently performing.

The purposes of Ctrl (Control) and Alt (Alternate) are defined by the software you are using. Some computers may have other special-purpose keys.

4.4.2   Light Pen

A light pen is a pointing device used to select a displayed menu option on the CRT. It is a photosensitive pen like device. It is capable of sensing a position on the CRT screen when its tip touches the screen. When its tip is moved over the screen surface, its photocell-sensing element detects the light coming from the screen and the corresponding signals are sent to the processor. The menu is a set of programmed choices offered to the user. The user indicates his choice by touching light pen against a desired description of the menu. The signals sent by the light pen to the processor identify the menu option.

4.4.3 Mouse

A device that controls the movement of the cursor or pointer on a display screen. A mouse is a small object you can roll along a hard, flat surface. Its name is derived from its shape, which looks a bit like a mouse, its connecting wire that one can imagine to be the mouse's tail, and the fact that one must make it scroll along a surface. As you move the mouse, the pointer on the display screen moves in the same direction. Mouse contain at least one button and sometimes as many as three, which have different functions depending on what program is running. Some new mouses also include a scroll wheel for scrolling through long documents.

Invented by Douglas Engel Bart of Stanford Research Center in 1963, and pioneered by Xerox in the 1970s, the mouse is one of the great breakthrough in computer ergonomics because it frees the user to a large extent from using the keyboard. In particular, the mouse is important for graphical user interfaces because you can simply point to options and objects and clicks a mouse button.

Such applications are often called point-and-click programs. The mouse is also useful for graphics programs that allow you to draw pictures by using the mouse like a pen, pencil, or paintbrush.

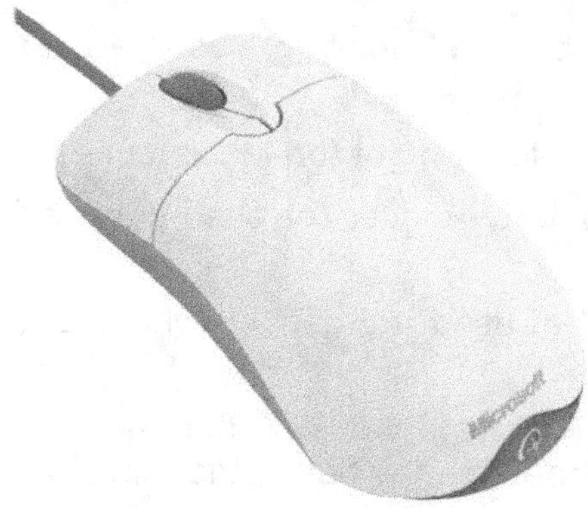

There are three basic types of mouse:

Mechanical: Has a rubber or metal ball on its underside that can roll in all directions. Mechanical sensors within the mouse detect the directed the ball is rolling and move the screen pointer accordingly.

Opt mechanical: Same as a mechanical mouse, but uses optical sensors to detect motion of the ball.

Optical: Uses a laser to detect the mouse movement. You must move the mouse along a special mat with a grid so that the optical mechanism has a frame or reference. Optical mouse have no mechanical moving parts. They responds more quickly and precisely than mechanical and opt mechanical mouse but they are more expensive.

4.4.4 Joystick

A joystick is also a pointing device. It is just like a lever that moves in all directions and controls the movement of a pointer or some other display symbol. A joystick is similar to a mouse, except that with a mouse the cursor stops moving as soon as you stop moving the mouse. With a joystick, the pointer continues moving in the direction the joystick is pointing. To stop the pointer, you must return the joystick to its upright position. Most joysticks include two buttons called triggers.

Joysticks are used mostly for computer games, but they are also used occasionally for CAD/CAM systems and other applications.

4.4.5 Trackballs

Trackball is also a pointing device. Essentially, a trackball is a mouse lying on its back. To move the pointer, you rotate the ball with your thumb, your fingers, or the palm of your hand. There are usually one to three buttons next to the ball, which you use just like mouse buttons.

The advantage of trackballs over mouse is that the trackball is stationary so it does not require much space to use it. In addition, you can place a trackball on any type of surface, including your lap. For both these reasons, trackballs are popular pointing devices for portable computers.

4.4.6 Scanners

Scanning device translate images of text, drawings, photos into digital form. Scanners are a kind of input devices. They are capable of entering information directly into the computer. The main advantage of direct entry of information is that users do not have to key the information. This provides faster and moves accurate data entry. Important types of scanners are optical scanners and magnetic-ink character readers.

Optical Scanners: The Optical Scanners are capable of reading information recorded on paper, employing light source and light sensors. The information to be scanned is typewritten information, information coded as ink or pencil marks or bars. The following are the commonly used optical scanners:

4.4.7 Optical Character Reader (OCR)

An optical character reader detects alphanumeric character printed or type written on paper. The text which is to be scanned is illuminated by a low frequency source. The light is absorbed by the dark areas and reflected from the lighted areas. The reflected light is received by photocells or CCDs (charged coupled devices), which provide binary data corresponding to dark and lighted areas. An OCR can scan several thousands of printed or typewritten characters per second. Optical character technology very useful in office automation and electronic documentation.

4.4.8 Optical Mark Readers (OMR)

Special marks such as squares or bubbles are prepared on examination answer sheets or questionnaires. The users fill in these squares with soft pencil or ink to indicate their choice. An optical mark reader detects these marks and the corresponding signals are sent to the processor. If a mark is present, it reduced the amount of reflected light. If a mark is not present, the amount of reflected light is not reduced. This change in the amount of reflected light is used to detect the presence of a mark. This method is used for analysis of objective type questions. For example, market survey, population survey, etc. where choice is restricted to one out of a few choices available.

4.4.9 Optical Bar Code Readers

This method uses a number of bars (lines) of varying thickness and spacing between them to indicate the desired information. Bar codes are used on most manufactured retails products. An optical bar reader can read such bars and convert them into electrical pulses to be processed by a computer. The most commonly used bar code is Universal Product Code (UPC). The UPC code uses a series of vertical bars of varying widths. These bars are detected as ten digits. The first five digits identify the supplier or manufacturer of the item. The second five digits identify the product. The code also contains a check digit to ensure that the information read is correct.

4.4.10 Magnetic Ink Character Readers (MICR)

MICR is widely used by banks in advanced countries to process large volumes of cheques and deposit forms written by customers every day. Special ink called magnetic ink (i.e. an ink which contains iron oxide particles) is used to write characters on cheques and deposit forms, which are to be processed by an MICR. MICR is capable of reading characters written with magnetic ink on paper. The magnetic ink is magnetized during the input process. The MICR reads the magnetic patterns of the written characters. To identify the characters these patterns are compared with special patterns stored in the memory. When a cheque is entered into an MICR, it passes through a magnetic field. The iron oxide particles are magnetized under the magnetic field. The read head reads the characters written with magnetic ink on cheque. It interprets the character and sends the corresponding data directly to the computer for processing. An MICR processes Up to 2,600 cheques per minute.

4.4.11 CCD Camera

In many applications it is desired that a computer should be able to see its environment. For example, a robot must be able to see to perform its job; a computer-controlled security system must be able to see its environment etc. To provide vision to computers, sensors like video cameras, CCD cameras, OPTICRAM cameras, etc. are employed. These cameras act as sensors to provide signals proportional to the intensity of light falling on various spots of the image of an object. The computer can process these signals and recognize and display the image of the object.

4.4.12   Sensors

A sensor is a type of input device that collects specific kinds of data directly from the environments and transmits it to a computer. Although you are unlikely to see such input devices connected to a PC in an office, they exist all around us, often in invisible form. Sensors can be used for detecting all kinds of things: speed, movement, weight, pressure, temperature, humidity, wind, current, fog, gas, smoke, light, shapes, images, and so on.

For example, in metros highways there are sensors that detect the speed and volume of traffic. These sensors send data to computers that can adjust traffic lights to keep cars and trucks away from grid locked areas. In aviation, sensors are used to detect ice buildup on airplane wings or to alert pilots to sudden changes in wind direction. Government regulators to monitor whether companies are complying with air-pollution standards also use sensors.

4.5   Output Devices

4.5.1 Softcopy Versus Hardcopy

Output devices translate information processed by the computer into a form that humans can understand. The two principal kinds of output are hardcopy, which is printed, and softcopy, such as material shown on a display screen. Output devices include display screens; printers, plotters, and multi function devices; audio-output devices; video-output devices; and virtual reality.

Hardcopy: Hardcopy refers to printed output, whether it is text or graphics.

Softcopy: Softcopy refers to data that is shown on a display screen or is in audio or voice form. This kind of output is not tangible; it cannot be touched.

There are several types of output devices.

- Display Screens
- Printers, Plotters, and multifunction devices
- Audio-output devices
- Video-output devices
- Virtual-reality devices

4.5.2 Display Screen or Monitor

The term monitor usually refers to the display screen. There are many ways to classify monitors. The most basic is in terms of colour capabilities, which separates monitors into three classes:

Monochrome: Monochrome monitors actually display two colours, one for the background and one for the foreground. The colour can be black and white, green and black, or amber and black.

Gray-Scale: A gray scale monitor is a special type of monochrome monitor capable of displaying different shades of gray. The use of many shades of gray to represent an image is called gray-scalling. Continuous-tone images, such as black-and-white photographs, use an almost unlimited number of shades of gray. Conventional computer hardware and software however can only represent a limited number of shades of gray (typically 16 or 256). Gray-scaling in the process of converting a continuous-tone image to an image that a computer can manipulate.

Colour: Colour monitors can display anywhere from 16 to over 1 million different colours. Colour monitors are sometimes called RGB monitors because they accept three separate signals – red, green, and blue.

After this classification, the most important aspect of a monitor is its screen size. Like televisions, screen sizes are measured diagonally in inches, the distance from one corner to the opposite corner diagonally. A typical size for small VGA monitors is 14 inches. Monitors that are 16 or more inches diagonally are often called full-page monitors. In addition to their size, monitors can be either portrait (height greater than width) or landscape (width greater than height).

Larger landscape monitors can display two full pages, side by side. The screen size is sometimes misleading because there is always an area around the edge of the screen that can't be used. Therefore, monitor manufactures must now also state the viewable area – that is, the area of screen that is actually used.

The resolution of a monitor indicates how densely packed the pixels are. In general, the more pixels (often expressed in dots per inch), the sharper is the image. Most modern monitors can display 1024 by 768 pixels, the SVGA standard. Some high-end models can display 1280 by 1024, or even 1600 by 1200.

Another common way of classifying monitors is in terms of the type of signal they accept: analog or digital. Nearly all-modern monitors accept analog signals, which is required by the VGA, SVGA, 8514/A, and other high-resolution colour standards.

A few monitors are fixed frequency, which means that they accept input at only one frequency. Most monitors, however, are multi-scanning, which means that they automatically adjust themselves to the frequency of the signals being sent to it. This means that they can display images at different resolutions, depending on the data being sent to them by the video adapters.

Other factors that determine a monitor's quality include the :

Bandwidth: The range of signal frequencies the monitor can handle. This determines how much data it can process and therefore how fast it can refresh at higher resolution.

Refresh Rate: How many times per second the screen is refreshed (redrawn). To avoid flickering, the refresh rate should be at least 72 Hz.

Interlaced or no interlaced: Interlacing is a technique that enables a monitor to have more resolution, but it reduces the monitor's reaction speed.

Dot pitch: The amount of space between each pixel. The smaller the dot pitch, the sharper is the image.

4.5.3 Video Display Unit (VDU)

Video Display Unit also called monitors, or CRTs, are output devices showing programming instructions and data as they are input and after it is processed. Sometimes a monitor is also referred to as a VDT (Vide display terminal), although technically a VDT includes both screen and keyboard.

Display screens are of two types: cathode-ray-tubes and flat-panel display.

Cathode-Ray Tubes (CRTs): The most common form of display screen is the CRT. A cathode-ray tube is a vacuum tube used as a display screen in a computer or video display terminal. This same kind of technology is found not only in the screen of desktop computers but also in television sets. Images are represented on the screen (whether CRT or flat-panel display) by individual dots or "picture elements" called pixels. A pixel is the smallest unit on the screen that can be turned on and off. A stream of bits defining the image is sent from the computer (from the CPU) to the CRT's electron gun, where the bits are converted to electrons. The inside of the front of the CRT screen is coated with phosphor. When a beam of electrons from the electron gun (deflected through a yoke) hits the phosphor, it lights up selected pixels to generate an image on the screen.

Flat-panel Displays: Flat panel display is much thinner, less weight and consumes less power and thus they are more useful in portable computers. Three types of technology used in flat panel display, liquid-crystal display, electro luminescent display and gas plasma display.

Clarity of Picture on a screen: Whether for CRT or flat-panel, screen clarity depends on three qualities: resolution, dot pitch, and refresh rate.

Resolution: Refers to the sharpness and clarity of an image. The term is most often used to describe monitors, printers, and bit-mapped graphic images. For graphics monitors, the screen resolution signifies the number of dots (pixels) on the entire screen. For example, a 640-by-480-pixel screen is capable of displaying 640 distinct dots on each of 480 lines, or about 300,000 pixels. This translates it into different dpi measurements depending on the size of the screen. For example, a 15-inch VGA monitor (640 x 480) displays about 50 dots per inch.

Monitors, scanners, and other I/O devices are often classified as high resolution, medium resolution, or low resolution. The actual resolution ranges for each of these grades is constantly shifting as the technology improves. In the case of dot matrix and laser printers, the resolution indicates the number of dots per inch. For example, a 300-dpi (dots per inch) printer is one that is capable of printing 300 distinct dots in a line 1 inch long. This means it can print 90,000 dots per square inch.

Dot Pitch: Dot pitch is the amount of space between pixels; the closer the dots, the crisper the image. This is a measurement that indicates the diagonal distance between like-coloured phosphor dots on a display screen. Measured in millimeters, the dot pitch is one of the principal characteristics that determine the quality of display monitors. The dot pitch of colour monitors for personal computers are ranges from about 0.15 mm to 0.30 mm. Another term for dot pitch is phosphor pitch.

Refresh Rate: Refresh rate is the number of times per second the pixels are recharged so that their glow remains bright. The refresh rate for a monitor is measured in hertz (Hz) and is also called the vertical frequency, vertical scan rate, frame rate or vertical refresh rate. The old standard for monitor refresh rates was 60 Hz, but a new standard developed by VESA sets the refresh rate at 75 Hz for monitors displaying resolutions of 640 x 480 or greater. This means that the monitor redraws the display 75 times per second. The faster the refresh rate is the image sharper.

Monochrome versus Colour Screens: Display screens can be either monochrome or colour.

Monochrome: Monochrome display screens display only two colours - usually black and white, amber and black, or gray and black.

Colour: Colour display screens can display between 16 and 16.7 million colours, depending on their type. Most software today is developed for colour, except for some pocket PCs.

Text Versus Graphics: Character-Mapped Versus Bitmapped Display: Another distinction in display screens relates to their capacity to display graphics. A screen lacking this capacity is referred to as character-mapped. A bitmapped screen can display graphics.

Character-Mapped: Character-mapped display screens display only text-letters, numbers, and special characters. They cannot display graphics unless a video adapter card is installed. Text is displayed in rows and columns, with rows measuring the height of the screen and columns measuring the width. Most computer screens display 25 rows and 80 columns, which means that a row or line can have up to 80 characters of text.

Bitmapped: A representation, consisting of rows and columns of dots, of a graphics image in computer memory. The value of each dot (whether it is filled in or not) is stored in one or more bits of data. For simple monochrome images, one bit is sufficient to represent each dot, but for colours and shades of gray, each dot requires more than one bit of data. The more bits used to represent a dot, the more colours and shades of gray can be represented.

The density of the dots, known as the resolution, determines how sharply the image is represented. This is often expressed in dots per inch (dpi) or simply by the number of rows and columns, such as 640 by 480.

To display a bit-mapped image on a monitor or to print it on a printer, the computer translates the bit map into pixels (for display screens) or ink dots (for printers). Optical scanners and fax machines work by transforming text or pictures on paper into bit maps.

Video Display Adapters

To display graphics, a display screen must have a video display adapter. A video display adapter, also called a graphics adapter card, is a circuit board that determines the resolution, number of colours, and how fast images appear on the display screen. Video display adapters come with their own memory chips, which determine how fast the card processes images and how many colours it can display. A video display adapter with 256 kilobytes of memory will provide 16 colours; one with 1 megabyte will support 16.7 million colours.

The video display adapter is often built on the motherboard, although it may also be an expansion card that plugs into an expansion slot. Video display adapters embody certain standards. New computer displays tend to favor VGA, SVGA or XGA standards;

VGA: Abbreviation of video graphics adapter, a graphics display system for PCs developed by IBM. VGA has become one of the de facto standards for PCs. In text mode, VGA systems provide a resolution of 720 by 400 pixels. In graphics mode, the resolution is either 640 by 480 (with 16 colours) or 320 by 200 (with 256 colours). The total palette of colours is 262,144.

Unlike earlier graphics standards for PCs MDA, CGA and EGA, VGA uses analog signals rather than digital signals. Consequently, a monitor designed for one of the older standards will not be able to use VGA. It is introduced in 1987, several other standards have been developed that offer grater resolution and more colours but VGA remains the lowest common denominator. All PCs made today support VGA, and possibly some more advanced standard.

SVGA: Short for Super VGA, a set of graphics standards designed to offer greater resolution than VGA. There are several varieties of SVGA, each providing a different resolution:

- 800 by 600 pixels
- 1024 by 768 pixels
- 1280 to 1024 pixels
- 1600 by 1200 pixels

All SVGA standards support a palette of 16 million colours, but the number of colours that can be displayed simultaneously is limited by the amount of video memory installed in a system. One SVGA system might display only 256 simultaneous colours while another displays the entire palette of 16 million colours. Monitor and graphics manufacturers called VESA develop the SVGA standards.

XGA: Short for extended graphics array, a high-resolution graphics standard introduced by IBM in 1990. XGA was designed to replace the older 8514/A video standard. It provides the same resolutions (640 by 480 or 1024 by 768 pixels), but supports more monitors to be non-interlaced.

For any of these displays to work, video display adapters and monitors must be compatible. Your computer's software and the display adapter must also be compatible. Thus, if you are changing your monitor or your video display adapter, be sure the new one will still work with the old.

4.5.4 Paper Output Devices: Printers, Plotters & Multifunction Devices

Printers, plotters and multifunction devices produce printed text or images on paper. Printers may be desktop or portable, impact or non-impact. Impact printers include daisywheel and dot matrix printers. Non-impact printers include laser, ink-jet, and thermal printers. Plotters are pen, electrostatic, and thermal. Multifunction devices combine capabilities, such as printing, scanning, copying, and faxing.

Printers are most popular output devices. They provide information in a permanent readable form. They produce printed outputs of results, programs and data. Printers used with computers can be classified as follows:

(a) Character printers (b) Line printers and (c) Page printers

A character printer prints one character of the text at a time. A line printer prints one line of the text at a time. A page printer prints one page of the text at a time.

The above classification of printers is based on as to how they print. There is one more classification based on the technology used in their manufacture.

Impact printers: An electro-mechanical that causes hammers or pins to strike against a ribbon and paper to print the text. Non-impact printers do not use any electro-mechanical printing head to strike against ribbon and paper. They use thermal, chemical, electrostatic, laser beam or inkjet technology for printing the text. Usually a non-impact type printer is faster than an impact type. The disadvantage of non-impact type printers is that they produce only a single copy of the text whereas impact printers produce multiple copies of the text.

Character Printers: Characters printers print one characters at a time. They are low speed printers. Their printing speed lies in the range of 60-600 characters per second. Two types of impact character printers are available: dot-matrix printers and letter quality printers.

Dot Matrix Impact Type Character Printers: A character is printed by printing the selected number of dots from a matrix of dots. The print head contains a vertical array of 9, 18 or 24 pins. A character is printed in a number of steps. One dot-column of the dot matrix is taken up at a time. The selected dots of a column (i.e. the column of dot-matrix) are printed by the print head at a time as it moves across a line.

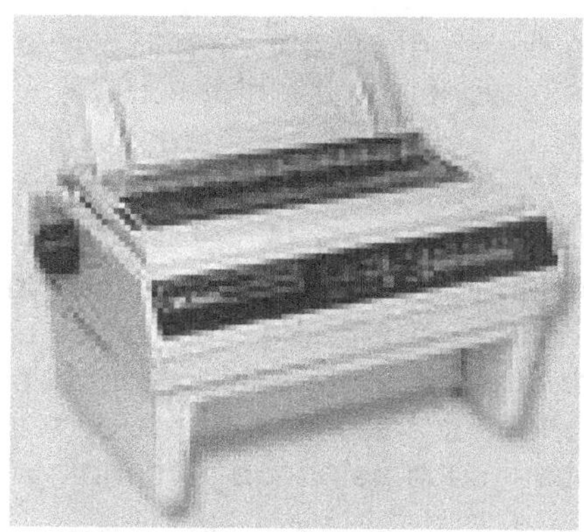

A dot-matrix printer is faster than a letter quality printer. Its printing speed lies in the range of 80-600 cps (character per second). Such printers operate at two or three speeds. The lower is the speed, the better the printing quality. Higher speed is for draft printing and the lower speed is for near-letter quality (NLQ) printing, i.e. printing is as good as that of a letter quality printer. Many dot matrix printers are bi-directional. A bi-directional printer prints one line a text from left to right and then it prints the next line from right to left.

Dot-matrix printers are very flexible. They do not have fixed character fonts. The term font is used to refer to a character set of a printer. As fonts are not fixed, a dot-matrix printer can print any shape of a character by software. This permits printing special characters such as @, Ω, $\sqrt{}$, Θ, Φ, β, ∞, $\subseteq$, $\Leftrightarrow$, Ψ etc; various sizes of print, bold or expanded characters, italics characters of any languages and ability to print graphics.

Letter Quality Impact Character Printer (Daisy Wheel Printers): An impact type letter quality printer is used where good quality of printing is needed. Such printers also called Daisy Wheel Printers. It is much slower compared to a dot-matrix printer. Its speed is in the range of 20-75 CPS. It is costlier than dot-matrix printer. Its font is of fixed type. It cannot print graphics; Two-to-three types of fonts are available with Daisy Wheel. One can select a font having the desire style of characters.

A daisy wheel printer has a removable print wheel, the flower like daisywheel consisting of spokes. Each spoke end with a raised character, which is turned to align the desired letter, and then struck with a hammer.

Non-impact Character Printers

This type of printers use thermal, electrostatic, chemical and inkjet technologies. They are briefly described below.

Thermal Character Printers: These types of printers use special heat sensitive paper. Such papers have a special heat sensitive coating. When a spot on the special paper is hearted, it becomes dark. A character is printed with a matrix of dots. A print head consists of 5 × 7 or 7 × 9 matrix of tiny heating elements. Electric current heats the heating element. To print a character, the printing head is moved first to the correct character position. Then the heating elements for the desired character are turned on. After a short time they are turned off. Therefore the print head is moved to the next Character position. Such printers have a speed about 200 characters per second (cps).

For people who want the highest quality colour printing available with desktop printers, thermal prints are the answer. However they are expensive and they require expensive paper. Thus they are not generally used for jobs requiring a high volume of output.

Ink-jet Character Printers: It uses dot-matrix approach to print text and graphics. Earlier ink-jet printers used one or more nozzles in print head that emit a steady stream of tiny ink drops. Each droplet is charged when it passes rough a valve. Then it passes through horizontal & vertical deflecting plates. These plates deflect ink drops to direct them to the desired spots on the paper to form the impression of a character. In this type of printers the continuous stream of ink-jet approach used. The speed of inkjet printers lies in the range of 40-300 cps. The average life of an ink-jet print head is about 10 billion characters, which is 5 times more than that of the print head of an impact type dot-matrix printer.

An Inkjet printer uses ink cartridges containing a column of tiny heaters. The print quality of such printers is very near letter-quality. Speed of such printers is in the same range as that of slow dot-matrix printers. Most colour printing is done on ink-jet because the nozzles can be hold four different colours.

Line Printers

The line printer prints one line of the text at a time. Its printing speed lies in the range of 300-3000 lines per minutes. It is used for large-volume printing jobs. It may be used with mini and mainframe computers.

(a) Drum Printer (b) Chain Printer (c) Band Printer

Drum Printer: A drum printer uses a rapidly rotating drum (cylinder) which contains a complete set of raised characters in each band around the cylinder. Each character position along the text line contains a band of raised character set. There is a magnetically driven hammer in each character position of the line. The printer receives all characters to be printed in one line of the text from the processor. The hammers hit the ribbon and paper against the desired character on the drum when it comes in the printing position. Its noise level is high. Its speed varies from 200 to 2000 lines per minute.

Chain Printer: Chain printer uses a rapidly rotating chain, which is called print chain. The print contains characters each link of the chain is character font. Magnetically driven hammers are located in each print position. The printer receives all the characters to be printed in one line from the processor. The printer prints one, line at a time. A chain may contain more than one character set. The desired character comes in the print position the hammer strikes the ribbon and paper against the character. The noise level of the printer is high. Its speed lies in the range of 400-2400 lines/m.

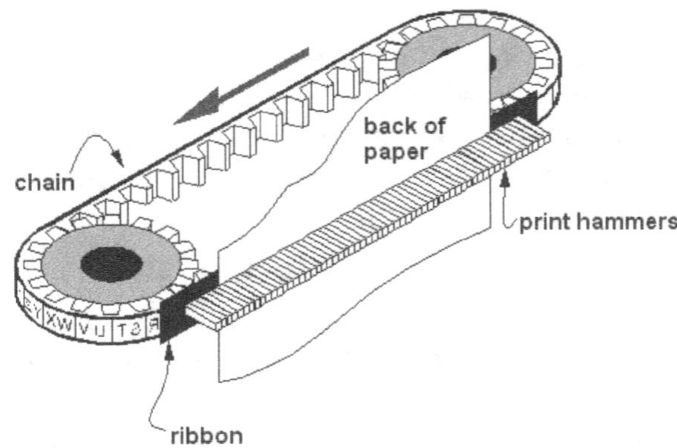

Band Printer: Band printer is just like a chain printer. It contains fast rotating steel print bands in place of chains. The print band contains a raised character set. Hammers strike the ribbon and the paper against the character to print the character. Some printers can print up to 3000 lines/m.

Laser Printers: This is a type of printer that utilizes a laser beam to produce an image on a drum. The light of the laser alters the electrical charge on the drum wherever it hits. The drum is then rolled through a reservoir of toner, which is picked up by the charged portions of the drum. Finally, the toner is transferred to the paper through a combination of heat the pressure. This is also used as a copy machines.

Because an entire page is transmitted to a drum before the toner is applied, laser printers are sometimes called page printers. There are two other types of page printers that fall under the category of laser printers even though they do not use lasers at all. One uses an array of LEDs to expose the drum, and the other uses LCDs. Once the drum is charged, however, they both operate like a real laser printer.

One of the chief characteristics of laser printers is their resolution how many dots per inch (dpi) they lay down. The available resolution range is from 300 dpi at the low end to 1,200 dpi at the high end. By comparison, offset printing usually prints at 1,200 or 2,400 dpi. Some laser printers achieve higher resolutions with special techniques known generally as resolution enhancement.

4.6   Units of Measurement for Storage

We will discuss the meanings of kilobytes, megabytes, gigabytes, and terabytes as unit of data storage, the same terms are also use to measure the data capacity of storage devices.

Bit: Short for binary digit, the smallest unit of information on a machine. A single bit can hold only one of two values: 0 or 1. More meaningful information is obtained by combining consecutive bits larger units. For example, a byte is composed of 8 consecutive bits.

Byte: To represent letters, numbers, or special characters (such as $ or *), bits are combined into groups. A group of eight bits is called a byte and a byte represents one character, digit, or any other value. (For example, in Binary scheme, 01001000 represents the letter P.) The capacity of a computer's memory of a floppy disk is expressed in terms of numbers of bytes.

Kilo Byte: In decimal systems, kilo stands for 1,000, but in binary systems, a kilo is 1,024 (2 to the 10th power). Technically, therefore, a kilobyte is 1,024 bytes, but it is often used loosely as a synonym for 1,000 bytes. For example, a computer that has 256 KB main memory can store approximately 256,000 bytes (or characters) in memory at one time.

Mega Byte: Megabyte is frequently abbreviated as MB. This is equal to 1,048,576 (2 to the 20th power) bytes or 1024 kilo bytes.

Gigabyte: Gigabyte is often abbreviated as GB. One gigabyte is equal to 1,024 megabytes, or 2 to the 30th power (1,073,741,824) bytes.

Terabyte: This is approximately 1 million bytes. 2 to the 40th power (1,099,511,627,776) bytes. A terabyte is equal to 1024 Gigabytes.

Petabyte: 2 to the 50th power (1,125,899,906,842,624) bytes. A petabyte is equal to 1.024 terabytes.

Exabyte: 2 to the 60the power (1,152,921,504,606,846,976) bytes. An exabyte is equal to 1,024 petabytes.

Zettabyte: 2 to the 70th power bytes, which is approximately 10 to the 21st power bytes. A zettabyte is equal to 1,024 exabytes. The name zeta was chosen because it's the last letter of the Latin alphabet and also sounds like the Greek letter Zeta.

Yottabyte: 2 to the 80the power bytes, which is approximately 10 to the 24th power bytes. A yottabyte is equal to 1,024 zettabytes. The name yotta was chosen because it's the second-to-last letter of the Latin alphabet and also sounds like the Greek letter iota.

4.7   Storage Devices

Storage is categorized as primary or secondary. Primary storage is main memory working storage or temporary storage. Secondary storage is permanent storage. Examples are floppy disk, hard disk, optical disks, flash memory cards, and magtietic tape.

4.7.1 Primary Storage

Physical memory that is internal to the computer. The word primary, internal or main is used to distinguish it from external mass storage devices such as disk drives. Another term for main memory is RAM.

The computer can manipulate only data that is in main memory. Therefore, every program you execute and every file you access must be copied from a storage device into main memory. The amount of main memory on a computer is crucial because it determines how many programs can be executed at one time and how much data can be readily available to the program.

Because computers often have too little main memory to hold all the data they need a technique called swapping, in which portions of data are copied into main memory when they are needed. Swapping occurs when there is no room in memory for the existing data. When one portion of data is copied into memory, in equal-sized portion is copied (swapped) out to make that memory block vacant.

Primary storage is the computer's small storage capacity, determining the total size of the programs and data files it can work with at any given moment. Primary storage, which is contained on RAM chips, is temporary. Once the power to the computer is turned off, all the data and programs within memory simply vanish. For this reason, primary storage is said to be volatile. Volatile memory is temporary memory; the contents are lost when the power is turned off. If you accidentally kick out the power cord underneath your desk, or a storm knocks down a power line to your house, whatever you are currently working on will immediately washout.

RAM

A RAM acronym of random access memory, a type of computer memory that can be accessed randomly; that is, any byte of memory can be accessed without touching the preceding bytes. RAM is the most common type of memory found in computers and other devices.

There are two basic types of RAM

- Dynamic RAM (DRAM)
- Static RAM (SRAM)

Dynamic RAM: A type of physical memory used in most personal computers. The term dynamic indicates that the memory must be constantly refreshed it will lose its contents.

Static RAM: Static RAM pronounced ess- RAM. SRAM is faster and less volatile than dynamic RAM, but it requires more power and more expensive.

ROM

ROM acronym for read only memory. Once data has been written onto a ROM chip, it cannot be removed and can only be read. Unlike main memory, ROM retains its contents even when the computer is turned off. ROM is referred to as being nonvolatile, whereas RAM is volatile. ROM stores critical programs such as the program that boots the computer.

Types of ROM

PROM: Pronounced prom, as acronym for programmable Read-Only Memory. A PROM is a memory chip on which data can be written only once. Once a program has been written onto a PROM, it remains there forever. The difference between RAM and PROM is that a ROM is programmed during the manufacturing process, where as a PROM is manufactured as blank memory.

EPROM: Erasable programmable read only memory is a special type of memory that retains its contents until is not exposed to ultraviolet light. The ultraviolet light clears its contents, making it possible to program. The memory write and erase an EPROM, you need a special device called a PROM burner.

EEPROM: Electrically erasable programmable read only memory is a special type of PROM that can be erased by exposing it to an electrical charges.

Cache

Cache pronounced cash is a special high-speed storage mechanism .It can be either a reserved section of main memory or an independent high-speed storage device. Two types of caching are commonly used in personal computers – memory caching and disk caching.

4.7.2 Secondary Memory or Secondary Storage

The earliest storage devices were punched paper cards, which were used as early as 1804 to control silk-weaving looms. Modern mass storage devices include all types of disk drives and tape drives. Mass storage is distinct from memory, which refers to temporary storage areas within the computer.

Secondary storage in non-volatile – that is, data and programs are permanent, or remain intact, when the power is turned off. The main types of secondary storage are:

4.7.3 Floppy Disks

Floppy disk is round pieces of flat plastic that store data and programs as magnetized spots. The two principal sizes are **3½ -inch** and **5¼--inch**. A disk drive copies or reads, data from the disk and writes, or records, data to the disk. Components of a floppy disk include tracks and sectors; disks come in various densities. All have write protect features. Card must be taken to avoid data corruption on disks and users are advised to back up, or duplicate, the data on their disks.

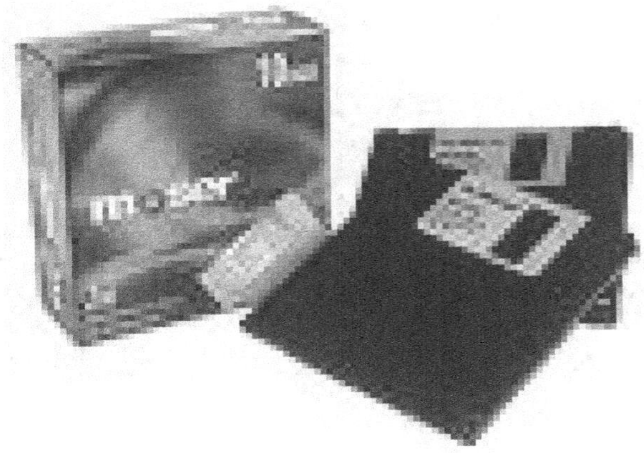

A floppy disk is a soft magnetic disk. It is called floppy because it flops if you wave it (at least, the 5¼-inch variety does). Unlike most hard disks, floppy disk (often called floppies or diskettes) is portable, because you can remove them from a disk drive. Disk drives for floppy disks are called floppy drives. Floppy disks are slower to access than hard disks and have less storage capacity, but they are cheaper and portable.

Floppies come in two basic sizes

5¼ inch: The common size for PCs made before 1987. This type of floppy is generally capable of storing between 100 K and 1.2 MB (megabytes) of data. The most common sizes are 360 K and 1.2 MB.

3½ inch: Despite their small size, microfloppies have a larger storage capacity than their cousins from 400 K to 1.4 MB of data. The most common sizes for PCs are 720 K (double-density) and 1.44 MB (high-density). Macintoshes support disks of 400 K, 800 K, and 1.2 MB.

Floppy Disk Drive

To use floppy disk we use a machine that reads data from and writes data onto a disk is called Floppy Disk Drive. A disk drive rotates the disk very fast and has one or more heads that read and write data. Disk drives can be either internal (housed within the computer) or external (housed in a separate box that connects to the computer). The process of READ and WRITE means the following:

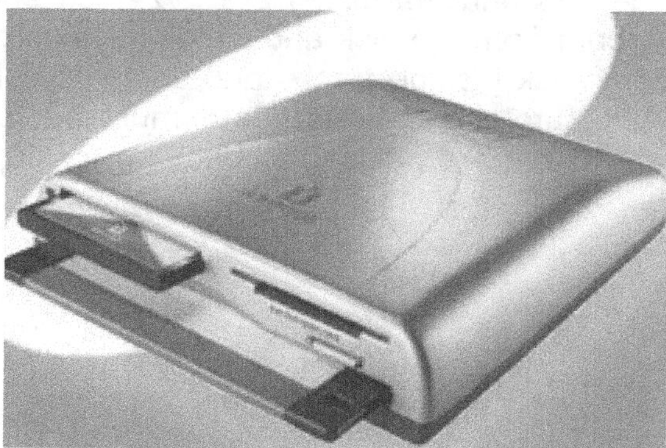

READ: to copy data to a place where it can be used by a program. The term is commonly used to describe copying data from a storage medium, such as a disk, to main memory for the purpose of using the data for processing.

WRITE: to copy data from main memory to a storage device, such as a disk. i.e. the data recorded onto the disk from the main memory for later use.

Characteristics of Floppy Disks: Both 5 ¼ inch and 3 ½ inch disks work in similar ways, although there is some difference. The characteristics of floppy disks are as follows:

Tracks and sectors: One a floppy disk data is recorded in rings called tracks. These tracks are not visible. A typical floppy disk has 80 (double density) or 160 (high-density) tracks. Each track is further divided into a number of sectors. Sector is the smallest unit that can be accessed on a disk. The tracks are concentric circles around the disk and sectors are segments within each circle. For example, a floppy disk might have 40 tracks, with each track divided into 10 sectors. The operating system and disk drive keep tabs on where information is stored on the together they are measured in terms of tracks per inch (TPI). For example, double-density 5.25-inch floppies have a TPI of 48, while high density floppies record 96 TPI. High-density 3.5-inch diskettes are formatted with 135 TPI.

Formatting: formatting means to prepare a storage medium, usually a disk, for reading and writing. When you format a disk, the operating system erases all book keeping information on the disk, tests the disk to make sure all sectors are reliable, makes bad sectors (that is, those that are scratched), and creates internal address tables that it later used to locate information. You must format a disk before you can use it.

Note that reformatting a disk does not erase the data of the disk, only the address tables. Do not panic, therefore, if you accidentally reformat a disk that has useful data. A computer specialist should be able to recover most, if not all, of the information on the disk. You can also buy programs that enable you to recover a disk yourself.

The previous discussion, however, applies only to high-level formats, the type of formats that most users execute. In addition, hard disks have a low-level format, which sets certain properties of the disk such as the interleave factor. The low-level format also determines what type of disk controller can access the disk (e.g. RLL or MFM)

Data capacity – sides and density: Density means how tightly information is packed together on a storage medium (tape or disk). A higher density means that data are closer together, so the medium can hold more information. Floppy disks can be single-density, double-density, high-density, or extra-high-density. To use a double-density, high-density, or extra-high-density disk, you have a disk drive that supports the density level. Density, therefore, can refer both to the media and the device.

Write protect feature: 'Write-Protect' means to marks a file or disk so that its contents cannot be modified or deleted. When you want to make sure that neither you nor user can destroy data, you can write-protect it. Many operating systems include a command to write protect files. You can also write-protect 5¼ inch floppy disks by covering the write protect files. 3½-inch floppy diskettes have a small switch that you can set to turn on write protection. Write protected files and media can only be read; you cannot write to them, edit them, append data to them, or delete them.

Backup of important data: Backup means to copy files to a second medium (a disk or tape) as a precaution in case the first medium fails. One of the cardinal rules in using computer is:

Back up your files regularly.

Even the most reliable computer is apt to break down eventually. Many professionals recommend that you make two, or even three, backups of all your files. To be especially safe, you should keep one backup in a different location from the others.

You can back up files using operating system commands, or you can buy a special-purpose backup utility. Backup programs often compress the data so that backups require fewer disks.

4.7.4 Hard Disk

Hard disk is a magnetic disk on which you can store computer data. The term hard is used to distinguish it from a soft, or floppy disk. Hard disks hold more data and faster than floppy disks. A hard disk, can store data from MB to TB whereas most floppies have a maximum storage capacity of 1.4 MB.

A single hard disk usually consists of several platters. Platter is a round magnetic plate that constitutes part of a hard disk. Each platter requires two read/write heads, one for each side. All the read/write heads are attached to a single access arm so that they cannot move independently. Each platter has the same number of tracks, and a track location that cuts across all platters is called a cylinder.

Removable Hard Disk

A type of disk drive system in which hard disks are enclosed in plastic or meta cartridges so that they can be removed like floppy disks. Removable disk derives combine the best aspects of hard and floppy disks. They are nearly as capacious and fast as hard disks and have the portability of floppy disks. Their biggest drawback is that they're relatively expensive.

Some Important terms related to Hard / Floppy Disk

Cylinder: A single-track location on all the platters making up a hard disk. For example, if a hard disk has four platters, each with 600 tracks, then there will be 600 cylinders, and each cylinder will consist of 8 tracks (assuming that each platter has tracks on both sides)

Track: A ring on a disk where data can be written. A typical floppy disk has 80 (double density) or 160 (high-density) tracks. For hard disks, each platter is divided into tracks, and a single-track location that cuts through all platters (and both sides of each platter) is called a cylinder. Each track is further divided into a number of sectors. The operating system and disk drive remember where information is stored by noting its track and sector numbers.

The density of tracks (how close together they are) is measured in terms of tracks per inch (TPI).

4.7.5 CD-ROM

CD-ROM abbreviation is Compact Disc-Read-Only Memory. This is a type of optical disk capable of storing large amounts of data – up to 1 GB, although the most common size is 650 MB (megabytes). A single CD-ROM has the storage capacity of 700 floppy disks, enough memory to store about 300,000 text pages.

The vendor stamps CD-ROMs, and once stamped, they cannot be erased and filled with new data. To read a CD, you need a CD-ROM player. All CD-ROMs conform to a standard size and format, so you can load any type of CD-ROM into any CD-ROM player. In addition, CD-ROM players are capable of playing audio CDs, which share the same technology.

CD-ROMs are particularly well suited to information that requires large storage capacity. This includes software applications, graphics, sound, and especially video.

CD-ROM Player

Also called a CD-ROM drive, a device that can read information from CD-ROM. CD-ROM players can be either internal, or external, which generally connect to the computer's SCSI interface or parallel port. Parallel CD-ROM players are easier to install, but they have several disadvantages: They're somewhat more expensive than internal players, they use up the parallel port which means that you can't use that port for another device such as a printer, and the parallel port itself may not be fast enough to handle all the data pouring through it.

There are a number of features that distinguish CD-ROM players, the most important of which is probably their speed. CD-ROM players are generally classified as single-speed or some multiple of single-speed. For example, a 4X player access data at four times the speed of a single-speed player.

Constant Linear Velocity, or CLV is a method used by older CD-ROM player to access data. With CLV, the rotation speed of the disk changes based on how close to the center of the disk the data is. For tracks near the center, the disk rotates faster and for data outside the disk rotates slower. The purpose of CLV is to ensure a constant data rate regardless of where on the disk the data is being accessed. Because less data can fit on the inside tracks, the disk needs to rotate faster for these areas. An alternative technology, which is becoming increasingly popular, is CAV (Constant Angular Velocity).

Constant Angular Velocity or CAV is a technique for accessing data off of rotating disks. With constant speed regardless of what area of the disk is being accessed. This differs from constant linear velocity (CLV), which rotates the disk faster for inner tracks. Disk drives use CAV, whereas CD-ROMs generally use CLV, though some new drives use a combination of CAV and CLV. The advantage of CAV is that it is much simpler to design and produce because the motor doesn't need to change speed. In addition, CLV runs into problems for very high-speed CD-ROMs because there's a brief latency whenever the drive needs to change the rotational speed.

CD-R drive: Short for compact Disk-Recordable drive, a type of disk drive that can create CD-ROMs and audio CDs. This allows users to "master" a CD-ROM or audio CD for publishing. Until recently, CD-R drives were quite expensive, but prices have dropped dramatically.

A feature of many CD-R drives, called multi session recording, and enables you to keep adding data to a CD-ROM over time. This is extremely important if you want to use the CD-R drive to create backup CD-ROMs.

To create CD-ROMs audio CDs, you'll need not only a CD-R drive, but also a CD-R software package. Often, it is the software package, not drive itself that determines how easy of difficult it is to create CD-ROMs.

CD-R drives can also read CD-ROMs and play audio CDs.

CD-RW DISK: Short for CD-Re-Writable disk, a type of CD disk that enables you to write onto it in multiple sessions. One of the problems with CD-R disks is that you can only write to them once. With CD-RW drives and disks, can treat the optical disk just like a floppy or hard disk, writing data onto it in multiple times.

WORM: Short for write once, read many, an optical disk technology that allows writing data onto a disk just once. After that, the data is permanent and can be read any number of times. WORM is also called CD-R.

Erasable optical disk: A type optical disk that can be erased and loaded with new data. In contrast, most optical disks, called CD-ROMs are read-only.

4.7.6   Digital Video Disk (DVD)

Short for digital versatile disc or digital video disc, a new type of CD-ROM that holds a minimum of 4.7 GB (gigabytes), enough for a full-length movie. CD-ROMs as well as VHS videocassettes and laser discs.

The DVD specification supports disks with capacities of from 4.7 GB to 17 GB and access rates of 600 KBps to 1.3 MBps. One of the best features of DVD drives is that they are backward compatible with CD-ROMs.

DVD-RAM: A new type of re-writable compact disc that provides much greater data storage than today's CD-RW systems. The DVD Consortium is still hammering out the specification for DVD-RAMs. Meanwhile, a competing group of manufactures led by Hewlett-Packard, Philips and Sony, have come up with a competing standard called DVD+RW. Whereas the DVD-RAM standard supports 2.6 GB per disk side, DVD+RW support 3 GB per side.

DVD-ROM: A new type of read-only compact disc that hold a minimum of 4.7 GB (gigabytes), enough for a full-length movie. Many experts believe that DVD-

ROMs will eventually replace CD-ROMs, as well as VHS videocassettes and laser discs. Currently, however, DVD-ROMs are more promise than reality. There are only a few DVD-ROM devices can play old CD-ROMs, CD-I disks, and video CDs, as well as new DVD-ROMs. Newer DVD players can also read CD-R disks.DVD-ROMs use MPEG-2 to compress video data.

4.7.7 Magnetic Tape

It is a magnetically coated strip of plastic on which data can be encoded. Tapes for computers are similar to tapes used to store music. This is the oldest storage media used till today.

Storing data on tapes is considerably cheaper than storing data on disks. Tapes also have large storage capacities, ranging from a few hundred kilobytes to several gigabytes. Accessing data on tapes is slower than accessing data on disks. Tapes are sequential-access media, which means that to get to a particular point on the taps, the tape must go through all the preceding points. In contrast, disks are random-access media because a disk drive can access any point at random without passing through intervening points.

4.7.8 Pen Drive

USB Pen Drive is a small key ring-sized device that can be used to easily transfer files between USB-compatible systems. Available in a range of capacities (and in some cases, with an MP3 player built-in) this handy little gizmo can save all those data-transfer hassles.

Plug it into the USB port of PC (or Mac!) and watch the system automatically detects the new device. Take a look at system drives... a new drive has been created! The operating system can now access USB Pen Drive just like any ordinary Hard Disk Drive.

Copy across all the required files to the new drive, wait for the Read/Write LED on the USB Pen Drive to stop flashing then disconnect it. That's it. Files are now safely stored on USB Pen Drive. If you want to copy those files to another PC/Mac, just plug it in the new machine, wait for it to be detected and copy them off again.

4.7.9 USB

For a good few years now, most Motherboards have been built with an on-board facility called USB.

USB - Universal Serial Bus, is a 'standard' developed by the computer industry to allow a vast number of different devices to be easily attached to one machine with the minimum requirement for extra drivers and software and still operate at an efficient speed.

Put simply, this means: plug a USB device in without switching the PC off, it will be automatically detected by the Operating System and will be ready for use in a few seconds. The USB Pen Drive *is* one of those devices.

CHAPTER 5

Fundamentals of Operating system

5.1 Definition and Need of Operating System

The operating system is the link between the hardware and software. An operating system (usually known as the OS) is an organised set or collection of software programs that controls the overall operation of the computer system. It controls and directs the flow of data and instruction from one part of the computer to another.

A computer itself is nothing but a collection of various hardware devices such as the keyboard, the visual display unit, Central Processing Unit (CPU). It is the operating system that makes these independent hardware devices, although interconnected by cables, a single entity which is both easy to use and manage. Operating system acts as an interface between the user and the computer system. It is only due to presence of the operating system that the user doesn't have to bother about the technical details and functional aspects of each of the hardware components of the system. All the user needs to do is to present the problem to the operating system in a language that can be understood by the operating system and get the results. The computer hardware provided the raw processing power or ability. It is the job of the operating system to make this ability conveniently available to the users.

5.2 Function of Operating System

An operating system (OS) is an integrated set of programs that is used to manage the various resources and overall operations of a computer system. It is designed to support the activities of computer installation. Its prime objective is to improve the performance and efficiency of a computer system, increase facility with which a system can be used. Thus, like a manager of a company, an operating system is moreover, it makes the computer system user friendly. That is, it becomes easier for people to interact with and make use of the computer.

Operating system is known by many different names, depending on the manufacture of the computer. Other terms used to describe the operating system are monitor, executive, supervisor, controller and master control programs. Operating System performs the following functions.

1. **Process Management:** That is assignment of processors to different tasks being performed by the computer system.

2. **Memory Management:** That is, allocation of main memory storage to the system programs.

3. **Input/Output management:** That is coordination and assignment of the different input and output devices while one or more programs are being executed.

4. **File management:** The storage of files on various storage devices and the transfer of these from one storage device to another. It also allows all files to be easily changed and modified through the use of text editors or some other file manipulation routines.

5. **Setting Priority:** It determines and maintains the order in which jobs are to be executed in the computer system.

6. Automatic transition from job to job, directed by special control statements.

7. Interpretation of commands and instructions.

8. Coordination and assignment of compilers, assemblers, utility programs, software.

9. Production of dumps, traces, and error message and other debugging and error detection aids.

10. Facilitates easy communication between the system and the computer operator.

5.3   Useful Terms of Operating System

5.3.1 Multi-Programming

Overlapped or interleaved execution of two or more processes is terms as multiprogramming. In other words, multiprogramming implies that two or more processes are active at the same time and are available for execution. The operating system may select one of these active programs for allocation to CPU or processor, on the basis of some selection technique. The next process in the queue is allocated to the CPU, when either of the following takes place.

(i)   The executing process issues an I/O request

(ii) The executing process completes execution, or

(iii) The time allocated to the executing process is over.

In this way, the CPU or the processor can be kept busy by the operating system, which switches from one process to a waiting process, whenever the first process either terminates or requests an I/O activity or its allocated time is over, while the I/O outputting the data. All active processes that are not executing are kept on the secondary storage and when one of these is to be executed, it is loaded from there along with the intermediate results that it had computed when the CPU was allocated to it, last time.

5.3.2 Multi-Processing

Multiprocessing is a term used with the processing on a system which contains more than one CPUs. In a system with more than one CPU, more than one instruction can be executed by the system at the same time. Thus more than one process can be simultaneously executed in such systems.

A Multiprocessing operating system is an operating system that has been designed for a Multiprocessor system, that is, a system having more than one CPUs output from system. It is the job of the Multiprocessing operating system to schedule and balance the input, output and the processing capabilities of a system to schedule processors. Since scheduling and coordinating the activities of multiple CPUs is a very complex task, a multiprocessing operating system is a very complex and sophisticated operating system.

5.3.3 Time Sharing Technique

A real time operating system is one in which the input data is to be processed and the result produced within a stipulated time period. That is, the processing of data should take very small amount of time. Real time operating systems are generally used in industry as monitors. Such systems are very useful in places where a close watch is kept on the surroundings of the system and some corrective action is to be taken in case one particular thing happens. For examples consider a heat furnace whose temperature is to be kept constant for, 30 hours at 300^0 Centigrade and that the maximum allowable temperature variation is $\pm 1^0$ centigrade. In such a situation, manual monitoring is virtually impossible. Here a real time system can be used very conveniently. Such a system (that is the one that can be used in such a situation) will have heat sensors, which will provide the input, that is the temperature of the furnace, to the system. The system will process this input and accordingly try to adjust the temperature of the furnace.

5.3.4 Real Time

In the manner in which processors working with higher speed were developed the technique of batch processing proved to be unproductive in view of the use of processing capacity. On one hand input and output applications work with a very slow speed and the time taken to read any information from the memory forces the processor to remain free. After doing other work and after sometime, again starts doing the first job from where it had left earlier. In this way the time of the processor can be fully utilized. The activities are assessed by the operating system.

If 16 terminals are attached with one system and work is going on all terminals then for sometime the computer does the work of one user and then serial wise of other users. It works with such high speed that every one feel that the computer is working method in which you don't have to wait is called online Processing technique the method in which computer does work of many users together and distributes it in time slices is known as time sharing technique.

5.4   MS-DOS

MS-DOS stands for Microsoft Disk Operating System developed by the Micro Soft Ltd.

Most of the DOS programs are stored in two files, namely IO.SYS and MSDOS.SYS. Another file, which contains DOS routines, is the COMMAND.COM. The IO.SYS and MSDOS.SYS are hidden files and are not visible to ordinary user. These are all present in the boot sector of the system.

The IO.SYS file contains the extensions to the ROM-BIOS. These may be additions to the exiting set of elementary routines stored in ROM and can be changed in already existing routines stored in ROM.

The MSDOS.SYS file contains the MS-DOS service routines. These routines provide better control over various peripheral devices. But these routines are not as flexible as the ROM-BIOS routines.

The COMMAND.COM files are the third part of the DOS. It contains the command interpreter of the DOS. This command interpreter first accepts any command that we give to the system. If what we have entered is correct and it exists as a command by the name then COMMAND.COM invokes the specified command. In case of an error, COMMAND.COM gives an appropriate error message. So any interaction that a user may have with the system or DOS can only be through COMMAND.COM.

5.5   Types of Operating System

On the basis of the number of users working on the system, O.S. can be classified into the following types.

5.5.1 Single User O.S

The O.S. on which one user can work at a time is known as single operating system. DOS belongs to this category.

5.5.2 Multi-User O.S

When two or more users can work on the same O.S. simultaneously it is known as multi-user O.S. Unix is a multi-user O.S. as two or more persons can work at a time in this type of O.S.

On the basis of the mode of working the O.S. are again classified into following types.

5.5.3 Character User Interface (CUI)

When the user operates the system by means of characters it is known as CUI. Ex: DOS, Here the USER gives command to the system by means of characters i.e. in order to copy a file we have to give exact syntax of copy command in DOS ex: Copy A: FILE 1 B: FILE1

5.5.4 Graphical User Interface (GUI)

When the user operates the system by means of pictorial or graphical representations it is known as GUI. Ex: Windows is an operating environment, which provides the feature of GUI. i.e., in order to copy a file in windows we have to select the option of copy and it will be copied.

5.6   Booting Process

The process of starting our computer is called booting. Typically, we will start computer at the beginning of the day and leave it on until you're done at the end of the day. At that time, exit any programs which running, return to the DOS command prompt, and turn off the power.

5.6.1 Warm Booting

If we reboot system, we have two options: a warm boot or a cold boot. A warm boot is "gentler" and often quicker because the computer stays powered on during the procedure. To perform a warm boot, press the key combination CTRL+ALT+DEL. To use this key combination, hold down the Ctrl Key, then hold down the Alt key, then hold down the Del key. Release all three keys after the screen clears and the computer restarts.

5.6.2 Cold Booting

If a warm boot doesn't seem to clear up the problem completely, then perform a cold boot. To do so, turn off the power, preferably using the switch on computer surge protector. Wait until the computer's hard disk has stopped rotating (counting to 30 slowly should do it!), then turn the power on again

5.7   Resource Management

5.7.1 Process Management

Process Scheduling: On multiprocessing systems, scheduling is used to determine which process is given control of the CPU. Scheduling may be divided into three phases: long-term, medium-term, and short-term. Long-term scheduling, or job scheduling, determines which jobs or processes may compete for systems resources. Typically, once the job scheduler makes a job active, it stays active until it terminates. The main objective of the job scheduler is to provide the medium-term scheduler with an appropriate number of jobs. Too few jobs and the CPU may sit idle because all jobs are blocked. Too many jobs then memory management system becomes overloaded, degrading system efficiency.

The medium-term scheduler, or swapper, swaps processes in and out of memory. Any memory management system that supports multiprocessing can use swapping to allow more processes to share a system than can physically fit in memory. Even memory management systems like paging may swap all process out of memory to limit the number of processes competing for memory.

The short-term scheduler, or dispatcher, allocates the CPU to a process that is loaded into main memory and ready to run. Typically, the dispatcher allocates the CPU for a fixed maximum amount of time. A process that must release the CPU after exhausting its time slot returns to the pool of processes from which the dispatcher selects the process to execute. On multithreaded systems, a variety of options exist for short-term scheduling. Instead of scheduling processes, the short- term scheduler can schedule threads. However, short-term scheduling can also be two-level scheduling: thread scheduling within process scheduling. Since threads within a process share memory and other resources, the overhead required to switch between threads in a process is less than the overhead when switching between heavyweight processes (or threads in different processes).

Process State: At its simplest, scheduling can consist of just short-term scheduling. On such a system a process exists in one of four states.

- **Blocked:** A process that is waiting for some event to occur before it can continue executing. Most frequently, this event is completion of an I/O operation. Blocked processes do not require the services of the CPU since their execution cannot proceed until the blocking event completes.
- **Ready:** A process that is not allocated to a CPU but is ready to run. A ready process could execute if allocated to a CPU.
- **Running:** A process that is executing on a CPU. If the system has n CPUs, at most n processes may be in the running state.
- **Terminated:** A process that has halted its execution but a record of the process is still maintained by the operating system

  Medium-term scheduling adds two additional process states

- **Swapped-Blocked:** A process that is waiting for some event to occur and has been swapped out to secondary storage.
- **Swapped-Ready:** A process that is ready to run but is swapped out to secondary storage. A swapped-ready process may not be allocated to the CPU since it is not in main memory.

Long-term scheduling adds the following state.

Held: A process that has been created but will not be considered for loading into memory or for execution. Typically only new processes can become held processes. Once a process leaves the held state, it does not return to it.

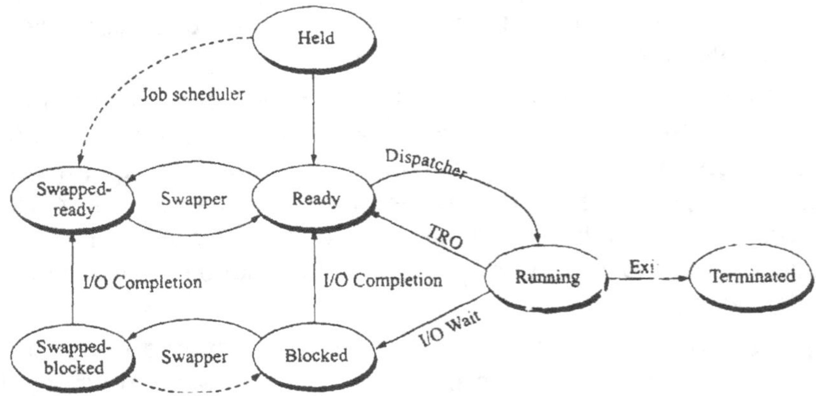

Process state transition diagram

Scheduling Criteria: The goal of a scheduling algorithm is to identify the process whose selection will result in the "best" possible system performance. Best performance is a subjective evaluation that comprises a mix of a number of criteria of varying relative importance. The scheduling policy determines the importance of each of the criteria. A number of algorithms have been used extensively to implement a scheduling policy.

Listed below are some commonly used scheduling criteria. In some cases, the different criteria are complementary; they use different techniques to measure the same basic performance characteristics. In other cases, the criteria are contradictory; improving performance according to one criterion will adversely affect performance as measured by another. It is impossible to design an algorithm that optimizes all the criteria simultaneously.

- **CPU Utilization:** The percentage of time the CPU is executing a process. The load on the system affects the level of utilization that can be achieved; high utilization is more easily achieved on more heavily loaded systems. The importance of this criterion typically varies depending on the degree the system is shared. On a single-user system, CPU utilization is relatively unimportant. On a large, expensive, time-shared system, it may be the primary consideration.

- **Throughput:** The number of processes the system can execute in a period of time. Evaluation of throughput must consider the average length of a process. On systems with long processes, throughput will be less than on systems with short processes.

- **Turnaround Time:** The average period of time it takes a process to execute. A process's turnaround time includes all the time it spends in the system, and can be computed by subtracting the time the process was created from the time it terminated. Turnaround time is inversely proportional to throughput.

- **Wait Time:** The average period of time a process spends waiting. One deficiency of turnaround time as a measure of performance is the time a process spends productively computing increases the turnaround time, lowering the performance evaluation. Wait time presents a more accurate measure of performance because it does not include the time a process is executing on the CPU or performing I/O: it includes only the time a process spends waiting.

- **Response Time:** On interactive systems, the average time it takes the system to start responding to user inputs. On a system where there is a dialog between process and user, turnaround time may be mostly dependent on the speed of the user's responses and relatively unimportant.

Of more concern is the speed with which the system responds to each user's input.

- **Predictability:** Lack of variability in other measures of performance. Users prefer consistency. For example, an interactive system that routinely responds within a second, but on occasion takes 10 s to respond, may be viewed more negatively than a system that consistently responds in 2 s. Although average response time in the latter system is greater, users may prefer the system with greater predictability.

- **Fairness:** The degree to which all processes are given equal opportunity to execute. In particular, do not allow a process to suffer from starvation. A process is a victim of starvation if it becomes stuck in a scheduling queue indefinitely.

- **Priorities:** Give preferential treatment to processes with higher priorities.

Scheduling Algorithms: Scheduling is divided into *nonpreemptive and preemtive; in nonpreemptive,* a process retained control of the CPU until the process blocked or terminated. This approach adequately served the needs of batch jobs where response time was of little or no concern. On today's interactive systems, *preemptive* scheduling is used. The scheduler may preempt a process before it blocks or terminates, in order to allocate the CPU to another process.

Lengthy execution without I/O by a process could monopolize the CPU, giving the processes in the ready queue no opportunity to respond to their users' inputs. Six scheduling algorithms have seen widespread use.

First-Come First-Served: The simplest scheduling algorithm *is First-Come First-Served* (FCFS). Jobs are scheduled in the order they are received. FCFS is nonpreemptive. Implementation is easily accomplished by implementing a queue of the processes to be scheduled or by storing the time the process was received and selecting the process with the earliest time.

FCFS tends to favor CPU-bound processes. Consider a system with a CPU-bound process and a number of I/O-bound processes. I/O-bound processes will tend to execute briefly, then block for I/O. A CPU-bound process in the ready state should not have to wait long before being made runnable. The system will frequently find itself with all the I/O-bound processes blocked and the CPU-bound process running. As the I/O operations complete, the ready queue fills up with the I/O-bound processes. Their wait time increases while I/O device utilization plummets.

Under some circumstances, CPU utilization can also suffer. In the situation described above, once a CPU-bound process does issue an I/O request, the CPU can return to process all the I/O-bound processes. If their processing completes before the CPU-bound process's I/O completes, the CPU sits idle, An algorithm that provides a better mix of CPU- and I/O-bound processing usually performs better than FCFS.

Shortest Job First: *Shortest Job First* (SJF) is another nonpreemptive algorithm. It selects the job (process) with the shortest expected processing time. In case of a tie, first-come first-served scheduling can be used. Originally implemented in a batch-processing environment, SJF relied on a time estimate supplied with the batch job.

SJF has been modified for short-term scheduling use in an .interactive environment. The algorithm bases its decision on the expected processor burst time. Expected burst time can be computed as a simple average of the process's previous burst times or as an exponential average. The exponential average for a burst can be computed using the equation.

$$e_{n+1} = Xt_1 + (1-a)e,$$

where e_n represents the nth expected burst, t_1 represents the length of the burst at time $n,$ and a constant that controls the relative weight given to the most recent burst (if cc is zero the most recent burst is ignored; with cc equal to one, the most recent purpose is the only consideration).

Clearly, SJF favors short jobs over long ones. In extreme cases, the constant arrival of small jobs can lead to starvation of a long job.

Shortest Remaining Time: *Shortest Remaining Time* (SRI) is a preemptive version of shortest job first. Any time a new process enters the pool of processes to be scheduled, the scheduler compares the expected value for its remaining processing time with that of the process currently scheduled. If the new process's time is less, the currently scheduled process is preempted. Like SJF, SRI favors short jobs, and long jobs can be victims of starvation.

Round Robin: *Round Robin* (RR) is a preemptive algorithm that selects the process that has been waiting the longest. After a specified time quantum, the running process is preempted and a new selection is made. Interrupts from an interval timer ensure that processing is suspended and control is transferred to the scheduling algorithm at the conclusion of the time quantum.

Round robin is used extensively in time-shared systems. Use of small time quantum allows round robin to provide good response time. However, short time quanta increase the number of switches between processes, decreasing efficiency. Hardware designed to perform rapid process switches facilitates use of round robin with a short time quantum.

Priority: Priority scheduling requires each process to be assigned a priority value. The process selected is the one with the highest priority. First-come first-served can be used in case of a tie. Priority scheduling may be preemptive or nonpreemptive.

Priority assignment mechanisms vary widely and include basing the priority on a process characteristic (memory usage, I/O frequency, the user executing the process, usage cost (CPU time for higher-priority jobs costs more), or a user- or administrator-assignable parameter. Some of the mechanisms yield dynamically changing priorities (amount of time running), while others are static (the priority associated with a user).

Although it may be intuitively appealing to have the priority value directly proportional to its actual selection priority, on some systems the processes with the lowest-priority values are afforded the highest-selection priority

Multilevel Feedback Queues: The major disadvantage with the five preceding algorithms is they basically treat all jobs the same. This results in each algorithm favoring certain kinds of processes. An algorithm using *Multilevel Feedback Queues* **(MFQ)** addresses this deficiency by customizing the scheduling of a process based on the process's performance characteristics.

5.8   Deadlock

Deadlock occurs when each process in a set of processes controls a resource that another process in the set has requested. Each process blocks, waiting for its requested resource to become available. For deadlock occur, four conditions must hold.

- **Mutual Exclusion:** Each resource may be allocated to only one process at any instant.

- **Hold and Wait:** Processes do not release previously granted resources while waiting for pending requests to be granted.

- **No Preemption:** Previously granted resources may not be taken away from the processes holding by them.

- **Circular Wait:** There exists a chain of two or more processes such that each process in the chain holds a resource requested by the next process in the chain.

5.8.1 Deadlock Prevention

Deadlock can be prevented by never allowing all four conditions to hold. By implementing a policy that makes one of the conditions impossible, the system will be assured to be deadlock-free. However, implementing such a policy may introduce more problems than it solves, as the following analysis shows.

Eliminating mutually exclusive access to any resource is not a practical solution. Some resources cannot be shared. However, in some cases, apparently non-shareable resources can be shared if direct access is not required. For example, a printer appears to be a non shareable resource. Two users cannot print on the printer simultaneously. However, the exact time that the printing takes place is typically not important. A spooling system allows processes to access a virtual printer simultaneously. The print jobs are sent to the actual printer in a non shared sequential fashion. Unless direct access to the actual printer is required, spooling eliminates the mutually exclusive access condition for the printer resource.

The hold-and-wait condition will never apply if requests for resources can only be made by processes holding no resources. One strategy enforces this restriction by requiring all resources to be requested before a process starts executing. There are two major disadvantages to this policy. First, a process may not know what resources it will require The resources needed may depend on its computation. A process requesting every resource it may conceivably need may request resources it never actually uses. Even if the resources are used, forcing the request to occur before the process starts may result in the process holding resources long before they are actually needed. This can lead to poor system performance due to low resource utilization. This strategy is also very susceptible to starvation. A process requesting a number of popular resources may never find them all available at one time.

Another hold-and-wait prevention strategy is to require processes to release all held resources when a request is made. Unfortunately, in most cases this strategy is not practical. For example, after a process has written data to a disk, to release the disk to request a printer the data on the disk. If the disk is allocated to another process, all the stored data could be lost.

Eliminating the non-preemption condition is even less practical than eliminating mutual exclusion. Preempting a resource is essentially forced sharing. Preemption can be applied to devices whose state can be saved and then later restored. For example, a process can be preempted from using a CPU by saving the CPU state. However, the device characteristics necessary to do this are essentially the same as the characteristics needed for creating a shared virtual device for which mutually exclusive access is not required.

Elimination of the circular-wait condition is perhaps the most promising of the prevention techniques One method for breaking the cycle is to associate each resource with a unique priority number. Processes may only request a resource if its priority is higher than all currently held resources. Using this strategy, any resource can be requested. If the resource does not have a higher priority than all currently held resources, the currently held resource with a higher priority must first be released. In those situations, this approach is similar to the one used to eliminate the hold-and-wait condition, but this strategy is more flexible, allowing resources to be held under some circumstances when an additional request is made. If the priority numbers are chosen wisely, this system may accommodate the needs of many processes. However, it will not work in all cases. Then typically is no priority number that will match the needs of all processes.

5.8.2 Deadlock Avoidance

Rather than prevent one of the conditions that must be present for deadlock to exist, deadlock can be avoided by never allocating a resource if it may eventually lead to deadlock. A simple way to do this is to allocate resources to only one process at a time. Although not efficient, deadlock clearly cannot occur. In the future, a more generous allocation policy can be implemented with additional information about potential resource needs of all processes.

A system is said to be in a safe state if there is a *safe execution sequence*. An execution sequence is an ordering for process execution such that each process, when executed, runs until it terminates or is blocked, and all requests for resources are immediately granted if the resource is available. A safe execution sequence is an execution sequence in which all processes run to completion.

An *unsafe* state is a state that is not safe, not necessarily a deadlocked state. An unsafe state may currently not be deadlocked, but there is at least one sequence of requests from processes that would make the system deadlocked. If that sequence of requests occurs, no set of responses to those requests would allow the operating system to avoid a deadlocked state.

An algorithm for determining whether or not a state is safe must be supplied with the following information: the current allocation of resources to each process, the maximum number of each resource a process might request, and the total number of each resource currently available in the system.

The *banker's algorithm* makes decisions on granting a resource based on whether or not granting the request will put the system into an unsafe state. When a request is received, the algorithm first checks that the process is not requesting more resources than its specified maximum allocation, raising an error exception for an invalid request. Given a valid request, the number of resources requested is compared to the number of resources available. If not enough resources are available, the request is denied. If sufficient resources are available, the algorithm creates a modified version of the current state that reflects the effect of granting the resource. The algorithm then checks if the modified version of the system state is safe. The resource is granted if and only if the modified version of the system state is safe. While very elegant in design, the banker's algorithm has one major disadvantage. It requires knowledge of the maximum number of resources each process might request. Such information is not available on most systems. Thus, few systems use the banker's algorithm.

5.8.3 Deadlock Detection

Instead of trying to prevent or avoid deadlock, systems could allow deadlock to happen (hoping it occurs infrequently), and recover from deadlock when it does occur. Such a strategy requires mechanisms for detecting and recovering from deadlock.

A resource allocation graph may be used to model the state of resource allocations and requests. In such a graph, processes are drawn is circles, resources as rectangles. Within a resource rectangle, a dot is drawn for each instance of that resource. For each pending resource request, a direct arrow is drawn from the process to the resource rectangle. For each granted request, a direct arrow is drawn from a resource dot to the process.

5.8.4 Recovery from Deadlock

Three approaches to recover from deadlock are automatic preemption, automatic termination, or manual intervention. With **automatic preemption** the operating system preempts a subset of the allocated resources. Three major issues must be resolved to implement such a strategy.

- **Selection:** Which resources from which processes are to be preempted? If the decision is made to preempt one resource from a process, should all its other resources also be preempted? Other factors in making the decision could include:
  1. A process's priority
  2. How long a process has been executing
  3. How long a process still needs to execute
  4. How many resources a process currently holds
  5. The size of the different sets of resources that, if released, would break the deadlock
  6. How many processes would be affected

- **Consequence:** What happens to the processes that have resources preempted? Can the system maintain state information about processes such that if they are victims of preemption, they can be rolled back to an earlier state? Maintaining such information can be costly in terms of both time and storage space. Even rolling a process back to its starting state may not be practical. Some input data may be unrecoverable. Unless that data was captured and saved when the process was first run, the ability to process that information will have been lost.

- **Starvation:** If the same process is repeatedly a victim of preemption, constant rollbacks could preclude it from terminating. Will the selection mechanism preclude the possibility of starvation? One solution is to use a preemption counter. Each time a process is rolled back, the preemption counter is incremented. Should deadlock occur, no resources would be preempted from the process with the highest preemption counter.

Instead of preempting resources, **automatic termination** eliminates deadlock by terminating processes. All deadlocked processes could be terminated, or the system could select, a subset of the deadlocked processes to terminate. Although more drastic, terminating all processes can be done quickly on systems where fast resolution is important. If only a subset of processes are to be terminated, the same factors encountered in automatic preemption may be considered in selecting the processes to be terminated. It should also be noted that the termination of one process may have effects beyond that process. Processes dependent on the terminated process's computation may be adversely affected, and partially updated files may be left in inconsistent states.

The **manual intervention** approach turns responsibility for resolving the problem over to the system operator. Given the limitations of the automatic approaches, in many cases this is an attractive option. But some systems run without a full-time (or even part-time) operator and others must react to a deadlock situation within moments of its detection. In such cases, manual intervention is not a practical solution.

5.9   File Management

The file management function of the operating system involves handling the file system which consists of two parts - a set of files, and a directory structure. File is a collection of related information, has a name, and is stored on a secondary storage. It is the smallest named unit that can be written to a secondary storage device. Data cannot be stored on the secondary storage if it is not in the form of a file. A file has attributes like its name, location, size, type, time, and date of creation etc. The information stored in a file can be accessed in different ways – sequential access (access is in a sequential order from start to end) and direct access (the file can be accessed in any order). Directory structure provides information about the files stored on the secondary storage. Directory contains information about all the files within it. The information about the files is kept as entries in the directory of device. A directory further may have a sub-directory defined within it. Directory contains the name, location, size, and type of all the files defined on the device. The tree-structured directory is the commonly used directory structure. The file manager is responsible for the maintenance of secondary storage (e.g., hard disks). Nutt describes the responsibility of the file manager and defines the file, the fundamental abstraction of secondary storage:

Each file is a named collection of data stored in a device. The file manager implements this abstraction and provides directories for organizing files. It also provides a spectrum of commands to read and write the contents of a file, to set the file read/write position, to set and use the protection mechanism, to change the ownership, to list files in a directory, and to remove a file. The file manager provides a protection mechanism to allow machine users to administer how processes executing on behalf of different users can access the information in files. File protection is a fundamental property of files because it allows different people to store their information on a shared computer, with the confidence that the information can be kept confidential.

In addition to these functions, the file manager also provides a logical way for users to organize files in secondary storage. Brookshear [1997] elaborates:

"For the convenience of the machine's users, most file managers allow files to be grouped into a bundle called a directory or folder. This approach allows a user to organize his or her files according to their purpose by placing related files in the same directory. Moreover, by allowing directories to contain other directories, called subdirectories, a hierarchical organization can be constructed. For example, a user may create a directory called Records that contains subdirectories called Financial Records, Medical Records, and Household Records. Within each of these subdirectories could be files that fall within that particular category. A sequence of directories within directories is called a directory path"

While users may need to store complex data structures in secondary storage, most storage devices including hard disks are capable of storing only linearly addressed blocks of bytes. Thus, the file manager needs to provide some way of mapping user data to storage blocks in secondary storage and vice versa. These blocks can be managed in at least three different ways: as a contiguous set of blocks on the secondary storage device, as a list of blocks interconnected with links, or as a collection of blocks interconnected by a file index. These three methods are commonly referred to as Contiguous Allocation, Linked Allocation, and Indexed Allocation.

The operating system manages the storage media like the disk and implements the abstract concept of the file. System calls are an interface between the process and the operating system. Operating system provides system calls for creating, reading, and writing, deleting, repositioning, and truncating a file. Some of the operations that can be performed on a directory are – search for a file, create, delete and rename a file, list a directory, and traverse the file system within the directory. The user simply uses the system calls like "dir", "list" to perform operation on a file or directory, without going into the details of its working.

5.9.1 Objectives for a File Management System

- Minimize or eliminate the potential for lost or destroyed data
- Provide a standardized set of I/O interface routines
- Provide I/O support for multiple users

5.9.2 Methods of File Allocation

Contiguous Allocation Method: In this method data in a file is stored in a contiguous section of the disk (that is, the file occupies a linear sequence of disk blocks). The directory entry for each file contains the file name, start block number and the file size.

Advantages:
1. Simple to implement
2. Allows linear and sequential access with the same ease

Disadvantages:
1. Does not allow simple expansion of files
2. Risk of external fragmentation
3. Solving the fragmentation problem requires compaction, a time consuming process
4. The kernel must allocate and reserve contiguous space when the file is first created

Linked Allocation Method: Here the data blocks of a file can be scattered anywhere on the disk. The directory entry of a file contains the start block number and the file name. Each data block uses 4 bytes of its space for a pointer to the next block of the file. This continues until the last block which has a special end-of-file (EOF) value.

Advantages:
1. No external fragmentation. Any free block can be used to satisfy the request

2.   A file can expand. No need to declare the file size when the file is first created

3.   No need to compact disk space

Disadvantages:

1.   Direct-access is very inefficient

2.   The pointers take up some space

3.   Scattering the pointers all over the disk poses a reliability problem

Indexed Allocation Method: In this allocation method an index block is allocated for each file that is created. The index block of a file contains all the pointers that point to the data blocks of that file. The directory entry contains the index block number and the file name.

Advantages:

1.   Grouping all the pointers into one location solves the problem of reliability.

2.   Direct-access is efficient. The 'i'th entry in the index block points to the 'i'th block of the file.

Disadvantages:

1.   The pointers may waste a lot of space since an entire disk block must be allocated to hold them even if few pointers are actually used.

5.10   Memory Management

Memory management is primarily concerned with allocation of physical memory to requesting processes. Certain amount of memory is required for activating the process .The memory management divided into

1.   Contiguous allocation
2.   Noncontiguous allocation

5.10.1 Contiguous Allocation

Contiguous allocation means that each logical object is placed in a set of memory locations with strictly consecutive addresses. A common approach with contiguous allocation is to partition the available physical memory while relocating suitable free partition, if available. Memory partition may be divided static partition or dynamic partition.

In static partition memory is wasted in each portion where an object of smaller size than the partition is itself is loaded. Wasting of memory within a partition called internal fragmentation. Dynamic partitioning eliminates internal fragmentation by making each partition only as large as necessary to satisfy is request for space for an object.

Swapping: Removing suspended or permitted process from memory and subsequent bringing back is called swapping. Swapping is help full for improving processes in partitioned memory environments by increasing the ratio of ready to resident processes.

When the schedule decided to admit few process for which no suitable free partition can be found the swapper invoked to vacate such a partition. Swapper responsibilities are:

1. Selection of process to swapper out
2. Selection of process to swapper in
3. Allocation and management of swapper space

5.10.2 Non Contiguous Allocation

Non contiguous allocation means that memory is allocated in such a way that's part of a single logical object may be placed in non contiguous areas of physical memory.

Paging: Paging is the memory management scheme that removes the requirement of contiguous allocation of physical memory. The physical memory is conceptually divided into a number of fixed size slots, page frames. The virtual address space of process is also split into fixed size blocks of the same size, called pages.

CHAPTER 6

Microsoft Office

6.1   Microsoft Word

Microsoft Word is a powerful tool to create documents. Word processing software which allows writing articles, letter, edit them and print them after formatting. It has all the possible options of a word processor in the form of font style and size; indents; the spacing; margins; spell check and grammar checkers to name few.

Starting Microsoft Word

Double click on the Microsoft Word icon on the desktop.

Or

Click on Start --> Programs --> Micro office --> Microsoft Word

6.1.1 Toolbars

The toolbars in Microsoft Word provide easy access and functionality to the user. There are many shortcuts that can be taken by using the toolbar. First, make sure that the proper toolbars are visible on the screen.

1. Click **View**
2. Select **Toolbars**
3. Select **Standard, Formatting, and Drawing**
4. Other toolbars can be selected if you wish

Standard Toolbars

This entire toolbar could become a floating window by double-clicking on the control bar at the far left end of this toolbar. That gives the following window, which can be placed anywhere on the screen:

This toolbar can be restored to its original position by clicking in the gray bar at the top and dragging it back to the top of the screen. Push the top of the window up to the bottom of the menu bar.

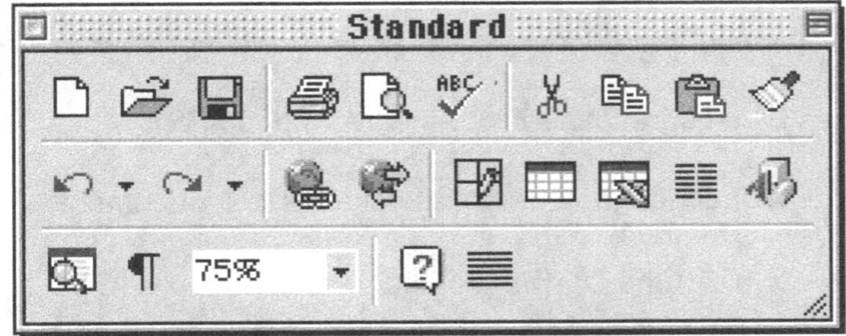

Commonly used buttons:

Creates a new blank document

Open a file

Saves the active file with its current file name, location and file format

Prints the active file

Print preview

Spelling, grammar and writing style checker

Cut - Removes the selection from the document and places it on the clipboard

Copy - Copies the selected item(s) to the clipboard

Paste - Places the content of the clipboard at the insertion point

Format painter - Copies the format from a selected object or text and applies to other objects or text

Undo - Reverses the last command,

Redo - Reverses the action of the Undo button

Displays the Tables and Borders toolbar

Insert a table into the document, or make a table of selected text

Insert an Excel spreadsheet into the Word document

Columns - Changes the number of columns in a document

Displays or hides the Drawing toolbar

Zoom - Enlarge or reduce the display of the active document.

6.1.2 Creating and Opening Documents

There are several ways to create new documents, open existing documents, and save documents in Word:

Create a New Document

1.   Click the New Document button on the menu bar.
2.   Choose **File New** from the menu bar.
3.   Press **CTRL+N** on the keyboard.

Open an Existing Document

1.   Click the Open File button on the menu bar.
2.   Choose **File Open** from the menu bar.
3.   Press **CTRL+O** on the keyboard.

Each method will show the Open dialog box. Choose the file and click the **Open** button.

Save a Document

1.   Click the Save button on the menu bar.
2.   Select **File Save** from the menu bar.
3.   Press **CTRL+S** on the keyboard.

Renaming Documents

To rename a Word document while using the program, select **File Open** and find the file you want to rename. Right-click on the document name with the mouse and select **Rename** from the shortcut menu. Type the new name for the file and press the **ENTER** key.

Working on Multiple Documents

Several documents can be opened simultaneously for editing multiple documents at once. All open documents are listed under the **Window** menu.

Close a Document

Close the current document by selecting **File Close** or click the Close icon if it's visible on the Standard Toolbar.

6.1.3 Editing a Document

Typing and Inserting Text

To enter text, just start typing! The text will appear where the blinking cursor is located. Move the cursor by using the arrow buttons on the keyboard or positioning the mouse and clicking the left button. The keyboard shortcuts listed below are also helpful when moving through the text of a document:

Move Action	Keystroke
Beginning of the line	**HOME**
End of the line	**END**
Top of the document	**CTRL+HOME**
End of the document	**CTRL+END**

Selecting Text

To change any attributes of text it must be highlighted first. Select the text by dragging the mouse over the desired text while keeping the left mouse button depressed, or hold down the **SHIFT** key on the keyboard while using the arrow buttons to highlight the text. The following table contains shortcuts for selecting a portion of the text

Selection	Technique
Whole word	Double-click within the word
Whole paragraph	Triple-click within the paragraph
Several words or lines	Drag the mouse over the words, or hold down **SHIFT** while using the arrow keys
Entire document	Choose **Edit Select All** from the menu bar, or press **CTRL+A**

Deselect the text by clicking anywhere outside of the selection on the page or press an arrow key on the keyboard.

Deleting Text

Use the **BACKSPACE** and **DELETE** keys on the keyboard to delete text. Backspace will delete text to the left of the cursor and Delete will erase text to the right. To delete a large selection of text, highlight it using any of the methods outlined above and press the **DELETE** key.

Formatting Text

The formatting toolbar is the easiest way to change many attributes of text. If the toolbar as shown below isn't displayed on the screen, select **View Toolbars** and choose **Formatting**.

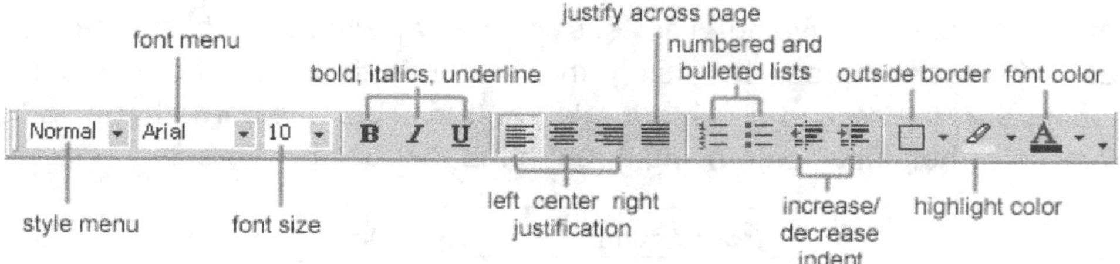

- **Style Menu** - Styles are explained in detail later in this tutorial.
- **Font Face** - Click the arrowhead to the right of the font name box to view the list of fonts available. Scroll down to the font you want and select it by clicking on the name once with the mouse. A serif font (one with "feet" circled in the illustration below) is recommended for paragraphs of text that will be printed on paper, as they are most readable. The following graphic demonstrates the difference between *serif* (Times New Roman on the left) and *sans-serif* ("no feet", Arial on the right) fonts.
- **Font Size** - Click on the white part of the font size box to enter a value for the font size or click the arrowhead to the right of the box to view a list of font sizes available. Select a size by clicking on it once..
- **Font Style** - Use these buttons to bold, italicize, and underline text.
- **Alignment** - Text can be aligned to the left, center, or right side of the page or it can be justified across the page.
- **Numbered and Bulleted Lists** - Lists are explained in detail later in this tutorial.
- **Increase/Decrease Indent** - Change the indentation of a paragraph in relation to the side of the page.
- **Outside Border** - Add a border around a text selection.

- **Highlight Colour** - Use this option to change the colour behind a text selection. The colour shown on the button is the last colour used. To select a different colour, click the arrowhead next to the image on the button.
- **Text Colour** - This option changes the colour of the text. The colour shown on the button is the last colour chosen. Click the arrowhead next to the button image to select another colour.

Moving (Cutting) Text

Highlight the text that will be moved and select **Edit Cut** from the menu bar, click the **Cut** button on the standard tool bar, or press **CTRL+X** at once. This will move the text to a clipboard.

To move a small amount of text a short distance, the drag-and-drop method may be quicker. Highlight the text you want to move, click the selection with the mouse, drag the selection to the new location, and release the mouse button.

Copying Text

To copy text, choose **Edit Copy**, click the **Copy** button on the standard toolbar, or press **CTRL+C** to copy the text to the clipboard.

Paste Text

To paste, cut or copied text, move the cursor to the location you want to move the text to and select **Edit Paste** from the menu bar, click the **Paste** button on the standard toolbar, or press **CTRL+V**. Document when at once Paste, click the **Clear Clipboard** button (the icon with an "X" over the clipboard image) to clear the contents of the clipboard.

Columns

To quickly place text in a column format, click the **Columns** button on the standard toolbar and select the number of columns by dragging the mouse over the diagram.

For more column options, select **Format Columns** from the menu bar. The **Columns** dialog box allows you to choose the properties of the columns. Select the number and width of the columns from the dialog box.

Lists

Bulleted and Numbered Lists

1. Click the **Bulleted List** button or **Numbered List** button on the formatting toolbar.

2. Type the first entry and press **ENTER**. This will create a new bullet or number on the next line. If you want to start a new line without adding another bullet or number, hold down the **SHIFT** key while pressing **ENTER**.

3. Continue to type entries and press **ENTER** twice when you are finished typing to end the list.

Use the **Increase Indent** and **Decrease Indent** buttons on the formatting toolbar to create lists of multiple levels.

Formatting Lists

Using the Bullets and Numbering dialog box can change the bullet image and numbering format.

1. Highlight the entire list to change all the bullets or numbers, or place the cursor on one line within the list to change a single bullet.

2. Access the dialog box by selecting **Format Bullets and Numbering** from the menu bar or by right clicking within the list and selecting **Bullets and numbering** from the shortcut menu.

3. Select the list style from one of the seven choices given, or click the **Picture** button to choose a different icon. Click the **Numbered** tab to choose a numbered list style.

4. Click **OK** when finished.

TABLES

Tables are used to display data and there are several ways to build them in Word. Begin by placing the cursor where you want the table to appear in the document and choose one of the following methods.

Insert a Table

There are two ways to add a table to the document using the Insert feature:

1. Click the **Insert Table** button on the standard toolbar. Drag the mouse along the grid, highlighting the number of rows and columns for the table.

2. Or, select **Table |Insert| Table** from the menu bar. Select the number of rows and columns for the table and click **OK**.

Draw the Table

A table can also be drawn onto the document:

1. Draw the table by selecting **Draw Table** from the menu bar. The cursor is now the image of a pencil and the **Tables and Borders** toolbar has appeared.

2. Draw the cells of the table with the mouse. If you make a mistake, click the **Eraser** button and drag the mouse over the area to be deleted.

3. To draw more cells, click on the **Draw Table** button . Inserting Rows and Columns

Once the table is drawn, insert additional rows by placing the cursor in the row you want to be adjacent to. Select Table **|Insert| Rows Above** or **Rows Below**. Or, select an entire row and right-click with the mouse. Choose **Insert Rows** from the shortcut menu.

Much like inserting a row, add a new column by placing the cursor in a cell adjacent to where the new column will be added. Select **Table |Insert| Columns to the Left** or **Columns to the Right**. Or, select the column, right-click with the mouse, and select **Insert Columns**.

GRAPHICS

Adding Clip Art

To add a clip art image from the Microsoft library to a document, follow these steps:

1. Select **Insert|Picture|Clip Art** from the menu bar.

2. To find an image, click in the white box following **Search for clips**. Delete the words "Type one or more words . . ." and enter keywords describing the image you want to use.

OR

Click one of the category icons.

3. Continue selecting images to add to the document and click the **Close** button in the top, right corner of the **Insert ClipArt** window to stop adding clip art to the document.

Add An Image from a File

Follow these steps to add a photo or graphic from an existing file:

1. Select **Insert|Picture|From File** on the menu bar.

2. Click the down arrow button on the right of the **Look in:** window to find the image on your computer.

3. Highlight the file name from the list and click the **Insert** button.

Auto Shapes

The AutoShapes toolbar will allow you to draw many different geometrical shapes, arrows, flow chart symbols, stars, and banners on the document. Activate the AutoShapes toolbar by selecting **Insert|Picture|AutoShapes** or **View|Toolbars|AutoShapes** from the menu bar, or clicking the **AutoShapes** button on the Drawing toolbar. Click each button on the toolbar to view the options for drawing the shape.

- **Lines** - After clicking the Lines button on the AutoShapes toolbar, draw a *straight line*, *arrow*, or *double-ended arrow* from the first row of options by clicking the respective button. Click in the document where you would like the line to begin and click again where it should end. To draw a *curved line* or *freeform shape*, select curved lines from the menu (first and second buttons of second row), click in the document where the line should appear, and click the mouse every time a curve should begin. End creating the graphic by clicking on the starting end or pressing the **ESC** key. To *scribble*, click the last button in the second row, click the mouse in the document and hold down the left button while you draw the design. Let go of the mouse button to stop drawing.

- **Basic Shapes** - Click the Basic Shapes button on the AutoShapes toolbar to select from many *two- and three-dimensional shapes*, *icons*, *braces*, and *brackets*. Use the drag-and-drop method to draw the shape in the document. When the shape has been made, it can be resized using the open box handles and other adjustments specific to each shape can be modified using the yellow diamond handles.

- **Block Arrows** - Select Block Arrows to choose from many types of *two- and three-dimensional arrows*. Drag-and-drop the arrow in the document and use the open box and yellow diamond handles to adjust the arrowheads. Each AutoShape can also be rotated by first clicking the **Free Rotate** button on the drawing toolbar. Click and drag the green handles around the image to rotate it. The tree image below was created from an arrow rotated 90 degrees.

- **Flow Chart** - Choose from the flow chart menu to add *flow chart elements* to the document and use the line menu to draw connections between the elements.

- **Stars and Banners** - Click the button to select *stars*, *bursts*, *banners*, and *scrolls*.

- **Call Outs** - Select from the *speech and thought bubbles*, and *line call outs*. Enter the call out text in the text box that is made.

- **More AutoShapes** - Click this button to choose from a list of clip art categories.

Each of the submenus on the AutoShapes toolbar can become a separate toolbar. Just click and drag the gray bar across the top of the submenus off of the toolbar and it will become a separate floating toolbar.

Spelling and grammar check

Auto Correct

Word automatically corrects many commonly misspelled words and punctuation marks with the AutoCorrect feature. To view the list of words that are automatically corrected, select **Tools|AutoCorrect**. This may be a hidden feature so click the double arrows at the bottom of the **Tools** menu listing if the AutoCorrect choice is not listed.

Many options including the accidental capitalization of the first two letters of a word and capitalization of the first word of the sentence can be automatically corrected from this page. If there are words you often misspell, enter the wrong and correct spellings in the **Replace** and **with** fields.

Spelling and Grammar Check

Word will automatically check for spelling and grammar errors as you type unless you turn this feature off. Spelling errors are noted in the document with a red underline. Grammar errors are indicated by a green underline. To disable this feature, select **Tools Options** from the menu bar and click the **Spelling and Grammar tab** on the dialog box. Uncheck **"Check spelling as you type"** and **"Check grammar as you type"**, and click **OK**.

To use the spelling and grammar checker, follow these steps:

1. Select **Tools Spelling and Grammar** from the menu bar.

2. The **Spelling and Grammar** dialog box will notify you of the first mistake in the document and misspelled words will be highlighted in red.

3. If the word is spelled correctly, click the **Ignore** button or click the **Ignore All** button if the word appears more than once in the document.

4. If the word is spelled incorrectly, choose one of the suggested spellings in the **Suggestions** box and click the **Change** button or **Change All** button to correct all occurrences of the word in the document. If the correct spelling is not suggested, enter the correct spelling in the **Not in Dictionary** box and click the **Change** button.

5. If the word is spelled correctly and will appear in many documents you type (such as your name), click the **Add** button to add the word to the dictionary so it will no longer appear as a misspelled word.

   As long as the **Check Grammar** box is checked in the **Spelling and Grammar** dialog box, Word will check the grammar of the document in addition to the spelling. If you do not want the grammar checked, remove the checkmark from this box. Otherwise, follow these steps for correcting grammar:

1. If Word finds a grammar mistake, it will be shown in the box as the spelling errors. The mistake is highlighted in green text.

2. Several suggestions may be given in the **Suggestions** box. Select the correction that best applies and click **Change**.

3. If no correction is needed (Word is often wrong more than it is right), click the **Ignore** button.

6.1.4 Page Formatting

Page Margins

The page margins of the document can be changed using the rulers on the page and the **Page Setup** window. The ruler method is discussed first:

1. Move the mouse over the area where the white ruler changes to gray.

2. When the cursor becomes a double-ended arrow, click with the mouse and drag the margin indicator to the desired location.

3. Release the mouse when the margin is set.

*The margins can also be changed using the **Page Setup** dialog box:*

1. Select **File Page Setup** and choose the **Margins tab** in the dialog box.

2. Enter margin values in the **Top**, **Bottom**, **Left**, and **Right** boxes. The **Preview** window will reflect the changes.

3. If the document has **Headers** and/or **Footers**, the distance of this text appears from the edge of the page can be changed.

4. Click **OK** when finished.

Page Size and Orientation

Change the orientation page within the Page Setup dialog box.

1. Select **File Page Setup** and choose the **Paper Size** tab.

2. Select the proper paper size from the drop-down menu.

3. Change the orientation from **Portrait** or **Landscape** by checking the corresponding radio button.

Headers and Footers

A header is text that is added to the top margin of every page such as a document title or page number and footer is text added to the bottom margin. Follow these steps to add or edit headers and footers in the document:

1. Select **View Header and Footer** from the menu bar. The Header and Footer toolbar will appear and the top of the page will be highlighted.

2. Type the heading in the **Header** box. You may use many of the standard text formatting options such as font face, size, bold, italics, etc.

3. Click the **Insert AutoText** button to view a list of quick options available.

4. Use the other options on the toolbar to add page numbers, the current date and time.

5. To edit the footer, click the **Switch between Header and Footer button** on the toolbar.

6. When you are finished adding headers and footers, click the **Close button** on the toolbar.

Page Numbers

1. Select **Insert Page Numbers** from the menu bar then dialog box will appear.

3. Select the position of the page numbers by choosing "Top of page" or "Bottom of page" from the **Position** drop-down menu.

4. Select the alignment of the page numbers in the **Alignment** drop-down menu.

5. If you do not want the page number to show on the first page (if it is a title page, for example), uncheck the **Show number of first page** box.

6. Click **OK** when finished.

Print Preview and Printing

Preview your document by clicking the Print Preview button on the standard toolbar or by selecting **File Print Preview**. When the document is ready to print, click the Print button from the Print Preview screen or select **File Print**.

6.2 Power Point 2000

Microsoft PowerPoint is a powerful tool to create professional looking presentations and slide shows. PowerPoint allows user to construct presentations from scratch or by using the easy to use wizard.

Starting Microsoft PowerPoint

- Two Ways

  1 Double click on the Microsoft PowerPoint icon on the desktop.

  Or

  2. Click on Start --> Programs --> Microsoft PowerPoint

6.2.1 Creating and Opening a Presentation

After you open up Microsoft PowerPoint, a screen pops up asking if you would like to create a New Presentation or Open an Existing Presentation.

Auto Content Wizard

- Creates a new presentation by prompting for information about content, purpose, style, handouts, and output. The new presentation contains sample text that you can replace with own information. Simply follow the directions and prompts that are given by Microsoft PowerPoint.

Design Template

- Creates a new presentation based on one of the PowerPoint design templates supplied by Microsoft.

Blank Presentation

- Creates a new, blank presentation using the default settings for text and colours. Go to next step: Creating a Blank Presentation.

Opening an Existing Presentation

1. Select **Open An Existing Presentation** from the picture above
2. Click on your presentation in the white box below step 1

   o If you do not see your presentation in the white box, select **More Files** and hit OK.

   o Locate your existing Presentation and click the **Open** button

Create a Blank Presentation

After select Blank Presentation a window pops up asking to select the layout of the first slide.

Pre-Designed Slide Layouts (Left to Right)

- Title Slide
- Bulleted List
- Two Column Text
- Table
- Text & Chart
- Chart & Text
- Organizational Chart
- Chart
- Text & Clip Art
- Clip Art & Text

- Title Only
- Blank Slide

Slide Manipulation

- Inserting A New Slide
    1. Click **Insert** at top of screen
    2. Select New Slide
- Formatting A Slide Background

format your slide to make it look however you would like, whether it is a background colour, picture, or a design template built into Microsoft PowerPoint. The next step will show you how to apply a Design Template, but the other items mentioned above can be accomplished the same way.

1. Click **Format** at the top of the screen
2. Select Apply Design Template.
3. Select Design you wish to apply
4. Click Apply Button

Inserting Clipart & Pictures

1. Display the slide to add a picture to.
2. Click Insert at the top of the screen
3. Select Picture
4. Select Clip Art
5. Click the category you want
6. Click the picture you want
7. Click Insert Clip on the shortcut menu
8. When finished using the Clip Gallery, click the Close button on the Clip Gallery title bar

Adding Transitions to a Slide Show

You can add customized transitions to slide show that will make it come alive and become appealing to audience. Follow these steps when adding Slide Transitions.

1. In **slide or slide sorter view**, select the slide or slides to add a transition to.
2. On the **Slide Show** menu at the top of the screen, click **Slide Transition.**

3. In the Effect box, click the transition, and then select any other options if required.

4. To apply the transition to the selected slide, click Apply.

5. To apply the transition to all the slides, click Apply to All.

6. Repeat the process for each slide you want to add a transition to.

7. To view the transitions, on the Slide Show menu, click Animation Preview.

Viewing the Slide Show

View slide show by any of the following ways:

1. Click Slide Show at the lower left of the PowerPoint window.

2. On the Slide Show menu, click View Show.

3. On the View menu, click Slide Show.

4. Press F5 on the keyboard

Navigating While In Slide Show

- **Forward Navigation**
  - simply click on the left Mouse Button or click the Enter Button on your

Keyboard

- **Reverse Navigation**
  - click the Backspace on the keyboard
- **Exiting the show**
  - click the Esc Button on the keyboard

Pack up a presentation for use on another computer

1. Open the Presentation

2. On the **File** menu, click **Pack and Go**

3. Follow the instructions in the Pack and Go Wizard.

Unpack a presentation to run on another computer

1. Insert the disk or connect to the network location packed the presentation to

2. In My Computer, go to the location of the packed presentation, and then double-click **Page setup**

3. Enter the destination.

6.2.2 Common Tasks

Common Tasks Options

- To add a new slide, click the Common Tasks, New Slide to see the New Slide dialog box. New slides are added below the current slide.

    o The Slide Layout Tool applies, or re-applies the selected layout and uses almost the same dialog box as New Slide. Slide Layout reapplies the selected current master style and is useful when moved Placeholders or decided to change the format of a slide and need to return to (or apply) a specific layout format. To apply or re-apply a layout, click the Slide Layout Tool and make layout choice.

    o To change the applied template, click and select a different template. All slides in presentation will have the newly chosen design applied, and any charts created will be updated with the new colour scheme.

View

The View Toolbar is located in the lower left corner of the screen and lets you quickly move through different views of the presentation:

Normal	**Default view**
Outline	View for textual development
Slide	View for graphical development
Slide Sorter	View of a thumbnail of each slide
Slide Show	Displays on-screen presentation

Text

Options on the Text Toolbar allow you to make choices affecting highlighted text.

Note: Keep in mind that some options may be hidden. To access those, click the double-headed or drop-down arrow on the toolbar.

Text Toolbar

Drawing

The Drawing Toolbar contains the tools (each is described in detail later in this tutorial) to incorporate objects into a presentation:

Drawing Tools Toolbar

- **Inserting New Slides:** New slides are added after the current one. To add a new slide below the current one, click the New Slide Tool. Then choose the layout of the new slide from the New Slide Auto Layout dialog box.

- **Understanding Apply to All and Apply:** On many dialog boxes, when making option selections in PowerPoint, are seen two choices: Apply to all and apply. When choose Apply to all, each slide in the presentation will change according to the selections made, both existing and future slides. When choose Apply only current slide is changed.

- **Applying Design Templates:** PowerPoint calls its built-in colour schemes Design Templates. These can apply a Design at any point during development, but most of will prefer to establish the Design from the outset so that you see the effects of development. On the basis of interest apply a different Design at any time.

  For adding previous versions of Microsoft Office templates to use in addition to those found in the new version. To do so, on the Office CD where the templates are located, find the directory containing the templates, and then copy the individual templates into the directory on workstation containing the current version's templates. They will then appear in the selection list alongside the current templates.

- **To apply a Design, click the Apply Design Tool:** Though you can apply only a single Design to a presentation, you still can affect the appearance of individual slides within the presentation by altering the slide colour scheme and the background. These two options available in the Format menu.

- **Setting up Presentation Masters:** Masters allow making design decisions that will then affect each slide or page in the presentation. There are masters for Slides, Title Slide, Handouts and Notes.

Sample Slide Master

Master slide is including placement, font styles and sizes; bullet styles; footers; objects; and images. Individual slides can derivate from the master but each new slide will follow the master specifications.

First set up the master before building any slides. When create the master first, all slides add to the presentation will be based on that master. If, build slides before establishing the master, some items on the slides may not change to conform. Any text or object you place on the master will display on every slide in the presentation in the location that placed it on the Master.

- **Text Guidelines**

  To make font changes on the master, highlight the text that you want to change, and then make the changes using the tools on the Text Toolbar. For example to change the title text to 44-point Arial, highlight the words "Click to edit Master title slide," then choose Helvetica and 44 from the font face and type size boxes, respectively.

  When making choices about fonts in the presentation, keep these guidelines in mind:

- Text will be easier to read when formatted in a sans serif font such as Arial or Helvetica.

- Slide titles should be not less than 44-point type.

- Body text should be not less than 30-point type in order to remain clearly readable to all audience.

Headers and Footers

The Slide Master shows the default location of any date, slide number, or textual footer that you choose to use.

To insert text into the footer,

1. Choose VIEW: Header and Footer.

2. Make sure that Footer is check marked, and then type the text in the Footer text box.

To insert a date,

1. Choose VIEW: Header and Footer.

2. Make sure that the Date and time option is checked.

3. Choose either Update automatically or fixed.

4. Update automatically updates the date and time on your presentation slides each time when open the presentation.

5. Fixed allows to type a specific date into the box that will be displayed on slide.

To insert a slide number,

1. Choose VIEW: Header and Footer.

2. Click the checkbox for Slide Number.

To insert objects, images, and diagrams that will appear on each slide in your presentation, create or insert the object, size it, and move it to the location on the Slide Master where you want it to display on each slide.

Background

Choose FORMAT: Background to make changes to the "wallpaper" of the slide. The drop-down box allows to change colours, patterns, gradients, and other fill effects.

Every object on a Slide Master, including the design on the Design Template itself, is considered a Master Item. You can choose not to display Master items on the current slides, or all slides by clicking the option to omit background graphics from master.

To omit all Master Items, choose FORMAT: Background. Click Omit background graphics from master. Click on either Apply or Apply to all.

Navigating during Development

To navigate through the slides during development, you can use the Scroll Bar on the right of the screen. Press and drag the Slider to move continuously through the presentation. An indicator shows the slide are currently passing and the title of that slide. Release the Slider to move to the indicated slide.

Sample Slider Image

To move one complete slide forward or backward, click the appropriate double-headed arrow at the bottom of the Scroll Bar. Another option is to move directly to the desired slide by clicking on the slide itself in the Outline pane. All Auto Layouts but two (Blank and Large Object) have a Placeholder for Title. The Slider demonstrates one reason why it is important to always use a layout that contains a Title Placeholder and to always title each slide—the title helps orient you to the location within the presentation.

In addition, the bottom left corner of the PowerPoint screen shows the current slide, out of the total number of slides, as well as the name of the Design Template applied to the presentation.

Creating Bulleted Lists

To create a bulleted list from the Auto Layout, choose the Bulleted List layout. Click in the main Placeholder and begin typing. Each time press ENTER, the cursor is automatically placed in the next bulleted point. If the text you type in a bulleted item is longer than a single line, the text will automatically wrap to subsequent lines and indent appropriately.

Each new bullet appears somewhat "grayed out" or Dim prior to typing the first character in the item. This is because the bullet will not appear on the slide unless it has accompanying text.

Each slide should contain no more than seven (7) bulleted points. Multiple-line items should have no more than 2-3 lines each. You should decrease the number of bulleted points in proportion to multiple-line entries.

- To create subsequent indented levels, make sure the cursor is in the line in which the next level to begin, click the Demote Tool.

- Each consecutive point will remain on the current level until click the Promote Tool to return to a previous level or the Demote Tool to indent one level further.

Bullet Styles

Although you can set Bullet Styles in the Master, you also can change the bullet style on any slide or on any bulleted point. When you change the bullet style, every subsequent bullet on that slide, whether promoted or demoted, will have that style until you change back to the default or change to a different slide. To change the bullet style, make sure the cursor is in the line of text in which you wish to change the bullet, choose FORMAT: Bullet.

- **Adding / Removing Bullets**

  The Bullet Tool is a toggle. Click it once to place a bullet at the beginning of the current line of text (the one in which the cursor is flashing). Click it again to remove the bullet. This way add bullets to text have typed without using the Bullet Auto Layout.

- ***Working with Text***

  Any time wish to make formatting changes to text, you must highlight the text to be changed. Making a selection from the Text Toolbar affects the highlighted text only. In addition to the standard text formatting tools of font choice and size, bold, italics, and underline, you also can align text left, center, or right. Other special tools are described below.

- **Shadowed Text**

  The Shadow Text Tool places a slight shadow behind the text. Although the effect is not prominent, this is an excellent tool to use to give more definition to title text. Remember should not shadow all body text since this makes it very "muddy" to read.

- **Increase/Decrease Font Size**

  Increase or decrease the font size of highlighted text by clicking on the Increase Font Size or Decrease Font Size Tool, respectively. Size is incremented and decremented by the standard font sizes.

- **Text Colours**

  To choose text colours with the Font Colour Tool located in the Drawing Toolbar. Highlighted text will change to the colour displayed in the band beneath the A.

To make additional colour choices or to see additional non-scheme colours used in this presentation, click the drop-down arrow beside the A.

Animating the Presentation

To animate a single object on a PowerPoint slide

1. Select the object.
2. Choose SLIDE SHOW: Preset Animation.
3. Select the animation effect you desire for the selected object.

Preset Animation Dialog Box

Animated Layers or Slides

It is useful to bring a layered object into a presentation one layer at a time, building it on-screen. To animate a layered object or to animate each object on a slide,

1. Choose SLIDE SHOW: Custom Animation.
2. In the Custom Animation dialog box, each object is identified in the Check to animate slide objects list. If don't remember what a particular object is, click the object's name in the list; that object appears selected in the preview window.
3. Click in the object's checkbox to animate that object. It will be added to the Animation order list.
4. To change the order that the animated objects appear, select the object in the Animation order list, then click the up or down arrow to move the object through the list.
5. Choose whether the object appears only on a mouse click or after a specified number of seconds.

Layer Animation Dialog Box

To choose other effects such as sound effects and how the object appears on the slide during the on-screen presentation, click on the Effects tab.

To animate text,

1. Click on the Effects tab.

2. In the Introduce Text section, from the drop-down box, choose whether the text is introduced all at once, by word, or by letter.

To animate charts click the Chart Effects tab. It is to choose to introduce the data by series, categories, or elements.

Printing the Presentation

When print a presentation, several options are available. print all the slides at a time, the current slide, or a selection of slides. Selections can be comma separated or dash separated, i.e., 2, 3, 5-9.

Format of the printed output.

- Slides—prints a single page per slide on 11 x 8 1/2 paper.
- Notes Pages—prints a single page of notes on 8 1/2 x 11paper.
- Outline—prints the outline of the presentation on 8 1/2 x 11paper.
- Handouts—the most popular option for handouts is to print the presentation three slides per page. This option prints three slides down the left margin and a lined area to the right of each slide on which to take notes. If choose to print two slides per page, each page will contain half-sheet views of two consecutive slides. Printing six or nine slides per page will print six (or nine) equally sized consecutive slides on each page. These options don't include space for note taking.

Print Dialog Box

To give definition to printed slides, you can choose to frame the slides. This prints a simple box around each slide. If you are printing a colour presentation on a black and white printer, the printer will interpret all the colours as shades of gray. Another choice is to click the   black and white printer option. The printer then will eliminate all shading.

6.3 Ms Excel

Microsoft Excel is allows to create professional spreadsheets and charts. It performs numerous functions and formulas to assist a projects. This program is designed to make your number crunching needs easy to accomplish. In Microsoft Excel, a spreadsheet is divided into boxes called cells. Microsoft Excel is the Microsoft Office spreadsheet application. Excel allows you to create spreadsheets, embed formulas that perform calculations, create charts, and analyse data. Microsoft Excel to do such projects as budgets, result analysis etc..

Excel is the mainly spreadsheet application in the world and one of the most popular microcomputer applications till date. It was also the first spreadsheet that allowed user to modify or specify the cell appearance.

6.3.1 Features

- Auto complete
- Point-and-Click Formulas
- Sorting
- Filtering
- Design and editing charts
- Pivot table
- Macro applications

6.3.2 Structure

When Excel is launched it opens as a new Excel Workbook. The Excel application window looks like a Photo frame which includes standard title bar & toolbars. The task pane is displayed on the right side of application window. Below the toolbars is a strip that contains the name box and the formula bar. Excel status bar displays information about current selections, commands operations etc.,

A workbook is a multi-page Excel document with each page called a work sheet, and the active worksheet being displayed in the document window. By default each workbook contains three worksheets and depending on user requirement more sheets could be added or removed. At the left end of the horizontal scroll bar the *sheet tabs* and navigation buttons are present which are used to move to another worksheet. Each work sheet is divided into columns and rows separated by gridlines. Columns are vertical divisions and marked as A, B, C and so on. Horizontal rows are numbered. Thus a worksheet has 256 columns (A to IV) and 65,536 rows. The intersection of this column and row is called a cell i.e., the intersection of column A and row 1 is called *A1* cell.

6.3.3 Managing Numbers

In excel two types of data could be entered directly namely Text and Numbers. Text could be entered easily in cell which could be enlarged to hold the full information. The text could be aligned to right, left or centre although if you select default alignment for text is right justified and for numbers is left. Other data could also be incorporated into worksheets, including maps, graphics, hyperlinks, text copied from word documents. However the behavior of this information would be different from the data directly fed into the excel sheet.

Excel has an auto complete feature which keeps track of text entered in a column and can complete other entries in the same column. For instance on repeating of Syllabub in another cell in the same column, excel can automatically fill it with known and already used text. For eg. if the term 'Year' has been used in the worksheet and the syllabub 'Y' is repeated, an auto suggestion of 'Year' is displayed for auto completion. If many entries begin with the same character then a list if provided for picking the correct term. Right-click in the cell for choosing the appropriate term from list is a shortcut method.

Working with numbers

The main objective and the major strength of the spreadsheet called Excel is to work with numbers. It performs all calculation accurately using standard computer operation symbols for mathematical and logical operations. For e.g. the various operations and appropriate symbols used in Excel are as follows:

Addition	+
Subtraction	-
Multiplication	×
Division	/
Exponentiation on (to the power of)	^
Equal to	=
Not equal to	<>
Greater than	>
Less than	<

Using these operations it is possible to work with numbers using more than one operation in a formula.

Using formulas is easy with Excel. There are two ways of using them *Point – and – click Formulas* and the traditional method. The former is a highly reliable and commonly used method.

1. ***Point –and – click Formulas:*** In this one starts with equal symbol ('=') in the cell where the results are required.

2. **Traditional method:** Under this method we type the entire formula without selecting any cells i.e., by manually entering the cell references. This also starts with the equal ('=') symbol. For instance cell *E2* and *G2* contain data of total seed cost and Fertilizer cost respectively required by the farmer indicated in cell *A2*. Using these two cells *E2* and *G2*, ratio of Seed cost and Fertilizer cost can be calculated by typing '= *E2 / G2* 'in cell *A2*.

Sorting

To sort the data in a database, the first step is to select any cell or range of cells in it. Next from the Data menu Sort option is selected. This provides a sort dialog box. In this dialog box the fields are selected by which one wants to sort the database. It is possible to select more than one field for sorting sequentially.

6.3.4 Filtering a Database

Filtering helps to create a subset which is a group of records from the database. For instance, from the aforementioned example if only need the Farmer's information belonging to treated watershed, a *filter* could be used to select the records that meet the specific criteria while temporarily hiding all other records.

Excel can set up an AutoFilter by selecting any cell in the database and Choosing from a drop down list box from data menu the option *Filter*. With in the Filter option,

6.3.5 Graphics

Excel is a tool that helps bridge the gap between figures in spreadsheets and the text document from MS word. The graphical representation of data gives better description of the data, even for lay persons. It supports a broad selection of chart types, depending on data and the information that needs to be conveyed by using graphs, pie diagram, bar charts etc.

Pie charts are used to show the relationships between pieces of an entity. The implication is that the pie chart includes all components of an entity and hence it can include only one data series at a time. If we select more than one data series at any point of time, Excel uses the first series of data and ignores all others and no error message appears either.

Using Series charts we can chart more than one set of data series. These charts can be used to compare data points in one series with that in the other series. There are several types of series charts which can be used to improve the usefulness of charts. For example, *Column chart* can be used to draw simple, compound or complex bar diagram. To draw a column chart we need to select Chart icon from the standard tool bar. When the chart wizard is available. In the Excel worksheet Column chart has to be selected. Depending on our requirement and data a chart type is to be selected. Preview of chart sample is available with 'Press and Hold to View Sample' button. After preview the Next button has to be pressed. Automatically Excel would display the chart previously selected for the data range. Otherwise a new set of the data range can be specified for preparation of chart. For this Row or Column has to be selected in series and the process start again. To illustrate or label a chart like 'Title', 'Axes', 'Gridlines, etc., are available where chart title, X-axis label, Y-axis label, etc., can be typed. Finally one is prompted to store the chart in a separate worksheet or as an object in the same worksheet which is open currently. In a similar manner Bar chart, Line chart, Radar chart etc., can also be drawn

6.3.6 Adding/Deleting a Data Series

Excel charts can be modified quickly and easily. If we have an existing series chart we can simply select and drag the excluded series of data to add them to a chart. Steps for adding a data series to a chart is simple. First a chart object or chart worksheet is to be selected and right clicked. Next a list of options viz., Format Chart Area, Chart Type, Source Data, Chart Options, etc., is to be selected along with Source data. In the displayed Source data window, we need to indicate the Data Range and Series tabs. In the Series tab we can add or delete a Series into the existing data series.

6.3.7 Data Analysis

The popularity of Excel is due to the simplicity it renders to data analysis. Besides graphical presentation, it helps in drawing trend lines, using formulas for analysis of data series and many other aspects. Data forms provide an easy way to enter or search for data without corrupting the original data set. For adding and deleting records with a Data Form one has to select any cell in a database and then choose Data ➤ Form from the menu bar in order to open the data form. To add a record, new button is to be clicked or scroll is to be used till the end of the database. Entering record using the data from text box controls the Tab between controls. Press Enter to open a New Record form. Pressing the Up Arrow or scroll bar on the database frame to close the New Record form. To delete record displayed in the form, click Delete button. When prompted, click OK to delete the row that contains the record.

Searching for Records is also simple. After opening the data form if it is not already open, Click the Criteria button and enter the search criteria for one or more fields in the text box controls. Click Find Next to find the first record that meets the criteria. Use Find Next and Find Prev to view the records that meet the search criteria and finally click the scroll bar to view all records in the database.

6.3.8 Creating Pivot Tables

Pivot tables are the most powerful tool for data analysis in Excel. A *pivot table* summarizes the columns of information in a database in relationship to one other

Creating a PivotTable requires a few sequential steps

1. Selection of any cell in the database.
2. Choosing Data ➤ PivotTable and PivotChart Report from the menu bar to open the PivotTable Wizard.
3. Selection of type of data source you may want to use for the table. After clicking next verifying whether entire database has been selected. If not, selection of correct range for the database is essential. Click Next.

4. Dragging field buttons to the Pivot Table layout areas, we may place a field in the Data, Column, and Row areas, but Page area is optional.

5. To choose another summary method for a data field, double-click the field button in the data area to open the PivotTable Field dialog box. Select a summarization method from the Summarize by list. To use a custom calculation, click the Options button to extend the dialog box, and then choose a function and Base field and Base item if required. Click Ok to return to the PivotTable Wizard. Click Next.

6. Enter a starting cell location for the table, or leave the location blank to have Excel insert a new worksheet for the table. Enter a name for the table or leave the default name.

7. Select the PivotTable options we want to use, then click the Finish button to close the Wizard and create the PivotTable Report.

6.3.9 Macro Applications

Excel 2002 is more than mere a spreadsheet or data analysis tool with the most powerful Excel tool of all – its *Programmability* with macros and VBA; we can create our own software and programming the Excel to do exactly what we want it to do. There are two ways to create a VB program. The simplest method is to *record macros* – VB programs that run within Excel. Otherwise, if we familiar with Visual Basic, we can create Excel *macros* by opening the Visual Basic interface and typing the code.

As in Word and PowerPoint, we can use Macro Recorder to create *macros*. For this, one needs to select Tool ➤ Macro ➤ Record New Macro which would help display Record macro dialog box. After filling the entries it would turn on the recorder, and complete the steps for before saving the macro. However caution must be taken before as recording a macro, once begin recording, all actions are recorded including mistakes caused.

Procedure for creating macro is relatively simple. Select Tools menu, then Macro option it will display Record New Macro option, when we select this option it will display Record Macro dialog box. In this dialog box we have to specify Macro name which can be up to 255 characters log and can contain numbers, letters and underscores but not space or other punctuation characters, and they must begin with a letter. It is not case sensitive. Enter a new description. If other user will have access to the macro, include any related information.

For Storing a Macro use the Store Macro in drop-down list. Select the document you want the macro stored in. In Excel, a macro's storage location determines how you'll be able to access and run it during subsequent sessions.

If select the current workbook, the macro will only be available in that workbook. If you want to use the same macro else where you'll have to copy or re-create it. Macros that are stored in a workbook, including a template, are called *local macros*.

Storing an Excel macro in the Personal Macro. Workbook created a *global macro*, which is available to all workbook created in the Excel. All global macros are loaded each time one launches Excel which consumes valuable space. Also macro names used globally can't be reused in individual workbooks, and hence it is a best practice to store it locally.

CHAPTER 7

Programming Concepts

Programming closely relates to problem solving. With a problem solving attitude, logic can be developed for the solution to a problem. To encode logic various aids in the form of decision tree, flowchart, algorithm, and pseudo code are available. While developing logic to solve a problem intricacies of programming languages can be avoided. Once the logic is designed and represented in a flow chart, algorithm, or pseudo code it is easy to translate this into a program written in a programming language. A Program is executed in a computer, a flow chart, an algorithm, or pseudo code is the aid to program development.

7.1   Decision Tables

Decision tables are graphic method for describing the logic of decisions. In a tabular format, the decision table lists a set of conditions plus a set of actions and identifies different combinations of decisions, which lead to different combination of actions. These different combinations are termed rules.

A decision table is simply a table showing the various actions to be taken for different combination of conditions. Since it specifies only the logic rules involved, and says nothing about the procedure used, a decision table is more problem oriented than a flowchart (which is solution oriented). The tables are more useful than flowcharts as an aid to program design.

The four basic elements of a decision table are:

- Condition stub
- Condition entry
- Action stub
- Action entry

The condition stub and condition entries describe the conditions to be tested, while the action stub and action entries concern the actions to be taken. In a decision table these four elements form quadrants, as shown below:

Condition stub	Condition entries
Action stub	Action entries

Fig. 7.1 Layout of Decision tables

The table lists all the conditions relating to a procedure, one below the other, in the condition stub; the action stub lists all possible actions. The condition entries and actions entries together constitute one or more "rules", which run vertically through the two right-hand quadrants. Each rule indicates the actions needed when a particular set of conditions applies.

There are two types of decision tables:

1. Limited Entry Table

- It gives the simple conditions as Yes / No so the actions related are: "execute" or 'do not execute".

2. Extended Entry Table

- It has conditions more than two possible states Yes/No. So there are many options of actions related.

Conditions and actions are connected by "if...then..." relationship. If the specified condition exists then perform the indicated action.

If condition is met   (Yes)

If condition is not met   (No)

If conditions is in between   (-)   (neither Yes nor No)

Another form of decision table is Mixed table in which all values like (Y), (N) & (-) are entered.

A decision table may be used in conjunction with flowchart. For example, the flowchart may have a section that is more clearly represented by a decision table. As shown in the margin, a predefined process box in the flowchart represents this section , which references the decision table.

The decision table may be used both for manual procedures and for computer program logic. It is very useful when collecting data from users on the logic they wish to have applied to a problem to organize it into a decision table. It helps to bring out any undefined rules (conditions without specified actions) and is more understandable to the users than a flowchart.

1. List conditions and actions.

2. Combine conditions that describe both possibilities.

3. Make yes or no responses (Y or N)

4. Mark actions to be taken for each rule with X.

5. Check for completeness

6. Combine redundant rules to simplify table.

7. Record table for most understandable order of rules.

Example

A university has the following criteria for deciding to admit students to its graduate schools.

Admit a student who has undergraduate grades of A or better, has test scores on the admission test of over 500, and has a grade average of A or better for the past two years. Also admit if the overall grade average is less than A but the last two-year's average is A or better and the test score is over 600. Admit on probation if the overall and 2-year grade averages are A or better but test score is 600 or less. Admit on probation if overall grade is A or better and test score is above 600 but last 2 years are below A. Also admit on probation of overall grades are less than A average and test score is 600 or less, but grades for past two years are A or better. Refuse to admit all others.

Solution:

Step first: to write down all of the conditions and actions.

Conditions

1. Undergraduate grades of A or better.

2. Test scores of over 600

3. Grade average of A or better in past 2 years

4. Test score of 600 or less

5. Grades less than A last 2 years

6. Overall grade average less than A

Action

1. Admit

2. Admit on probation

3. Do not admit

In second step we will combine conditions, which describe the only two possibilities of a single condition. In this case, "Test scores over 600" and "test scores of 600 or less" can be combined. A single condition "test scores over 600" can represent both because a "No" answer means test score 600 or below. The same reasoning allows the combination of 1 and 6 and also 3 and 5. There are thus only three conditions.

1. Undergraduate of A or better.
2. Test scores of over 600
3. Grade average of a better past 2 years.

Step three is to prepare the yes and no responses using Y and N all possible combinations & conditions. Then for each set of conditions mark the actions(s) to be taken with an X. The number of rules to be handled in the step is 2" where N is the number of conditions. In the example there are three conditions, so there will be 2,3 or 8 rules. The Y's and N's can be inserted in any order, but a systematic method will reduce the effort of filling in the table and then alternating between N and Y. Writing two Y's and four N's fill in the row above this. This doubling of the sets of Y's and N's continues until the table is complete. Then analyze each rule and fill in the action entries. Fig 7.2 shows the completed table at this stage.

Graduate school admission	1	2	3	4	5	6	7	8
Undergraduate grades of A or better.	Y	Y	Y	Y	N	N	N	N
Test scores of over 600	Y	Y	N	N	Y	Y	N	N
Grade average of A or better in past 2 years	Y	N	Y	N	Y	N	Y	N
Admit to graduate school	X				X			
Admit on probation		X	X				X	
Do not Admit				X		X		X

Fig. 7.2 Condition Table

The next action is to combine rules there are redundancies. Two rules can be combined into a single rule if all of the conditions except one have the same Y and N (or -) condition entries and the actions are the same for both. Combine the two rules into one and replace the condition entry of Y and N with a dash (-), which means the condition does not affect the actions to be taken. Using these procedure rules 1 and 5 can be combined, as shown in the margin. In other words, if grades are A or better in the past two years, the student is admitted without regard to overall average.

The completed table with only five rules must represent the eight possible rules. To check for completeness of the rules, analyse as follows:

1. Count number of dashes in the condition entries for each rule. The number of rules "represented" by each rule is 2" where m is the number of dashes.

Where there are no dashes, the number represented is 20, or 1. A single dash means two rules have been combined (21-2), etc.

2. Sum the number of rules represented by the different rules as computed above.

3. Compare the number of rules represented by the table with the number to be accounted for, which are 20 (n-number of conditions). If they are equal (and all other features are correct), the table is complete.

In the example, rules 1,3 and 4 have one dash (21 for each, or 6), and rules 2 and 5 have two dashes (20 for each, or 2). The sum of 6 plus 2 is equal to 2,3 or 8, rules required by the three conditions.

7.1.1 Advantages of Decision Tables

The decision table has a number of advantages as a tool for analysis and communication.

1. The table provides a framework for a complete and accurate statement of processing or decision logic.

2. The table is compact and easily understood, making it very effective for communication between analysts or programmers and others.

3. The table allows mechanization of some programming tasks.

4. Decision tables can serve as a compact means of describing or specifying operations. How compact they are depends on the number of conditions included, and on the number of different actions to be taken. In general, the compactness of decision tables decreases in proportion to the sum of the number of variables included and the number of possible actions.

5. The decision table provides a convenient way of tersely stating logically complex problems. Larger decision tables can be split and linked together. The procedures for creating decision tables' problems. Larger decision tables can be split and linked together. The procedures for creating decision tables provide rules for checking for four types of possible errors: completeness, size, redundancy, and inconsistency.

   These offer valuable aids in systems design and programming, but people must go through the elaborations process of doing most of the checking work.

6. Decision tables can be used to summarize much information in documentation, but in this case they are sometimes regarded as being too concise. In programming, their precision and conciseness are major advantages, when supported with additional documentation.

7.1.2 Disadvantages of Decision Table

Decision tables have no theoretical size limit, but there are real practical limits imposed by people.

1. Large decision tables become incomprehensible, and can be neither checked nor used well by people. Fortunately, the size usually is reduced by rule consolidation.

2. Decision tables do not reduce the human labor of thinking or discovery. Human beings still must do the work of defining, specifying, and following to its logical consequences, watch chain of conditions and actions. Decision tables take away from people none of this arduous work, but they can be used to pinpoint where that work can be best concentrated.

3. Decision tables ignore the delicate interleaving of logic and action that seems so natural when people think about conditions and actions to be taken. Decision tables force the human user to consider conditions separately from actions.

The advantages of decision tables are drawing an increasing number of supporters, but their groups of users are fairly small. Typically, the experience of the first-time user is that he must increase the time and effort he puts in, in order to prepare the decision table. This additional investment may pay off in less debugging and in more efficient user or decision tables, but the additional investment by the user is difficult to justify.

7.2   Flowcharts

For writing algorithm for solving problems, we take the help of flow charts. A flow-chart is a diagrammatic representation of the various steps involved in the solution of a problem. Flow-chart is a diagrammatic representation of the logic paths contained within a solution to the given problem. Flow-charts are drawn up as a pictorial guide for assisting in writing of an algorithm.

The flow-chart indicates the direction of flow of a process, relevant operations and computations, points of decisions and other information which are a part of the solution. Once developed and properly checked, flow-chart provides an excellent guide for writing the program.

Flowcharts are of two types

- System flowcharts and
- Program flowcharts.

A system flowchart describes the data flow and operations for a data processing system. The flowchart shows how the data processing is to be accomplished. A program flowchart describes the sequence of operations and decisions for a particular program. Program flowcharts are sometimes referred to as block or logic diagrams.

After the program has been defined and the processing system designed, the first step in the programming for the application is the preparation of a description of the computer procedures required performing the required processing. Program flow-chart are usually the most convenient methods of preparing this description. Program flowcharts are prepared in the same way as for lower-level language programs, except that less detail is required for describing higher-program steps.

7.2.1 Flowchart Symbols

A flowchart is a drawing giving a suitable step-by-step solution of a problem, using suitable annotated geometric figures (having predefined meanings) connected by flow lines. The flowcharts are used for designing and documenting a process of a program. They represent the program logic and the sequence of steps to be performed for writing the program.

Each symbol in the flowchart has a well-defined shape and meaning and expresses and operation or flow of data. Sufficient annotation is incorporated within the symbols to make a flowchart self-explanatory. Templates are available for drawing the flowchart symbols. Flowcharts are helpful in devising algorithms for solving problems.

There is sufficient creativity and flexibility in the design of flowcharts, so much, that no two people will draw them exactly alike.

Flowcharts go by many other names like the diagram, system chart, run diagram, process chart, procedure chart, and logic chart. As a programming aid, flowcharts are often prepared by systems analysts and designers to describe systems and to specify the work to be accomplished by programs. Programmers use flowcharts as a basis for writing programs and as a means of communication among each other, particularly when the programming is done as a team effort. Programmers as well as systems analysts also use flowchart as a source of information for maintenance work on program and systems.

Flow chart is more widely used than decision tables, publication languages, or abstract notations. This popularity is due to their advantages.

The flowchart provides an excellent means for depicting the flow of program logic. In this diagram different types of boxes represent the different steps. These boxes and other symbols used in flowchart are shown in Table along with their use/meaning.

In flow-charting, it is customary to label each box to show the action performed by it. For example, the adjoining figures indicate the start of a process or procedure and its end.

Symbol	**Name**	**Meaning/Use**
	Terminal Box	A flattened oval box. It denotes 'start' and 'stop' of a program. A flowchart starts from it and ends into it.
	Input / Output Box	A parallelogram shaped box, showing the location where data is required to be input into the program and the point where the results are output by the program.
	Processing Symbol	A rectangular box, used for indicating the types of process or action which result in singular outcome. They indicate arithmetic processes, assignment statements, macro instructions. It can also be a command for moving data from one place of storage to another.
	Decision Box	It is a diamond (rhombus) shaped box. It contains a logical question with a Yes or No (True of False). The branch followed by the program depends on the outcome of the questions.
	Connector	Long flow charts spanning more than a sheet of paper can be terminated at the bottom of the sheet and labeled with a number. The activity can begin at another connector with the same number on the next sheet. Exit connectors and entry connectors are depicted as shown.
	Flow lines	Flow lines connect symbols to show the sequence of logical steps. An arrowhead indicates the direction of flow. Usually the direction of flow is indicated but in the absence of an arrow head flow is assumed from top to bottom and from left to right.
	Preparation Symbols	The symbol indicates the preparation for some procedure like initializing certain variables. Some programmers indicate a preparation by the process symbol – a rectangular box.

7.2.2 Rules for making a Flowchart

1. Only those symbols should be used which are discussed above. Using conventional symbol the flowcharts are easy to understand.

2. The arrows in flow-chart represent the direction of flow or data in the problem.

3. The logic of a program flowchart should flow from top to bottom and from left to right. This follows Standard English convention and imposes consistency upon the drawing.

4. Normally flow lines should not cross each other.

5. Horizontal arrow inside the box indicates that the terms on both sides of the arrow are synonyms. It can be taken as symbol for the words "Let the term on left hand side represent the expression on right hand side" or let the number be incremented by one".

6. Each symbol (except decision box) used in program flowchart should have one entry point and one exit point. A computer thinks linearly- i.e., one step at a time in a sequential fashion. This rule forbids multiple exits from processing symbols or input / output symbols. The one exception to this rule is the decision symbol, which, by definition, is a branching symbol with more than one exit.

7. As far as possible, the instructions within the symbols of a program should be independent of any particular programming languages. Sometimes , it is not known what computer language will be used to write a particular program. At other times, a program will be written in one language and then, rewritten in another language. This rule keeps the flowchart at the logic level rather at the language-coding level that follows.

8. All decision branches should be labeled. Decisions usually ask questions that require labels like "Yes" and "No" or "True" or "False". Without labels, the different logic paths that data processing can take remain undefined.

7.2.3 Where to use Decision Tables and Where Flowcharts?

The decision table is best for presenting a problem with many conditions; it is not well suited to show the flow of processing where there are few decisions. Decision tables have been used much less frequently than flowcharting. The reasons for this are partly the fact that many applications do not lend themselves to decision tables, but also the lack of training in their uses. On balance, than, the decision table is a very useful tool for some applications and should therefore be one of the methods that the analysts or programmer can use when appropriate.

7.2.4 Examples of Flowcharts

Example 1

Fig 7.3 is a flowchart for finding the sum S, the average A, and the product P of three numbers X, Y, and Z. Observe that three assigning the large number to BIG and the smaller number to SMALL. Observe the two arrows leaving the decision "Is A > B?", one labeled "NO" and the other labeled "YES".

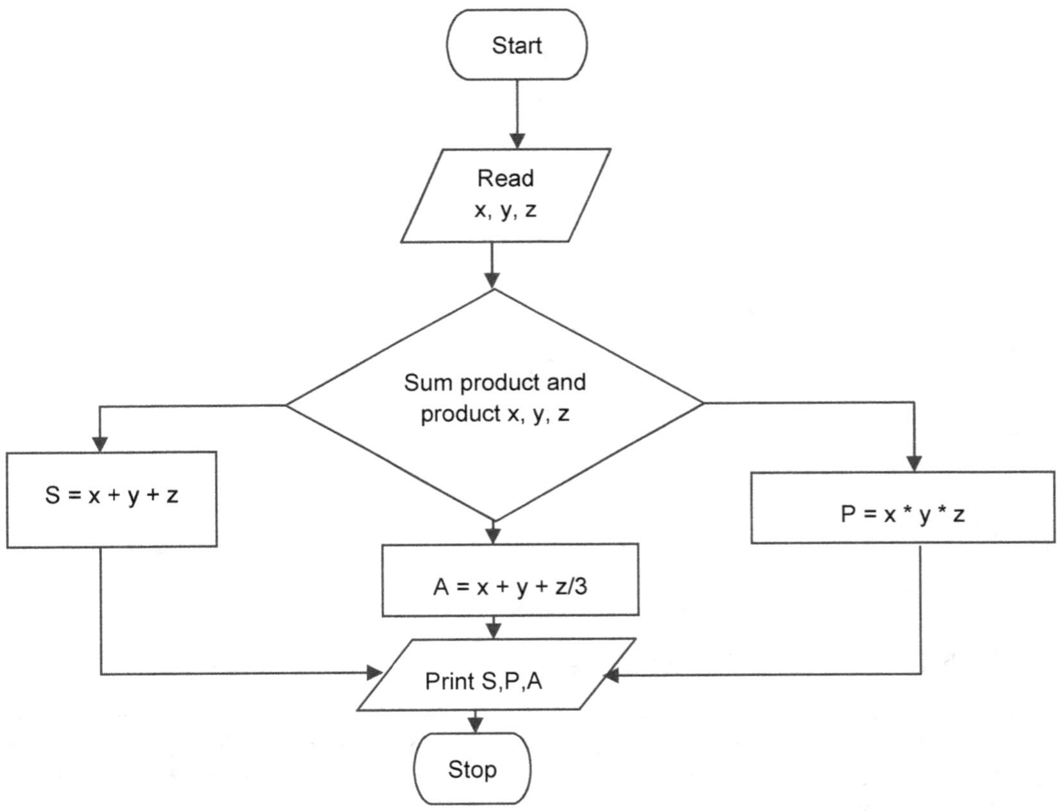

Fig 7.3 Flowchart for Sum product and average

Example 2

Fig 7.4 shows a flowchart which reads two numbers, A and B and prints them in decreasing order, after assigning the larger number to BIG and the smaller number to SMALL. Observe the two arrows leaving the decision "Is A > B ?" One labeled "No" and the other labeled "YES".

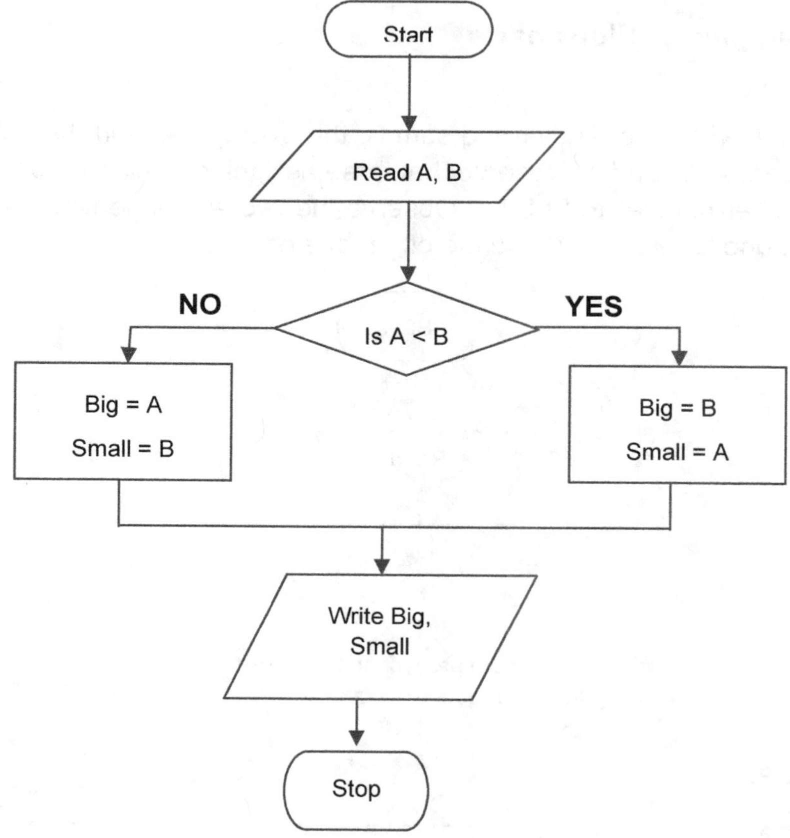

Fig 7.4 Flowchart for condition

7.2.5 Advantages of Flowcharts

Flowcharts are used for a broad variety of applications in different types of work. For example, they are as convenient to use in administrative file handing as in scientific or engineering computation. This popularity, born out of wide applicability, generates further so much so that flow-charting is a lingua among persons of various disciplines working with computers.

- Flowcharts give a clear graphical/ pictorial representation of the various paths that must be followed to perform the acts to accomplish the goals of the program.

- Flowcharts are invaluable at the time when modifications must be made to the original program to perform additional services not planned originally. It helps to locate the exact sports in the program where the changes should be made. A good flow chart enables the programmer to visualize whether or not such changes might upset program features.

- Flowcharts are languages independent. Knowledge of a programming language is not normally necessary to be able to use them or to create them. This is always true for the pictorial part of flowcharts, and ideally should be true for the wording inside the symbols in a flowchart.

- Flowcharts are constraining and precise in ways that the useful to programmers and analysts. These are a limited means of description that force the user to give attention to many significant matters while suppressing attention to a host to less important details.

- Flowcharts are a visual representation, and hence provide a convenient alternative to the usual narration description for a program or system. This enables a more rapid scan or search of a flowchart than is possible with a description when particular items of information are sought. The graphic format enables an user to comprehend a lot in a single glance.

- Flowcharts offer a controllable level of details. They are usable from the most summary systems level to the most detailed programming level. The wide range of detail options greatly enhances the communication value of the flowchart. It is generally concluded that the flowchart is more valuable to the summary than what is provided by the programming language (for flow diagrams) or in the English language narrative (for system charts). For this reason, arranged from very summary to quite detailed, so that the user may choose the level for detail most convenient for his particular purposes. In this regard it should be noted that the system chart variety of flowchart inherently provides a more summary view than does the flow diagram variety of flowchart.

7.2.6 Disadvantages of Flowcharts

- On the disadvantages side, some programmers and analysts complain that flowcharts are a waste of time, since people do not think in graphic terms. In their view, a flowchart an unnatural means of communication.

- Flow charts are something new and strange to work with for beginners. They are reluctant to accept them.

- When modifications are made in the original program corresponding changes must be made in the flow charts of the program in the documentation. If the programmer is too busy, or otherwise, forgets to up-data the flow charts each time.

- It is often difficult to draw the line as to the extent of details of the program to be incorporated in the flowchart. When too many details are included in the flowchart it may become obscure to other programmer.

- Flow charts may not reveal significant steps to be followed in actual coding. Also, they do not guide the programmer, how to code a step as given by the flow chart.

- Flowcharts are often cumbersome to use and costly to produce. Because of their graphic format, flowcharts may devote more than a page of space to present what may requires from a few lines to less than a half-page of equally detailed description in some other format. Manual preparation of flowcharts is slow, although detailed flow diagrams can be prepared by computer if the program to be flow-charted exists in source form.

- Flowcharts do not constitute programming languages. They are person-to-person means of communication, not person-to-computer. No translators exist for accepting program systems described in flowchart form.

- The flow diagram variety of flowchart does not fit well with all programming languages. Although flow diagrams go well with Cobol, Algol, PL/1, and Basic. They seem less compatible with Snobol, Comit, Lisp, and IPL-V.

- Flowcharts may not highlight what is important. Each operation commonly receives as much attention in a flowchart as any other, given the level of detail at which the flowchart is prepared. Yet, intuitively, people feel that some operations are more significant than others. The flowchart does not possess any convenient, automatic way to highlight these.

- Flowcharts are difficult to produce at a summary level. No consistent logical rules have yet been developed to aid the process of producing meaningful summary flowcharts.

7.2.7 Types of Flowcharts

Presently two major varieties of flowcharts are used in practice :

- System chart

- Program flow diagram.

The flow diagram in figure connects rates on part of what a system chart shows. The unit of data transformation for the two is thus very different. For a flow diagram, the unit of data translation is usually an operation or short sequence of operations that a computer can perform (such as an instruction or a series of instructions that comprise a subroutine). An example is testing for the presence of leading zeros in a number.

By contrast, in a system chart the unit of data transformation is usually the work done by an entire computer program. Example are : sorting a file of data, inverting a matrix, or producing a report. Flow diagrams commonly have an algorithmic orientation, stressing how data is transformed, whereas systems charts primarily identify inputs and outputs to algorithms, stressing what data is used or produced at various point in a sequence of operations.

7.2.8 Uses of Flowcharts

Flowcharts are the most widely used graphic method for describing computer operations. They are adaptable to wide from the early days of the computer programming.

The major use of flowcharts is in documentation and programming. As a documentation device, the flowchart is a way of communicating, from one person to another, the nature of the operation to be performed and of the data upon which it is to another, regardless of the programming language or computer used. Since a flowchart is a graphic means of communication, this feature makes it a good choice for use the usual programming languages and English language.

All the flow charts we have drawn, which give details of each step of a process or procedure. But these are more common in the flowcharts of large engineering project. Micro-level flowcharting is seldom used in computer programming.

7.3   Algorithm

In our daily life we encounter with a number of problems, which can be solved by two methods.

- Algorithms

- Heuristic

In algorithm, there is set procedure to solve the problem in such a manner that solution is definitely obtained. Heuristic is the method of obtaining optimum solution of the problem intuitively by experienced guess.

For solving a problem by computer, we have to be very clear in writing the instructions for the computer. The set of instructions is known as program. The solution is obtained by breaking the contents of the problem and given data in such a manner, that all instructions are given in sequence. This procedure is known as algorithm and has to be devised prior to the actual coding of the computer program. Actual computer program is written in coded languages, known as programming language. Algorithm is thus a design or plan of obtaining a solution to the problem. It is logical process of analyzing a mathematical problem and data step by step so as to make it easier to understand and implement solution to the problem. Certain operations must be performed on data for producing the required results. In order that a computer can perform an operation, it must be converted into a form that the computer is able to execute. Moreover the operations must be carried out in a specific sequence. In our day-to-day work, the brain automatically performs the algorithms by experience but not in a systematic and error-free way. But for processing on computer, one has to be systematic and to the point, as computer does not know alternatives. For example we must read a record before using its content in calculations. Sometimes it is necessary to perform an operation only if the data satisfies a particular condition. For example, income tax must be deducted from the salary of an employee only if income exceeds a certain limit.

Writing algorithm for solution of a problem is a method of successive iterations. Algorithm is first roughly estimated and written. Then it is carefully gone through a number of times and refined each time. The final form of an algorithm emerges through a number of stepwise refinements carried out successively, till the detailed steps become precisely clear to the person or machine, which is going to execute the steps. In an algorithm, all items of instructions are listed in the order in which they are to be carried out. This is done with the help of flow charts.

However the complex problems may be (Numeric, or non-numeric), it can always be broken into a set of smaller sequence of steps and procedures. We can always think it to be solved with the help of a systematic step problem solving procedure, which if following meticulously, will lead us to a definite solution. This step-by-step procedure is technically known as algorithm. In contract to this, there are heuristic procedures, which most of the time may offer a person some optimum solution to correct solution or any solution at all will be achieved all the time. Algorithm may constitute of sequence, selections and repetitions. Therefore, it is necessary that all these terms be understood.

7.3.1 Efficient Algorithms

The following points must be born in mind before writing an efficient algorithm.

- Every procedure should carefully specify the input and output variable.
- The meaning of all variables should be defined.
- The flow of the program should generally be forward except for normal looping and unavoidable instances.
- Indentation rules should be established and followed, so that computation units of program text can more easily be identified.
- Documentation should be short, but meaningful. Avoid commands like "J is increased by one."
- Use subroutines, where appropriate.

Let us see method of evolving by writing the steps for solving certain day to day problems.

It is not sufficient that only the method of solving a problem is written and solution is obtained through computer. But we expect that computer also prints results in a systematic manner such that the user is able to identify the set of results. Suppose in a problem we want to calculate the value of three variables A,B and C and get the results printed. Now computer will print 3 values, but it may not be easy for user to identify which is the value of A out of these 3 results. So for this purpose remarks such as "Answer A=", or "Answer: Temp in Celsius is" are also printed.

Example

Develop an algorithm for converting given temperature in Celsius scale into Fahrenheit scale.

From our knowledge of physics, we know the relationship between temperature in the two given scales i.e. temperatures in Fahrenheit and Centigrade. This is

$$C / 5= (F\text{-}32) / 9$$

First we have to write this formula in such a way so that values of temperature in degree Fahrenheit are equated to value in centigrade, namely.

$$F = 1.8*C + 32$$

Now we can write down steps for writing the algorithm for solving this in such a manner that any person with average intelligence can go on follow the procedure and come to definite solution. The algorithm shall be similar to following algorithm:

1. Read (obtain) the given values of C i.e. temperature in Celsius.

2. Multiply this value with 1.8 and equate it equal of F i.e. F=1 8*C.

3. Now replace this value of F by F+32

4. Write the Answer

5. STOP

Explanation

1. For deriving or obtaining any value from the given problem, we have written "Read" because in most of the computer programming languages, "Read" is a statement which causes the computer to read the given value of a data item. We have to feed this value in computer's memory and computer will read this value in the program automatically as and when necessary.

2. The value of F is in two parts which are 1.8*C and + 32. In computer applications it is customary to calculate the value in part and equate them equal to the required parameter and store this part value in memory. This

part value is further added with remaining part and replaced with original value.

3. It is customary to write stop at the end, otherwise sometimes due to mistake in designing the algorithm the computer may continue to work infinitely. Now we will define the algorithm by writing.

Refined Algorithm

1. Read value of C
2. F = 1.8*C
3. F = F + 32
4. Print "Answer: The value of F is = ; followed by the calculated value of F.
5. STOP

Explanation

1. In second step of the algorithm we have written F = 1.8 C instead of F=1.8*C to indicate that computer is to replace value in storage location F by 1.8*C which is its part value. In next step it replaces this part value of F i.e. F = 1.8*C by any value of F which is equal to F=1.8 C + 32 in the same location.

2. The calculated value i.e. result obtained, if printed simply numerically will not make any sense on the paper unless we write the words "The answer is equal to"; and fill in the blanks with the answered value. For making the computer to print these words' it is necessary that they are written under the quotes "..." because computer understands either the numeric values written without quotation marks or the strings of words written under quotation marks. This is one of the rules of BASIC Programming language.

3. Observe carefully that we have placed semi-colon, symbol immediately after quote marks. This is necessary according to rules of the programming languages like BASIC that allow the answered value to be printed immediately after the result after a space. Here the computer will not print the quote marks, or the semicolon. Actually these two symbols are a part.

7.4   Pseudo Code

Pseudo-code is a series of statements in unambiguous English that describes the actions to be taken by the program to produce that output required by the program. Pseudo implies that the program code is not written in any high-level language but in brief English phrases. At this stage programmers are not encumbered with the rule of the computer language but are free to write, in their nature language, statements, which will guide the flow of control in the program.

The objective of pseudo-code is to set up a structure for the program so that the goals will be achieved in the most efficient manner possible. The first level of pseudo-code gives the overall outline of the program. Additional levels of refinement may be developed to guide the details of the program.

Pseudo-code has not been standardized; hence, a programmer is free to write the plan for the program in natural phrases. The thoughts, plans and ideas contained in the pseudo-code phrases written by one programmer are equally understandable by other programmers.

Pseudo-code use phrases such as, if-then-else, repeat, until, while-do, read, print, copy etc. It also uses variable names and assignment symbol. Common logical and mathematical symbols are shown in the table.

Symbols used in pseudo code

Symbol	Example	Meaning
<	a<b	"a is less than b".
<=	a <=b	"a is either less or equal to b".
=	a = b	"a is equal to b".
>	a > b	" a is greater than b".
> =	a > = b	" a is greater or equal to b".
< >	a < > b	"a is not equal to b".
< -	a <- b	" a is assigned the value b, destroying the old value of a".

Some symbols, operators, key words and constructs enumerated below are used in writing pseudo-code;

(a) The assignment symbols "<-" means "takes the value of";

C <- A+B

Means C takes the value of A plus B.

(b) The sequencing operator (say;) delimits each statement in a compound statement;

DO this; DO that; DO the- other;

(c) Key words allow data input to and output from the program;

Read: to input data from memory, e.g., READ next – Value of A

WRITE: to output data to memory, e.g., WRITE Result

ACCEPT: to input data from a keyboard, e.g. ACCEPT operator-response;

DISPLAY: to output data to a screen, e.g., DISPLAY Result

PRINT: to output data to a printer, e.g. PRINT Data

(d) There are various looping constructs;

REPEAT a command sequence;

UNTIL condition;

WHILE condition

DO a command sequence;

ENDDO;

FORIFROM a to b (STEP x)

DO a command sequence;

ENDDO; P

(e) Conditional branching may use the IF-THEN-ELSE Construct;

IF Condition

THEN

Command sequence 1;

ELSE

Command sequence 2;

ENDIF;

(f) We call procedures using the PERFORM or CALL key words;

PERFORM label; or

CALL label;

(g) We obtain branching (or selection) with nested If;

IF conditions 1   or we can use the CASE structure

(Which better);

THEN   DO CASE OF index

Command sequence 1; CASE index condition 1

Command sequence 2

THEN   command sequence 1;

ELSE IF condition 2;   CASE index condition 2

THEN....   CASE index condition.

:

ELSE   CASE index condition N

Default command sequence;   command sequence N;

ENDIF; OTHERWISE

Default command sequence;

END CASE;

7.4.1 Logical Constructs in Pseudo-Code

A pseudo-code program consists of a list of statements. Some of these statements are among those used in flowcharts, e.g. Read statements, Write statements, Assignment statements, Condition. However, instead of arrows of flow lines to indicate the logic an algorithm, the pseudo code program uses three types of organization.

- Sequential logic
- Selective logic, and
- Iterative logic
1. Sequential Logic

    Under this logic, and instructions in a pseudo code program are executed in order, from the top to the bottom. Although it is not necessary to have Start statement or Stop statement (since the program begins sort at the top and ends at the bottom), we frequently signal the completion of a pseudo code program by writing END at the bottom of the program.

    Read NAME, PRINCIPLE, RATE

    INTEREST = PRINCIPAL x RATE

    Write NAME, INTEREST

    END

    Sometimes we begin the program with a title, e.g. here "Calculating Interest".

2. Select ional Logic

    This logic employs a number of structures, called IF-structures, each of which is essentially a selection of one out of several alternatives. Each such structure begins with a statement of the form.

    IF condition

    And ends with statement

    END IF

Single alternative: The appropriate structure is called an IF THEN structure; That is, IF the condition holds, THEN procedure A, the coding of which may involve one or more statements, is executed; otherwise procedure A is skipped, and control transfers to the first, statement following the ENDIF statement.

The following pseudo code program, which calculates an employee's WAGES given his hourly RATE of pay and number of HOURS worked, used an IF THEN structure:

```
Read NAME, RATE, HOURS
WAGES = HOURS x RATE
IF HOURS > 40
WAGES = WAGES + (HOURS – 40) x 0.5 RATE
END IF
Write NAME, WAGES
END
```

In other words, WAGES equals HOURS times RATE, but if the employee has worked overtime (more than 40 hours), then there is an additional payment at half rate for those hours over 40. Observe that the IF-procedure is indented, a pseudo code convention that makes programs much easier to read.

Double Alternative: An IF THEN ELSE structure is used for decision involving two distinct alternative. Observe that a THEN ELSE statement separates two procedures. As indicated by the flowchart, IF the condition holds, THEN procedure A (above the ELSE statement) is executed; ELSE procedure B (below the ELSE statement) is executed.

Example: Following is a pseudo code program for (Whose flowchart appears in Fig. 7.4)

```
Read A, B
IF A < B
BIG = B
SMALL = A
ELSE
BIG = A
SMALL = B
ENDIF
Write BIG, SMALL
END
```

Again observe how the procedure blocks are indented for easier reading.

Multiple alternatives. Decisions that involve more than one alternatives may be handled by means of nested. If structures, where in one IF- Structure is contained in the procedure component of another IF-Structure. An example is the ELSE IF structure use one or more statements on the form.

ELSE IF Condition between the IF ELSE statements. Observe that only one of the procedures will be executed, the one the follows the first condition which holds. If none of the conditions holds, then the procedure following the ELSE statement is executed. If this procedure is empty, then the ELSE statement itself may be omitted.

Again observe the indented procedure block.

Iteration Logic

This logic refers to structure involved loops, of which there are three types. One type, begin with a DO statement, which has the form.

DO K = 1 TO N or DO K = INIVAL = End value and INCR = Increment.

7.4.2 Advantages of Pseudo Code

The pseudo code possesses the following major advantages:

1. The pseudo code instructions are midway between English and high level languages but free ambiguities of English language. That is way pseudo code is often called structured English. The pseudo code displays the programming logic beautifully and can be converted to complete programs very easily.

2. Pseudo code consisting of simple sentences in English and mathematical symbols and are easier to write and understand. On the other hand, charts are cumbersome to draw.

3. Pseudo code, being very closed to high languages, can easily be translated to a computer program whereas flow charts cannot be coded directly into a computer program very easily.

7.5   Programming Paradigms

When computers were invented and subsequently programming began, major focus was done on getting the problems solved. There were no guidelines as how the programs should be written. In those days, usually scientists wrote programs for themselves for scientific computations. As the application of the computer increased in other areas like in business and in organizations, a new breed of professionals called programmers started writing program for others. These high in demand programmers switched companies. When large complex programs needed updates due to errors in a software or to meet the changes in business or process, programmers found it difficult because with the lapse of time, many things washed off from their minds. The situation was horrible if the author of the program had switched the company. This was the time software scientists thought of documenting the programs and programming paradigms started getting evolved.

The concept of Procedure oriented programming suited well to program most of the application areas for many years. Gradually computers became more versatile and with its increased power entered into more complex applications like multimedia, interactive gaming, robotics and many more. A new programming paradigm called Object Oriented Programming (OOP), evolved to meet the changing needs. OOP helped immensely in visual programming, event driven programming, component based programming etc. OOPS is the buzz word today but Procedure Oriented Programming too is popular.

Procedure oriented programming Top Down approach whereas OOP follows Bottom Up approach. However in practical implementations, a sandwiched approach may be needed sometimes.

CHAPTER 8

Programming Languages

A myriad of programming languages are available for writing programs. Choice of the programming language is usually based upon the nature of the program and choice of the programmer. Programming languages are classified into various levels ranging from machine level, assembly level, high level, 4GL, 5GL and up to natural languages. A language which is easy for the computer to understand but difficult to write a computer program is said to be low level language. Level of the language moves to higher level when it is easy for the programmer to write a program into a language. As the level of programming language said to increase, it becomes difficult for the computer to understand the program. To ease the understanding of the program by the computer, system software like assembler and compilers come into play. Hence it will always be effort of scientists to make programming easier for the human programmers.

A language is a system of communication. With a natural language such as Hindi, we can communicate to one another our ideas and emotions. Similarly, a computer language is a means of communication. With the help of a computer language, a programmer tells a computer what he wants it to do. A Computer Programming Languages is a set of rules that tells the computer what operations to perform. All Natural languages (Hindi, French, German etc.) use a standard set of symbols for the purpose of communication. Everyone using those languages understands these symbols. We normally call this set of symbols the vocabulary of that particular language. All computer languages have a vocabulary of their own. Each symbol of the vocabulary has a definite unambiguous meaning, which can be looked up in the manual of that language. Hence, each symbol of a computer language is used to tell the computer to do a particular job. The main difference between a Natural language and a computer language is that computer language uses a very limited or restricted vocabulary. This is mainly because a programming language by its very nature and purpose does not need to say too much. Each and every problem to be solved by a computer has to be broken down into discrete (simple and separate), logical steps which basically comprise four fundamental operations – input and output operations, arithmetic operations, movement of information within the CPU, and logical or comparison operations.

The symbols of a particular computer language must also be used as per prescribed rules, which are known as the syntax rules of the language. Computers, being machines are receptive only to exact vocabulary used correctly as per syntax rules of the language. Thus, in case of a computer language, we must stick by the exact rules of the language if we want to be understood by the computer. As yet, no computer is capable of correcting and deducing meaning from incorrect instructions. Computer languages are less verbose, precise and simpler than natural languages but they have to be used with great precision. Unless a programmer adheres exactly to the syntax rules of a programming language, even down to the correct punctuation marks, the computer will not understand his commands.

8.1 Characteristics of Programming Language

A programming language should possess the following characteristics to be considered as a good high-level language:

(a) The language should be relatively independent of a given computer system. That is, instead of being machine based, it should be oriented more towards the problem to be solved.

(b) Each statement of the language should be a macroinstruction that gets translated into many machine language instructions.

(c) The language should enable the programmers to write instructions using familiar words and mathematical symbols. It should be natural and should use abbreviations and words used in everyday communication.

(d) The language should be independent of machine language instructions and other pieces of system software except for the compiler or the interpreter.

(e) The language should not be experimental in nature and should exist on more than one computer system.

8.2 Types of Programming Languages

Programming languages have improved just as computer hardware improved. They have progressed from machine-oriented languages that use strings of binary 1's and 0's to problem-oriented languages that use common mathematical and/or English terms. However, all computer languages can be classified in the following five broad categories:

Machine languages (First Generation Languages – 1945)

Assembly languages (Second Generation Languages – mid 1950s)

High-level languages (Third Generation Languages – early 1960s)

Fourth Generation languages (Very High Level Languages or SQL – early 1970s)

Fifth Generation languages (Natural Languages – early 1980s)

8.2.1 Machine Languages

The set of instruction codes, whether in binary or decimal, which can be directly understood by the CPU of a computer without the help of a translating program, is called a machine code or machine language. This is the basic language of the computer, representing data as 1s and 0s. Machine language programs varied from computer to computer. i.e. they were Machine Dependent.

Advantages and Limitations of Machine Languages

Machine Language is the fundamental language of a computer and is normally written as strings of binary 1s and 0s. The circuitry of a computer is wired in such a way that it immediately recognizes the machine language and converts it into electrical signals needed to run the computer. An instruction prepared in any machine language has a two-part. The first part is the command or operation, and it tells the computer what function to perform. The second part of the instruction is the operand, and it tells the computer where to find or store that data or other instructions that are to be manipulated. Thus, of the data field that is involved in the operation. Typical operations involve reading, adding, subtracting, writing, and so on.

As all computers use binary digit (0s and 1s) for performing internal operations, most computers' machine language consists of strings of binary numbers and this is the only number system the CPU directly understands. When stored inside the computer, the symbols, which comprise the machine language program, are made up of 1s and 0s. For example, a typical program instruction to print out a number on the printer might be look like.

10110011111101000011000011000

The program to add two numbers in memory and print the result might look something like the following

00110011111000111000011001

11000100001111000011000011

00011000010000000100001000

100001000001000001000000100

This is obviously not a very easy language to learn, because it is difficult to read and understand and it is written in a number system with which we are not familiar.

Programs written in machine language can be executed very fast by the computer. This is mainly because machine instructions are directly under-by the CPU and no translation of the program is required. However, writing a program in machine language has several disadvantages, which are discussed below.

Machine Dependent: The internal design of every type of computer is deferent from every other type of computer and needs different electrical signals to operate; the machine language differs from computer to computer.

Difficult to Program: Although easily used by the computer, machine languages is difficult to program. It is necessary for the programmer either to memorize the dozens of code numbers for the commands in the machine's instruction set or to constantly refer to a reference card.

Error Prone: For writing program in machine language, since a programmer has to remember the opcodes and he must also keep track of the storage location of data and instructions, it becomes very difficult for him to concentrate fully on the logic of the problem. This frequently results in program errors. Hence, there is a large likelihood to make errors while using machine code.

Difficult to Modify: It is difficult to correct or modify machine language programs. Checking machine instructions to locate errors is as tedious as writing them initially. Similarly, modifying a machine language program at a later data is so difficult that many programmers would prefer to code the new logic afresh instead of incorporating the necessary modifications in the old program.

8.2.2 Assembly Language

Assembly languages are one step ahead of machine languages. Assembly language is a language that allows a programmer to use abbreviations or easily remembered words instead of binary numbers. Each assembly language statement is translated into one-machine instructions by the assembler program. To program in an assembly language, we have to be well versed in the computer's architecture. Unless well documented, assembly language programs can be extremely difficult to maintain.

Assembly languages are hardware dependent; there is a different assembly language for each CPU series, and their language statements are quite different. In the part, systems software (operating systems, database managers, etc.) was written in assembly language to maximize the machine's performance.

Advantages of Assembly Languages over Machine Languages

Assembly languages have the following advantages over machine languages:

Easier to understand and use: Assembly languages are easier to understand and use because mnemonics are used instead of numeric op-codes and suitable names are used for data. The use of mnemonics means that comments are usually not needed; the program it self is understandable. Symbolic programming also saves a lot of time and effort of the programmer because it is easier to write as compared to machine language programs.

Easy to Locate and Correct Errors: While writing programs in an assembly language, fewer errors are made, and those that are made are easier to find and correct because of the use of mnemonics and symbolic field names. Furthermore, assemblers are so designed that they automatically catch errors. If we use an invalid mnemonic or a name that has never been defined, the assembler will print out an error indication. For example, suppose one instruction in the symbolic program reads ADD SUM, and we forget to define what SUM is, the assembler will look through its table to find whether SUM is earlier defined or not. If not, it will indicate the error.

Easier to Modify: Assembly language programs are easier for people to modify than machine language programs. This is mainly because they are easier to understand and hence it is easier to locate, correct, and modify instructions as and when desired. Moreover, insertion or removal of certain instructions from the program does not require change in the address part of the instructions following that part of the program. This is required in case of machine languages.

No need to track Addressee: One of the greatest advantages of assembly language is that it relieves us of worrying about addresses for instructions and data. This is more important than it seems at first glance. Suppose we have written a long machine language program involving many steps and many reference to itselt within the program, such as looping, and address modifications, and so on. At the very end we may suddenly discover that we have left out an instruction in the middle. If we insert that entire program to check any reference to other steps. This is a tedious job. But if we write the same program in symbolic language, we merely add the extra instruction at their right place, and the assembler will take care of step numbering automatically.

Easily Reloadable: Suppose that an assembly language program starts at address 2000 and we suddenly find that we have another program to be used with this program and this program also starts at location 2000. Obviously, one of the two programs will have to be rewritten to be moved somewhere else. In machine language, this can be a complicated job. But in case of assembly language, we merely have to change the first statements; for example instead of:

START PROGRAM AT 2000 AND START DATA AT 3000

We merely change this first statement to :

START PROGRAM AT 3000 AND START DATA AT 4000 and run the symbolic program once more through the assembler.

Efficiency: In addition to the above-mentioned advantages, an assembly language program also enjoys the efficiency of its corresponding machine code because there is one-to-one correspondence between the instructions of an assembly language program and its corresponding machine language program. There is one-to-one relationship between symbolic and machine codes.

Limitations of assembly languages:

Machine Dependent: Because each instruction in the symbolic language is translated into exactly one machine language instruction, assembly languages of the processor being used.

Knowledge of Hardware required: Since assembly languages are machine dependent, so the programmer has to be aware of particular machines' characteristics and requirements as the program is written. An assembly language programmer must known how his machine works and should have a good knowledge of the logical structure of his computer in order to write a good assembly language program.

Machine Level Coding: In case of an assembly language, instructions are still written at the machine-code level i.e. one assembler instruction is substituted for one machine-code instruction.

Machine and assembly languages being machine dependent, are referred to as low-level language. In general, assembly languages are termed one-for-one in nature, i.e. each assembly language instruction will result in one machine language instruction.

A language in which each statement is directly translated into a single machine code is known as a low-level language. Examples of low-level languages are assembly languages of various processors.

8.2.3 High Level Languages

To overcome the difficulties associated with assembly languages, high-level or procedure-oriented languages have been developed. High level languages permit programmers to describe tasks in a form, which is problem oriented rather than computer oriented. One can formulate problems more efficiently in a high-level language. The programmer does not need to have a precise knowledge of the architecture of the computer he is using.

The instructions written in high-level languages are called statements. The statements more clearly resemble English and mathematics as compared to mnemonics in assembly languages. Examples of high-level languages are BASIC, PASCAL, FORTRAN, COBOL, ALGOL, PL-II, PROLOG, LISP, ADA, SNOBOL, etc.

Advantages of High Level Languages: high-level languages enjoy the following advantages over assembly and machine languages:

Machine Independence: High-Level languages are machine independent. This is a very valuable advantage. Thus a program written in a high-level language can be run on many different types of computers with very little or practically no modification.

Easy to Learn and Use: These languages are very similar to the languages normally used by us in our day-to-day life. Hence they are easy to learn and use. The programmer need not learn much about the computer he is using. The programmer does not have to necessarily know the machine instructions, the data format, and so on.

Few Errors: In case of high-level languages, since the programmer need not write the entire small steps carried out by the computer, he is much less likely to make errors. The computer takes care of all the little details, and will not introduce any error of its own unless something breaks down. Furthermore, compilers are so designed that they automatically catch and point out the errors made by the programmer. Hence, diagnostic errors, if any, can be easily located and corrected by the programmer.

Lower Preparation Cost: Writing programs in high-level language require less time and effort, which ultimately leads to lower program preparation cost. Generally, the cost of all phases of program preparation (coding, debugging, testing, etc.) is lower with a high-level language than with an assembly language or with a machine language.

Better Documentation: A high-level language is designed in such a way that its instructions may be written more like the language of the problem. Thus a person familiar with the problem can easily understand the statements of a program written in a high-level language. For the documentation of such programs, very few or practically no separate comment statements are required.

Easier to Maintain: Programs written in high-level languages are easier to maintain than those in assembly languages or machine languages. This is mainly because high-level language programmes are easier to understand and hence it is easier to locate, correct, and modify instructions as and when desired. Insertion or removal of certain instructions from a program is also possible without any complication. Thus, major changes can be incorporated with very little effort.

Limitations of high-level languages: Two disadvantages of high-level languages are:

Lower Efficiency: Generally, a program written in an assembly language of machine language is more efficient than the one written in a high Level language.

That is, the programs written in high-level languages take more time to run require more main memory.

Lack of Flexibility: Because the automatic features of high-level languages always occur and are not under the control of the programmer, they are less flexible than assembly languages. An assembly language provides programmers access to all the special features of the machine they are using. This lack of flexibility means that some tasks cannot be done in high-level language, or can be done only with great difficulty.

In most cases, the advantages of high-level languages far outweigh the disadvantages. Most computer installations use a high-level language for most programs and use an assembly language for doing special tasks that cannot be easily done otherwise.

8.2.4 Difference Between Assembly Languages and High-Level Language

One statement of a high-level language corresponds to many instructions of the assembly language program. Hence, a high Level program is much shorter compared to an assembly language program.

Many high-level languages have been developed; some are for general purpose and some for special purposes. For example, PASCAL, PL-II and ADA are general-purpose languages. FORTRAN and APL are for scientists and engineers. They are designed to solve mathematical problems. COBOL is for business applications. BASIC is for newcomers to programming. PROLOG is based on logical reasoning and used for artificial intelligence (i.e. expert system). SNOBOL is suitable for text processing. APT is used in manufacturing applications to control machine tools.

8.2.5 Brief Description of Some Popular High-Level Languages

Ada: A high-level programming language area developed in the late 1970s and early 1980s for the United States Defense Department. Ada was designed to be a general-purpose language for everything from business applications to rocket guidance systems. One of its principal features is that it supports real-time applications. In addition, Ada incorporates modular techniques that make it easier to build and maintain large systems. Since 1986, Ada has been the mandatory development language for most U.S. military applications. In additions, Ada is often the language of choice for large systems that require real-time processing, such as banking and air traffic control systems.

Ada is named after Augusta Ada Byron (1815-52), daughter of Lord Byron, and Countess of Lovelace. She helped Charles Babbage develop programs for the analytic engine, the first mechanical computer. She is considered by many to be the world's first programmer.

BASIC: It is an abbreviation for Beginners All-purpose symbolic Instruction Code. It is a very simple and easy language. It is suitable for scientific computations. But it is not as powerful as FORTRAN. It was introduced in 1965 by Dartmouth College, UK. It is a widely used language for simple computations and analysis. It is the most popular high-level language used in personal computers. To translate BASIC instructions into machine language codes interpreters are frequently used in PC systems. BASIC language compliers are also available for these systems.

FORTRAN: It is an abbreviation for Formula Translation. IBM introduced it in 1957. It is a very useful language for scientific and engineering computations as it contains many functions for complex mathematical operations. It is a compact programming language. Huge libraries of engineering and scientific programs written in FORTAN are available to users. It is not suitable for processing large business files like COBOL. It has a number of versions. Earlier, FORTRAN IV was very popular. In 1977 the American National Standard Institute (ANSI) published a standard for FORTRAN called FORTRAN 77 that all manufacturers could use the same form of the language. The latest version is in known as FORTRAN 90.

APL: IBM has developed APL. It is a very powerful language. It permits users to define instructions. It contains a large library of predetermined functions. It is used with personal computers and also with larger systems. It can perform complex arithmetic-logic operations with a single command. It is designed for mathematical work and provides more facilities than FORTRAN. It is very complex and has no commercial applications. Mathematician uses it. It requires special keyboards and terminals because its instructions entirely consist of geometric shapes and symbols.

C Language: A high-level programming developed by Dennis Ritchie and Brian Kernighan at Bell Labs in the mid 1970s. Although originally designed as a systems programming language, C has proved to be a powerful and flexible language that can be used for a variety of applications, from business programs to engineering. It is a popular language for personal computer programmers because it is relatively small – it requires less memory than other languages.

The first major program written in C was the UNIX operating system, and for many years C was considered to be inter linked with UNIX. However, C is important independent language of UNIX.

Although it is a high-level language, C is much closer to assembly languages than other high-level languages. This closeness to the underlying machine language allows C programmers to write very efficient code. The low-level nature of C, however, can make the language difficult to use for some types of applications.

C++: A high-level programming language developed by Bjarne Stroustrup at Bell Labs. C++ adds object-oriented features to its predecessor; C. C++ is one of the most popular programming languages for graphical applications, such as those that run in Window and Macintosh environments.

PROLOG: It is a suitable for developing programs involving complex logical operations. It is used primarily for artificial intelligence applications. It was developed in France. The Japanese have chosen this language as a standard language for their fifth generation computer project. It is quite suitable for handling large databases and for producing rules-based expert systems applications. PROLOG stands for programming in Logic. It is based on mathematical logic. Most of high-level languages like BASIC, COBOL, FORTRAN or PASCAL are not based on the principles of mathematical logic. These languages were designed to provide efficient computation and data manipulation. They enable us to use computers for computations and data manipulation purposes. But today computers are also being used to provide conclusions based on intelligent resonating. For such a purpose, programming languages based on the principle of mathematical logic are needed. PROLOG is based on the first order predicate calculus. PROLOG consists of a set of facts and rules that describe objects and relations between objects in a given domain. The statement that are unconditionally true are called facts, while rules provide properties and relations which are true depending on given; while rules provide properties and relations which are true depending on given conditions. Many expert systems have been developed. They perform operations based on logical reasoning and provide conclusions.

LISP: It stands for LIST processing. McCarthy developed this language in the early 1960s. It is suitable for non-numeric operations involving logical operations. It is used extensively in artificial intelligence and pattern recognition. It is also used in game playing theorem proving etc. It is capable of searching, handling and sorting long string of lists of text. So it has often been used to implement computerized translators. It is used primarily on larger computers but LISP compilers are also available for PCs.

SNOBOL: It stands for String Oriented Symbolic language. A group led by Griswold in the mid 1960s developed this language. It can manipulate strings of characters and hence it is used in text processing. It is capable of performing various types of operations on strings of characters such as combining strings, splitting strings, matching strings etc.

LOGO: Seymour Papert and his colleagues at MIT developed it in the late 1960s. It has also been popularized as a first educational language that children can use to achieve intellectual growth and problem-solving skills. LOGO has graphics capability. Children can easily use it to make drawings. They can draw colour and animate images. It runs on PCs. It is used to compose music, manipulate text, manage data, etc.

APT: It stands for Automatically programmed Tooling. It is used in manufacturing applications to control machine tools.

MODULA-2: Nicklaus Wirth, the creator of PASCAL, has developed it. Although it retains the merits of PASCAL, it is more powerful and easier to use. PASCAL programs can easily be translated into MODULO-2 codes. It is a strongly structural language. It is easier for the compiler to find programming errors than it is with other languages. Structured programming also results in well-planned program steps, which produces more efficient and trouble-free software.

JAVA: A high-level programming language developed by Sun Microsystems. Java was originally called OAK, and was designed for handheld devices and set-top boxes. OAK was unsuccessful so in 1995 Sun changed the name to Java and modified the language to take advantage of the World Wide Web.

Java is an object-oriented language similar to C++, but simplified to eliminate language features that cause common programming errors. Java source code files (files with a java extension) are compiled into a format called byte code (files with a class extension), which can then be executed by a Java interpreter. Compiled Java code can run on most computers because Java interpreters and runtime environments, known as Java Virtual Machines (VMs), exist for most operating systems, including UNIX, the Macintosh OS, and Windows. Byte code can also be converted directly into machine language instructions by a just in time compiler (JIT). Java is a general purpose programming languages with a number of features that make the language well suited for use on the World Wide Web. Small Java applications are called Java applets and can be downloaded from a Web server and run on your computer by a Java-compatible Web browser, such as Netscape Navigator or Microsoft Internet Explorer.

8.2.6 Fourth Generation Languages (4GLs)

A very high-level language is often a 4GL (4th generation language). 4GLs are much more user-oriented and allow programmers to develop programs with fewer commands compared with third-generation languages. 4GLs are called nonprocedural because programmers do not write the programs, they need only tell the computer what they want to be done, not all the procedures for doing it. That is, they do not have to specify all the programming logic or otherwise tell the computer how the task should be carried out. This saves programmers a lot of time because they do not need to write as many lines of code as they do with procedural languages.

Fourth generation languages consist of report generations, query languages, application generators, and interactive database management system (DBMS) programs. Some 4GLs tools are applicable for end-users and some for programmers.

8.2.7 Difference Between 4GLs and High-Level Languages

(i)   The 4GLs are often easier to use than high-level languages.

(ii)   The 4GLs are not supported by the industry standards. They offer less control over output results than do high-level languages.

(iii)   4GLs do not use hardware resources as efficiently as do the high-level languages. Therefore, most application programs are written in high level languages only.

4GLs will probably not replace third-generation language because they are usually focused on specific tasks, hence offer options. Still, they improve productivity because programs are easy to write.

8.2.8 Fifth Generation: Natural Languages

Natural languages of two types: The first are ordinary human languages: Hindi, English, German, French, Spanish, and so on. The second are programming languages that use human language to give people a more natural connection with computers. Some of the query languages mentioned above under 4GLs might seem pretty close to human communication, but natural languages – which are still in their infancy – try to be even closer.

An example of a request in 4GL FOCUS, for example, might be:

Sum Sales by State by Date

Natural languages allow questions or commands to be framed in a more conversational way or in alternative forms. For example, with a natural language, you might be able to state:

I want the sales of personal computers for Madhya Pradesh and Chhatisgarh broken down by city for January and February. Also, I need January and February sales list by cities for laser printers sales in Keral and Madhya Pradesh.

Natural languages are part of the field of study known as artificial intelligence. Artificial intelligence (AI) is a group of related technologies that attempt to develop machines to emulate human like qualities, such a learning, reasoning, communicating, seeing and hearing.

8.2.9 Source Language and Object Language

The language in which a programmer writes programs is called source language. It may be a high-level language or an assembly language. The language in which the computer works is called object language or machine language. Machine codes are also known as object codes. A program written in a source language is called a source program. When a source program is converted into machine codes by an assembler or a compiler, it is known as an object program. In other words, a machine language program ready for execution is called an object program.

Report generation: A report generator, also called a report writer, is a program for end users that are used to produce a report.

The report may be a printout or a screen display. It may show all or part of a database file. You can specify the format in advance – columns, headings, and so on – and the report generator will then produce data in that format. An example of a report generator is Crystal Report. Report generators were the precursor to today's query languages.

Query languages: A Query language is an easy-to-use language for retrieving data from a database management system. The query may be expressed in the from of a sentence or the query may be obtained from choices on a menu.

Examples of query languages are SQL (Structured Query Language), QBE (Query-By-example), and Intellect. For example, with Intellect, which is used with IBM mainframes, you can pose an English- language command such as 'Tell me the number of employees in the purchase department.'

Application generations: An application generator is a programmer's tool that allows a person to give a detailed explanation of what data needs to be processed. The software then generates the code needed to create a program to perform the task. The benefit is that the programmer does not need to specify how the data should be processed. The application generator is able to do this because it consists of modules that have been preprogrammed to accomplish various tasks. Programmer use application generators to help them to create parts of other programs. For example, the software is used to construct on-screen menus or types of input and output screen formats.

- Examples of application generations are NOMAD and FOCUS, two relational database management systems.

CHAPTER 9

Program Design

9.1 Introduction

Systems analyst, familiar with both management and data processing, would probably be assigned the responsibility for working out a detailed, technical solution that satisfies the user.

The first event leading to the preparation of a computer task is someone's decision that here is a need for information – perhaps management requests the preparation of a report, or operating personnel may request a new or improved record-keeping procedure to prove data for decision making, or it may be as subsystem in the master information system development. The starting point for the design of any computer program must be a proper specification of its intended behaviors. It is most usual to describe this behaviors pattern in terms of the necessary inputs and the required outputs. The programmer's problem is then to design a process (or algorithm), which will, give the correct inputs, derived from them the required output.

In addition to the descriptions of these input and outputs, a program specification may include a description of any constraints, which must apply to the solution. These may include details of run time and/or space limitations available equipment and utilities, as well as project deadlines.

Within a program specification, the definitions of the inputs and outputs must include a description of their meaning, so that the programmer can understand the relationship between them.

For instance, one may need a program to find the area of a triangle given the lengths of its three sides. Such statement of the problem is almost a complete specification – the programmer needs to know only the properties of triangles in order to handle it. The problem as stated has meaning only because we understand the terms "triangle" "area" and "side", and their inter-relationships. If, on the other hand, the specification is "given X, Y and Z, compute A". It would be meaningless without a definition of A, X, Y and Z.

A program needs to be fully specified, because it is part of a larger system and its design must be consistent with the method used overall. In a commercial environment, the specification would come from a systems analyst, or systems manager, who studies user requirements and is responsible for the design and co-ordination of a software project. The analyst hands over the specifications to a team of programmers, each of who works on a set of programs.

To help a programmer to understand a particular program's position, the entire system should be clear. Since an overall systems specification should be known before individual programs are specified, all the programmer needs to do is study the documentation. He or she should find, among other things, an overall system description in diagrammatic form. This may take the form of a system run chart, showing all files and programs involved – or it may be a data flow diagram, in which specific files are not mentioned. In either case the role played by the particular program under consideration should be clear.

The program gains a name according to the naming in use; also, in addition to a description of the program inputs and outputs in the form of details record formats, the programmer will probably receive a description of the function of the program in some form.

9.2   Task Analysis

Any program written in a business environment is part of a software system to carry out a certain processing task. An actual data processing package would consist of a large number of programs, each handling one activity. For example, in a software package used by a sales department, one program may enter daily sales into data files. Another program uses the records to these data files to produce a particular report.

Information is the basis for action both by personnel within an organization and by persons outside (e.g. customers, suppliers, government agencies). The analysis of need and development of specification should involve both a systems analyst and the people who will use the program. The participation of those who need the data is important because of their knowledge of the function being studied and because of the human relations problems, which develop, if a system is designed for their use without them handling it.

Participation by a systems analyst early in the definition stage is important because he or she has the background to perceive ways in which the full power of the computer may be used to assist the decision process. Frequently, a program is designed from the specifications furnished by the users without considering the decisions to be made and other uses for the output. The resulting programs have frequently been found to be inadequate because the definition was incomplete or did not consider the use of new computer based analytical and computation techniques.

Based on the rough specifications for the application, the programmer designs a program which best meets the need considering the limits imposed by the facilities and personnel which can be used and the costs which can be justified by the value of the results to be achieved. Programmer must make decisions with respect to processing method, types of file media, frequency of processing, etc., to balance the cost and value or alternative approaches. In all matters affecting the users, he or she should consult with them so that these decisions will be understood and accepted.

Some of the questions, which need to be answered in the task analysis and design phase, are.

For Source Documents

- What source documents must be provided, how often, any by whom?
- How will information on the source document be transcribed to machine-readable forms?
- What is the layout of the source document and computer input form?

For Files

- Which computer files will be maintained?
- What type of file media and file organization will be used?
- What will be the size of the file and the growth rate?
- What is the layout of the computer record and the computer file?

For Processing

- What processing, computerized or mechanical is required?
- How frequently must processing be performed?
- What volume of transactions must be processed?
- What processing approach will be used?
- What off-line equipment will be necessary?

For Output

- What is format of the report?
- To whom will the report be distributed?

The result of this analysis of need is a set of specifications outlining the information needs. The specifications describe the problem, the data to be provided, the persons to receive the output, the frequency of output, and an estimate of the volume of transactions to be processed. Essentially, it is a statement of user needs.

9.3   Data Analysis and Input Design

Input Design is the process of converting an external, user-oriented description of the inputs into a machine-oriented format. In most business systems, devices operated by humans generate inputs. In these cases, the input design must take into account the human element in order to ensure rapid and accurate data entry from a source document. This will prevent error and speed of data entry. Two important rules to follow in designing source documents for data entry are:

1. Lay out the data elements in sequence so that the data entry operator can follow easily. The normal sequence of data entry is from left to right and from top to bottom of the page.

2. Group the data elements to be entered separately from those that are not to be entered. This means that the data entry operator does not have to hesitate while skipping over fields that are not to be stored or processed.

It must be remembered that digital computers do not make any mistakes. This implies that computer errors can generally be traced to incorrect input data or unreliable programs. Both caused by human failures; not due to computer fragilities.

9.4   Designing

It is essential that the overall program strategy should be completely charted out before the detailed programming actually begins. The way the programmer can concentrate initially on the general program logic, without bothering for the syntactical details of the individual instructions. This overall planning process may then be repeated several times, with more programming detail added at each stage. Thus, the programmer can gradually shift his or her attention from the overall computation strategy to the details of the individual instructions. Such an approach is often referred to as "top-down" programming.

A problem specification is generally given in terms of a desired relation between inputs and outputs, which specifies what is to be computed. An algorithm or program for a given problem specifies how the given relation between inputs and outputs is to be achieved. It is the task of the programmer to convert "static" input/output specifications of what is to be computed into dynamic specifications that specify how the computation is to be performed.

A given input/output relation may be realised by a wide variety of different algorithms, and each algorithm may in turn be realized in a variety of different programming languages. There is thus considerable freedom in developing a program for the solution of any given problem. This freedom of choice in developing programs leads to the notion that programming is an art rather than a science.

Although the set of all programs for realising a given problem specification is in general infinite, there are a number of criteria other than correctness, which may be used to restrict the class of acceptable programs that realise a given problem specification.

A good program should economize both computation time and the storage space required to represent the program and data structures. A well-defined sub program should specify it. Modular design of a program is important because it makes the program easier to understand, facilitates debugging, and allows modifications to be made more easily. It is usually worth paying a price in computation time and memory space in order to achieve greater modularity. Modular construction is especially important in large programs. Since the human mind is severely limited in the complexity it can handle, and systematic modularity reduced the number of factors the human mind must handle at any given moment, thereby allowing the understanding of a large system than would otherwise be possible.

Programming is the process of converting broad system specifications into usable machine instructions that produce desired results. Programmers must answer the following questions during the program design.

1. Have the problem specifications been spelled out clearly & completely? Little significant progress can be made until the programmer can answer "yes" to this question.

2. Am I familiar with a solution method that will solve the problem?

    If the programmer knows a procedure that will solve the problem, the solution may then be coded in a selected language. If this is not the case, the next question must be considered.

3. Can I locate a solution method to solve the problem from other people or from books or journals? If a method can be located, the solution may be coded. Otherwise, the next question must be answered.

4. How can I develop a procedure that will solve this problem?

This question often challenges programmers, and a modular design approach (considered below) is often used at this time to reduce a large (and seemingly unmanageable) problem into smaller tasks that are easier to solve.

Several programming analysis tools are available to help people develop problem solutions. One such tool is the program flow chart. It is a detailed chart to represent steps to be carried out within the machine to produce the needed output.

A commercial program is designed to meet the needs of the customer who will be its ultimate user. The outputs and reports, the screen messages and questions, and the inputs required – the user must understand all these and find them similar to those already in use. The users should therefore have as close connection as possible with specifying the requirements. When they are satisfied, they will generally have to issue a formal "acceptance" of the specifications, by signing relevant documents. Because the programmer may not get a chance to interact with the users themselves, they must be able to understand the specifications and follow them rigidly. Any improvements, which they would like to suggest, should be raised at the appropriate meetings.

Moreover, because he or she is part of a team, the programmer must document his or her programs in a predetermined way, so that the rest of the team can easily understand them. This sometimes means that programmers who are new to a team have the additional burden of adapting to the standards for specifications and documentation that are already in use by the team as a whole.

Following steps are involved in designing the solution:
1. Planning the program
2. Coding of instructions
3. Translation (compilation)
4. Debugging
5. Documentation

9.5   Data Validation

All data entry programs must also have routines that validate the data input. As one of the safeguards against incorrect entries, it is necessary to accumulate and display data-entry statistics giving the number of records entered and the errors found. The data entry operator can then check these incorrect records against the original source. Control totals (a sort of data entry check) should also be shown to ensure all data has been entered.

A good practice in a data entry program is to present some kind of key to the latest value entered- a operator often has to continue to work through interruptions which cause the last entry made to be forgotten.

Outputs also have to be validated, particularly those, which are little unusual, such as, the nil statement and the multi page Invoice. Testing is a vital but time-consuming activity. It is inevitable that errors will be found. These may be due to incorrect programming, misunderstanding of specifications or simply omissions in the original design. The programmer must code the amendments required, and the programs and system retested. This retesting is very important because the requested amendments may have caused unwanted side effects and so new errors and problems may appear. One of the most common sources of faults in programs is the fixing of other faults!

9.5.1 Input Validation

At the point data is entered into the computer, it should be subjected to input validation procedures in which data is tested for errors to the extent possible or appropriated in the light of the consequences of input errors. A separate input validation run or input editing run is usually performed in systems where the data is not entered directly and comes from intermediate processing, the erroneous transaction or record found to contain and error, is shunted rather than stopping the computer on the console typewriter or printer explaining why item rejected. There will thus usually be a file of rejects and an error run should be carefully controlled to make sure they are corrected and reentered at a later run.

In the case of on-line processing of unmatched transactions, data items are tested in the same manner the batch processing validation run. An error message to the input station describing the error is the basis for rejecting the transaction and requesting a resubmission of a correct input (or submission of a correction to one or more fields of the input record).

Before testing the data items themselves, the input validation run should test that the file being used is the correct one (correct data, correct records). Checking the internal file label does this. A file label is a record at the beginning and also possibly at the end of the file which contains identification or master file is used and that the entire file has been processed. At the beginning is the header label, which identifies the file. Typical contents are:

- Name of file
- Creation data
- Purge date
- Identification number
- Reel number (for magnetic tape)

The input validation tests seek to establish that the data is within the limits established for valid data. Some examples of programmed checking which can be done are:

- **Valid Code:** If there is only limited number of valid codes, say for coding expenses, the code being read may be checked to see if it is one of the valid codes.

- **Valid Character:** If only certain characters are allowed in a data field, the computer can test the field to determine that no invalid characters are used.

- **Valid Field Size, sign, and composition:** If a code number should be specified number of digits in length, the computer may be programmed to test the field size as is specified. If the sign of the field must always be positive or always negative, a test may be made to determine that the field does indeed contain a proper composition of characters.

- **Valid Transaction:** There is typically a relatively small number of valid transactions which are processed with a particular file. There is a limited number, for example, of transaction codes, which can apply to accounts receivable file updation. As part of input error control, the transaction code can be tested for validity.

- **Valid Combinations of Field:** In addition to each of the individual fields being tested, combinations may be tested for validity. For example a salesman code, may be associated with only a few territory codes, this can be checked.

- **Missing Data Test:** The program may check the data field to make sure that all data fields necessary to code a transaction have data field necessary to code a transaction have data in them.

- **Check Digit:** Check digit are one or more digits carried within a unit item of numerical data to provide information about the other digits in the unit in such a manner that, if a transaction or transposition error occurs in subsequent data entry, the check tails, and an indication of error is given.

- **Sequence Test:** In batch processing the data to be processed must be arranged in a sequence, which is the same as the sequence of the file. Both the master file and the transaction file may be tested to ensure that they are in a proper sequence, ascending or descending as the case may be. The sequence check can also be used to account for all documents, if these are numbered sequentially.

- **Limit of Reasonableness Test:** This is a basic test for data processing accuracy. Input data should usually fall within certain limits. For example, hours worked should not be less than zero and should not be more than, say, 50. The upper limit may be established from the experience of the particular firm. Input data may be compared against this limit to ensure that no input error has occurred or at least no input error exceeding certain reestablished limits.

Examples: The total amount of a customer order may be compared with his average order amount. If this order exceeds, say, three times the amount of his average order, then an exception notice may be printed. A material receipt, which exceeds two times the economic order quantity established for particular item, might be subject to question. A receiving report amount may be compared with the amount requested on the purchase order. If there is more than a small percentage variance, then there is an assumption of error in the input data. In a utility billing, consumption is checked against prior periods to detect possible errors or trouble in the customer's installation.

9.6   Coding the Program

Writing the program involves translating the algorithm or flowchart into a programming language. This processing is known as coding. The language chosen depends upon what the program is expected to do and what facilities are available to the programmer.

The programming activity continues with coding of the logic described in the flowchart into statements in the language being used. These are usually written on coding paper designed for the particular language. These source language statements are then typed using a keyboard, line by line. The resulting group of lines form source program.

The translation phase begins with the loading of the translator and routine of the compiler into the computer memory. This routine reads the source program codes, interprets their meaning, and produces an object program on some machine-readable output medium such as magnetic disk. A listing of the program is printed on the line printer or typewriter. This listing includes any error diagnostic, which the translator routine detects. The errors, which can be detected, are mainly textual errors involving improper use of the language. If errors are found, these must be corrected and the translation process repeated.

Programming is sometimes contrasted with coding generally refers to the writing and debugging of programs for given programs specifications. The text of a program is sometimes referred to as code, and lines of program text are refereed to as lines of code, especially in the case of machine-language programs.

9.7   Debugging

When a program is compiled or executed it may produce a number of errors. Errors may become discouraged because of bugs, but this should not be the case. Debugging should be considered to be a part of programming.

Thus debugging is the process of checking the correctness of the program either manually or through facility of compiler program error checking. How, then to get rid of the bugs? When test data produces incorrect output, it is necessary to trace through the logic to find out how and where the program has failed. You can examine the values of memory variables by introducing additional PRINT or DISPLAY statements at selected points. Then use some variation of the dry run to trace through the code and see how these values are being produced. At the end, ensure that to remove such statements added for de-bugging purposes properly after the error has been corrected.

On inspecting the code, a few pointers may be helpful.

(a) It is important to be able to approach the code with a fresh and open mind, even when looking at it for the last time. Never believe even yourself; it is surprising how easy it is to make assumptions. The code must be seen from the viewpoint of an obedient and "dumb" computer.

(b) Only the output of a program is relevant while analyzing a failure. The error in the output is a direct indication of what has failed, and however impossible it may seem at first (or even second) glance, the error must exist at a relevant point.

(c) In case of an elusive error, keep in mind that an error can escalate and show up at a point far from where it was caused. The total picture must, therefore, be re-examined at such times.

(d) It sometimes helps to be able to "image" the problem, especially when it is connected with one of the input or output devices or with a file transfer. While considering each statement, try to imaging exactly what would be happening on the computer in response.

A high-level language usually simplifies debugging. The coding is normally not as lengthy and logic of the program is easier to follow. The programmer first does desk checking of his program, tracing through the logic to see if it does what is intended. The program is then ready for a test run. If it does not run correctly, corrections are made in the source, and the program is translated again.

9.8   Types of Errors

In general, bugs can be detected during compilation while the second is detected during or after execution. If the rules of syntax are violated, then the program will not compile. On the other hand, the program may be syntactically perfect but there can be a logical error. Thus the three types of errors that can occur in a program are.

(a) Syntax error, or syntactical errors,

(b) Run-time errors,

(c) Logic errors, or logical errors.

Syntax Errors: Syntax errors occur when there is a violation in any of the rule of language formation. Errors causes by misunderstanding or misinterpreting the syntax and type rules of the programming language are trivial mistakes may arise due to applying rules of one higher language to another like a student who has learnt BASIC can FORTRAN first and now leaning PASCAL may tend to apply rules of these two languages into the statements being written in PASCAL. A person habituated BASIC may tend to write the assignment statement MARK=5 instead of MARK: = 5 and PRINT instead of WRITELN of PASCAL. These errors are usually easy to correct because the compiler will point out where an error has occurred. The Pascal compiler produces these error messages while it is attempting to translate a Pascal program into machine language. Any grammatical mistake will cause problems when the translation is performed. The complier will attempt to produce a message indicating where the mistake is and what it believed the mistake to be.

Disk Checking: It's unusual for complex programs to run to completion on the first attempt. In fact, the time spent in DEBUGGING and testing often equals or exceeds the time spent in program coding. To reduce the number of errors, the programmer should carefully check the coding for accuracy before entering it into the computer. This desk-checking process should include an examination of program logic and program completeness. For this, typical input data should be manually traced through the program processing paths to identify possible errors. After desk checking, an attempt is made to convert the source program into object program form. Compiler programs and interpreters contain error-diagnostic features, which detect (and print messages about) mistakes caused by the incorrect application of the language used to prepare the source program.

When changes have been made, in response to errors detected, a re-compilation can be ordered. This process may continue until all detected syntax errors have been remedied.

9.9   Testing

During the programming stage, each programmer or programming team will perform their own program testing to the specifications laid down by the designer. The completed programs are then passed to the designer for further testing. He will be anxious not only to examine the delivered programs but also to prove their interfaces with the rest of the system. Testing will be performed by both desk checking comparing the program flowcharts with the original specifications and by running the program using test data.

Test data should be manually compiled and the results produced by the system compared with the appropriate clerical figures or the current computer system. For example, in a system designed to produce and print examination certificates, a sample of student's data should be taken and entered into the new computer system. The generated certificates can then be compared with their clerically produced counter parts and discrepancies investigated.

It is also important that the system correctly identifies errors and omissions and testing for these is especially critical. Common error tests include the input of:

- Oversize and undersize data items.
- Incorrect formats

When testing a program take care to select the test data so that it tests all cases. eq. Pick a set of data which will cover all possible selections. Large programs are very difficult to test completely once they are completed because of their complexity and the time needed to try all possible cases. If top-down programming is adopted it should be possible to test program modules thoroughly at each step along the way.

Despite all these testing methods programs may still be faulty when they are tried out on the computer. Well-tested programs sometimes work for a while and then suddenly produce a fault. This may happen because some combination of circumstances has occurred which the program designer had not taken into account while designing the program.

The purpose of testing is to determine whether the results are correct. The testing procedure involves using the program to process input test data that will produce known results. The items developed for tested should include:

- Typical data, which will test the generally used program paths.
- Unusual but valid data, which will test the program paths used to handle exceptions.
- Incorrect, incomplete, or inappropriate data, which will test the program error handling capabilities.

A testing procedure that's often followed is to separately test different portions of a program. This helps to isolate detected errors to a particular program segment.

The use of a modular programming approach is better procedure. Another technique that's often used is to entrust much of the testing to someone other that the programmer who wrote the code. A fresh outlook is often helpful, and errors that are missed by a programmer who is "too familiar" with the code may be easily picked up by someone else.

- It is good practice to test a program as it is being written and before it is tried out on the computer.
- How will the system be tested to ensure its readiness for use?
- How is the system to be implemented in terms of conversion?
- How is the system controlled for errors?

To centre heading on a line, count the number of characters on the heading, including spaces between words, Subtract this number from the number of available print positions on each line (80) to get the total number of blank spaces around the heading. Dividing this number by 2 gives the number of spaces that should be inserted in front of the heading.

1. **Levels of testing:** One of the most difficult questions with regard to testing is how much is enough? Although the aim of testing is to reveal errors, it is likely that some will get through the testing process without being found. Also, experience shows that, while it is fairly easy to find say, 95 % of the errors in a piece of code, it becomes more and more costly and difficult to find and correct the remaining errors. This has led to something of a compromise between what is desirable and what is achievable in terms of programs correctness, and has led to a distinction between different "levels" of correctness.

   The way most testing works is to input a set of values, then compare the expected results with the actual ones. If the output produced by a test run is correct; it shows the programs have correctly processed that set of data. Depending on the type of data input, we can identify three levels of program correctness – possible, probable correctness and absolute correctness.

   - Possible correctness follows obtaining correct output for some arbitrary input. If the outcome of such a test is wrong, the program cannot possibly be correct.

   - Probable correctness involves obtaining correct output for a number of carefully selected inputs. If all potentially problematic areas are checked in this way, the program is probably correct.

   - Absolute correctness can be demonstrated only by a test that involves every possible combination of inputs. Such a test would take a huge amount of time; it is therefore not practicable.

   Coding errors will not occur very often if you adopt a systematic approach. When they do occur, they almost invariably follow a misuse of the language facilities. This is usually due to an inadequate understanding of, or familiarity with, the languages in use. All programmers should ensure that they understand fully all aspects of the languages. All programmers should ensure that they understand fully all aspects of the languages they use, rather than "muddle through" using sometimes an inappropriate subset.

2. **Difference between Testing and Debugging:** It is very easy to make mistakes when writing programs, and so programs often fail to work the first

time they are tried. If a program has been well designed the faults should be easier to find and correct. The program faults are called "bugs" and getting rid of these faults by making appropriate changes to the program is called debugging.

Debugging is often regarded as a "patching up job". In fact alterations made to programs in order to get rid of bugs are often called "patches" or "fixed". Treating debugging in this way is rather a risky way to do things, because in patching one bug, another bug may be introduced. A more sound approach to debugging is to return to the program design process, and all stages in programming, so that the previously unforeseen circumstances are wholly incorporated into the design.

Testing is part of the procedure that ensures the program corresponds with the original specification, and that it works in its intended environment. We have already come across some similar verification and validation techniques. Dry running the code helps to ensure its logical correctness, and inspections and walk-through are to confirm that no errors follow the transition from stage to stage, e.g. specification to design.

The difference between these activities and testing is that they are "static", while testing is "dynamic". Dynamic in this situation means the process uses executable code, rather than listings or documents while describe the code. Testing should form a major part of any verification and validation activity on any software project. Static methods can be used to very good effect, and contribute significantly to the discovery of errors at a early stage – but they can never replace dynamic testing.

Most programmers, asked to define testing, say something like "Testing is the process of checking a program to show there are no errors". This type of definition concentrates on errors being absent – implying that successful test is one that shows no errors, and a failed test is one that finds no error. However, this approach is wrong. The aim of testing is to find errors so that can be corrected: resulting in a more reliable, and better quality final program.

CHAPTER 10

Fundamentals of Programming in C++

10.1 Introduction to C++

C++ is an object oriented extension of the programming language C. It is the superset of C. Whatever statements valid in C are also valid in C++ but its vice versa is never true as C++ contains some additional features which are, not in C. Whatever we have used in C are still useful in C++. Along with them, some more features like Inheritance and polymorphism are used as Data abstraction is already a feature of C language and exists in form of structures. We will be using the same data abstraction concept of C structures in the form of C++ classes with some modifications and much more power. Data abstraction refers to a programmer defined data type together with a set of functions that can be performed on the data. Data abstraction in C++ is an encapsulation of data and member functions that can manipulate data together in one single entity is called class. A class is very similar to a structure used in C, in fact it is enhanced version of C structures.

C++ is derived from C Language. C++ is an object oriented extension of the programming Language C. It has all the powers of C language plus all the power of object oriented programming system.

10.2   Procedure Oriented Vs Object Oriented Programming

10.2.1 Procedure Oriented Programming

In Procedure oriented programming the task was thought of a set of many smaller tasks called procedures or functions. In Procedural programming, program is composed of one or more procedures which are invoked in a particular order to achieve the desired result. Every procedure is a set of instructions representing a specific task. Here procedure to solve the problem is of prime importance and data design plays secondary role. Data is provided to functions as per procedure need, no much thought is given to data design. Top-down design and modular approach are central to Procedure oriented programming.

Top down design: This approach is also a natural approach of problem solving by human being. The complex problem is broken into smaller problems. Smaller problems are broken into further smaller problems; this process is repeated until problem becomes so small that solutions become visible. In top down design approach complexity is exposed in top down manner. In programming jargon it can be stated that in top down programming, 'called modules are implemented first and 'calling ones' later.

Modular Approach: Modular approach suggests that the problem should be divided into small modules or task. Modules are also synonymously termed as functions or procedures. Some programming languages do differentiate modules, procedures and functions with subtleties. Modularizing problems make solving them easier. Modular programming reduces 'ripple effect', i.e. making changes in small area of program does not affect the whole program. Programs are made up of modules, which are parts of a program that can be coded and tested separately, and then assembled to form a complete program. So, when you make changes in a small module it does not impact the larger program. Modules communicate by passing parameters and return values.

10.2.2 Object Oriented Programming (OOPs)

Oops concept is build around objects. An object binds data and functions together. Unlike procedure oriented programming, here objects interact with one another by message passing. Functions do not interact directly. The concept has been borrowed from real life. If, different students are considered as objects, we can draw an analogy. When a student is asked to utter his or her name one tells it. Nobody can change the name of a student without his or her consent. They are the owners of their data. 'Student' is an example of real life object.

OOPs have dramatically improved programming by increasing code reuse with increased portability. OOPs programming follows bottom up design, wherein available solutions are searched and are made to fit in the program structure. The concept of reusability of code is exercised more in OOPs.

Main differences between procedure oriented programming and object oriented programming are summarized in following table.

Procedure oriented programming	Object oriented programming
Emphasis is on algorithms i.e. on procedure to solve the problem	Emphasis is also on data. Data design is important
Larger programs are divided into smaller modules	Division of program is into various objects consisting of data and functions
Data is not bound with functions	Data and functions bound together
Data can move freely from function to function in the system	Objects move and communicate with each other through message passing
Follows top down approach	Follows bottom up approach
Function overloading is not possible	In OOP, function overloading is possible
No feature for supporting Polymorphism and inheritance	OOP has exceptional feature like polymorphism, inheritance
Older programming languages support this paradigm like BASIC, FORTRAN, COBOL, Pascal, older versions of Visual BASIC, C.	OOPs is supported by modern programming languages like java,C#,C++, VB.net

10.3 C++ Programming Basics

Basic program construction: Consider the following DISPLAY program

```
#include <iostream.h>
void main()
{
cout <<"Hello world ";
}
```

10.3.1 Function

Functions are one of the fundamental building blocks of C++. The DISPLAY Program consists of single function called main (). The parenthesis following the word main are distinguishing features of a function The word **void** preceding the function name indicates that this particular function does not have a return type. The body of the function is surrounded by curly brackets or braces. These braces mark the beginning and the end of the function which contains body of function. Every function must use these pair of brackets .When you run C++ program the first statement executed will be at the beginning of a function called main(). The program may consist of many - functions, classes and other program elements but the start of program control - always goes to main().

Program Statement: Program statement is the fundamental unit of C++ programming. There is only one statement in FIRST program

cout <<"Hello world";

This statement tells the computer to display the quoted phrase. The identifier **cout** is actually an object. It is predefined in C++ to correspond to the standard output stream. A stream refers to flow of data. The operator, << is called insertion or put operator. It directs the contents of the variable on its right to the object on its left in FIRST it directs the string constant "Hello World" to **cout** which sends it to display.

A semicolon signals the end of statement. This is the crucial part of the syntax.

Preprocessor Directives: The first line of DISPLAY Program,

#include <iostream.h>

Might look like a program statement, but it is not part of a function body and doesn't end with a semicolon, as program statements must start with a number sign hash(#). It is called a preprocessor directive which is an instruction to the compiler itself. A part of compiler called the preprocessor deals with these directives before it begins the real compilation process. The # include directive tells the compiler to insert another file into your source file. In effect, the # include directive is replaced by the contents of the file indicated. All preprocessor directives are identified with initial # sign.

Header File: Header files are included with preprocessor directive #include. In the DISPLAY program the header file used is iostream.h. It contains declarations that are needed by **cout** identifier and <<operator. Without header file declaration the compiler will not recognise them.

Comments: Comments are an important part of any program. They help the person writing a program, and, anyone else who reads the source file, to understand what is going on. The compiler ignores comments, they do not add to file size or execution time of the executable program.

Comment Syntax
1.   Comments start with a double slash symbol // and terminate at the end of the line
2.   Second type of comment syntax begins with /* character pair and ends with */ and between them. One can type multi-line syntax using this syntax.

Variable: Variables are the most fundamental part of any language. A variable is a symbolic name that can be given to a variety of values. When a variable is given a value, the value is actually placed in the memory space occupied by the variable. Most popular languages use the general variable types, such as integers, floating point numbers and characters.

Integer Variables: Integer variables exist in several sizes, but most commonly used type is **int**. This type of variable requires two bytes of storage. Int variable is declared as - int variable name; These declarations must be terminated with a semicolon. The variable name can use upper case and lower case letter, and the digits from 1 to 9, underscore can also be used. The first character of the variable name must be a letter or underscore. They can be as long as you like, but only the first 32 characters will be recognised. The compiler distinguishes between an upper case and lower case letters and is case sensitive. hence 'Bar' is not same as 'bar or BAR'. You can't use a C++ keyword as a variable name. A keyword is the identifier for a language feature like **int**, **class**, **if**, **while** and so on.

Character Variables: Variable of this type occupy only one byte of memory. Character variables are sometimes used to store numbers that confine themselves to range of (-128 to 127), but they are more commonly used to store ASCII characters. The character constants use single quotation marks around a character. When C++ compiler encounters such a character constant, it translates it into the corresponding ASCII codes. The constant 'a' will be stored as 97.

Floating Point Variables: Floating point variables represent numbers with a decimal place. They represent real numbers, which have both an integer part , to the left of decimal point and fractional part to the right. There are 3 kinds of floating point variables in C++, **float**, **double** and **long double**. **Float** requires 4 bytes of memory.

Long: Type long is a type of integer variable. Type long can also be written as **long int**. It is used when type **int** is too small for the values being stored. Variables of type **long** occupy 4 bytes of memory.

Thus we have seen that there are 3 integer types **char**, **int** and **long** and three floating point types: **float**, **double** and **long double**. Type double occupies 8 bytes and stores floating point number which has much larger range and precision. Floating point type long double occupies 10 bytes, and has only slightly greater range and precision than type double.

Input with cin: Now we have seen some variable types in use, Lets see how a program accomplishes input. The next sample program asks the user for a temperature in degrees and converts it to Celsius and displays the result .

```
#include <iostream.h>
void main()
{
int ftemp;
cout << "Enter temperature in Fahrenheit";
cin >> ftemp;
```

```
    int ctemp = (ftemp-32)*5/9;
    cout <<"Equivalent in celsius is" <<ctemp;
}
```

The statement cin >>ftemp; causes the program to wait for the user to type in a number. The resulting number is placed in the variable ftemp. The keyword cin is an object predefined in C++ to correspond to standard input stream. This stream represents data coming from keyboard. The >>is the extraction or get from operator. It takes the value from the stream object on its left and places it in the variable on its right.

The program has several new things besides its input capabilities. The variable ctemp is defined not at the beginning of program but at the end where it is used to store the result of arithmetic operation. So you can define variables, throughout a program and not just at the beginning. Defining the variables where they are used can make the listing easier to understand, since you don't need to refer repeatedly to the start of the listing to find the variable definitions. However the variables that are used in many places in a function are probably better defined at the start of the function.

The extraction operator << is used repeatedly in second cout statement in program. The program first sends the phrase "Equivalent in centigrade" in **cout** and then sends the value of ctemp. The insertion operator >> can be cascaded with **cin** in the same way, allowing the user to enter a series of values.

Expression: An arrangement of variables and operators that specifies computation is known an expression. Thus ftemp+5, (ftemp-32) *beta/ 9 are expressions where the computations specified in the expression are performed, the result is usually a value. Parts of expressions may also be expressions. Thus (ftemp-32) and beta/9 are expressions by themselves. Even single variables and constants like beta and 32 are considered to be expressions. Expressions aren't same as statements. Statements ask the compiler to do something and terminate with a semicolon, while expressions specify computation. There can be several expressions in a statement.

Manipulators: Manipulators are the operators used with the insertion operator << to modify or manipulate the way data is displayed. Most common are **endl** and **setw**. The declarations for the manipulators are not in the usual iostream.h header file, but in separate header file called iomanip.h. When manipulators are used, iomanip.h should be included in the program file.

endl Manipulator: This manipulator causes a linefeed to be inserted into the stream. It has same effect as sending the single '\n' character.

setw Manipulator: The setw manipulator causes the number (or string) that follows it in the stream to be printed, within a field n characters wide, where n is the argument to setw(n). The value is right justified within the field.

10.4 Type Conversion

C++, like C compiles without error, expressions involving several different data types. It can multiply variables of 2 different types and stores result in another type. Types are considered higher or lower, based roughly in the order shown below-

Data Type	Order
long double	Highest
double	
float	
long	
int	
char	Lowest

When two operands of different type are encountered in the same expression, the lower type of variable is converted to higher type variable. This is automatic data conversion. The language provides with a choice for explicitely specifying how values are to be converted in mixed-mode expression. This is done by using a cast operator. The name of the data type to which the conversion is to be made (such as int or float) is enclosed in parenthesis and placed directly to left of the value to be converted. The word cast is used.

10.5 Arithmetic Operators

C++ employ usual arithmetic operators +,-,*, and / for addition, subtraction, multiplication and division. These operators work on all data types, both integer and floating point. Apart from these, there is another operator that works only with integer variable called the modulus operator represented by °%. This operator returns the remainder when one number is divided by another, for example; 2%4=2, 3%4=3, 4%4=0, 5% 4=1, 6%4=2.

10.5.1 Arithmetic Assignment Operator

Consider following statement

$$total = total + item;$$

In this situation you add something to an existing value. The arithmetic assignment operator combines the arithmetic operator and assignment operator and eliminates the repeated operand. Here is a statement that has exactly the same effect as the one above

```
total += item.
```

There are arithmetic assignment operators corresponding to all the arithmetic operators: +=,-=,*=,/= and %=. Consider the following program

```
#include <iostream.h>
void main()
{
int arts = 27;
arts += 10;
cout <<arts <<endl;
arts -= 7;
cout <<ans <<endl;
 arts *= 2;
 cout <<arts <<endl;
 arts /= 3;
cout <<arts <<endl;
arts %= 3;
cout <<arts <<endl;
}
```

Output
```
37
30
60
20
02
```

10.5.2   Increment Operators

The increment ++ operator adds one to the argument. Example. Count = Count + 1 is similar to ++COUNT. The increment operator can be used in two ways: as a prefix meaning that the operator precedes the variable; and as a postfix meaning that operator follows the variable. Often a variable is incremented within a statement that performs some other operation on it. For eg.

```
total = avg * ++ count.
```

In this case count is incremented first because prefix notation is used. If we use postfix notation, count++, the multiplication would have been performed first, then count would be incremented.

10.5.3   Decrement Operator

Decrement operator --, behaves much like increment operator, except that it will subtract one from its operand.

10.6   Loops and Decisions

Many programs do not execute all their statements in strict order from beginning to end. Most programs decide what to do in response to changing circumstances. The flow of control jumps from one part of the program to another, depending on calculations performed in the program. Program statements that cause such jumps are called control statements. There are two major categories: loops and decisions. How many times a loop is executed, or whether a decision results in the execution of section of code, depends on whether certain expressions are true or false. These expressions involve a kind of operator called a relational operator, which compares two values.

10.7   Relational Operators

A relational operator compares two values. These values can be any, built in C++ data type such as char, int, float, or as we will see later - they can be user defined classes. The comparison involves such relationships as equal to, less than, greater than and so on, result of the comparison is true or false. Here is a complete listing of C++ operators -

Operator	Meaning
>	Greater than
<	less than
= =	Equal to
!=	not equal to
> =	greater than or equal to
< =	less than or equal to

Now let us look at some expressions that use relational operators, and also look at the value of each expression. The first two lines are assignment statements that sets the value of variables nikky and nishu -

```
nishu = 42            //      assignment statement
nikky = 12            //      assignment statement
(nishu == nikky)      //      false
(nikky >= 12)         //      true
(nishu > 44)          //      false
(nikky !=12)          //      false
```

(7 < nikky)	//	true
(0)	//	false (by definition)
(44)	//	true (since it is not 0)

Note that the equals operator ==, uses two equal signs. A common mistake is to use single 'equals to sign', the assignment sign as a relational operator. This is a nasty bug since compiler won't notice anything wrong. However, your program won't do what you want. Although C++ generates 1 to indicate true, it assumes that any value other than 0 (sixty as -7 or 44) is true, only 0 is false .

10.7.1 Conditional Operator (?:)

This is a ternary operator that needs three arguments to operate. Consider following statement S

```
        if (alpha < beta)

                min = alpha;

        else

                min = beta;
```

This sort of construction can be expressed in a compressed way by using conditional operator. This operator consists of two symbols which operate on three operands. Equivalent of above program statement using a conditional operator is,

min =(alpha <<beta) ? alpha : beta

The part of this statement to the right of equals sign is the conditional expression. The question mark and colon make up the conditional operator. The expression before the expression, (alpha <beta) is the test expression. Test expression, alpha, beta are operands. If the test expression is true, then the conditional expression takes the value of the operand following the question mark, *alpha* above. If the test expression is false the conditional expression takes the value of following colon, *beta* in above statement. The conditional expression can be assigned to another variable, or used anywhere as a value can be.

10.7.2   Logical Operator

The logical AND (&&) operator and logical OR operator (II) combines two Boolean accessions to yield another expression.

The logical NOT operator (!) changes the Boolean value from true to false or from false to true

goto Statement: goto statement causes unconditional jump to the program flow.The goto statement sends the control to a label. You insert a label in your code at the desired place i.e. destination for the goto. The label is always terminated by a colon. The keyword goto is followed by this label name. The goto statement is included in C++, just for the sake of completion. In modern programming languages use of goto is avoided as it spoils the structure of the program. Use of goto was very popular before the advent of structured programming paradigm.

Precedence of operators: Precedence specifies which kinds of operations will be carried out first, while computing an expression. The order is:

unary → arithmetic → logical → conditional → assignment operator

10.8 Loops

Loops causes a section of your program to be repeated a certain number of times. The repetition continues while a condition is true. When the condition becomes false the loop ends and control passes to the statements following the loop. There are 3 kinds of loops, **for**, **while** and **do** loop.

10.8.1 for Loop

In **for** loop, all its loop control elements are gathered in one place. **for** loop executes a section of code, a fixed times. It is usually used when you know, before entering the loop, how many times you want to execute the code. Consider the following example-

```
void main()
{
int j;
 for (j=0; j<10; j++)
 cout << i*i<< "        ";
}
```

Output

```
0   1    4     9    16    25    36    49    64    81
```

for statement controls the loop. It consists of keyword for, followed by parenthesis that contains three expressions separated by semicolons. These three expressions are the initialization expression, the test expression and the increment expression. These three expressions usually involve same variable which is called loop variable. In the above program loop variable is j. It is defined before loop begins. The body of loop is the code to be executed each time through the loop. In the above program body consists of single statement: cout <<j*j<<"   ";.

for statement is not followed by a semicolon. That is because for statement and the loop body are together considered to be a program statement. If you put a semicolon after for statement, the compiler will think there is no loop body.

Now let's consider the three expressions of for loop. The initialization expression- This expression is executed only once when the loop starts. It gives the loop variable an initial value. The test expression usually involves a relational operator. It is evaluated each time through the loop just before the body of loop is executed. It determines whether loop will be executed again. If the text expression is true, loop is executed one more time. If it's false, the loop ends and control passes to the statements following the loop. The increment expression changes the value of the loop variable, often by incrementing it. It is always executed after the end of loop, after the loop body has been executed.

Multiple statements in loop body- You may want to execute more than one statement in the loop body. Multiple statements are delimited by braces just as functions are.

for loop variation: The Increment expression doesn't need to increment loop variable; it can perform any other operation also. In the following example uses decrements operation for the loop variable. The given program calculates factorial of a given number-

```cpp
#include <iostream.h>
void main()
{
unsigned int num;
 unsigned long fact = 1;
cout <<"Enter a number";
cin >>num;
for(int j=num; j>0; j--)
fact *=j;
 cout <<" factorial is "<<fact;
}
```

10.8.2   while Loop

for loop does something a fixed number of times. If you don't know how many times the loop should be executed then we use while loop. In the Following example we ask the user to enter a series of numbers, when entered 0, the loop terminates. Notice that there is no way for a program to know, in advance, how many numbers will be typed before the 0 appears, that is up to the user of the program

```cpp
#include <iostream.h>
void main ()
    {
        int n=99; // make sure n isn't initialized to 0
        while (n != 0)
        {
        cin >>n;
        cout >>"\n  ">>n;
        }
    }
```

Output

1

9

7

55

0

Above output is produced assuming that, he user enters some numbers say 1,9, 7, 55 and 0. Then the loop continues until 0 is entered at his point the program terminates.

The while loops looks like a simplified version of for loop. It contains test expression but no initialization or increment expressions. As long as test expression is true the loop will continue to execute. Although there is no initialization expression, the loop variable must be initialized before the loop begins. The loop body must also contain some statement that changes the value of loop variable; otherwise the loop will never end.

10.8.3 do while Loop

In a while loop, the test expression is evaluated at the beginning of the loop. If the test expression is false when the loop is entered, the loop body won't be executed at all. But in some situations you want to guarantee that the loop gets executed at least once, no matter what is the initial state of the test expression. When this is the case you should use the do loop, which places the test expression at the end of loop. In the following program the user is supposed to enter two numbers, a dividend and a divisor. It then calculates the quotient and the remainder

```cpp
#include <iostream.h>
void main ()
{
 int dividend, divisor;
char ch;
do
        {
        cout <<"\nEnter dividend "; cin >>dividend;
        cout <<"\nEnter divisor ";  cin >>divisor;
        cout <<" \nQuotient is "<<dividend /divisor ;
        cout <<"\n Remainder is " <<dividend % divisor;
        cout <<"\n Do another (y/n)";
        cin >>ch;
        }
    while (ch!='n');
    }
```

Most of the program resides in do loop. First the keyword do marks the beginning of loop. Then, as with the other loop, braces delimit the body of the loop. Finally a statement provides the test expression and terminates the loop.

An execution of the program produces following output.

```
Enter dividend 11
Enter divisor 3
Quotient is 3
Remainder is 2
Do another (y/n)y
Enter dividend 222
Enter divisor 17
```

Quotient is 13

Remainder is 1

Do another (yin) n

10.8.5   If Statement

Decisions: Programs also need to make one time decision. In a program a decision causes one time jump to a different part of the program, depending on the value of an expression. Decisions can be made in C++ in several ways. Most important is with the **if-else** statement, which chooses between two alternatives.

if statement can be used without **else** as a simple if statement. Look at the following simple example

```
#include <iostream.h>
void main ()
{
 int x;
 cout <<"\n Enter number:";
 cin >>x;
if (x >100)
        {
        cout <<"\nThe number "<<x;
        cout <<"is greater than 100\n";
        }
}
```

if keyword is followed by a test expression in parenthesis. The syntax of **if** is very much like to that of **while**. The difference is that the statements following **if** are executed only once if the test expression is true , the statements following **while** are executed repeatedly until the test expression becomes false. The output of the program is -

Enter number:1500

The number 1500 is greater than 100

10.8.6 Nested if within Loop Statement

The loop and decision structure seen so far can be nested inside one another. You can nest **ifs** inside loops, loops inside ifs, ifs inside ifs and so on. In the following example if is nested within a for loop. The program prints all even numbers less than equal to the entered number.

```
# include <iostream.h>
void main()
{
unsigned long n,j;
cout <<"\n Enter a number ";
cin >> n;
cout <<"\n All even numbers less than "<< n;
cout << "\n";
for(j=2; j<=n; j++)
    if (j%2==0)
            cout <<" "<<j;
}
```

Output

```
Enter a number:13
All even numbers less than 13
  2 4 6 8 10 12
```

if else Statement

The if statement lets you do something if a condition is true, the if-else statement lets you do one thing if a condition is true and do something else if it is false. It consists of statement followed by a statement or block of statements, else followed by another statement or block of statements. Consider the following program-

```
#include <iostream.h>
#include <conio.h>
void main()
{
int chcount = 0;

int wdcount =1;
```

```
        char ch ='a';
        while (ch !='\r')
          {ch =getche ();
           if (ch=="  ")
              wdcount ++;
            else
              chcount ++;
           }
        cout <<"\n words ="<<wdcount <<endl;
        cout << letters =" <<chcount-1;
        }
```

So far we have used **cin** and >> for input. This approach required that, the user always presses the <enter> key to inform program that input is complete. However in the above example, a program often needs to process each character typed by the user without waiting for an <enter>. The getch () library function performs this service. It returns each character typed, as soon as it is typed. It takes no arguments and requires the conio.h header file. Another function, getch (), is similar to getche() but it doesn't echo the character to the screen. The if else statement cause the word count wdcount to be incremented if the character is a space, and the character count chcount to be incremented if the character is anything but a space. Thus anything that isn't a space is assumed to count as a character. Here is some sample interaction with the program-

        string is for while and do

        words=6 letters= 21

The test expression in the while statement checks to see if ch is the '\r' character, which is the character received from keyboard when the <<enter>>key is pressed.

10.9   The switch Statement

If you have a large decision tree and all the decisions depends on the value of same variable, then use switch statement instead of a series of **if else** conditions. **switch** is a multi way branching statement.

Consider the following program-

```
        #include <iostream.h>
```

```
void main()
{
 int n;
cout <<"Enter n :";
cin >>n;
switch (n%2)
{
case 0:
cout <<   "Number is even";
 break;
case 1:
cut <<"Number is odd";
 break;
}
}
```

This program prints one of the two possible messages, depending on the value of the expression. The keyword switch is followed by the **switch** variable or an expression in parenthesis.,**switch (n%2):**

The braces then delimit number of **case** statements. Each **case** keyword is followed by a constant, which is not in parenthesis but is followed by a colon. Before entering the switch, the program should assign value to the switch variable. This will usually match a constant in one of the case statements. When it is matched, the statements following case keyword will be executed, until a break is reached.

The break keyword causes the entire switch statement to exit. The control goes to the first statement following the end of switch construction. The break keyword is also used to escape from loops.

The output of program is-

Enter n : 4

Number is even

Default Keyword: The default keyword is used at the end of switch construction. This keyword gives the switch statement a way to take an action if the value of the loop variable doesn't match any of the case constants. No break is necessary after default, since we are at the end of switch statement.

Following program makes use of multi-way branching and use of default case

```cpp
#include <iostream.h>
void main()
{
 int n;
cout <<"Enter n (1 to 7) :";
cin >>n;
switch (n)
    {
    case 1:
            cout <<"Monday";
            break;
    case 2:
            cout <<"Tuesday";
             break;
    case 3:
            cout <<"Wednesday";
             break;
    case 4:
            cout <<"Thursday";
             break;
    case 5:
            cout <<"Friday";
            break;
    case 6:
            cout <<"Saturday";
             break;
    case 7:
            cout << "Sunday";
            break;
    default:
            cout <<"Invalid input";
             break;
    }
```

Output

Enter n (1 to 7) :1Monday

Enter n (1 to 7) :7Sunday

Enter n (1 to 7) :8Invalid input

Above output is produced by three different run of the program. Input of '1' resulted the selection of case that produces output as Monday, similarly, input '7' resulted output as Sunday. Since, there is not matching case for input as '8', default case is selected and out is produced as 'Invalid input.

10.10 Structures

Using **structures** it becomes convenient, to organise simple variables into more complex entities. A structure is a collection of simple variables. The variables in a structure can be of different types like some can be **int**, some can be **float** and so on. The data items in a structure are called —members of the structures. The structures are often considered as an advance feature, but for C++ programmers, structures are one of the two important building blocks in the understanding of objects and classes. In fact, the syntax of a structure is almost identical to that of a class. A structure is a collection of data, while a class is a collection of data and functions.

Simple Structure

Consider following example program.

```
# include <iostream.h>
struct distance
{
int feet
float inches :
} ;
void main()
{
distance d1;
d1.feet = 11;
d1.inches =6.75;
cout <<"\n feet "<<dl.feet;
cout <<",inches "<<dl.inches ;
}
```

Specifying a Structure

The structure specifier tells how the structure is organised. It specifies what members the structures will have. In the above example

```
struct distance
{
int feet;
 float inches ;
};
```

This construction is called structure declaration.

Syntax of the Structure Specifier: The keyword **struct** introduces the **specifier**. Next comes the structure name or tag, which is distance. The declarations of the structure members – feet and inches are enclosed in braces. The semicolon follows the closing brace, terminating the entire structure

Use of Structure Specifier: The specifier serves as a blue print for the creation of variables of type distance. The specifier does not itself define any variables. Its merely a specification for how such structure variables will look when they are defined.

Defining a Structure Variable

The first statement in main (),

```
distance d1
```

Defines a variable d1 of type structure distance. This definition reserves space in memory for d1. In some ways, we may think of the distance structure as a specification for a new data type.

Accessing structure members: Once a structure variable has been defined, its members can be accessed using the dot operator. The first member is given a value:

```
d1.feet =11;
```

The structure member is written in three parts – the name of the structure variable $d1$, the dot operator, which consists of a period (.), and the member name (feet). This means feet is the member of dl and a value which is 11 in the given example.

Other Structure Features

Now let us look at some additional features of structure syntax and usage

Combining Specifier and Definition: Consider the following program which combines the structure specifier and the definition into a single statement.

```cpp
#include <iostream.h>
struct
{
int feet;
float inches;
}d1;
void main ()
{
 dl.feet=11;
 d1.inches =6.75;
 cout <<"\n feet "<<d1.feet;
 cout <<"\n inches"<<d1.inches;
 }
```

In this program there is no separate statement for the structure definition:

distance d1;

Instead, the variable name *d1* is placed at the end of the specifier. The tag name in the structure specifier can be removed , if no more variables of this structure type will be defined. Merging the structure specification and definition this way is a short hand approach that can save a few program lines. But it is less clear and less flexible than using separate specifiers and definitions

Initializing Structure Variables

Structure members can be initialised when the structure is defined. The following program shows that you can have more than one variable of a given structure type

```cpp
# include <iostream.h>
struct part
{
int modelnumber :
int partnumber;
float cost;
```

```
            } ;
            void main ()
            {
            part  part1 = { 284,  675,  217. 35 };
            part part2;
            cout <<"\n   model "<<part1.modelnumber;
            cout <<"    part "<<part1.partnumber;
            cout<<"    costs Rs."<<part1.cost;
            part2=part1;
            cout <<"\n    model"<<part2.modelnumber;
            cout <<"    part "<<part2.partnumber;
            cout<<"    costs Rs."<<part2.cost;
            }
```

This program defines two variables of type part: *part1* and *part2*. It initialises *part,* prints out the values of its members, assigns part1 to part2, and prints out its members.

Here is the output-

```
     model 284     part 675     cost Rs. 217.35
     model 284     part 675     cost Rs. 217.35
```

The same output is repeated since one variable is made equal to the other.

Initialising Structure Variables: The part1 structure variable members are initialised when the variable is defined:

```
     part  part1 = { 284,  675,  217. 35 } ;
```

The values to be assigned to the structure members are surrounded by braces and separated by commas. The first value in the list is assigned to the first member, the second to the second member and so on.

Structure variables in Assignment statements: Once structure variable's members are initialised then the variable is defined.

```
     part2=part1;
```

The values of each member of part1 are assigned to the corresponding member of part2. Note that one structure variable can be assigned to another only when they are of the same structure type

Structures within Structures: You can nest structures within other structures. Consider the following program in which we want to create a data structure that stores dimensions of a room, its length and width. So we use two variables of type Distance as the length and width variables, like this

```
//Program that uses room structure-
# include<iostream.h>
struct Distance
{
int feet;
float inches ;
};
Struct Room
{
Distance length;
Distance width;
}
void main()
{
Room dining;
dining.length.feet=13;
dining.length.inches=6.5;
dining.width.feet=10; .
dining.width.inches=1.2;
float l = dining .length.feet + dining .length. inches/12;
float w = dining .width.feet + dining .width.inches/12;
cout<<\n Dining room area is "<<l*w <<" Square feet " ;
}
```

10.11 Functions

A function groups a number of program statements into a unit and gives it a name. This unit can then be invoked from other parts of the program. The functions help in the conceptual organisation of a program. Dividing the program into functions is one of major principles of structured programming. Another reason to use functions is to reduce the program size. The function's code is stored in only one place in memory; even through the function is executed many times in the course of the program.

Simple Functions: The following program generates a table, and lines of asterisks are used to make the table more readable.

```
#include<iostream.h>
void starline();
void main()
{starline();
cout <<" Data type Range\n";
starline ();
cout <<" char -128 to 127";
cout <<"\n int -3276862 to 32767\n";
starline ();
}
void starline ()
{
for (int j=0; j<<35; j++)
     cout <<'*';
cout <<"\n";
}
```

The output of the program is -

```
***********************************
Data type Range
***********************************
char -128 to 127
int -3276862 to 32767
***********************************
```

This program consists of two functions: main() and Starline(). The components necessary to add a function to a program are the function declaration, the call to the function and the function definition

The Function Declaration: The most common approach is to declare the function at the beginning of the program. In the program function is declared as-

```
void starline ();
```

The keyword void specifies that the function has no return value and the empty parenthesis indicate that it takes no argument. The function declaration is terminated with a semicolon. It is a complete statement. Function declarations are also called prototypes.

Calling the function: The function is called three times from main (). Each of the three calls looks like -

```
starline () ;
```

That is all we need to call the function :the function name, followed by parenthesis. The call is terminated by a semicolon. Executing the call statement causes the function to execute, i.e., control is transferred to the function.

Function Definition

The definition of function contains the actual code for the function .

```
void starline ()          // declarator
{
for (int j=0;j<35; j++)
        cout <<'*';                    // body
cout <<'\n';
}
```

The definition consists of a line called declarator followed by the function body. The function body is composed of statements that make up the function, delimited by the braces. The declarator must agree with the declaration. When the function is called, control is transferred to the first statement in the function body. The other statements in the function body are then executed, and when closing brace is encountered, control returns to the calling program .

Passing Arguments to Functions

Consider the following program-

```
#include<iostream.h>
int power (int,int );
void main ()
{
int num1,num2;
 cout<<"\nEnter number";
cin>>num1;
cout<<"\nEnter  power";
cin >>num2;
```

```
    power (num1, num2);
    }


    int power (int base, int pow)
    {
    int i;
    int p = 1;
    for (i = 0; i <= pow; i++)
        p =  p*base;
    cout <<"\npower is " <<p;
    }
```

The function name is power(). The items in the parenthesis are the data types of the arguments that will be sent to power(), are **int** type. The calling program takes arguments from the keyboard and passes them to the function. The variables used within the function to hold the argument values are called parameters, in power() they are base and power.

If a function uses default arguments, it need not include all the arguments shown in the declaration. Default values supplied by the function are used for the missing arguments.

Returning values from functions: Upon completion, a function can return a single value to the calling program. Usually, this return value consists of an answer to the problem that the function has solved. Consider following program :

```
    #include<iostream.h>
    float pound-to-kg (float);
    void main ()
    {
    float p,kg;
    cout <<"\nEnter weight in pounds:"; cin >>p;
    kg=pound-to-kg (p);
    cout <<"\nWeight in kilograms is :"<<kg;
    }
    float pound-to-kg (float pounds)
    {
     float kilograms = 0.45*pounds;
    return kilograms;
    }
```

This program returns the weight in kilograms, after weight is given in pounds. Here's the sample output of this program:

    Enter weight in pounds: 182

    Weight in kilograms is : 82.553741

When a function returns a value, the data type of this value must be specified. The function declaration does this by placing the data type, float in this case, before the function name in the declaration and the definition.

When a function returns a value, the call to the function

    pound-to-kg(p);

is considered to be an expression that takes on the value returned by the function. We can treat this expression like any other variable; in this case we use it in an assignment statement:

    kg=pound-to-kg(p);

This causes the variable kg to be assigned the value returned by pound-to-kg().

The Return Statement: The function pound-to-kg() has passed an argument representing a weight in pounds, which it stores in the parameter pounds. It calculates the corresponding weight in kilograms by multiplying this pounds value by a constant; the result is stored in the variable kilograms. The value of this variable is then returned to the calling program using a return statement-

    return kilograms;

Both main() and pound-to-kg() have a place to store the kilogram variable: kg in main(), and kilograms in pound-to-kg(). When the function returns, the value in kilograms, it is copied into kg. The calling program does not access the kilograms variable in the function; only the value is returned.

While many arguments may be sent to a function, only one argument may be returned from it. This is a limitation when you need to return more information.

10.12 Arrays

In computer languages we also need to group together data items of the same type. The mechanism that accomplishes this is the array. Arrays can hold a few data items, or thousands of items. The data items grouped in an array can be simple types like int or float, or they can be user-defined types like structures and objects. Arrays are like structures in that they group a number of items into a larger unit. But while a structure usually groups items of different types, an array groups items of the similar type. More importantly, the items in a structure are accessed by name, while those in an array are accessed by an index number. Using an index number to specify an item allows easy access to a large number ot items stored in a array.

Consider the following program

```
#include <iostream.h>
{
void main()
 int age[4];
cout <<endl;
 for(int j=0; j<4; j++)
{
cout <<"\nEnter an age:";
cin >>age [j] :
}
 for (int  j=0;j<4;j++)
cout "\nentered " << age[j];
}
```

Output

```
Enter an age : 44
Enter an age: 23
Enter an age : 68
entered 44
entered 23
entered 68
```

The first for loop gets the ages from the user and places them in the array, while the second for reads them from the array and displays them.

Defining Arrays: Like other variables in C++, an array must be defined before it can be used to store information. And, like other definitions, an array definition specifies a variable type and a name. But it includes another feature: a size. The size specifies how many data items the array will contain. It immediately follows the name, and is surrounded by square brackets.

```
int age [8]
```

Array Elements: The items in an array are called elements. All the elements in an array are of the same type. Since each element in age is an integer, it occupies two bytes. As specified in the definition, the array has exactly four elements. Notice that the first array element has the index 0. Thus, if there are four elements, the last index is number 3.

Accessing Array Elements: In the above program we access each array element twice. The first time, when we insert a value into the array, and the second time, we read it out with the line. In both cases the expression for the accessing array element is

age [j]

This consists of the name of the array, followed by brackets delimiting a variable j. Which of the four array elements is specified by this expression depends on the value of j; age[0] refers to the first element, age[1] to the second, age[2] to the third, and age[3] to the fourth. The variable (or constant) in the brackets is called the array index. Since j is the loop variable in both for loops, it starts at 0 and is incremented until it reaches 3, thereby accessing each of the array elements in turn.

10.12.1 Multidimensional Arrays

So far we have looked at arrays of one dimension: A single variable specifies each array element. But arrays can have higher dimensions. Following program defines a two dimensional array called sales.

```cpp
#include <iostream.h>
#include <iomanip.h>
const int DISTRICTS = 5;
const int MONTHS = 7;
void main()
{
int d, m;
float sales[DISTRICT][MONTHS];
cout <<endl;
 for (d=0; d<DISTRICTS; d++)
 for (m=0; m<MONTHS; m++)
 {
cout <<"Enter sales for district" <<d+1 ;
cout <<" and month" <<m+1 << " : " ;
cin >>sales[d][m];
```

```
            }
            cout <<"\n\n";
            cout <<" Months 1,2,3...";
            cout <<" 1 2 3 4 5 6 7";
            for(d=0; d<DISTRICTS; d++)
            {
            cout <<"\nDistrict <<d+1;
            for (m=0; m<MONTHS: m++)                // display array values
            cout <<setiosflags(ios::fixed)          // not exponential
                <<setiosflags (ios::showpoint)      // always use point
                <<setprecision(2)                   // digits to right
                << setw(10)                         // field width
                 <<sales[d][m];                     // get number from array
            }
            }
```

Defining Multidimensional Arrays

The array is defined with two size specifiers, each enclosed in brackets:

```
        float sales[DISTRICTS][MONTHS];
```

One way to think about this statement is that sales is an array of array. It is an array of DISTRICTS elements, each of which is an array of MONTHS elements.

Accessing Multidimensional Array Elements

Array elements in two-dimensional arrays require two indexes:

```
        sales[d][m]
```

Notice that each index has its own set of brackets. A common error is to write like sales[d,m].

10.12.2 Arrays of Structures

Arrays can contain structures as well as simple data types. In the following program we will see array of structures.

```
        #include <iostream.h>
        const int SIZE = 4;
        struct part
        {
```

```cpp
 int modelnumber;
int partnumber;
float cost;
};
void main()
{
Int n;
part apart[SIZE];
for(n=0; n<SIZE; n++)
{
cout <<endl;
cout <<"Enter model number:";
cin >>apart[n].modelnumber;
cout <<"Enter part. number
cin >>apart[n].partnumber
cout <<'Enter cost:";
cin >>apart[n].cost;
}
for (n=0; n<SIZE; n++)
{
cout <<"\nModel " <<apart[n].modelnumber;
cout <<" Part "<<apart[n].partnumber;
cout <<" Cost " <<apart[n].cost;
}
}
```

The user types in the model number, part number and cost of a part. The program records this data in a structure. However, this structure has only one element in an array of structures. The program asks for the data for four different parts, and stores it in the four elements of the part array. It then displays the information.

CHAPTER 11

Object Oriented Programming in C++

11.1 Introduction to Object Oriented Programming

The Object Oriented Programming popularly called OOP or OOPs has become one of the common words in the software industry. On one hand, OOPs is a programming principle in its own right and on the other, it is a set of tools to build more reliable and reusable systems.

Structured programming and Object oriented programming are equally popular today but they differ in the following way: The structured programming views the core elements of any program data and functions as two separate entities, where as OOPs views them as a single entity. In structured programming we can group the data of various types into a single entity but in object oriented programming we group the data of various types and various functions within an object. Then these functions will operate on the data that is bound into a single entity called object. That is the reason behind the object oriented programming playing an increasingly significant role in the analysis, design and implementation of software systems. Programs developed using these features are more reliable, easier to maintain, easier to reuse and enhance.

The OOPs is designed around the data being operated upon. Instead of making certain types of data fit to specific and rigid computer operations, these operations are designed to fit to the data. Its power lies in the fact that the programmer can create modular, reusable code and as a result formulate a program by composition and modification of the existing modules. Flexibility is gained by being able to change or replace modules without disturbing other parts of the code.

The fundamental features of OOPs are the following:

Encapsulation: It is the mechanism that combines the code and the data it encapsulates into a single unit and keeps them safe from external interference and misuse. In C++, this is supported by a construct called class. An instance of a class is known as an object, which represents a real world entity.

Data abstraction: The technique of creating new data types that are well suited to an application to be programmed is known as data abstraction. It provides the ability to create user defined data types for modeling a real world object, having the properties of built in data types and a set of permitted operators.

Inheritance: In a real world a child inherits many properties from its ancestors, such as a surname from his father. This concept is implemented in OOPs through inheritance. It allows the extension and reuse of existing code without having to rewrite the code from scratch. Inheritance involves the creation of new classes known as derived classes from the existing ones called base classes and thus enabling the creation of a hierarchy of classes. The new derived class inherits the members of the base class and also adds its own. Two popular forms of inheritance are single and multiple inheritance. Single inheritance refers to deriving a class from a single base class. The multiple inheritance refers to deriving a class from more than one base class.

Polymorphism: A word in English may change its meaning when the context is changed. For example, in following two sentences, the word 'saw' has different meanings.

I saw a beautiful bird.

I cut the wood with a saw.

Polymorphism, similarly, allows a single function name to be associated with different operations depending upon the type of data passed to it. A single function can perform different operations in different circumstances. In C++, it is achieved by function overloading, operator overloading and virtual functions.

Message passing: It is the process of invoking an operation on an object. In response to a message, corresponding method or function is executed in the object.

Extensibility: It is a feature, which allows the extension of the functionality of the existing software components. In C++ this is achieved through abstract classes and inheritance.

11.2 Objects and Classes

The world is full of objects around us. Look around you, there are books, pens, cars and many other objects. Even living objects are there for example students and teachers. In railway station book stall, we look at the collection of books. Books have different titles, authors, etc. Different books have names, authors etc.

This is how we differentiate them. Generally books have common attributes and different values for these attributes.

Look at the following table showing different values of attributes for two books.

Attributes	Book 1	Book 2
	Value	Value
Title	You Can Win	Three Mistakes of My Life
Author	Shiv Kheda	Chetan Bhagat
Category	Self Help	Fiction

Column1 of the table identifies properties of a class called 'Book' and to differentiate different books, it defines a set of attributes that every book should have.

Column 2 and Column 3 of above table are the two examples of 'Book' Class. These examples are created when we give values to attributes. Column 2 is a popular book you might have read. Column 3 is a book on which movie Three Idiots was made. You can have many examples of 'Book' Class. You can add many more attributes to Book Class, such as number of pages, edition etc. Attributes are also known as properties.

Omitting complexities here for simplicity, these examples of a class are known as 'objects'. You get objects when you give values to the attributes of a class. This is also called class initiations. Hence objects are also known as instances of a class. Observe that objects have their existence such as book "You Can Win" and "Three Mistakes of My Life", whereas classes are only the concept. Hence classes have no physical existence; they are data types.

Now identify classes and objects from following collection.

Nokia Lumia 1020, iphone, mobile, Samsungs s4.

It is easy to make out that Mobile is a class and rest of them are objects of mobile class.

There are more to classes. Take examples of Martin, Rahul and Hina three students of BE I Year. We can observe that Martin, Rahul and Hina are objects of class student. Class student has attributes like their Enrollment No., Name, Branch, Date of Birth, etc.

Now if Martin, Rahul and Hina are objects with certain properties, they can do many things. They can read, write, jump, sing so on and so forth. When we relate same concept to object oriented programming our objects can also do many things.

Formally we say objects have attributes and methods. Alternatively we say objects have properties and functions.

If we make a computer game for car racing we can, define a class car as follows:

Class car

Attributes/ Properties
    Car_Name, Color,Max Speed..
Methods or function or events
    Start ( ), run ( ), jump ( ), halt ( ) etc

There can be examples/ objects/ instances like

Object 1: Ferrari, Red, 350.

Object 2: Bugati Veron, Blue, 400.

Different students may have same methods like sing, dance but they all sing and dance differently. Similarly in OOP our objects of the same class can do the same things but on their own data.

Now we define class and object.

A class defines a new data type that binds its attributes and methods together.

An object is an instance of a class. An object is created by instantiating a class.

Class implementation: Our first program contains a class and two objects of that class. The program shows the syntax and general features of classes in C++. Here is the listing of a program.

Example

```
#include <iostream.h>
class smallobj
{
private:
        int somedata;
public:
        void setdata(int d)
            {
            somedata = d;
            }
        void showdata()
            {
```

```
                              cout « "\n Data is " « somedata;
                              }
              } ;

              void main()
              {
                      smallobj  s1, s2;        // define two objects of class
                      s1.setdata(1066);        // call member function to set data
                      s2.setdata(1776);
                      s1.showdata();           //call member function to display  data
                      s2.showdata();
              }
```

Output:

```
        Data is 1066
        Data is 1776
```

Observations/explanation: The class smallobj in this program contains one data item and two member functions. These functions provide the only access to the data item from outside the class. The first member function sets the data item to a value, and the second displays the value.

Placing data and functions together into a single entity is the central idea of object-oriented programming.

An object has the same relationship to a class that a variable has to a data type. The class smallobj is first specified in the program. Later, in main(), we declare two objects, s1 and s2, as the instances of class smallobj.

Each of the two objects is given a value by invoking setdata() member function, and each displays its value by invoking showdata().

Specifying the Class: In this program, the specifier starts with the keyword class, followed by the class name-smallobj,. Like a structure, the body of the class is delimited by braces and terminated by a semicolon. Data constructs like structures and classes end with the semicolon, while control constructs like functions and loops do not.

Visibility modes Private and Public: The body of the class contains two unfamiliar keywords: private and public. A key feature of object-oriented programming is data hiding. It means that data is concealed within a class, so that it cannot be accessed mistakenly by functions outside the class. The primary mechanism for hiding data is to put it in a class and make it private. Private data and functions can only be accessed from within the class. Public data or functions, on the other hand, are accessible from outside the class.

Class Data: The **smallobj** class contains one data item **somedata,** which is of type int. There can be any number of data items in a class. Just as there can be any number of data items in a structure. The data item **somedata** follows the keyword private, so it can be accessed from within the class, but not from outside.

Member Functions: Member functions are functions that are included within a class. There are two member functions in smallobj: setdata() and showdata(). Because setdata() and showdata() are within public section of the class, they can be accessed from outside the class. Therefore we have been able to invoke them from main(), which is a non member function.

Usually the data within a class is private and the functions are public. Public functions form the interface of the class, like a switch is our interface to our ceiling fan. The data is hidden so that it will be safe from accidental manipulation, while the functions that operate on the data are public so they can be accessed from outside the class. However, there is no rule that data must be private and functions public, in some circumstances you may find, you will need to use private functions and public data. Private data is like internal parts of same ceiling fan. If a public function is large and is to be broken into small functions, then these smaller functions can be kept private as these will be invoked only by this public function which is a part of public interface.

Using CLASS in main(): Now that the class is specified, lets see how main() makes use of it.

Defining Objects: The first statement in main(),

> **smallobj s1, s2;**

defines two objects, s1 and s2, of class smallobj. Remember that the specification of the class smallobj does not create any objects. It is the definition that actually create objects that can be used by the program. Defining an object is similar to defining variable of any data type. Space is set aside for objects in memory

Calling Member Functions: The next two statements in main() call the member function setdata()

      s1.setdata(1066);

      s2.setdata(1776);

These statements do not look like normal function calls. This syntax is used to call a member function that is associated with a specific object. Because setdata() is a member function of the smallobj class, it must always be called in connection with an object of this class. It doesn't make sense to say

      setdata(1066);

by itself, because a member function is always called to act on a specific object, not on the class in general.

To use a member function, the dot operator (the period) connects the object name and the member function. The syntax is similar to the way we refer to structure members, but the parenthesis signal that we are executing a member function rather than referring to a data item. The dot operator is also called the class member access operator.

11.3   Scope Resolution Operator

Scope resolution operator : : is added in C++. It was not present in C operators set.

To understand the concept of scope resolution operator one should have the idea of global and local variable names.

Let's take a real life example. If somebody says "Today, Sachin played well", everybody knows, Sachin (Tendulkar) is being talked about. But if there is a Sachin Das in your college Cricket team and your team plays a match today. Within your college team the above statement shall imply that Sachin is "Sachin (Das)". That is to say that famous Sachin has global scope where as Sachin in your team has local scope.

In the context of C++ programming, when you declare a variable outside of a function it has a bigger scope and variable declared within a function has a local scope. But when names of some global variable and local variable are same, confusion may occur. Consider following program

Example

```
# include <iostream.h>
int count = 10; // this is global variable
int size  = 50;
void main ( )
```

```
{ int count = 1000;  // this is a local variable
cout < < "\n "<<count;
cout < < "\n "<<size;
}
```

Output

```
1000
50
```

Observation/Explanation: There are two variables with the name count. Global variable count has value 10 and local variable count has value 1000.

```
count < < cout;
```

it displays what?

It displays 1000 because when local and global variables share common name then within the function preference is given to local variable. Therefore value of local variable will be displayed.

So within a function local variable is given preference.

```
count < < sizes;
```

outputs 50 because there is no conflict and there is single variable named size.

Now, if you are particular that within the function output should be the value of global variable count, scope resolution operator (: :) comes into play. Look at following program

Example

```
# include <iostream.h>
  int count = 10;
  void main ( )
{ int count = 1000;
  count < < : : count;
}
```

Output

```
10
```

Observation/Explanation: Here output is 10, the value of global variable. When : : is prefixed to a variable's name, (like : : count) it enables us to reference a global variable.

Scope resolution operator also helps to explicitly label the class name with the definition of member function name. When we define the member's function of class outside its scope, name of the class to which function belongs must be specified in following general form.

```
return_type      class_name : : function_name (argument declaration)
            {

                 —

                 —

                 —

            }
```

11.4 Function Overloading

C++ allows polymorphism. C++ implements polymorphism by function overloading. You can overload a function name by declaring more than one function with the same name within same scope. Overloaded functions differ by their signatures. The signature of function is its prototype declaration. Overloaded functions must differ from each other by the types and/or the number of arguments in the argument list. When you call an overloaded function, the correct function is selected by comparing the argument list of the function call with the parameter list of each of the overloaded functions.

Consider following program listing for understanding function overloading

Example:

```
#   include <iostream.h>
void show(int i)
{
cout << " \n One integer is passed as  " << i ;
}
void show(int i, int j)
{
cout << " \nTwo integers are passed as  " << i << " and "<<j;
}
void show(char* w) {
cout << " \n A word is passed as " << w;
}
void main()
```

```
        {
        show(10,20);
        show(100);
        show("overloading");
        }
```

Output

        Two integers are passed as 10 and 20

        One integer is passed as 100

        A word is passed as overloading

Key observations/Explanation: In main(), show() is invoked three times with different argument list. Depending upon the context/parameters passed, correct version of function gets executed that matches the type and number of arguments. Hence the output is the result of execution of the second definition, first definition and third definition in order.

   Another example with class usage

Example

```
# include <iostream.h>
class quadrilateral
        {
        int  areais;
        public:
        void area( int x);          // overloaded  function for square
        void area(int x, int y);   // overloaded  function for rectangle
        void show();
        };
void quadrilateral :: area( int x)  // overloaded  function for square area
        {
        areais = x*x;
        }
void quadrilateral ::  area( int x, int y)  // overloaded function for rectangle area
        {
        areais = x*y;
        }
void quadrilateral :: show()                // Member function definition
```

```
            {
            cout << "\n area  = "<<areais;
            }
void main( )

            {
            quadrilateral q1;
            q1.area(10,20);        // function is invoked that calculates area of
                                        rectangle

            q1.show();
            q1.area(10);           // function is invoked that calculates area
                                        of square

            q1.show();
            }
```

Output

```
        area = 200
        area = 100
```

Key observations/Explanation: In main(), object q1 is declared of quadrilateral type. Object q1 invokes area two times, first with two parameters and second with one parameter. First time, area is calculated with the area function definition that takes two parameters and calculates area of a rectangle. Second time, area is calculated with the area function definition that takes one parameter and calculates area of a square. Member function show() is invoked show the value of areais at that moment.

11.5   Constructors and Destructors

Objects are instances of classes and these are created and destroyed during program execution. Objects are runtime entities that consume memory for being stored. Constructors and Destructors are special member functions of class which are automatically executed at the time of object creation and object deletion respectively.

11.5.1 Constructors

In a class, constructor is a member function, which has its name same as to that of the class. For example if class name is counter, its constructor will be named as counter ( ).

Constructor function executes automatically when an object is created. Constructor function is like any other member function and it can contain any logic. But constructor function is written generally, to give initial values to member data of that object. Initializing variables is always a good idea, so that variables never have garbage value.

Look at following code

Example

Class counter

```
{   int count;
    public :
    counter (void);
    void show ( );
    } ;
    counter : : counter (void)
    {
    count = 0;
    }
    void counter : : show ( )
    {
    cout < < "count = "< < count;
    }
    void main()
    {       counter c1;
    c1. show();
    }
```

Output

```
            count = 0
```

Observation/Explanation: Output is 0 because we initialized the count variable to 0 through constructor. What will be the output of the same program if we do not write the constructor program counter()? In the absence of constructor data member count would not have initialized to 0 and output would have been some garbage value in place of 0.

Observe, constructors do not need a return type.

Types of Constructors: Function over loading applies to constructors too. A class can have multiple constructors. Common types of constructors are:

- Default constructor: This constructor is used when initial default values are to be assigned to data members, hence no parameters are required to be passed. We also call this type of constructor as empty constructor.

- Parameterized constructor: This type of constructor can be passed one or more parameters, so that values of these parameters can be assigned to data members.

- Copy constructors: In copy constructor, an existing object of the same class is passed as a parameter to the constructor. The code in constructor copies values of member data of passed object to the member data of object being created.

We modify the above mentioned simple example of constructor to accommodate all above type of constructors. We make it well commented so that it becomes self explanatory

Class counter

```
{   int count;
    public :
    counter ();                        // default constructor declared
    counter (int x);                   //parameterized constructor
                                          declared

    counter (counter& y);              //copy constructor declared
    void show (  );
    } ;
    counter : : counter ()             // default constructor defined
    {
    count = 0;
    }
    counter : : counter (int x)        // parameterized constructor
                                          defined

    {
    count = x;                         // copy value of parameter  x
    }
    counter : : counter (counter& y)   // copy constructor defined
    {
    count = y.count;                   // copy data from passed object
```

```
        }
        void counter : : show ( )
        {
        cout < < "\n count = "< < count;
        }
        void main()
    {   counter c1;        // syntax for default constructor
        counter c2(10);  // syntax for copy parameterized  constructor
        counter c3(c2);  // syntax for copy constructor
        counter c4=c3;  // alternative syntax for copy constructor
        c1. show();
        c2. show();
        c3. show();
        c4. show();
        }
```

Output

```
        count = 0
        count = 10
        count = 10
        count = 10
```

Observation/Explanation: Within main() four objects are declared.

In object c1 default constructor is invoked and object c1 is assigned value 0 for its member data x.

In object c2, parameterised constructor is invoked and object c2 is assigned parameter value 10 for its member data x.

Using object c3 and c4, copy constructor is invoked and object c3 and c4 are assigned values to their member data from objects c2 and c3 respectively. In copy constructor object is passed by reference.

Finally, show() is invoked by each of these objects to display value of its member data.

You can observe two different syntax of declaring objects while initialising through existing objects through copy constructors.

11.5.2 Destructors

Destructors are member functions with the same name as that of the class name but the character ~, pronounced as tilde, is attached as first character of destructors name. For example if class is counter, its destructor is named as ~counter (). Destructors have no arguments and return no values.

Destructors perform the reverse role to that of a constructor. Destructor is a member function that is invoked when object is being destroyed. It contains the logic that is needed while object is being destroyed. Generally it is used to free memory if any memory has been allocated dynamically to variables.

When you do not specify a destructor, the compiler generates a default destructor for you. Hence it is not mandatory to explicitly code destructors.

When a class uses pointer variable as member data and allocates memory dynamically, it becomes important to write the constructor. If we do not free the memory allocated to pointer variables, it is not returned to operating system and remains unused. This logic of freeing the memory can be implemented in the destructor.

11.6   Friend Functions

A friend function is not a member function of a class still it has the right to access all private and protected members of the class. Friend functions are normal external functions that are given special access privileges. A friend function is defined outside the scope of a class, only its prototype preceded by the keyword **friend**, has to appear within the class, to which it is a friend. A friend function can be declared within private or public visibility modes, it does not matter. Friend function is called with a normal function call syntax, it doesn't need an object name for invocation.

Example:

```
#  include <iostream.h>
   class A
{
   int x, y;
   public:
   void setxy( int, int );          // Member function
   friend void sum(A);              // friend function

};
   void A::setxy(int m, int n )      // Member function definition
```

```
        {
            x = m;
            y = n;
        }
            void sum( A a )                    // friend function definition
        {
            cout << "\n sum = "<< a.x + a.y;
        }
            void main( )
        {
            A a1;
            a1.setxy(10,20);                   // invoke member function
            sum(a1);                           // invoke friend function
        }
```

Output:

```
        Sum = 30
```

Key observations/Explanation: setxy() is a member function hence invoked in main() through an object a1 of the class.

Member function setxy() directly accesses its member data x and y in its body.

sum() is a friend function hence invoked in main() directly without the need of an object to precede with. sum() accesses private data of object a1 as it has the right to access, being the friend of class A. But observe in the statement within sum()

```
        cout << "\n sum = "<< a.x + a.y;
```

friend function has to access member data through its object.

Friend functions are great help to act as bridge between two different classes, when some operations require data from the objects from two different classes. They also implement operator overloading in an elegant way in C++. To understand the concept of operator overloading first let us consider summing two objects of above defined class A. Let us define sum of the two objects of A1 class as creation of third object of class A whose x value is sum of x values of both the objects and y value is obtained as sum of y values of both the objects. See the following example program

Example:

```
        #  include <iostream.h>
```

```cpp
class A
{
    int x, y;
    public:
    void setxy( int, int );                 // Member function
    void show();
    friend A sum(A, A);                       // friend function
};
    void A::setxy(int m, int n )            // Member function definition
{
    x = m;
    y = n;
}
    void A::show()                          // Member function definition
{
    cout << "\n x = "<<x;
    cout << "\n x = "<<y;
}
    void sum( A p, A q) // friend function definition
{
    A r;
    r.x = p.x + q.x;
    r.y = p.y + q.y;
    return r;
}
    void main( )
{
    A a1,a2,a3;
    a1.setxy(10,20);                        // invoke member function
    a2.setxy(20,30);                        // invoke member function
    a3 = sum(a1,a2);                        // invoke friend function
    a1.show();                              // display the data within object a1
    a2.show();                              // display the data within object a2
    a2.show();                              // display the data within object a3
}
```

Output:

```
        X=10
        y=20
        x=20
        y=30
        x=30
        y=50
```

Key observations/Explanation: Here, friend function is passed two objects of same class, within the definition of friend function a local object a3 is created, computed sum and returned as the sum of two objects. This returned object is received in a3 in the main function. Rest of the program is self explanatory.

Operator overloading as a Friend function

Look at following code segment

```cpp
        void main( )
    {
        int i,j,k;
        A a1,a2,a3;

        ..

        ..

        k = I + j;
        a3 = sum(a1,a2);     // invoke friend function

        ..

        ..

    }
```

In the above segment of the code, I can write k = i + j. Here, i, j, k are integer variables and operator + has built in definition to add integers.

It is already defined the addition of objects of above defined class A, now if we wish that for adding a1 and a2, I should be able write a3 = a1 + a2 instead of writing a3 = sum(a1,a2).

C++ permits this. You can give definitions to operators for your own data types which you have created by declaring classes. It can be done through member functions or through friend functions. In case of operator overloading, friend function will need one object for unary operators, two objects for binary and so on. If operator overloading is done through member function instead of a friend function, member function shall need one less object. For example, if + operator is overloaded through friend function it will need two objects to be passed and if same is overloaded through member function it will need one object

If we do it through friend function in the code in our previous example, following changes are required.

Within class declaration of friend function sum() and definition of friend function sum(), replace its signatures friend A sum(A, A); with friend A operator +(A, A);

Within main() replace invocation statement a3 = sum(a1,a2); with a3 = a1 + a2;

That's all. It works. Look at the elegance.

In some way friend functions concept available in C++, violate OOP principles, as it allows non member function to access private members of a class. May be, for this reason this feature is not provided in OOP language java.

Finally we summarise features of Friend function

- Friend function can access the private or protected members of the class in which they are declared to be friend but Friend function access members through objects of class

- Friends are not the member's functions of the class to which they are friends hence they can be invoked directly without preceding an objects name

- Friend functions can be friend of more than one classes, hence they can be written to implement tasks that require data from objects of more than one class

- Friend can be declared anywhere in public, protected or private visibility mode the class.

- Usually, it has the objects as arguments

11.7　Inheritance

Inheritance is probably the most powerful feature of object oriented programming, after classes. Inheritance is the process of creating new classes, called derived classes, from existing base classes. The derived classes inherit all the capabilities of the base class but can add new features to it. The base class is unchanged by this process.

Inheritance has important advantages, as it permits code reusability. Once a base class is written and debugged, it can be adapted to work in different situations. Reusing existing code saves time and money and increases program's reliability. Inheritance can also help in the original conceptualization of a programming problem, and in the overall design of the program.

11.7.1 Derived Class and Base Class

Consider the following program

Example

```
#   include <iostream.h>
    class publication
    {
    protected:
    char title(30];
    float price;
    public:
    void getdata()
    {
    cout «"\n Enter title:";
    cin » title;
    cout « "\nEnter price:";
    cin » price;
    }
    void putdata()
    {
    cout « "\n Title :" « title;
    cout « "\n Price:" « price;
    }
    };
    Class book: public publication
    {
    private:
    int pages;
    public:
    void getdata ()
    {
    Publication :: getdata();
    cout « "Enter number of pages :";
```

```
        cin » pages;
    }
        void putdata( )
    {
        publication: putdata();
        cout « "\n Pages : "« pages;
    }
    } ;
        void main ()
    {
        book book1;
        book1. getdata ();
        bookl. putdata();
    }
```

Output

```
        Enter title: C++ programming
        Enter price: 322
        Enter number of pages: 400
        Title: C++ programming
        Price: 322
        Pages: 400
```

Key observations/Explanation: In this program we have a class publication which acts as a base class for class book. The class book derives all the features of class publication and it adds some new features.

Specifying Derived Classes: Inheriting class publication in the program is class book. This class has the same functions as the class publication, except that the function includes some additional statements. The first line of class book specifies that it is derived from publication.

class book: public publications

Here we use single colon followed by keyword public and the name of the base class publication. This sets up relationship between the classes. After this relationship is setup the derived class can refer to the functions and data of the base class but the base class has no access to the derived class.

11.7.2 Abstract Base Class

In above program example, you have noticed that objects of base class publication have not been defined. We use this as a general class whose purpose is to act as a base from which other classes are derived.

Classes used only for deriving other classes such as publication, are sometimes called abstract classes, meaning that no actual instances of this class are created. With the **protected** access specified, we have increased the functionality of a class without modifying it. We are familiar with the access specifiers private and public. Class members (which can be data or functions) can always be accessed by functions within their own class, whether the members are private or public. But objects of a class defined outside the class can access class members only if the members are public.

The object cannot access private members of other class.

This is all we need to know if we do not use inheritance. With inheritance, the question that concerns is, can member function of derived class access members of the base class. The answer is that member functions can access members of the base class if the members are public, or if they are protected. They can't access private members.

A protected member, can be accessed by the member functions in its own class or in any class derived from its own class. It cannot be accessed from functions outside these classes, such as main(). Protected members can be inherited further by derived classes. We know that public members can be inherited by derived class but private members cannot. If we wish that certain members of a class should remain private but should be inherited if needed by the derived class. To meet such requirement protected visibility mode is used. Protected members of a class are called inheritance ready. Classes can be derived public or private for example

> Class book : public publication

Or

> Class book : private publication

When inheritance is done using public specifier, public members of base class move to public visibility mode and protected members move to protected visibility mode in the inherited class. If inheritance is done using private specifier, public members and protected members move to private visibility mode in the inherited class.

11.7.3 Levels of Inheritance

Classes can be derived from classes that are themselves derived. Here is a small program that shows the idea:

```
class A
{ };
class B : public A
{ };
class C : public B
{ };
```

Here class B is derived from class A, and class C is derived from class B. The process can be extended to arbitrary number of levels.

Multiple Inheritance: A class can be derived from more than one base class. This is called multiple inheritance. The syntax for multiple inheritance is similar to that for single inheritance.

```
class A
  { };
class B
  { };
class C: public A, public B
  { };
```

The base classes from which C is derived are listed following the colon in C's specification; they are separated by commas. Thus the class C can be derived from A and B.

11.8 Virtual Functions

Functions are bound with code at compile time, this is known as **static binding** however with the help of virtual functions **dynamic binding** is possible. Dynamic binding is also referred as run time or on the fly binding.

Virtual functions implement concept of function overriding. Function overriding is different from function overloading. Overloaded functions are within same class and with different signatures. Overridden functions have same name and signatures but they are in base and inherited classes.

Example

```
class abase
```

```
    {
    public:
    virtual void afunction()

    {
    cout << "Hello, calling from base " ;

    }
    };
    class aderived: public abase

    {
    public:
    void afunction()

    {
    cout << "\n Hello calling from derived" ;

    }
    };
    void main()

    {
    aderived d1;
    abase* pa1;
    pa1=&d1;
    *pa1.afuntion();
    }
```

Output

```
        Hello calling from derived
```

Key observations/Explanation: In this program we have a base class abase and a derived class aderived. Virtual function afunction is defined differently in both of these classes. Now look at the main(), object *d1* is an instance of derived class and its address has been assigned to a pointer variable *pa1* of base class *abase*. This assignment will be on run time. But it is sensed that the pointer is referring to the object of derived class, hence function definition of derived class is executed. Late binding has taken place, output is produced accordingly.

Virtual function features are summarised below:

- Virtual functions implement function overriding
- Virtual functions implement runtime polymorphism
- With virtual functions the compiler can match a function call with the correct function definition at run time i.e., virtual functions implement dynamic binding.

- Virtual functions are declared in base class with keyword virtual
- A virtual function is a member function you may redefine for other derived classes,
- Compiler can ensure that the compiler will call the redefined virtual function for an object of the corresponding derived class
- Virtual functions make the program execution slow because of late binding of the code.

Chapter 12

Data Structures

12.1 Introduction

In computer science, a data structure is a way of storing data in a computer so that it can be used efficiently. Often a carefully chosen data structure will allow a more efficient algorithm to be used. The choice of the data structure often begins from the choice of an abstract data structure. A well-designed data structure allows a variety of critical operations to be performed, using as little resources, both execution time and memory space, as possible.

Different kinds of data structures are suited to different kinds of applications, and some are highly specialized to certain tasks. For example, B-trees are particularly well suited for implementation of databases, while routing tables rely on networks of machines to function.

In the design of many types of programs, the choice of data structures is a primary design consideration, as experience in building large systems has shown that the difficulty of implementation and the quality and performance of the final result depend heavily on choosing the best data structure. After the data structures are chosen, the algorithms to be used often become relatively obvious. Sometimes things work in the opposite direction - data structures are chosen because certain key tasks have algorithms that work best with particular data structures. In either case, the choice of appropriate data structures is crucial.

This insight has given rise to many formalized design methods and programming languages in which data structures, rather than algorithms, are the key organizing factor. Most languages feature some sort of module system, allowing data structures to be safely reused in different applications by hiding their verified implementation details behind controlled interfaces. Object-oriented programming languages such as C++ and Java in particular use objects for this purpose.

Since data structures are so crucial to professional programs, many of them enjoy extensive support in standard libraries of modern programming languages and environments, such as C++'s Standard Template Library, the Java API, and the Microsoft. NET framework.

The fundamental building blocks of most data structures are arrays, records, discriminated unions, and references. There is some debate about whether data structures represent implementations or interfaces. How they are seen may be a matter of perspective. A data structure can be viewed as an interface between two functions or as an implementation of methods to access storage that is organized according to the associated data type.

12.2   Common Data Structures

Here is a list of common data structures.

Linear data structures

    Array

        Dynamic array

        Parallel array

    List

        Linked list

        Skip list

        Unrolled linked list

        V List

        Associative array (a.k.a. dictionary or map)

        Hash table

        Stack

        Queue

            Priority queue

            D-queue

        Tree data structures

            M-Way Tree

                B-tree

        Binary search trees

            Self-balancing binary search trees

                AVL tree

                Red-black tree

                Scapegoat tree

                Splay tree

Graph data structures

> Adjacency list
>
> Disjoint-set data structure
>
> Graph-structured stack

12.3   Linear Structure

The most common organization for components is a linear structure. A structure is linear if it has these 2 properties:

Property P1

Each element is `followed by' at most one other element.

Property P2

No two elements are `followed by' the same element.

An array is an example of a linearly structured data type. We generally write a linearly structured data type like this: A->B->C->D (this is one value with 4 parts).

•Counter example 1 (violates P1) : A points to B and C B<-A->C •counter example 2 (violates P2) : A and B both point to C A->C<-B

Dropping Constraint P1: If we drop the first constraint and keep the second, we get a tree structure or hierarchy: no two elements are followed by the same element. This is a very common structure too, and extremely useful. We'll study it in considerable detail.

Counter example 1 is a tree, but counter example 2 is not.

More complex example:

A is followed by B C D B by E F, C by G. We are not allowed to add any more arcs that point to any of these nodes (except possibly A - see cyclic structures below).

Dropping both P1 and P2:

If we drop both constraints, we get a graph. In a graph, there are no constraints on the relations we can define.

12.4   Cyclic Structure

All the examples we've seen are acyclic. This means that there is no sequence of arrows that leads back to where it started. Linear structures are usually acyclic, but cyclic ones are not uncommon.

Example of cyclic linear structure: A B C D A

Trees are virtually always acyclic.

Graphs are often cyclic, although the special properties of acyclic graphs make them an important topic of study.

Example: Add an edge from G to D, and from E to A

12.5 Stack

Stack is one of the most useful concepts of data structures in Computer Science. In this section, we shall define stack algorithm and procedures for insertion and deletion and see why stacks play such prominent role in the area of programming. We also describe prefix, postfix and infix matrices for expression.

A stack is an ordered collection of items into which new items can be inserted and from which items may be deleted at only beginning of the list, shown in Fig. 12.1

<table>
<tr><td>E</td></tr>
<tr><td>D</td></tr>
<tr><td>C</td></tr>
<tr><td>B</td></tr>
<tr><td>A</td></tr>
</table>

Fig. 12.1 Stack Containing Stack terms

In computer science, a stack is a data structure that works on the principle of Last In First Out (LIFO). This means that the last item put on the stack is the first item that can be taken off, like a physical stack of plates. A stack-based computer system is one that is based on the use of stacks, rather than being register based.

The stack method of expression evaluation was first proposed by early German computer scientist F.L. Bauer, who received the IEEE Computer Society Pioneer Award in 1988 for his work on Computer Stacks.

Operations

The two main operations applicable in the stack are:

Push: An item is put on top of the stack, increasing the stack size by one. As stack size is usually limited, this may provoke a stack overflow if the maximum size is exceeded.

pop: The top item is taken from the stack, decreasing stack size by one. In the case where there was no top item (i.e. the stack was empty), a stack underflow occurs.

Some environments that rely heavily on stacks may provide additional operations, for example:

dup: The top item is popped and pushed again twice, so that an additional copy of the former top item is now on top, with the original below it.

peek: Check the topmost item. This is also called top operation in many articles.

Swap or exchange: The two topmost items are exchanged.

Rotate: The three topmost items exchange places in a rotary fashion. Two variants of this operation are possible, most often called left and right rotate.

Empty Stack

If a stack contains a single item and stack is popped, the resulting stack contains no items is called the empty stack. Although the push operation is applicable to any stack, the pop operation cannot be applied to the empty stack because such a stack has no elements to Pop. Therefore, before applying the Pop operator to a stack, we must ensure that the stack is not empty. The operation empty(s) determines whether or not a stack (S) is empty. If the stack is empty, empty(s) returns the value TRUE; otherwise it returns the value FALSE.

The Stack Abstract Data Type

Before discussions the ADT stack, we define system stack. System stack is used by a program at run time to process function causes. Whenever a function is invoked, the program creates a structure, referred to as an activation record or a stack frame and places it on top of the system stack. Initially the activation record for the invoked function contains only a pointer to the previous stack frame and return address. The previous stack frame pointer points to the stack frame of the invoking function, the return address contains the location of the statement to be executed after the function terminates. Since only one function executes at any given time, the function whose stack frame is on top of the system stack is chosen. If this function invokes another function, the local variables and the parameters of the invoking function are added to its stack frame. A new stack frame is created for the invoked function and placed terminates, its stack frame is removed and the processing of the invoking function, which is again on top of the stack, continues.

Since all functions are stored similarly in the system stack, it makes no difference if the invoking function calls itself. That being a recessive call requires no special strategy; the run time program simply creates new stack frame for each recursion call. However, recursion can consume a significant portion of the memory allocated to the system stack, it could consume the entire available memory.

The representation of a stack as an abstract data type is straightforward

abstract typ def <<elt type>> stack (elt type);

abstract empty (s)

stack (eltype) s;

post condition empty = = (lens(s)= =0);

abstract eltype pop(s)

stack (eltype)s;

precondition empty (s)= =false;

    Pop = = first (s)

    S = = sub (s,1, len (s) −1);

abstract push (s, elt)

Stack (eltype)s;

eltype elt;

Post condition S = = <elt> +s;

Applications

Now that we have defined a stack and have indicated the operations that can be performed on it, let us see how we may use the stack in problem solving. Consider a mathematical expression that includes several sets of nested parentheses : for example,

$$5-(A*(A+B)/(X-3)+B)/(4-2.5)$$

We want to ensure that the parentheses are nested correctly; that is, we want to check that

1. There are an equal number of right and left parentheses.

2. Every right parenthesis is preceded by a matching left parenthesis.

   Expressions such as

     ((X+Y) or X+Y(/Violate Condition 1 and expressions such as /) X+Y

     (-Z or (X+Y))-(X+Z /Violate Condition 2)

To solve this problem, think of each left parenthesis as opening a scope and each right parenthesis as closing a scope.

The two conditions that must hold if the parentheses in an expression from an admissible pattern are as follows:

1. The parentheses count at the end of the expression is O. This implies that no scopes have been left open or that exactly as many right parentheses as left parentheses have been found.

2. The parentheses count at each point in the expression is non-negative. This implies that no right parenthesis is connected for which a matching left parenthesis had not previously been encountered.

6-((X+Y)*X)

   12 1   0

((A+B)

12   1

2+3 (1) X+Y) -Z

   1 0   -1

12.6 Infix, Postfix and Prefix

This section examines a major algorithm that illustrates the different types of states and various operations and functions defined upon them. The example is also an important topic of computer science in its own right.

Consider the Product of X and Y. We think applying the operator "X" to operands X and Y and write it as X*Y. This particular representation is called infix. There are two alternate notations for expressing the product of X and Y using the symbols X, Y and *. These are

XY Prefix   XY Postfix

The 'Pre-,' "Post," and 'in-" refer to the relative position of the operator with respect to the operands. In prefix notation the operator precedes the two operands, in postfix notation the operator follows the two operands, and in infix notation the operator is between the two operands.

We consider binary operation. For these operators the following is the order of precedence (highest to lowest):

1. Exponentiation (!), unary (-), unary +, NOT

2. Multiplication (*), division (/), mod, AND (&&)

3. Addition (+), Subtraction (-), or (!)

4. $<, <=, =, <>, >=$

We give the following examples of converting from infix to postfix and prefix

1   X and Y OR NOT (A > B)

	Postfix	Prefix
T1 = A>B	AB>	>AB

X and Y or NOT T1

	Postfix	Prefix
T2 = NOT TI	TI NOT	NOT TI
T3 = X and Y	XY and	and XY
T4 = T3 OR T2	T3T2 OR	OR T3T2
	T3T1 NOT OR	OR T3 NOT T1
	XY AND AB> NOT OR	OR and XY NOT >AB

Take another example:

B↑ B * C - D + E|F/G+H

		Postfix	Prefix
T1 =	B↑B	BB↑	↑BB
T2 =	T1*C	T1C*	*T1C
T3 =	E|F/G	EF/G	|E/FG
T4 =	T2-D	T2D-	-T2D
T5 =	T4+T3	T4T3+	+T4T3
T6 =	T5+H	T5H+	+T5H
		T4T3+H+	++T4T3H
		T2D-EFIG/+H+	++-* TIC D|E/FG
		TIC * D-EF|G/+H+	++ - *↑ BBCD|E/FG
		BB↑C * D-EF|G/+H+	

Converting an Expression from Infix to Postfix

Procedure play an important role in transforming infix to postfix, let us assume the existence of a function (op1,op2), where op1 and op2 are characters representing operators. This function returns TRUE if op1 has precedence over op2 when op1 appears to the left of op2 in an infix expression without parentheses. Pred (op1,op2) returns FALSE otherwise.

The algorithm to convert an infix string without parentheses into a postfix string as follows:

Opstk=the empty stack;

While (not end of input)

{

symb=next input character;

if (symb is an operand add symb to postfix string)

else

{

while (! Empty (opstk) &&prcd(stacktop(opstk),symb))

{

topsymb   =   pop(opstk)

add topsymb to the postfix string;

} /*end while*/

push (opstk, symb);

} /*end else*/

}/* end while*/

/* output any remaining operators */

while (empty (opstk))

{

topsymb   =   pop(opstk);

add topsymb to the postfix string;

add topsymb to the postfix string;

}/*endwhile*/

We illustrate this algorithm with example:

Example 1:   A + B * C

The contents of symb, the postfix string, and opstk are shown after scanning each symbol. Opstk is shown with its top to the right

S. No.	Symb	Postfix string	Opstk
1	A	A	
2	+	A	
3	B	AB	+
4	*	AB	+ *
5	C	ABC	+*
6	ABC		+
7		ABC *	+

Lines 1, 3 and 5 correspond to the scanning of an operand; therefore, the symbol (symb) is immediately placed on the postfix string. In line 2 an operator is scanned and the stack is found to be empty and the operator is therefore placed on the stack.

In line 4, the precedence of the new symbol (*) is greater than the precedence of symbol on the top of the stack (+), therefore the new symbol is pushed onto the stack. In steps 6 and 7, the input string is empty, and the stack is therefore popped and its contents are placed on the postfix string.

Modified algorithm to convert any infix string into a postfix string is as follows: -

Opstk = the empty stack;

While (not end of input)

{

   symb = next input character;

      if (symb is an operand add symb to postfix string)

      else

      {

      while (! Empty (opstk) &&prcd(stacktop(opstk),symb))

      {

      topsymb   =   pop(opstk)

      add topsymb to the postfix string;

      } /*end while*/

      If (empty (opstk) II symb!=')')

      Push (opstk, symb);

      Else /* pop the open parenthesis and discard if */

Top symb=pop (opstk);

while (empty (opstk))

{

topsymb   =   pop(opstk);

add topsymb to the postfix string;

add topsymb to the postfix string;

}/*endwhile*/

Example 2:   (X+Y)*Z

Symb	postfix string	opstk
(		(
X	X	(
+	X	(+
Y	XY	(+
)	XY+	*
*	XY+	*
Z	XY+Z*	

In this example, when right parenthesis is encountered the stack is popped until a left parenthesis is encountered, at which point both parenthesis are discarded. Using parenthesis forces order of precedence different than that of the default, the order of appearance of the operators.

12.7 Array

In computer programming, an array, also known as a vector or list, is one of the simplest data structures. Arrays hold a series of data elements, usually of the same size and data type. Individual elements are accessed by index using a consecutive range of integers, as opposed to an associative array. Some arrays are multi-dimensional, i.e. they are indexed by a fixed number of integers, for example by a tuple of four integers. Generally, one- and two-dimensional arrays are the most common.

Most programming languages have arrays as a built-in data type. Some programming languages (such as C, Fortran, and Java) generalize the available operations and functions to work transparently over arrays as well as scalars, providing a higher-level manipulation than most other languages, which require loops over all the individual members of the arrays.

Uses

Although useful in their own right, arrays also form the basis for several more complex data structures, such as heaps, hash tables, and V Lists, and can be used to represent strings, stacks and queues. They also play a minor role in many other data structures. All of these applications benefit from the compactness and locality of arrays.

One of the disadvantages of an array is that it has a single fixed size, and although its size can be altered in many environments, this is an expensive operation. Dynamic arrays or grow able arrays are arrays which automatically perform this resizing as late as possible, when the programmer attempts to add an element to the end of the array and there is no more space. To average the high cost of resizing over a long period of time, they expand by a large amount, and when the programmer attempts to expand the array again, it just uses more of this reserved space.

In the C programming language, one-dimensional character arrays are used to store null-terminated strings, so called because the end of the string is indicated with a special reserved character called a null character.

Some applications where the data are the same or are missing for most values of the indices, or for large ranges of indices, space is saved by not storing an array at all, but having an associative array with integer keys. There are many specialized data structures specifically for this purpose, such as Patricia tries and Judy arrays. Example applications include address translation tables and routing tables.

12.7.1 Multi-Dimensional Arrays

Ordinary arrays are indexed by a single integer. Also useful, particularly in numerical and graphics applications, is the concept of a multi-dimensional array, in which we index into the array using an ordered list of integers, such as in a [3,1,5]. The number of integers in the list used to index into it is always the same and is referred to as the dimensionality of array, and the bounds on each of these are called the dimensions of array. An array with dimensionality k is often called k-dimensional. One-dimensional arrays correspond to the simple arrays discussed thus far; two-dimensional arrays are a particularly common representation for matrices. In practice, the dimensionality of an array rarely exceeds three.

Mapping a one-dimensional array into memory is obvious, since memory is logically itself a one-dimensional array. When we reach higher-dimensional arrays, however, the problem is no longer obvious.

A few common representations include:

Row-major order. Used most notably by statically declared arrays in C. The elements of each row are stored in order.

1 2 3 4 5 6 7 8 9

Column-major order. Used most notably in Fortran. The elements of each column are stored in order.

1   5   7   2   4   8   3   6   9

Arrays of arrays: Multi-dimensional arrays are represented by one-dimensional arrays of references to other one-dimensional arrays. The sub arrays can be either the rows or columns.

The first two forms are more compact and have potentially better locality of reference, but are also more limiting; the arrays must be rectangular, meaning that no row can contain more elements than any other. Arrays of arrays, on the other hand, allow the creation of ragged arrays, also called jagged arrays, in which the valid range of one index depends on the value of another, or in this case, simply that different rows can be different sizes. Arrays of arrays are also of value in programming languages that only supply one-dimensional arrays as primitives.

In many applications, such as numerical applications working with matrices, we iterate over rectangular two-dimensional arrays in predictable ways. For example, computing an element of the matrix product AB involves iterating over a row of A and column of B simultaneously. In mapping the individual array indexes into memory, we wish to exploit locality of reference as much as we can. A compiler can sometimes automatically choose the layout for an array so that sequentially accessed elements are stored sequentially in memory; in our example, it might choose row-major order for A, and column-major order for B. Even more exotic orderings can be used, for example if we iterate over the main diagonal of a matrix.

12.7.2 Advantages and Disadvantages

Arrays permit efficient constant time, random access but not efficient insertion and deletion of elements. Linked lists have the opposite trade-off. Consequently, arrays are most appropriate for storing a fixed amount of data that will be accessed in an unpredictable fashion, and linked lists are best for a list of data that will be accessed sequentially and updated often with insertions or deletions.

Another advantage of arrays that has become very important on modern architectures is that iterating through an array has good locality of reference, and so is much faster than iterating through (say) a linked list of the same size, which tends to jump around in memory. However, an array can also be accessed in a random way, as is done with large hash tables, and in this case this is not a benefit.

Arrays also are among the most compact data structures; storing 100 integers in an array takes only 100 times the space required to store an integer, plus perhaps a few bytes of overhead for the whole array. Any pointer-based data structure, on the other hand, must keep its pointers somewhere, and these occupy additional space. This extra space becomes more significant as the data elements become smaller. For example, an array of ASCII characters takes up one byte per character, while on a 32-bit platform, which has 4-byte pointers, a linked list requires at least five bytes per character. Conversely, for very large elements, the space difference becomes a negligible fraction of the total space.

12.7.3 Types of Array

Dynamic array

A dynamic array, grow able array, resizable array, dynamic table, or array list is a data structure, an array that is automatically expanded to accommodate new objects if filled beyond its current size. It may also automatically de allocate some of its unused space to save memory. They have become a popular data structure in modern mainstream programming languages, supplied with most standard libraries.

Note that in this article, a dynamic array is not the same thing as a dynamically allocated array, which is just an ordinary fixed-size array whose size is selected at runtime.

One of the main disadvantages of a simple array is that it has a single fixed size, and although its size can be altered in some environments this is an expensive operation that may involve copying the entire contents of the array. Dynamic arrays automatically perform this resizing as late as possible, when the programmer attempts to add an element to the end of the array and there is no more space. However, if we added just one element to the array each time it runs out of space, the cost of the resizing operations rapidly becomes prohibitive. To deal with this, we instead resize the array by a large amount, such as doubling its size. Then, the next time we need to enlarge the array, we just expand it into some of this reserved space. The amount of space we have allocated for the array is called its capacity, and it may be larger than its current logical size.

Performance

In most ways, the dynamic array performs similar to an array, with the addition of new operations to add and remove elements from the end :

*Getting or setting the value at a particular index.

*Iterating over the elements in order.

*Add an element to the end.

*Remove an element from the end.

Dynamic arrays benefit from many of the advantages of arrays, including good locality of reference and data cache utilization, compactness (low memory use), and random access. They usually have only a small fixed additional overhead for storing information about the size and capacity. This makes dynamic arrays an attractive tool for building cache-friendly data structures.

The main disadvantage of dynamic arrays compared to normal arrays is that when they grow they reserve a great deal of space (linear space in fact) that may never be used. This becomes especially problematic when there are a large number of such arrays. There are variants however, which waste only space at any time.

Global array

The Global Arrays toolkit provides an efficient and portable "shared-memory" programming interface for distributed-memory computers. Each process in a Multiple Instruction, Multiple Data (MIMD) parallel program can asynchronously access logical blocks of physically distributed dense multi-dimensional arrays, without need for explicit cooperation by other processes. Unlike other shared-memory environments, the Global array model exposes to the programmer the non-uniform memory access (NUMA) characteristics of the high performance computers and acknowledges that access to a remote portion of the shared data is slower than to the local portion. The locality information for the shared data is available, and a direct access to the local portions of shared data is provided.

Global arrays have been designed to complement rather than substitute for the message-passing programming model. The programmer is free to use both the shared-memory and message-passing paradigms in the same program, and to take advantage of existing message-passing software libraries. Global arrays are compatible with the Message Passing Interface (MPI).

Parallel array

In computing, a parallel array is a simple data structure for representing arrays of records. It keeps a separate, homogenous array for each field of the record, each having the same number of elements. Then, objects located at the same index in each array are implicitly the fields of a single record. Pointers from one object to another are replaced by array indices. This contrasts with the normal approach of storing all fields of each record together in memory. For example, one might declare an array of 100 names, each a string, and 100 ages, each an integer, associating each name with the age that has the same index.

Example

```
int  ages[ ]  = {0,        27      23       4       25};
char *names[ ] = {"None",    "Mike",   "Billy",   "Tom",      "Stan"};
int  parent[ ] = {0 /*None*/, 4/*Tom*/, 2/*Mike*/, 0 /*None*/, 4/*Tom*/};
for(i = 1; i <= 4; i++) {
printf("Name: %s, Age: %d, Parent: %s \n",
names[i], ages[i], names[parent[i]]);
}
```

Advantages

- They can be used in languages, which support only arrays of primitive types and not of records (or perhaps don't support records at all).

- Parallel arrays are simple to understand and use, and are often used where declaring a record is more trouble than its worth.

- They can save a substantial amount of space in some cases by avoiding alignment issues. For example, one of the fields of the record can be a single bit, and its array would only need to reserve one bit for each record, whereas in the normal approach many more bits would "pad" the field so that it consumes an entire byte or a word.

- If the number of items is small, array indices can occupy significantly less space than full pointers, particularly on architectures with large words.

- Sequentially examining a single field of each record in the array is very fast on modern machines, since this amounts to a linear traversal of a single array, exhibiting ideal locality of reference and cache behavior.

Disadvantages

- They have significantly worse locality of reference when visiting the records sequentially and examining multiple fields of each record, which is the norm.

- They obscure the relationship between fields of a single record.

- They have little direct language support (the language and its syntax typically express no relationship between the arrays in the parallel array.)

- They are expensive to grow or shrink, since each of several arrays must be reallocated.

Sparse array

A sparse array in computing is an array where only very few indices are used in practice. Arrays are data structures used in programming languages. They map integer positions, or indices, less than the array's length, to values. A typical implementation allocates space for the entire array, even if only a few indices are ever used. If the sparsely is known in advance, more space-efficient implementations can be used; only allocating space for the entries that are actually used.

Associative array

In computing, an associative array, also known as a map, lookup table, or dictionary, is an abstract data type very closely related to the mathematical concept of a function with a finite domain. Conceptually, an associative array is composed of a collection of keys and a collection of values, and each key is associated with one value. The operation of finding the value associated with a key is called a lookup or indexing, and this is the most important operation supported by an associative array. The relationship between a key and its value is sometimes called a mapping or binding. For example, if the value associated with the key "bob" is 7, we say that our array maps "bob" to 7.

From the perspective of a programmer using an associative array, it can be viewed as a generalization of an array. While a regular array maps integers to arbitrarily typed objects (integers, strings, pointers, and, in an OO sense, objects), an associative array maps arbitrarily typed objects to arbitrarily typed objects. (Implementations of the two data structures, though, may be considerably different.)

Examples

One can think of a telephone book as an example of an associative array, where names are the keys and phone numbers are the values. Another example would be a dictionary where words are the keys and definitions are the values.

12.8 Queue

A queue is a linear list in which additions are made only at one end of the list (the 'rear') and deletions only at the other end (the 'front'). This is a first in, first out (FIFO) list since it is clear that an element, once added to the rear of the list, can be removed when and only when all earlier additions have been removed.

When a receptionist makes a list of the names of patients who arrive to see a doctor, adding each new name at the front of the list and crossing the top name off the list as a patient is called in, her list of names has the structure of a queue. The word 'queue' is also used in many other everyday examples. Such as the queue of traffic at a road junction, but it should be noted that in many cases (the traffic queue is one), the example is not true queue.

A queue is a linear list where additions and deletions may take place at either end of the list, but never in the middle. A queue, which is both input-restricted and output-restricted, must be either a stack or a queue.

Operations on Queue

Similar to stack operations, operations that define a queue are given below:

1. Create a queue
2. Check whether a queue is empty
3. Check whether a queue is full
4. Add item in the rear of queue (in queue)
5. Remove item from front of queue (dequeue)

12.8.1 Circular Queue

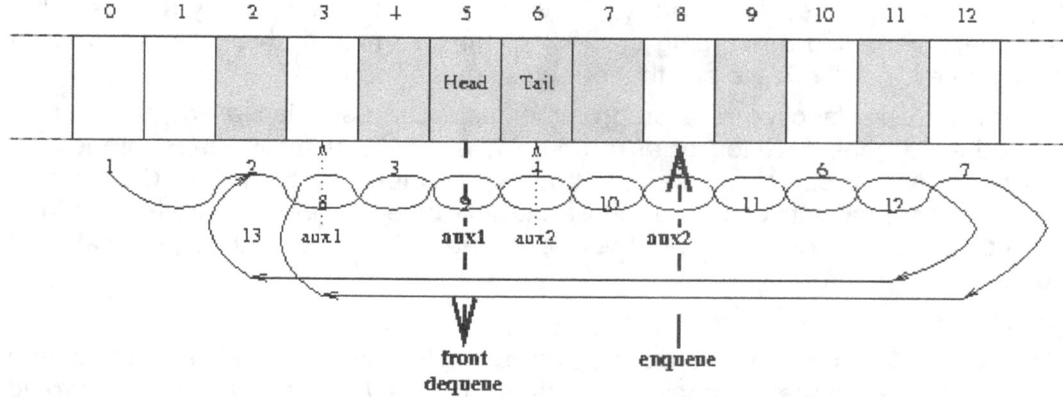

Fig. 12.2 Circular Queue

Now if we try to insert, an overflow may occur even though some cells are free. To avoid this drawback, we can arrange the elements in a circular fashion. It is then called a circular array representation. We may depict a circular queue as given in Fig. (12.2).

Applications

Queues are important in simulation models. They serve roles: as repetitive for scheduled events, as holding areas for entities through the system.

In a computer network, messages from one to another computer are generally created as asynchronously. These messages therefore need to be buffered until the receiving computer is ready for it. These communication buffers make extensive use of queues by storing these messages in a queue. Also the messages need to be sent to receiving computer in the same order in which they are created i.e. First in First out order.

Priority Queue

The priority queue is a data structure in which the intrinsic ordering of the elements dues determines the results of its basic operations. There are two types of priority queues:

1. Ascending priority queue

2. Descending priority queue

An ascending priority queue is a collection of items into which items can be inserted arbitrarily and from which only the smallest item can be removed.

A descending priority queue is similar but allows deletion of any largest item.

12.9   Lists

Lists like arrays are used to store ordered data. A list is a linear sequence of data objects of the same type. Real-life events such as people waiting to be served at a bank counter or at a railway reservation counter may be implemented using list structures. In computer science, lists are extensively used in data base management systems, in process management, in operating system, in editors etc.

We shall discuss lists, linked lists such as singly, doubly and circularly linked lists, and their implementations; using arrays and using pointers.

In computer science, a list is usually defined as an instance of an abstract data type (ADT) formalizing the concept of an ordered collection of entities. For example, an ADT for un-typed, mutable lists may be specified in terms of a constructor and four operations:

An example of a list - a single linked-list, with 3 integer values

In practice, lists are usually implemented using arrays or linked lists of some sort; due to lists sharing certain properties with arrays and linked lists. Informally, the term list is sometimes used synonymously with linked list. A sequence is another name, emphasizing the ordering and suggesting that it may not be a linked list.

Base Terminology

A linear list is an ordered set consisting of a variable number of elements to which addition and deletion can be made. A linear list displays the relationship of physical adjacency.

The first element of a list is called head of list and the last element is called tail of list.

The next element to the head of list is called its Successor. The previous element to the tail of the list is called its Predecessor. A head does not have a predecessor and tail does not have successor. Any other element of list has both one successor and one predecessor.

Characteristics

Lists have the following properties:

- The size and contents of lists may or may not vary at runtime, depending on implementations.
- Random access over lists may or may not be possible, depending on implementations.

Equality of lists

In mathematics, sometimes equality of lists is defined simply in terms of object identity: two lists are equal if and only if they are the same object.

In modern programming languages, equality of lists is normally defined in terms of structural equality of the corresponding entries, except that if the lists are typed, then the list types may also be relevant.

Lists may be typed. This implies that the entries in a list must have types that are compatible with the list type. It is common that lists are typed when they are implemented using arrays.

Operations of the Lists

Following are some of the basic operations that may be performed on a list:

- Create a list
- Check for an empty list
- Search for an element in a list
- Search for a predecessor or a successor of an element of a list
- Delete an element from a list
- Add an element at a specified location of a list
- Retrieve an element from a list
- Update an element of a list
- Sort a list
- Print a list
- Determine the size or number of elements
- Delete a list

More complex operations may be performed on a list, however a complex operation would generally turn out to be a combination of two or more of the above basic operations.

Specification

With the specification of collection complete, let's turn to lists. Our specification of List is a small extension of collection, taking into account the two special properties of lists:

1. In a list, there is a linear order (called followed by, or next) defined on the elements: every element (except for one, called the last element) is followed by one other element, and no two elements are followed by the same element. There is exactly one element in a list (the first element) that does not follow after any element.

2. It is possible to access individual elements of a list. Having a window on the list provides this access; when we define the abstract type List, we will also have to define Window.

The implications of list i.e. a special kind of collection are two-fold: Any operation that is applicable to a collection is applicable to a list. A list is a collection.

However, lists are special kinds of collections - they have two special properties. We have to add extra post conditions to the operators in order to say how these properties are affected by the operations.

12.9.1 Linked List

What are the drawbacks of using sequential storage to represent stacks and queues? One major drawback is that a fixed amount of storage remains allocated to the stack or queue even the structure is actually using a smaller amount or possibly no storage at all. Further, no more than that fixed amount of storage may be allocated, thus introducing the possibility of overflow.

In a sequential representation, the items of a stack or queue are implicitly ordered by the sequential order of storage. Thus, if q items [X] represent an element of a queue, the next element will be q items [X+1]. Suppose that the items of a stack or a queue were explicitly ordered, that is, each item contained within itself the address of the next item. Such an explicit ordering gives rise to a data structure pictured in Fig. 12.3, which is known as a linear linked list. Each item in the list is called a node and contains two fields, an information field and a next address field. The information field holds the actual element on the list. The next address field contains the address of the next node in the list.

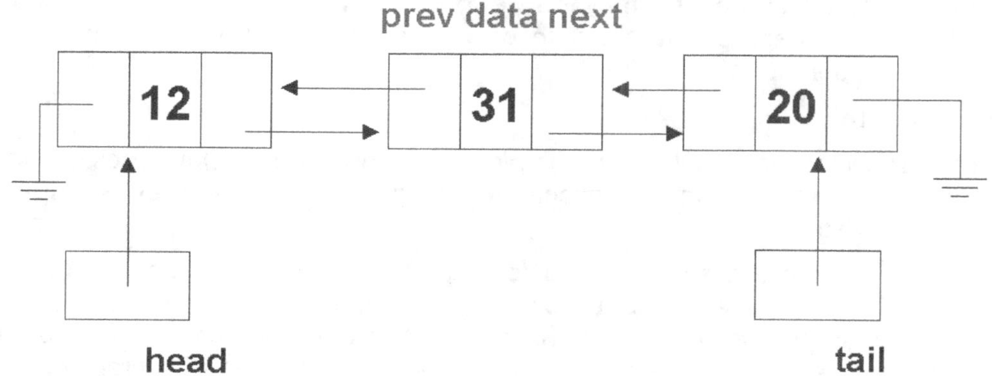

Fig. 12.3 Linked List

Such an address, which is used to access a particular node, is known as a pointer. The next address field of the last node in the list contains a special value, known as null, which is not a valid address. This null pointer is used to signal the end of a list.

The list with no nodes on it is called the empty list or the null list. The value of the external pointer list to such a list is the null pointer. A list can be initialize to the empty list by the operation list = null.

In computer science, a linked list is one of the fundamental data structures used in computer programming. It consists of a sequence of nodes, each containing arbitrary data fields and one or two references ("links") pointing to the next and/or previous nodes. A linked list is a self-referential data type because it contains a pointer or link to another data of the same type. Linked lists permit insertion and removal of nodes at any point in the list in constant time, but do not allow random access. Several different types of linked list exist: singly linked lists, doubly linked lists, and circularly linked lists.

Linked lists can be implemented in most languages. Languages such as LISP and Scheme have the data structure built-in, along with operations to access the linked list. Procedural languages such as C, C++, and Java typically rely on mutable references to create linked lists.

Allen Newell, Cliff Shaw and Herbert Simon at RAND CORPORATION as the primary data structure developed linked lists in 1955-56 for their Information Processing Language. The authors to develop several early artificial intelligence programs, including the Logic Theory Machine, the General Problem Solver, and a computer chess program, used IPL. Reports on their work appeared in IRE Transactions on Information Theory in 1956, and several conference proceedings from 1957-1959, including Proceedings of the Western Joint Computer

Conference in 1957 and 1958, and Information Processing (Proceedings of the first UNESCO International Conference on Information Processing) in 1959. The now-classic diagram consisting of blocks representing list nodes with arrows pointing to successive list nodes appears in "Programming the Logic Theory Machine" by Newell and Shaw in Proc. WJCC, February 1957. Newell and Simon were recognized with the ACM Turing Award in 1975 for having "made basic contributions to artificial intelligence, the psychology of human cognition, and list processing".

The problem of machine translation for natural language processing led Victor Yngve at Massachusetts Institute of Technology (MIT) to use linked lists as data structures in his COMIT programming language for computer research in the field of linguistics. A report on this language entitled "A programming language for mechanical translation" appeared in Mechanical Translation in 1958.

John McCarthy created LISP, standing for list processor, in 1958 while he was at MIT and in 1960 he published its design in a paper in the Communications of the ACM, entitled "Recursive Functions of Symbolic Expressions and Their Computation by Machine, Part I". One of LISP's major data structures is the linked list.

By the early 1960s, the utility of both linked lists and languages, which use these structures as their primary data representation, was well established. Bert Green of the MIT Lincoln Laboratory published a review article entitled "Computer languages for symbol manipulation" in IRE Transactions on Human Factors in Electronics in March 1961, which summarized the advantages of the linked list approach. A later review article, "A Comparison of list-processing computer languages" by Bobrow and Raphael, appeared in Communications of the ACM in April 1964.

Several operating systems developed by Technical Systems Consultants (originally of West Lafayette Indiana, and later of Raleigh, North Carolina) used singly linked lists as file structures. A directory entry pointed to the first sector of a file, and succeeding portions of the file were located by traversing pointers. Systems using this technique included Flex (for the Motorola 6800 CPU), mini-Flex (same CPU), and Flex9 (for the Motorola 6809 CPU). A variant developed by TSC for and marketed by Smoke Signal Broadcasting in California, used doubly linked lists in the same manner.

The TSS operating system, developed by IBM for the System 360/370 machines, used a double linked list for their file system catalogue. The directory structure was similar to Unix, where a directory could contain files and/or other directories and extend to any depth. A utility flea was created to fix file system problems after a crash, since modified portions of the file catalog were sometimes in memory when a crash occurred. Problems were detected by comparing the forward and backward links for consistency. If a forward link was corrupt, then if a backward link to the infected node was found, the forward link was set to the node with the backward link. A humorous comment in the source code where this utility was invoked stated "Everyone knows a flea caller gets rid of bugs in cats".

Singly Linked List

The simplest kind of linked list is a singly linked list (or slist for short), which has one link per node. This link points to the next node in the list, or to a null value or empty list if it is the final node.

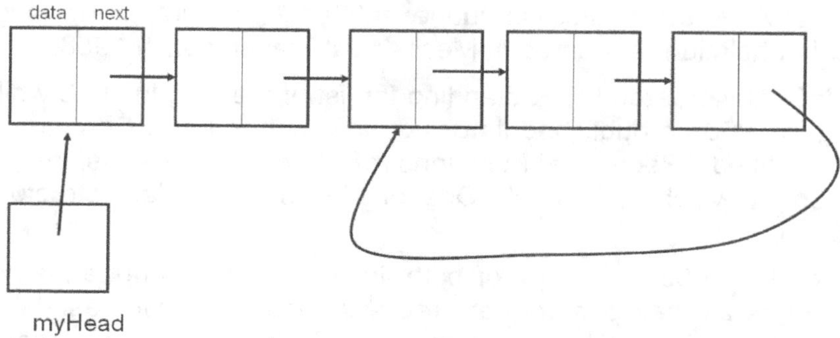

Fig. 12.4 A Singly-linked list

Operation on Link List

Let us see how an insertion algorithm works for inserting an element in a linked list.

1.   Check if list is empty, return of yes.
2.   Search for the element after which the insertion is to be done.
3.   Create a memory space for element to be inserted.
4.   Assign the data value to its data field.
5.   Assign its pointer to pointer of the success elements searched at step 2.
6.   Assign pointer of the element searched at step 2 to this new element created.

Deletion from a list

Deletion of an element from a single linked list requires.

1.   List to be checked for empty list.
2.   Search for the element with key value same as the element to be deleted.

3.   Its pointer to next element be saved and later assigned to next element of predecessor of the element searched at step 2.

4.   Despise the memory space held by the deleted element.

Doubly linked list: A more sophisticated kind of linked list is a doubly linked list or two-way linked list. Each node has two links: one points to the previous node, or points to a null value or empty list if it is the first node; and one points to the next, or points to a null value or empty list if it is the final node.

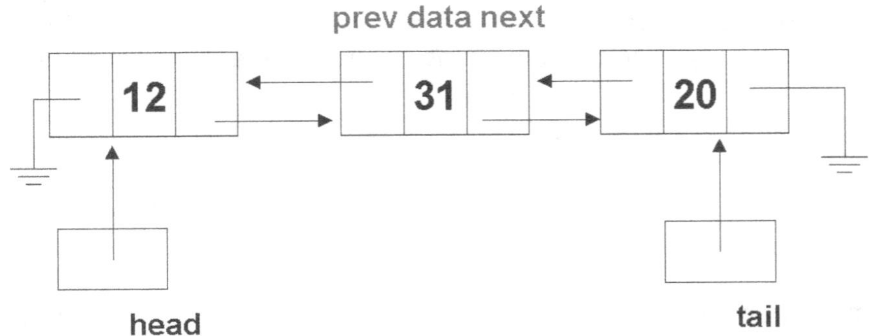

Fig. 12.5 Doubly-linked list

In some very low level languages, Xor-linking offers a way to implement doubly-linked lists using a single word for both links, although the use of this technique is usually discouraged.

Doubly-linked lists are a special case of multi-linked lists; it is special in two ways:

- Each node has just 2 pointers

- The pointers are exact inverses of each other

In a general multi-linked list, each node can have any number of pointers to other nodes, and there may or may not be inverses for each pointer.

Example 1: Multiple Orders of One Set of Elements

The standard use of multi-linked lists is to organize a collection of elements in two different ways. For example, suppose my elements include the name of a person and his/her age. e.g.,(Nakul, 19) (Shadev, 16) (Arjun,21) (Bhim, 18)

I might want to order these elements alphabetically and also order them by age. I would have two pointers - NEXT-alphabetically, NEXT-age - and the list header would have two pointers, one based on name, the other on age.

Inserting into this structure is very much like inserting the same node into two separate lists. In multi-linked lists, it is quite common to have back-pointers, i.e. inverses of each of the forward links; in our example, this would mean that each node had four pointers.

Example 2: Sparse Matrices

A second very common use of multi-linked lists is sparse matrices. A sparse matrix is a matrix of numbers, as in mathematics, in which almost all the entries are zero. These arise frequently in engineering applications. The use of a normal Pascal array to store a sparse matrix is extremely wasteful of space - in an N x N sparse matrix typically only about N elements are non-zero. For example:

```
X = 1  2  3
    ----------
Y = 1 |   0   88   0
Y = 2 |   0    0   0
Y = 3 |  27    0   0
Y = 4 |  19    0  66
```

We can represent this by having linked lists for each row and each column. Because each node is in exactly one row and one column, it will appear in exactly two lists - one row list and one column. So it needs two pointers: Next-in-this-row and Next-in-this-column. In addition to storing the data in each node, it is normal to store the co-ordinates (i.e. the row and column data is in the matrix). Operations that set a value to zero cause a node to be deleted, and vice versa.

12.9.2 Circular Linked Lists

In a circularly linked list, the first and final nodes are linked together. This can be done for both singly and doubly linked lists. To traverse a circular linked list, you begin at any node and follow the list in either direction until you return to the original node. Viewed another way, circularly linked lists can be seen as having no beginning or end. This type of list is most useful for managing buffers for data ingest, and in cases where you have one object in a list and wish to see all other objects in the list.

Singly-circularly-linked list

In a singly-circularly-linked list, each node has one link, similarly to an ordinary singly linked list, except that the next link of the last node points back to the first node. As in a singly linked list, new nodes can only be efficiently inserted after a node we already have a reference to. For this reason, it's usual to retain a reference to only the last element in a singly linked list, as this allows quick insertion at the beginning, and also allows access to the first node through the last node's next pointer.

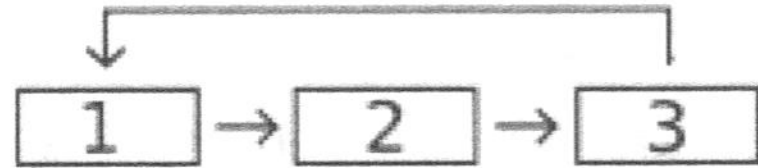

Fig. 12.6 singly-circularly-linked list

Doubly-circularly-linked list

In a doubly-circularly-linked list, each node has two links, similarly to doubly-linked list, except that previous link of the first node points to the last node and the next link of the last node points to the first node. As in doubly linked lists, insertions and removals can be done at any point with access to any nearby node.

Fig. 12.7 Doubly-circularly-linked list

Circular lists are usually preferable to non-circular ones, for two reasons:

- They provide easy access to both ends of a list: notice that we do not need the first pointer in the header, because we can easily reach the first node with L->last->next.

- The code for processing a circular list is often simpler than the code for processing a non-circular list - mainly because you don't have to constantly check if the next node is defined - it is always defined.

Applications of Linked Lists

Linked lists are used as a building block for many other data structures, such as stacks, queues and their variations.

The "data" field of a node can be another linked list. By this device, one can construct many linked data structures with lists; this practice originated in the LISP programming language, where linked lists are a primary (though by no means the only) data structure, and is now a common feature of the functional programming style.

Sometimes, linked lists are used to implement associative arrays, and are in this context called association lists. There is very little good to be said about this use of linked lists; they are easily outperformed by other data structures such as self-balancing binary search trees even on small data sets However, sometimes a linked list is dynamically created out of a subset of nodes in such a tree, and used to traverse that set more efficiently.

12.9.3 Linked Lists vs. Arrays

Linked lists have several advantages over arrays. Elements can be inserted into linked lists indefinitely, while an array will eventually either fill up or need to be resized, an expensive operation that may not even be possible if memory is fragmented. Similarly, an array from which many elements are removed may become wastefully empty or need to be made smaller.

Further memory savings can be achieved, in certain cases, by sharing the same "tail" of elements among two or more lists — that is, the lists end in the same sequence of elements. In this way, one can add new elements to the front of the list while keeping a reference to both the new and the old versions — a simple example of a persistent data structure.

On the other hand, arrays allow random access, while linked lists allow only sequential access to elements. Singly linked lists, in fact, can only be traversed in one direction. This makes linked lists unsuitable for applications where it's useful to look up an element by its index quickly, such as heap sort. Sequential access on arrays is also faster than on linked lists on many machines due to locality of reference and data caches. Linked lists receive almost no benefit from the cache.

Another disadvantage of linked lists is the extra storage needed for references, which often makes them impractical for lists of small data items such as characters or Boolean values. It can also be slow, and with a naïve allocate, wasteful, to allocate memory separately for each new element, a problem generally solved using memory pools.

A number of linked list variants exist that aim to ameliorate some of the above problems. Unrolled linked lists store several elements in each list node, increasing cache performance while decreasing memory overhead for references.

A good example that highlights the pros and cons of using arrays vs. linked lists is by implementing a program that resolves the Josephus problem. The Josephus problem is an election method that works by having a group of people stand in a circle. Starting at a predetermined person, you count around the circle n times. Once you reach nth person, take them out of the circle and have the members close the circle. Then count around the circle the same n times and repeats the process, until only one person is left. That person wins the election. This shows the strengths and weaknesses of a linked list vs. an array, because if you view the people as connected nodes in a circular linked list then it shows how easily the linked list is able to delete nodes (as it only has to rearrange the links to the different nodes). However, the linked list will be poor at finding the next person to remove and will need to recursive through the list till it finds that person. An array, on the other hand, will be poor at deleting nodes (or elements) as it cannot remove one node without individually shifting all the elements up the list by one. However, it is exceptionally easy to find the nth person in the circle by directly referencing them by their position in the array.

Doubly Linked vs. Singly-Linked

Double-linked lists require more space per node (unless one uses XOR-linking), and their elementary operations are more expensive; but they are often easier to manipulate because they allow sequential access to the list in both directions. In particular, one can insert or delete a node in a constant number of operations given only address of that node. Some algorithms require access in both directions. On the other hand, they do not allow tail sharing, and cannot be used as persistent data structures.

Circularly Linked List vs. Linearly-Linked LIST

Circular linked lists are most useful for describing naturally circular structures, and have the advantage of regular structure and being able to traverse the list starting at any point. They also allow quick access to the first and last records through a single pointer (the address of the last element). Their main disadvantage is the complexity of iteration, which has subtle special cases.

12.10 Trees

In computer science, a tree is a widely used computer data structure that emulates a tree structure with a set of linked nodes. Each node has zero or more child nodes, which are below it in the tree (in computer science, unlike in nature, trees grow down, not up). A node that has a child is called the child's parent node. A child has at most one parent; a node without a parent is called the root node (or root). Nodes with no children are called leaf nodes.

In graph theory, a tree is a connected acyclic graph. A rooted tree is such a graph with a vertex singled out as the root. In this case, any two vertices connected by an edge inherit a parent-child relationship. An acyclic graph with multiple connected components or a set of rooted trees is sometimes called a forest.

There are many different ways to represent trees; common representations represent the nodes as records allocated on the heap with pointers to their children, their parents, or both, or as items in an array, with relationships between them determined by their positions in the array (e.g., binary heap).

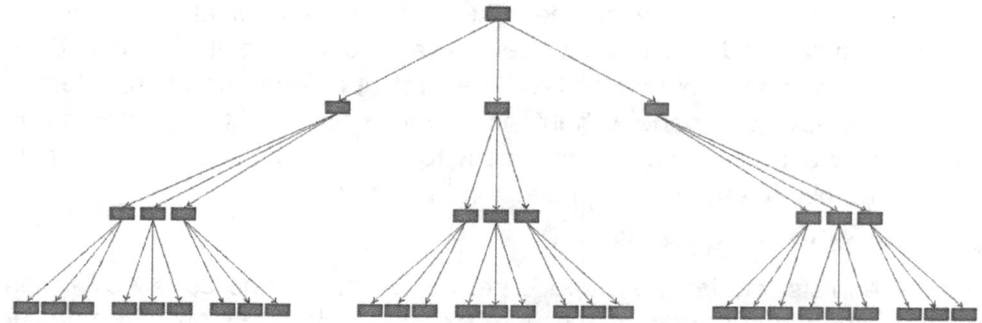

Fig. 12.8 Tree

Definition of Trees

Trees are as common and important as lists. There are many variations of trees like lists - binary search trees, balanced trees, and heaps are the main ones we will look at.

Recall that a list is a collection of components in which:

1.   Each component (except one, the first) has exactly 1 predecessor.

2.   Each component (except one, the last) has exactly 1 successor.

a tree is very similar: it has property (1) but (2) is slightly relaxed.

Each component has some number of successors.

If there is a limit on the number of successors that a node can have, the tree is called a general tree.

If there is a maximum number M of successors for a node, then the tree is called an M-way tree. In particular, a binary (2-ary) tree is a tree in which each node has 0, 1, or 2 successors.

The unique node with no predecessor is called the root of the tree. A node with no successors is called a leaf - there will usually be many leaves in a tree. The successors of a node are called its children; the unique predecessor of a node is called its parent. If two nodes have the same parent, they are called brothers or siblings. In a binary tree, the two children are called the left and right.

Common Operations on Trees

- Enumerating all the items;
- Searching for an item;
- Adding a new item at a certain position on the tree;
- Deleting an item;

- Removing a whole section of a tree (pruning);
- Adding a whole section to a tree (grafting);
- Finding the root for any node.

Common Uses for Trees

- Manipulate hierarchical data;
- Make information easy to search;
- Manipulate sorted lists of data.

Drawing Trees

The root is at the top; below it are its children. An arc connects a node to each of its children: we sometimes draw arrowheads on the arc, but they are optional because the direction parent->child is always top->bottom.

Then, we continue in the same manner, the children of each node are drawn below the node.

In general, each child of a node is the root of a tree ``within the big tree''. For example, B is the root of a little tree (B,D,E), so is C. These inner trees are called sub trees. The sub trees of a node are the trees whose roots are the children of the node, e.g. the sub trees of A are the sub trees whose roots are B and C. In a binary tree, we refer to the left sub tree and the right sub tree.

Path of Tree

A path is any linear subset of a tree, e.g. A-B-E and C-F are paths. The length of a path could be counted as either the number of nodes or the number of edges on the path - we will count the nodes; e.g. A-B-E has length 3. But be careful: there is no agreed definition! The textbook defines path length as the number of edges.

There is a unique path from the root to any node. Simple as this property seems, it is extremely important: all our algorithms for processing trees will depend upon it. The depth or level of a node is the length of this path. When you draw a tree, it is very useful if all the nodes in the same level are drawn as a neat horizontal row. The depth or height of a tree is the maximum depth of the nodes in the tree.

Ordered Trees

There are two basic types of tree. In an unordered tree, there is no distinction between the various children of a node - none is the "first child" or "last child". A tree in which such distinctions are made, is called an ordered tree, and data structures built on them are called ordered tree data structures. Ordered trees are by far the most common form of tree data structure. A simple example is binary tree.

Binary search trees are one kind of ordered tree, and there is a one-to-one mapping between binary trees and general ordered trees.

A tree is ordered if there is some significance to the order of the sub trees.

In, family tree, there could be no significance to left and right. In this case, the tree is unordered, and we could redraw the tree exchanging sub trees without affecting the meaning of the tree. On the other hand, there may be some significance to left and right - may be the left child is younger than the right... or (as is the case here) may be the left child has the name that is earlier in the alphabet. Then, the tree is ordered and we are not free to move around the sub trees.

For now, we will restrict ourselves to ordered trees. Like lists, ordered M-way trees have a nice recursive structural definition:

12.10.1 Structural Definition of Binary Trees

A binary tree is either empty or it has 3 parts:

- a value

- a left sub tree

- a right sub tree

Whenever a data structure has a recursive definition like this, most of the `properties' of the data structure can be computed in a recursive manner, which exactly mirrors the definition.

For example, here is a function to compute the number of nodes in a binary tree:

```
int size(binary_tree *t)

{

return is_empty(t) ? 0 : 1 + size(t->left) + size(t->right);

}
```

With lists we had an alternative to recursion - we could scan through a list as easily with normal loops (while, do ... while) as with recursion. This is not true for trees. It is possible to scan through a tree non-recursively, but it is not nearly as easy as scanning recursively.

12.10.2 Binary Trees

A binary tree is a tree, which is, either empty or consists of a root node and two disjoint trees called the left sub tree and right sub tree.

In a binary tree, no node can have more than two children (Fig. 12.9).

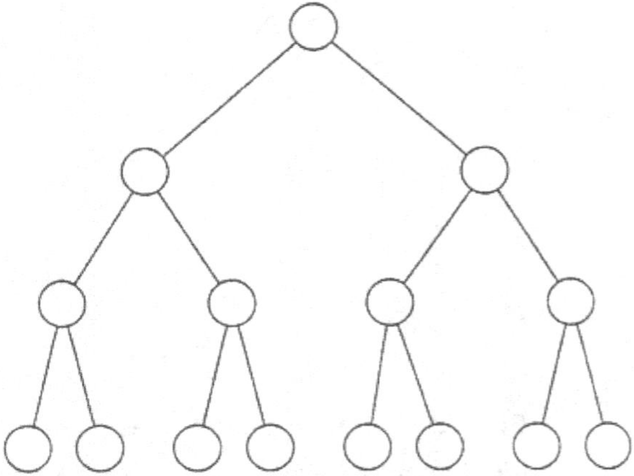

Fig. 12.9 A Binary Tree

Properties of binary tree

1. A binary tree with N internal nodes has maximum of (N+1) external nodes: Root is considered as an internal node.

2. The external path length of any binary tree with N internal nodes is 2N greater than the internal path length.

The height of a full binary tree with N internal nodes is about $\log_2 N$.

A full binary tree or a complete binary tree is a binary tree in which all internal nodes have same degree and all leaves are at the same level.

Linked lists most commonly represent binary trees. Each node can be considered as having 3 elementary fields: a data field left pointer, pointing to left sub tree and right pointer pointing to the right sub tree.

12.10.3 Binary Search Tree

In computer science, a binary search tree (BST) is a binary tree where every node has a value, every node's left sub tree contains only values less than or equal to the node's value, and every node's right sub tree contains only values that are greater than or equal. (Depending on the application of the binary search tree, equal values may not be allowed in either the left or right sub tree). This requires that the values have a linear order. New nodes are added as leaves. Sort algorithms and search algorithms exist for binary search trees. The values of a binary search tree can be retrieved in ascending order using an in-order traversal.

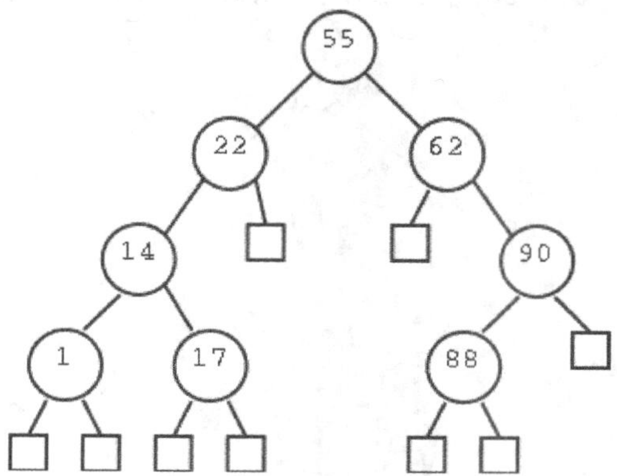

Fig. 12.10 Binary Search Tree

A binary search tree, BST, is an ordered binary tree T such that either it is an empty tree or:

- Each value in its left sub tree less than the root value.
- Each data value in its right sub tree greater than the root value, and
- Left and right sub trees are again binary search trees.

12.10.4 B-Tree

In computer science, B-trees are tree data structures that are most commonly found in databases and file systems. B-trees keep data sorted and allow amortized logarithmic time insertions and deletions. B-trees generally grow from the bottom up as elements are inserted, whereas most binary trees grow down.

The idea behind B-trees is that internal nodes can have a variable number of child nodes within some pre-defined range. As data are inserted or removed from the data structure, the number of child nodes varies within a node and so internal nodes are coalesced or split so as to maintain the designed range. Because a range of child nodes is permitted, B-trees do not need re-balancing as frequently as other self-balancing binary search trees, but may waste some space. The lower and upper bounds on the number of child nodes are typically fixed for a particular implementation. For example, in a 2-3 B-tree (often simply 2-3 tree), each internal node may have only 2 or 3 child nodes. A node is considered to be in an illegal state if it has an invalid number of child nodes.

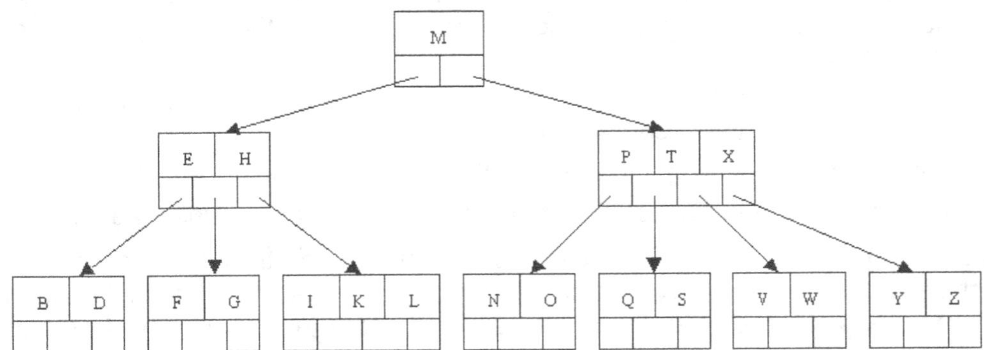

Fig. 12.11 B Tree

B-trees have substantial advantages over alternative implementations when node access times far exceed access times within nodes. This usually occurs when most nodes are in secondary storage such as hard drives. By maximizing the number of child nodes within each internal node, the height of the tree decreases, balancing occurs less often, and efficiency increases. Usually this value is set such that each node takes up a full disk block or an analogous size in secondary storage.

The B-tree's creator, Rudolf Bayer, has not explained what the B stands for. The most common belief is that B stands for balanced, as all the leaf nodes are at the same level in the tree. B may also stand for Bayer, or for Boeing, because he was working for Boeing Scientific Research Labs.

Algorithms

Search

Search is performed in the typical manner, analogous to that in a binary search tree. Starting at the root, the tree is traversed top to bottom, choosing the child pointer whose separation values are on either side of the value that is being searched. Binary search is typically used within nodes to determine this location.

Insertion

For a node to be in an illegal state, it must contain a number of elements which are outside of the acceptable range.

1. First, search for the position into which the node should be inserted. Then, insert the value into that node.

2. If no node is in an illegal state then the process is finished.

3. If some node has too many elements, split it into two nodes. Continue this process recursively up the tree. If you split the root node, create a new root

node. You must select the minimum and maximum number of elements such that the minimum is no more than one half of (the maximum plus one) in order for this to work.

4. First, search for the value, which will be deleted. Then, remove the value from the node, which contains it.

5. If no node is in an illegal state then the process is finished.

6. If some node is in an illegal state then there are two possible cases:

Its sibling node, a child of the same parent node, can transfer one or more of its child nodes to the current node and return it to a legal state. If so, after updating the separation values of the parent and the two siblings the process is finished.

Its sibling does not have an extra child because it is on the lower bound. In that case both siblings are merged into a single node and we recurse onto the parent node, since it has had a child node removed. This continues until the current node is in a legal state or the root node is reached, upon which the root's children are merged and the merged node becomes the new root.

12.10.5 AVL Tree/Height Balanced Tree

A binary tree of height h is completely balanced or balanced if all leaves occurs at nodes of level h or h-1 if all nodes at levels lower than h-1 have two children. According to this definition, the tree shown in fig12.12 is balanced, because all leaves occur at level 3 considering at level 1 and all nodes at levels 1 and 2 have two children.

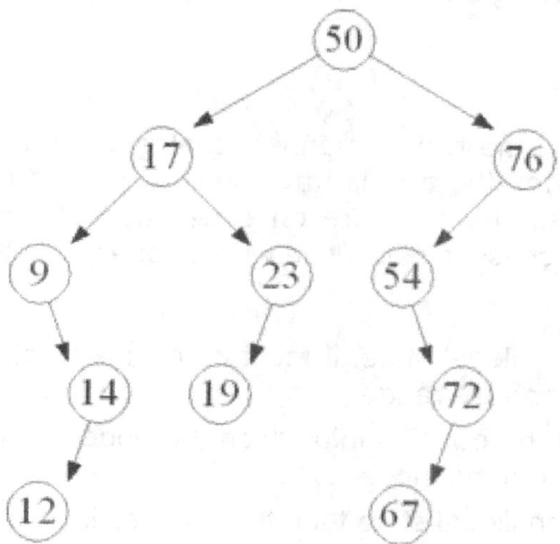

Fig. 12.12 AVL Tree

More precisely a tree is height balanced if, for each node in the tree, the height of the left sub tree differs from the height of the right sub tree by 1,0,-1.

An almost height balance tree is called an AVL tree. AVL tree may or may not be perfectly balanced tree.

12.10.6 M-Way Search Trees

A binary search tree has one value in each node and two sub trees. This notion easily generalizes to an M-way search tree, which has (M-1) values per node and M sub trees. M is called the degree of the tree. A binary search tree, therefore, has degree 2.

In fact, it is not necessary for every node to contain exactly (M-1) values and have exactly M sub trees. In an M-way sub tree, a node can have anywhere from 1 to (M-1) values, and the number of (non-empty) sub trees can range from 0 (for a leaf) to 1+(the number of values). M is thus a fixed upper limit on how much data can be stored in a node.

The values in a node are stored in ascending order, V1 < V2 < ... Vk (k < = M-1) and the sub trees are placed between adjacent values, with one additional sub tree at each end. We can thus associate with each value a `left' and `right' sub tree, with the right sub tree of Vi being the same as the left sub tree of V(i+1). All the values in V1's left sub tree are less than V1 ; all the values in Vk's sub tree are greater than Vk; and all the values in the sub tree between V(i) and V(i+1) are greater than V(i) and less than V(i+1).

In our examples, it will be convenient to illustrate M-way trees using a small value of M. But it is to be bear in mind that, in practice, M is usually very large. Each node corresponds to a physical block on disk, and M represents the maximum number of data items that can be stored in a single block. M is maximized in order to speedup processing: to move from one node to another involves reading a block from disk - a very slow operation compared to moving around a data structure stored in memory.

The algorithm for searching for a value in an M-way search tree is the obvious generalization of the algorithm for searching in a binary search tree. If we are searching for value X and are currently at node consisting of values V1...Vk, there are four possible cases that can arise :

1.   If X < V1, recursively search for X in V1's left sub tree.

2.   If X > Vk, recursively search for X in Vk's right sub tree.

3.   If X=Vi, for some i, then we are done (X has been found).

4.   The only remaining possibility is that, for some i, Vi < X < V(i+1). In this case, recursively search for X in the sub tree that is in between Vi and V(i+1).

Other algorithms for binary search trees - insertion and deletion - generalized in a similar way. As with binary search trees, inserting values in ascending order will result in a degenerate M-way search tree; i.e. a tree whose height is O(N) instead of O(logN). This is a problem because all the important operations are O(height), and it is our aim to make them O(logN). One solution to this problem is to force the tree to be height-balanced.

12.10.7 Threaded Binary Tree

We consider the linked representation of a binary tree T. Approximately half of the entries in the pointer fields LEFT and RIGHT will contain null elements. Replacing the null entries to it other type of information may more efficiently use this space. Specifically we will replace certain null entries by special pointers, which point towards higher in tree. These special pointers are called threads, and binary tree must be distinguished are called threaded binary trees.

In threads in a threaded tree must be distinguished in some way from ordinary pointers. The threads in diagram of a threaded tree must be distinguished by dotted lines in computer memory an extra 1 bit TAG field may be used to distinguished thread from ordinary pointer or alternatively threads may be denoted by negative integers, when ordinary pointers are denoted by positive integers.

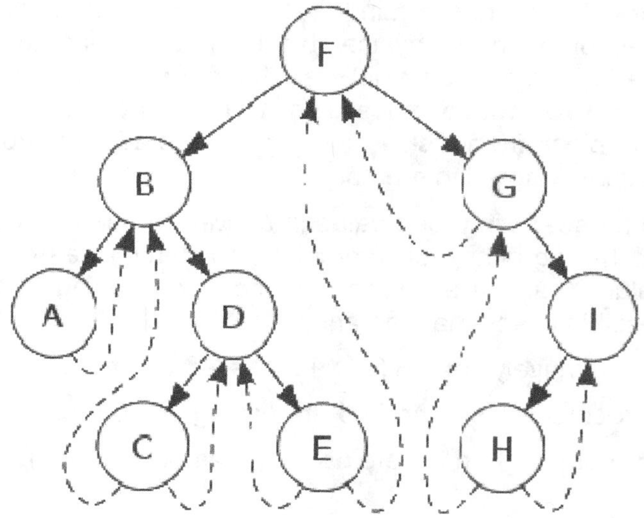

Threading may choose one way threading or two way threading. Accordingly one way threading of T, a thread will appear in the right face of a node and will point to the next node in the nodes traversal of T and in the two way threading of T, at thread will also appear in the left field of the first node and the right pointer of the last node. There is an analysis one way threading of a binary tree T which corresponds to the preorder traversal of T on the other hand there is no threading of T which corresponds to the post order traversal of T.

12.11 Graph

A graph is a set of objects called vertices (or nodes) connected by links called edges (or arcs), which can be directed (assigned a direction). Typically, a graph is designed as a set of dots (the vertices) connected by lines (the edges).

Structures that can be represented, as graphs are ubiquitous, and many problems of practical interest can be represented by graphs. The link structure of a website could be represented by a directed graph: the vertices are the web pages available at the website and there's a directed edge from page A to page B if and only if A contains a link to B. The development of algorithms to handle graphs is therefore of major interest in computer science.

Assigning a weight to each edge can extend a graph structure. Graphs with weights can be used to represent many different concepts; for example if the graph represents a road network, the weights could represent the length of each road. Another way to extend basic graphs is by making the edges to the graph directional (A links to B, but B does not necessarily link to A, as in webpages), technically called a directed graph or digraph. A digraph with weighted edges is called a network.

Networks have many uses in the practical side of graph theory, network analysis (for example, to model and analyze traffic networks or to discover the shape of the internet see Applications below). However, it should be noted that within network analysis, the definition of the term "network" may differ, and may often refer to a simple graph.

One of the first results in graph theory appeared in Leonhard Euler's paper on Seven Bridges of, published in 1736. It is also regarded as one of the first topological results in geometry; that is, it does not depend on any measurements. This illustrates the deep connection between graph theory and topology.

In 1845, Gustav Kirchhoff published his Kirchhoff's circuit laws for calculating the voltage and current in electric circuits.

In 1852, Francis Guthrie posed the four-colour problem, which asks if it is possible to colour, using only four colours, any map of countries in such a way as to prevent two bordering countries from having the same colour. This problem, which was only solved a century later in 1976 by Kenneth Appel and Wolfgang Haken, can be considered the birth of graph theory. While trying to solve it, mathematicians invented many fundamental graph theoretic terms and concepts.

Definition

A Graph G consists of a set of vertices (nodes) and a set E of edges (arcs). We write:

G = (V,E) is a finite and non-empty set of vertices. E is a set of pairs of vertices; these pair is called edges. Therefore

V(G), read as V of G is set of vertices,

E(G), read as E of G is set of edges,

And edge e = (v,w) is a pair of vertices v and w.

A graph may be pictorially represented (Fig. 12.13) as

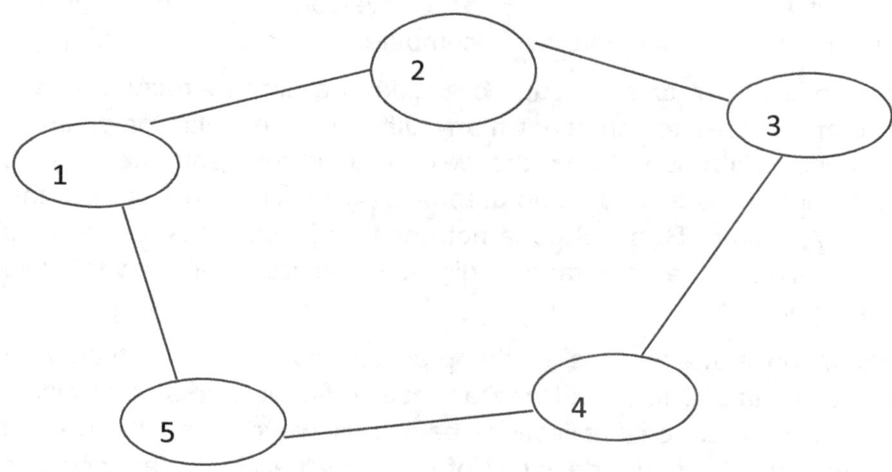

Fig. 12.13 A Graph

We could have write (1, 5) and (5,1) means ordering of vertices is not significant in an in-directed graph.

Thus, the sequence so generated is V2, V8, V3, V5, V6, V7. Here, we need a query instead of stack to implement it.

12.12 Sorting

General Sorting Strategy (Recursive)

A sorting algorithm is an algorithm whose input is any list and whose output is a list (or a change in the given list) that is sorted and has the same elements as the given list.

Most well known sorting algorithms are based on this general strategy. Given a list L

- If L has zero or one element, then it is already sorted, so nothing need be done;
- Otherwise
    1. Divide in L into two smaller lists, L1 and L2.
    2. Recursively sort each of the smaller lists. Result : L1 and L2 are now sorted.
    3. Combine L1 and L2. The result is a sorted version of the original list. How do we combine L1 and L2? As just discussed there's only one way to do so and produce a sorted list. We MERGE them.

This strategy works no matter how we do step (1). The pieces can be any size; they could be the same size, or they could be very different sizes; and it does not matter which elements of L we put together or in what order we put them into the pieces. We can divide up and scramble up the elements any way we like, and we will still sort L. In fact, we could even divide L into more than two pieces, we could divide it into 3, or 7, or whatever.

The one thing we must avoid is having one of the pieces equal to L; if this happens we would have an infinite loop. But that is the only thing we have to avoid.

We will now look at three specific versions of this general strategy : Merge Sort, Insertion Sort and Quick Sort.

12.12.1 Merge Sort

Although the general strategy uses MERGE to put the pieces back together, there is a specific version of the general strategy called Merge Sort. The defining feature of Merge Sort is that in step (1), the given list is divided into two equal size pieces (or as near equal as possible).

There are various ways of dividing L into 2 equal pieces, we will illustrate the algorithm by putting the first half of L in one piece and the second half of L in the other piece. We proceed until we're down to singleton or empty lists, which are always sorted, then we work our way back up the recursion by MERGING together the short lists into larger ones (which replace the list that we started with at that level).

Merge sort divides the array into two halves which are sorted recursively and then merged to form a sorted whole. The array is divided into equal sized parts (up to truncation) so there are log2(N) levels of recursion.

It is interesting to compare quick sort with merge sort; the former has a pre-order structure the latter a post-order structure. In fact there is also a bottom-up, breadth-first merge sort.

Complexity

Time

The best, average and worst case time-complexities of the (basic) algorithm are all the same, O(N*log(N)).

Space

The space complexity of the recursive algorithm is O(N+log(N)), N for the "working-space array" and log(N) for the stack space.

A naive non-recursive translation would still use O(N+log(N)) space, log(N) being for an explicit stack. However, because the array sections vary in a simple and systematic way, there is a non-recursive version that does not need any stack and requires O(N) space only (but there again, log(N)<<N, if N is large).

There are in fact in-situ merging algorithms that only use O(1) space but they are difficult!

Stability

Merge sort is stable if written carefully, it is a matter of a `<=' versus a `<'.

Once upon a time, computer programs were written in Fortran* and entered on punched cards, about 2000 cards to a tray. Fortran code was typed in columns 1 to 72 of each card, but columns 73-80 could be used for a card number. If you ever dropped a large deck of cards you were really in the pool, unless the cards had been numbered in columns 73-80. If they had been numbered you were saved+: They could be fed into a card sorting machine and restored to their original order.

12.12.2 Insertion Sort

In order to use INSERT instead of MERGE, it is clear what we have to do. We have to divide L so that one of the pieces is a singleton. This is easy - for example, just separate the head of L from its tail. Knowing that this piece is a singleton, we also can delete the recursive call that sorts it. This leads to the algorithm:

1. Divide L into two pieces, its HEAD and its TAIL.

2. Recursively sorts the TAIL.

3. INSERT the HEAD into the sorted TAIL.

This is called Insertion Sort.

Example: Given L = [56,35,42,29]:

1.   HEAD = 56. TAIL = [35,42,29].

2.   Recursively sort the TAIL. Result = [29,35,42]. (The details of this step are given below)

3.   INSERT 56 into [29,35,42]. Result = [29,35,42,56].

Step (2) is a recursive call, so it follows the same pattern, except for this computation, L = [35,42,29].

1.   HEAD = 35. TAIL = [42,29].

2.   Recursively sorts the TAIL. Result = [29,42].

3.   INSERT 35 into [29,42]. Result = [29,35,42].

So, we have succeeded in replacing the MERGE operation in step (3) with an INSERT operation, which is quite a bit more efficient. However, we have made a major sacrifice in efficiency in order to do this. Merge Sort happens to be one of the fastest sorting algorithms known; its speed is entirely due to the fact that it cuts the given list L into two equal size pieces. Insertion Sort gives up this source of efficiency, and as a result, it is much less efficient for large lists. We will see how to analyze the efficiency of algorithms later in the lecture.

12.12.3 Quick Sort

The idea behind Quick Sort is to replace the MERGE operation in step 3 with the very much faster JOIN operation. If this could be done, while still splitting the list more or less in half in step (1), we would have an algorithm that is clearly faster than Merge Sort. How can we change the way we do step (1) - SPLIT L into pieces - so that we can use JOIN instead of MERGE? This is the secret to Quick Sort.

When is it safe to JOIN two sorted lists L1 and L2?

When everything in L1 is smaller than everything in L2.

So that's how we cut our list in two. Pick a number, CUTOFF, and put all the elements less than CUTOFF into L1 and all the ones bigger than CUTOFF into L2.

How shall we choose the CUTOFF value? Does it matter?

We must keep 3 things in mind when we choose CUTOFF:

1. Its value must be fairly cheap to compute.

2. It must not be bigger than, or smaller than, all the values in the given list. Why? If it were, then one of the pieces would be identical to L and we'd be in an infinite loop.

3. Ideally, roughly half the values in L will be smaller than CUTOFF. Cutting-in-half will make Quick Sort very efficient.

Considering (2) and (3), the very best choice for CUTOFF is the median value in the given list. By definition the median of a list is the value in the list which is larger than exactly half the values in the list.

Let's illustrate Quick sort with the list [56, 29, 35, 42,15, 41, 75, 21], assuming that the median is chosen for splitting. At this point I'll also add one little wrinkle - Quick Sort actually splits the list into three pieces:

* L1 = {elements with keys strictly less than CUTOFF}

* LC = {elements with keys equal to CUTOFF}

* L2 = {elements with keys strictly greater than CUTOFF}

L1 and L2 are sorted recursively. Then, we join L2 to LC and then join the result to L1.

* L = [56,29,35,42,15,41,75,21]

* LC = [35] • L1 = [15,21,29], which happens to be sorted by a fluke.

* L2 = [56,42,41,75]

Recursively sort L1:

* L = [15,21,29]

* LC = [21]

* L1 = [15]. This is a singleton; so next recursive call will return it unchanged.

* L2 = [29] (ditto).

* JOIN: L1' LC L2' = [15,21,29]

We obtain L1' = [15,21,29].

Recursively sort L2.

- L = [56,42,41,75]
- LC = [42]
- L1 = [41]. This is a singleton; so next recursive call will return it unchanged.
- L2 = [56, 75]. Recursively sort L2.
  - L = [56,75]
  - LC = [56]
  - L1 = [ ], so next recursive call will return it unchanged.
  - L2 = [75], singleton, recursive call won't change it.
  - JOIN: L1' LC L2' = [56,75]
- L2' = [56, 75]
- JOIN: L1' LC L2' = [41, 42, 56, 75]

We obtain L2' = [41, 42, 56, 75]

JOIN L1' LC L2' = [15, 21, 29, 35 ,41,42,56,75]

Quick sort is very efficient if you use the median as the CUTOFF value, because the list is always split into two equal size pieces. But now we must consider, how efficiently can we compute the median of a list? There is no obvious way to do this quickly - in fact, all the obvious methods require you to sort the list! This obviously is no good - we are trying to use the median to do the sorting, so we can't sort the list in order to compute the median! There are some complex algorithms that do better than this, but in practice people do not use the median, they use something else that is easier to compute:

- The first element in the list.
- The mean (or average).
- The ``median of 3''. The way this is computed is to extract three elements from the list and use the middle of these 3 values as the CUTOFF.

What can go wrong? It can happen with these techniques that one of the pieces is empty - the CUTOFF value is removed from the list, and the other piece contains all the other values. For example, suppose you were unlucky and always used the smallest element in the list as the CUTOFF. L1 has all the elements smaller than this - there are none! In this case, called the worst case, Quick Sort is about the same efficiency as insertion sort.

Quick Sort is usually used with arrays. In this case, there is a special version of Quick Sort that sorts the array in place i.e. without using any extra memory (normally you would create L1 and L2 by copying the values out of L into them, so you'd need enough space for two whole copies of L). This is done by a complex method of shuffling around the values within the array: the basic idea is not too difficult to understand, but the code itself is very tricky.

Quick sort partitions the array into two sections, the first of "small" elements and the second of "large" elements. It then sorts the small and large elements separately.

Ideally, partitioning would use the median of the given values, but the median can only be found by scanning the whole array and this would slow the algorithm down. In that case, the two partitions would be of equal size; in the simplest versions of Quick sort an arbitrary element, typically the first element is used as an estimate (guess) of the median.

12.12.4 Two-Way Merge Sort

Merge sort is also of one `divide and conquer' class of algorithms. The basic idea into this is to divide the list into a number of sub lists, sort each of these sub lists and merge them to get a single sorted list. The recursive implementation of 2-way merge sort divides the list into 2 sorts the sub lists and then merges them to get the sorted list. This is also called concatenate sort. Merge sort is the best method for sorting linked lists in random order. The total computing time is of the order 0 (n log2 n).

The disadvantage of that it requires two arrays of the same size and type for the merge phase.

If   T1 (j) <   T2 (i)

then select T1 (j) and write into NT.

else select T2 (x) and write into NT.

CHAPTER 13

Computer Networks

13.1 Introduction

Computers are connected via a transmission media, are known as Computer Network. Suppose a server, which is kept in Office where all computers are connected together, means they can share their data & file. Fig 13.1 shows the data transmission over the network in the office. We can say all interconnected collection of autonomous computer is termed as computer network. Two computers are said to be interconnected if they are able to exchange the information. Computer network started its journey by Telegraph Network & Telephone network.

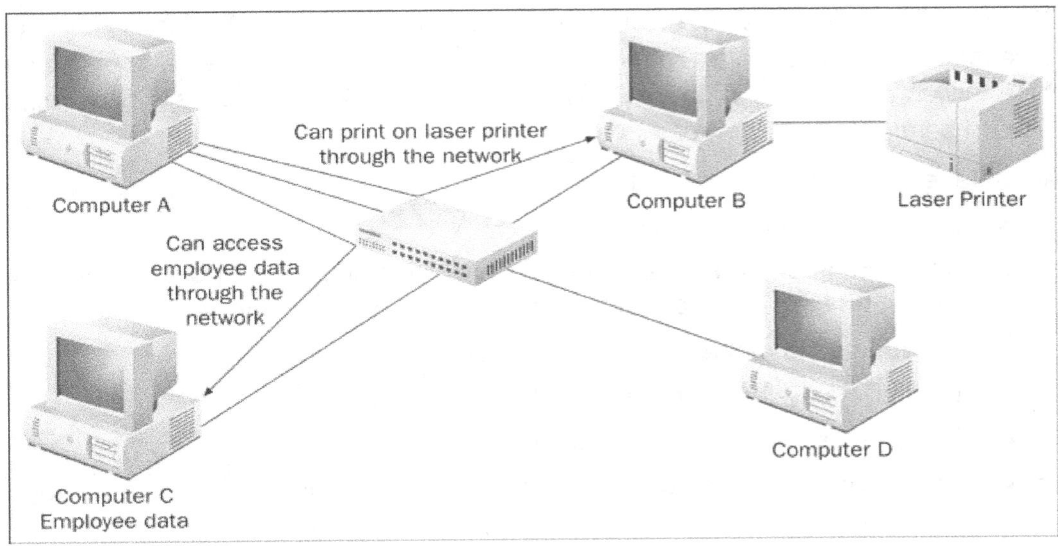

Fig. 13.1 Example of Network

In 1851 the first submarine cable was established between London and Paris. Eventually, networks of telegraph stations were established covering entire continents. In these networks a message or telegram would arrive at a telegraph station, and an operator would make a routing decision based on the destination address.

In 1875 Alexander Graham Bell invented **Telephone network,** which transmit voice signal. Now a days this is known as modern telephone service. It is connection oriented service because they require setting up of connection before the actual transfer of information can take place.

The first Computer Network was the Semi-Automatic Ground Environment **(SAGE)** system developed between 1950 and 1956 for air defense system. The system consisted of 23 computer networks, each network connecting radar sites, ground to air data links and other locations to a central computer. In the 1960s tree topology terminal oriented networks were developed to allow user terminals to connect to a single central shared computer.

The **ARPANET** (Advanced Project Research Network) was the first major effort at developing a network to interconnect computers over a wide geographical area. At the end of 1967 ARPA initiated a small contract with the Stanford Research Institute for the development of specifications for the necessary communications system. Elmer Shapiro was to be the key person on this study the first sites of the ARPANET were picked to provide either network support services or unique resources.

Advantages of Computer Networks:

- Sharing Individual computers
- Networked computers can share resources such as Printers, fax modems, scanners, hard disk, CD-ROMs, and DVDs can all be shared.
- Networks also make computer management easier
- Maximum utilization of H/W & S/W resources
- This reduces costs and the work of support staff
- Computer networks can help in improved communications through groupware.
- E-mail, electronic calendars, collaborative writing, and video conferencing are available.
- Computer networks allow computers to be managed from one central location.

13.2   Types of Network

According to the capacity of network is divided into following categories:

- Server-Based Network
- Local Area Network (LAN)
- Wide Area Network (WAN)
- Metropolitan Area Network (MAN)
- Wireless Network
- Internet
- Internet work

13.2.1   Server Based Network

This type of the network belongs to Client Server Model. It consists of one powerful machine which is known as server & rest are known as Clients. This is commonly used TCP/IP protocol to transfer their data.

- The network a special high-powered server controls.
- The server is dedicated to running the network.
- Print and file servers, application servers, communication servers, and directory service servers are common.

13.2.2   Local Area Network (LAN)

A local area network (LAN) is a group of computers and associated devices that share a common communications line or wireless link and typically share the resources of a single processor or server within a small geographic area (for example, within an office building). Usually, the server has applications and data storage that are shared in common by multiple computer users. A local area network may serve as few as (for example, in a home network) or as many as thousands of users (for example, in FDDI network).

- Network computers are located relatively close to each other.
- They are generally limited to buildings owned by one organization.
- They operate at high speeds.
- They are low-cost networks

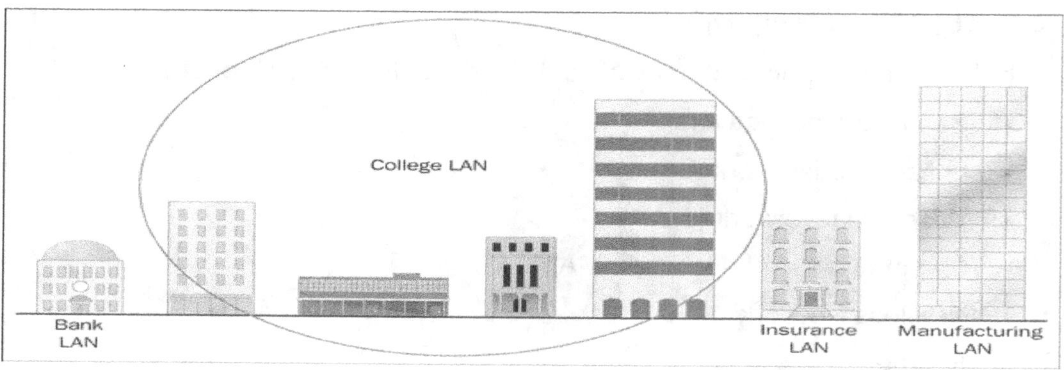

Fig. 13.2 Local Area Network (LAN)

FDDI: Ethernet is by far the most commonly used LAN technology. A number of corporations use the Token Ring technology. FDDI is sometimes used as a backbone LAN interconnecting Ethernet or Token Ring LANs. Another LAN technology, ARCNET once the most commonly installed LAN technology, is still used in the industrial automation industry.

Typically, a suite of application programs can be kept on the LAN server. Users who need an application frequently can download it once and then run it from their local hard disk. Users can order printing and other services as needed through applications run on the LAN server. A LAN server may also be used as a Web server if safeguards are taken to secure internal applications and data from outside access.

In some situations, a wireless LAN may be preferable to a wired LAN because it is cheaper to install and maintain.

13.2.3 Wide Area Network (WAN)

A *WAN* is a data communications network that covers a relatively broad geographic area and that often uses transmission facilities provided by common carriers, such as telephone companies. Typically, a WAN consists of two or more local-area networks (LANs). WAN technologies generally function at the lower three layers of the OSI reference model: the physical layer, the data link layer, and the network layer It connects computers and LANs over a larger geographical area. It crosses public thoroughfares such as roads, railroads, and water.

- Network computers are spread out over a larger area.
- They generally cross public thoroughfares.
- Public carriers often manage them.

- They operate at lower speeds.
- They are a higher-cost network

13.2.4 Metropolitan Area Network (MAN)

Networks that are serve an area of 3 to 30 miles, approximately the area of a typical city. MAN support high-speed disaster recovery systems, real-time transaction backup systems, interconnections between corporate data centers and Internet service providers, and government, business, medicine, and education high-speed interconnections. Fig 13.3 is showing MAN.

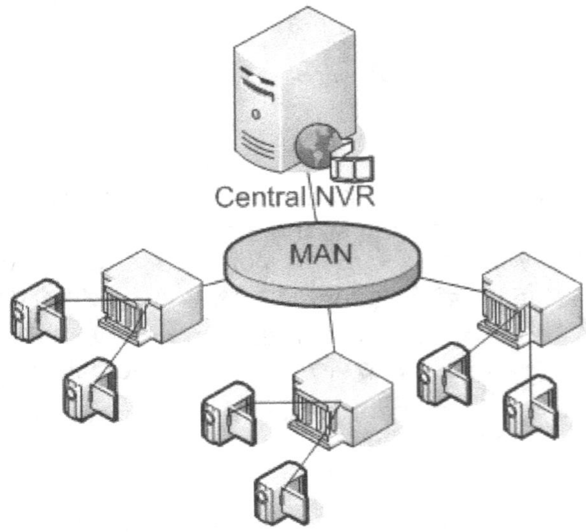

Fig. 13.3 Metropolitan Area Network (MAN)

13.2.5 Wireless Network

The term wireless networking refers to technology that enables two or more computers to communicate using standard network protocols, but without network cabling. A wireless network can also use an access point, or base station. In this type of network the access point acts like a hub, providing connectivity for the wireless computers. It can connect (or "bridge") the wireless LAN to a wired LAN, allowing wireless computer access to LAN resources, such as file servers or existing Internet Connectivity. An ad-hoc, or peer-to-peer wireless network consists of a number of computers each equipped with a wireless networking interface card. Each computer can communicate directly with all of the other wireless enabled computers. They can share files and printers this way, but may not be able to access wired LAN resources. Fig13.4 shows a wireless network, which can access from H/W access point.

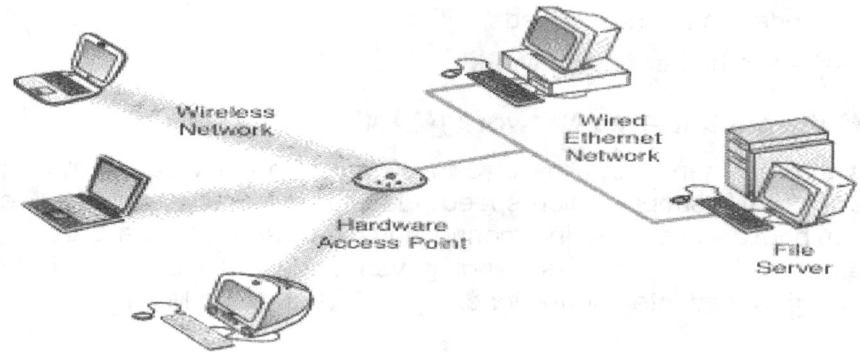

Fig. 13.4 Showing Wireless Network

13.2.6   Internet

The Internet uses high-speed data lines, called backbones, to carry data. Smaller networks connect to the backbone, enabling any user on any network to exchange data with any other user. Every computer and network on the Internet uses the same protocols (rules and procedures) to control timing and data format.

- The World Wide Web is a part of the Internet, which supports hypertext documents, allowing users to view and navigate different types of data.

- A Web page is a document encoded with hypertext markup language (HTML) tags. HTML allows designers to link content together via hyperlinks.

- Every Web page has an address, a Uniform Resource Locator (URL).

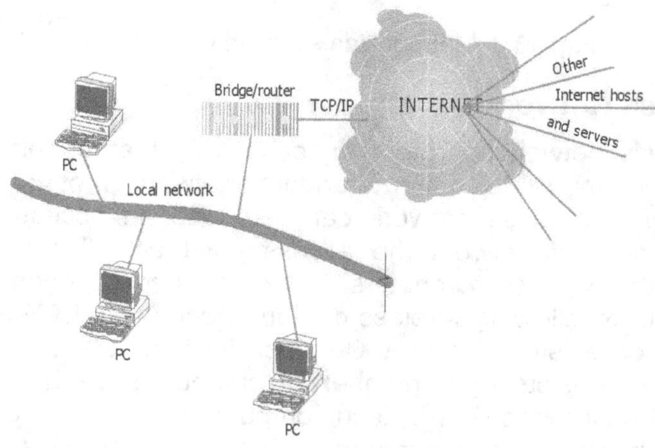

Fig. 13.5 Diagram of Internet

13.2.7 Intranet

A network connected within University, college or any organization to transfer data between that organizations are known as Intranet. It is usually a connected collection of LANs. It is also known as Internet work. An *Internet work* is a collection of individual networks, connected by intermediate networking devices, those function as a single large network. Internet working refers to the industry, products, and procedures that meet the challenge of creating and administering Internet works. For example a University having 5 Lab, i.e. Computer Lab, Physics Lab, Electronics Lab, Chemistry Lab & if they are connected from the LAN, so that is known as intranet.

13.3 Some Features of Networking

Hosts: A computer system that is accessed by a user working at a remote location. Typically, the terms are used when there are two computer systems connected by modems and telephone lines. The system that contains the data is called the host, while the computer at which the user sits is called the remote terminal.

Node: In networks, it is a processing location. A node can be a computer or some other device, such as a printer. Every node has a unique network address, sometimes called a Data Link Control (DLC) address or Media Access Control (MAC) address.

Download: To be copy data (usually an entire file) from a main source to a peripheral device. The term is often used to describe the process of copying a file from an online service or bulletin board service (BBS) to one's own computer. Downloading can also refer to copying a file from a network file server to a computer on the network.

Upload: To transmit data from a computer to a bulletin board service, mainframe, or network. For example, if you use a personal computer to log on to a network and you want to send files across the network, you must upload the files from your PC to the network.

13.4 Advantages of Networks

The following advantages are particularly true for LANs, although they apply to MANs and WANs as well.

Sharing of peripheral devices: Laser printers, disk drives, and scanners is examples of peripheral devices. A peripheral device is any piece of hardware the is connected to a computer. Any newly introduced piece of hardware is often quite expensive, as was the case with laser or colour printers. To justify their purchase, companies want them to be shared by many users. Usually the best way to do this is to connect the peripheral device to a network serving several computer users.

Sharing of programs and data: In the most organisations, people uses the same software and access same information. It could be expensive for a company to buy one copy of, say, a word processing program for each employee. Rather, the company will usually buy a network version of that program that will serve many employees.

Organistions also save a great deal or money by letting all employees have access to the same data on a shared storage device. This way the organisation avoids such problems as some employees updating customer addresses on their own separate machines while other employees remain ignorant of such changes.

Finally, network-linked employees can, using workgroup software, work together online one-shared projects.

Better communications: One of the greatest features of networks is electronic mail,With e-mail everyone on a network can easily keep others posted about important information. Thus, the company eliminates the delays encountered with standard interoffice mail delivery or telephone tag.

Security of information: Before networks became common place, an individual employee might be the only one with particular information, stored in his or her desktop computer. If the employee was dismissed – or if a fire or flood demolished the office – no one else in the company might have any knowledge of that information. Today such data would be backed up or duplicated on a networked storage device shared by others.

Access to databases: Networks also enable users to tap into numerous databases, whether the private databases of a company or the public databases of online services.

13.5 Local Area Networks (LANs)

A computer network that is spans a relatively small area. Most LANs are confined to a single building or group of building. However, one LAN can be connected to other LANs over any distance via telephone lines and radio waves. A system of LANs connected in this way is called a wide-area network (WAN).

Most LANs connect workstations and personal computer. Each node (individual computer) in LAN has its own CPU with which it executes programs, but it is also able to access data and devices anywhere on the LAN. This means that many users can share expensive devices, such as laser printers, as well as data. Users can also use the LAN to communicate with each other, by sending e-mail or engaging in chat sessions.

There are many different types of LANs; Ethernets being the most common for PCs. Most apple Macintosh networks are based on Apple's Talk network system, which is built into Macintosh computers.

The following characteristics differentiate one LAN from another:

Topology: The geometric arrangement of devices on the network. For example, devices can be arranged in a ring or in a straight line.

Protocols: The rules and encoding specifications for sending data. The protocols also determine whether the network users a peer-to-peer or client/server architecture.

Media: twisted-pair wire, coaxial cables, or fiber optic cables can connect devices. Some networks do without connecting media altogether, communicating instead via radio waves.

LANs are capable of transmitting data at very fast rates, much faster than data can be transmitted over a telephone line; but the distances are limited, and there is also a limit on the number of computers that can be attached to a single LAN.

LANs may be client-server or peer-to-peer and include components such as cabling, network interface cards, operating system, other shared devices, and bridges and gateways. The topology, or shape, of a network may take five forms: star, ring, bus, hybrid, or FDDL

Although large networks are useful, many organisations need to have a local network an in-house network – to tie together their own equipment. Here let's consider the following aspects of local networks:

- Types of LANs – client-server and peer-to-peer
- Components of a LAN
- Topology
- Impact of LANs

13.5.1 Types of LAN

Client/Server architecture: A network architecture in which each computer of process on the network is either a client or a server. Servers are powerful computer or processors dedicated to managing disk drives (file servers), printers (print servers), or network traffic (network servers). Clients are PCs or workstations on which users run applications.

Another type of network architecture is known as a peer-to-peer architecture because each node has equivalent responsibilities. Both client/server and peer-to-peer architectures are widely used, and each has unique advantages and disadvantages.

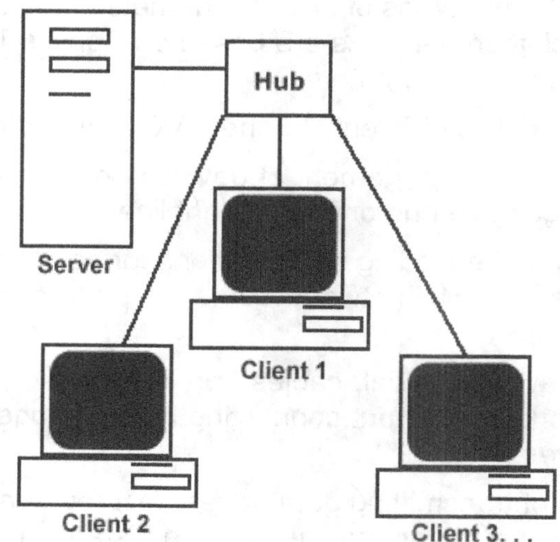

Fig. 13.6 Client/Server architecture

Peer-to-peer architecture, a type of network in which each workstation has equivalent capabilities and responsibilities. This differs from client/server architectures, in which some computers are dedicated to serving the others. Peer-to-peer networks are generally simpler and less expensive, but they usually do not offer the same performance under heavy loads.

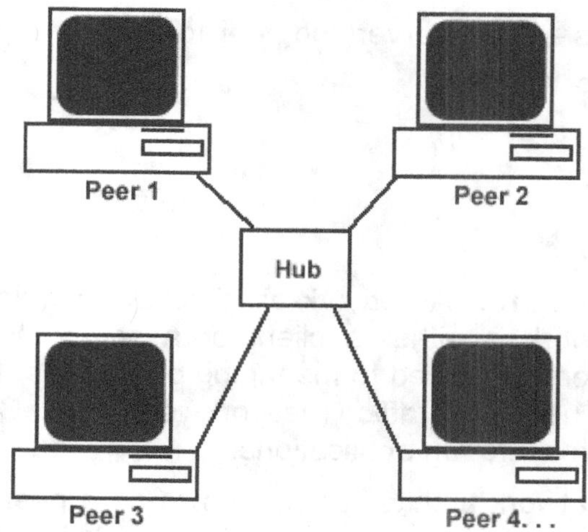

Fig. 13.7 Peer-to-peer architecture

13.5.2   Components of LAN

Media or cabling system: In computer networks, media refer to the cables linking workstations together. There are many different types of transmission media, the most popular being twisted-pair wire, coaxial cable (the type of cable used for cable television), and fiber optic cable (cables based on higher propagation).

Computer with Network Interface card: More than one computer are required to make a network interface card often abbreviated as NIC, an expansion board you insert into a computer so the computer can be connected to a network. Most NICs are designed for a particular type of network, protocol, and media, although some can serve multiple networks. The most popular NIC protocol is Ethernet.

Ethernet: A local-area network (LAN) protocol developed by Xerox Corporation in co-operation with DEC and Intel in 1976. Ethernet uses a bus or star topology and supports data transfer rates of 10 Mbps. The Ethernet specification served as the basis for the IEEE 802.3 standard, which specifies the physical and lower software layers. Ethernet uses the CSMA/CD access method to handle simultaneous demands. It is one of the most widely implemented LAN standards.

A newer versions of Ethernet, called 100Base-T (Fast Ethernet), supports data transfer rates of 100 Mbps. And the newest version, Gigabit Ethernet supports data rates of 1 gigabit (1,000 megabits) per second.

Network Operating System (NOS): An operating system that includes special functions for connecting computers and devices into a local-area network (LAN). Some operating systems, such as UNIX and the OS, has networking functions built in. The term network operating system, however, is generally reserved for software that enhances a basic operating system by adding networking features. For example, some popular NOS's for DOS and Windows systems include Novell Netware, Artisoft's LAN testic, Microsoft LAN Manager, and Windows NT.

Bridges: A device that connects two local-area networks (LANs), or two segments of the same LAN. The two LANs being connected can be alike or dissimilar. For example, a bridge can connect an Ethernet with a Token-Ring network.

Unlike routers, bridges are protocol-independent. They simply forward packets without analyzing and re-routing messages. Consequently, they're faster than routers, but also less versatile.

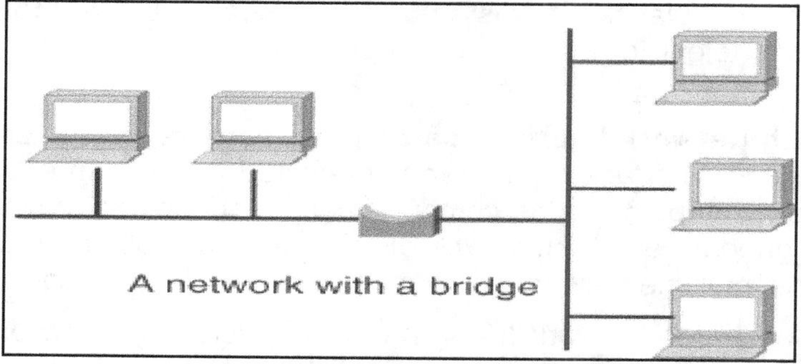

Fig. 13.8 Components of LAN

HUB: A common connection point for devices in a network. Hubs are commonly used to connect segments of a LAN. A hub contains multiple ports. When a packet arrives at one port, it is copied to the other ports so that all segments of the LAN can see all packets.

A passive hub serves simply as a conduit for the data, enabling it to go from one device (or segment) to another. So-called intelligent hubs include additional features that enable an administrator to monitor the traffic passing through the hub and to configure each port in the hub. Intelligent hubs are also called manageable hubs.

A third type of hub, called a switching hub, actually reads the destination address of each packet and then forwards the packet to the correct port.

Router: A device that connects two LANs. Routers are similar to bridges, but provide additional functionally, such as the ability to filter messages and forward them to different places based on various criteria.

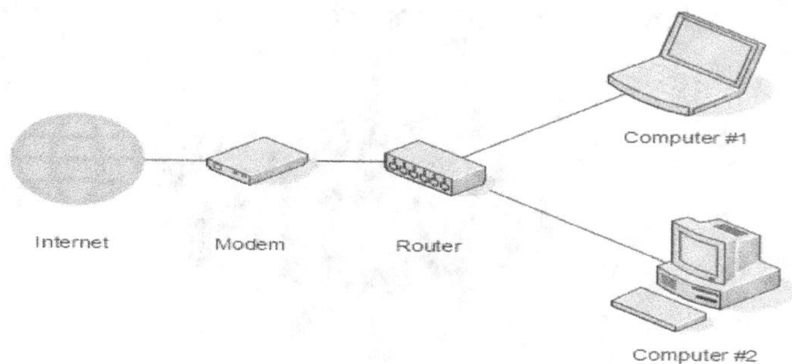

Fig. 13.9 Components of LAN

Router

Repeater: A network device used to regenerate or replicate a signal. Repeaters are used in transmission systems to regenerate analog or digital signals distorted by transmission loss. Analog repeaters frequently can only amplify the signal while digital repeaters can reconstruct a signal to near its original quality.

In a data network, a repeater can relay messages between sub-networks that use different protocols or cable types. Hubs can operate as repeaters by relaying messages to all connected computers. A repeater cannot do the intelligent routing performed by bridges and routers.

Gateway: In networking, a combination or hardware and software that links two different types of networks. Gateways between e-mail systems, for example, allow users on different e-mail systems to exchanges messages.

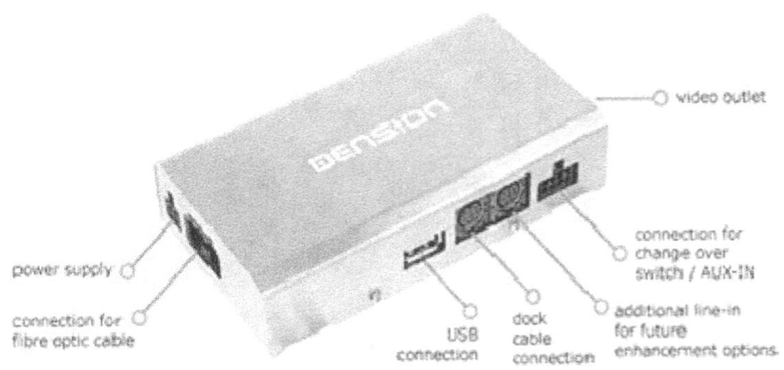

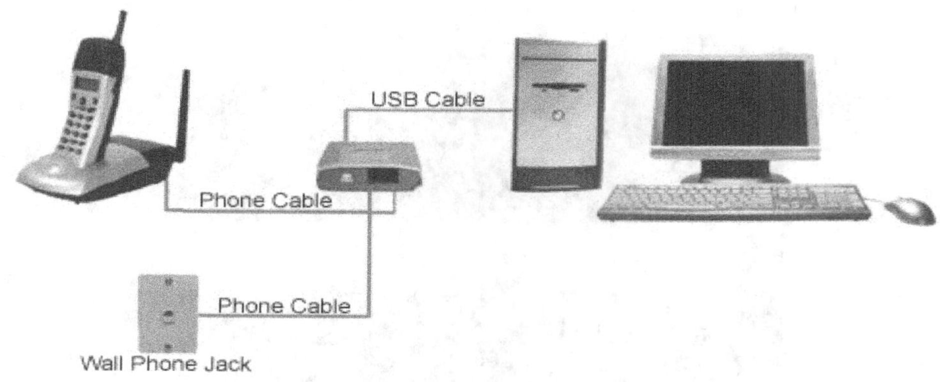

Fig. 13.10 Gateway

13.5.3   Topology of LAN

The geometric arrangement of a computer system or the shape of a local-area network (LAN) or other communications systems is called topology. There are three principal topologies used in LANs.

Bus topology: In Bus topology all devices are connected to a central cable, called the bus or backbone. Bus networks are relatively inexpensive and easy to install for small networks. Ethernet systems use a bus topology.

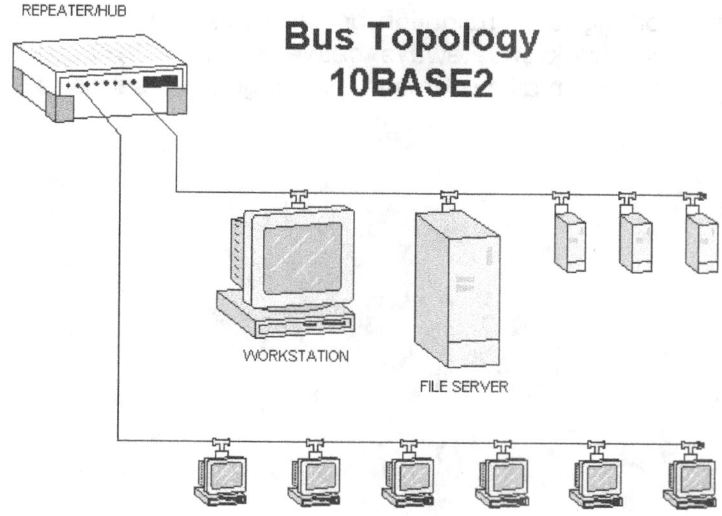

Fig. 13.11 Bus Topology

Advantages of Bus topology:

Short cable length and simple layout: Because there is a single common data path connecting all nodes, the bus topology allows a very short cable length to be used. This decreases the installation cost, and also leads to a simple, easy-to-maintain wiring layout.

Easy to extend: Additional nodes can be connected to an existing bus network at any point along its length. More extensive additions can be achieved by adding extra segments connected by a type of signal amplifier known as a repeater.

Resilient architecture: The bus architecture has an inherent simplicity that makes it very reliable from a hardware point of view. There is a single cable through which all data passes and to which all nodes are connected.

Disadvantages

Fault diagnosis is difficult: Although the simplicity of the bus topology means that there is very little that can go wrong, fault detection is not a simple matter. In most LANs based on a bus, control of the network is not centralized in any particular node. This means that detection of a fault may be performed from many points in the networks.

Fault isolation is difficult: In the star topology, a defective can easily be isolated from the network by removing its connection at the center. If a node is faulty on a bus, it must be rectified at the point where the node is connected to the network. Once the fault has been located, the node can simply be removed. In the case where the fault is in the network medium it self, an entire segment of the bus must be disconnected.

Nodes must be intelligent: Each node on the network is directly connected to the central bus. This means that some way of deciding who can use the network at any given time must be performed in each node. It tends to increase the cost of the nodes irrespective of whether this performed in hardware or software.

Repeater configuration: When a bus-type network has its backbone extended using repeaters, reconfiguration may be necessary. This may involve tailoring cable lengths, adjusting terminators etc.

Ring topology: In ring topology all devices are connected to one another in the shape of a closed loop, so that each device is connected directly to two other devices, one on either side of it. Ring topologies are relatively expensive and difficult to install, but they offer high bandwidth and can span large distances.

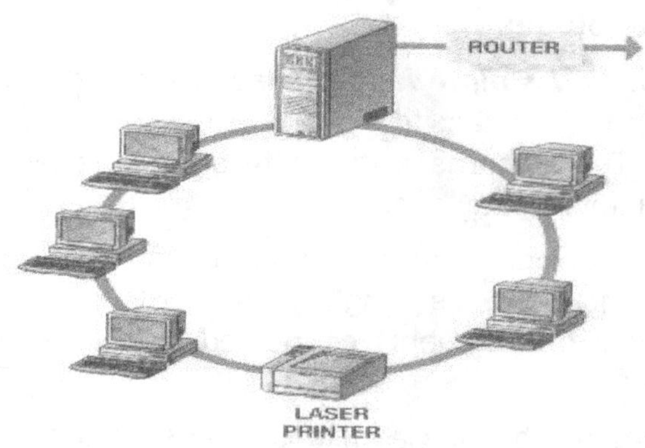

Fig. 13.12 Ring topology

Advantages

Short cable length: The amount of cabling involved in a ring topology is comparable to that of a bus and is small relative to that of a star. This means that fewer connections will be needed, which will in turn increase network reliability.

No wiring closet space required: Since there is only one cable connecting each node to its immediate neighbors, it is not necessary to allocate space in the building for wiring closes.

Suitable for optical fibers: Optical fibers offer the possibility of very high-speed transmission. Because traffic on a ring travels in one direction, it is easy to use optical fibers as a medium of transmission. Also, since a ring is made up of nodes connected by short segments of transmission medium, there is a possibility of mixing the types used for different parts of the network. Thus a manufacturing company's areas, where electrical interference may be a problem.

Disadvantages

Node failure causes network failure: The transmission of data on a ring goes through every connected node on the ring before returning to the sender. If one node fails to pass data through it the entire network has failed and no traffic can flow until the defective node has been removed from the ring.

Difficult to diagnose faults: The facts the failure or one node will affect all others has serious implications for fault diagnosis. It may be necessary to examine a series of adjacent nodes to determine the faulty one. This operation may also require diagnostic facilities to be built into each node.

Network reconfiguration is difficult: The all or nothing nature of the ring topology can cause problems when one decides to extend or modify the geographical scope of the network. It is not possible to shut down a small section of the ring while keeping the majority of it working normally.

Topology affects the access protocol: Each node on a ring has a responsibility to pass on data that is received. This means that the access protocol must take this into account. Before a node can transmit its own data, it must ensure that the medium is available for use.

Star topology: In a star topology several devices are connected to one centralized computer. In this topology none of the other computer can communicate with each other if the central computer breaks down. All the transmission between with each other of the network is through the central computer. This topology is used in the case where centralized record keeping is necessary, like in banking sector.

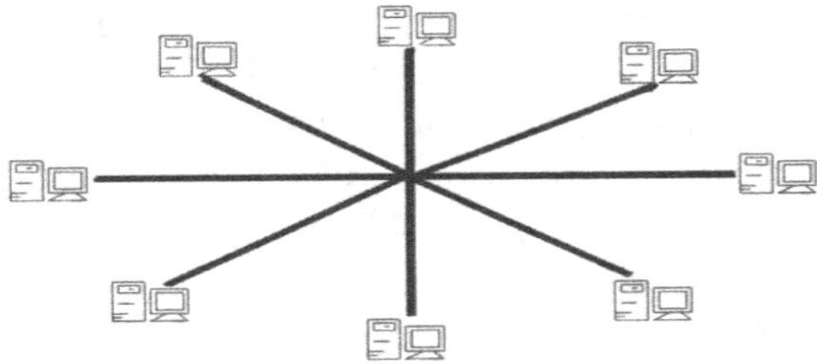

Fig. 13.13 State Topology

The star topology has found extensive application in areas where intelligence in the network is concentrated at the central node. The tendency in recent computer systems is away from host-based computing power, and the advent of microprocessor-based systems where all nodes possess a high level of processing power has led to a fall off in the use of this topology. Nevertheless, the technology is well understood and because It is currently the dominant configuration in traditional data communication, it Is likely to be with us for many years to come.

Advantages

Ease of service: That star topology has a number of concentration points, i.e. at the central node or at intermediate wiring closets. These provide easy access for service of reconfiguration of the network.

One device per connection: Connection points in any network are inherently prone to failure. In the star topology, failure of a single connection typically involved dis-connecting only one node from others.

Simple access protocols: Any given connection in a star network involves only the central node and one peripheral node. In this situation, contention for who has control of the medium for transmission purposes is easily solved. Thus, in a star network access protocols are very simple.

Centralised control/problem diagnosis: The fact that the central node is connected directly to every other node in the network means that faults are easily detected and isolated. It is a simple matter to disconnect failing nodes from the system.

Disadvantages

Long cable length: Because each node is directly connected to the center, the star topology necessitates a large quantity of cable. While the cost of the cable is often small, congestion in cable ducts and maintenance and installation problems can increase costs considerably.

Difficult to expand: The addition of a new node to a star network involves a connection all the way to the central node. Providing large numbers of redundant cables during the initial wiring usually caters for expansion. However, problems can arise if a longer cable length is needed or an unanticipated concentration of nodes is required.

Central node dependency: If the central node in a star network fails, the entire network is rendered inoperable. This introduces heavy reliability and redundancy constraints on this node.

Tree topology: In tree topology all devices are linked in a hierarchical fashion. This topology is also known as hierarchical topology. This topology is commonly used in the organisation where the headquarter communicate with regional offices and they communicated with branch offices and district offices and so on.

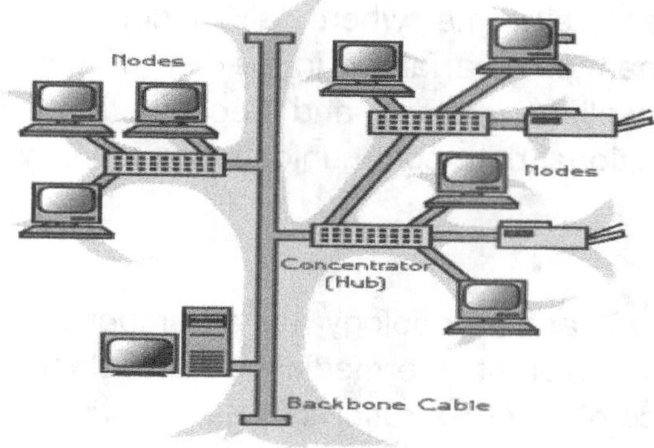

Fig. 13.14 Tree Topology

Advantages

Easy to extend: *Because* the tree is, of its very nature divided into subunits, it is easier to add new nodes or branches to it.

Fault isolation: It is possible to disconnect whole branches of the network from the main structure. This makes it easier to isolate a defective node.

Disadvantages

Dependent on the root: If the 'head end' device fails to operate, the entire network is rendered inoperable. In this respect the tree suffers from the same reliability problems as the star.

Mesh Topology: In mesh topology point-to-point connections have between every device in the network. Each device requires an interface for every on the network, mesh topologies are not usually considered practical. In addition, unless each station frequently sends signals to all the other stations, an excessive amount of network bandwidth is wasted. However, mesh networks are extremely fault tolerant, and each link provides guaranteed capacity.

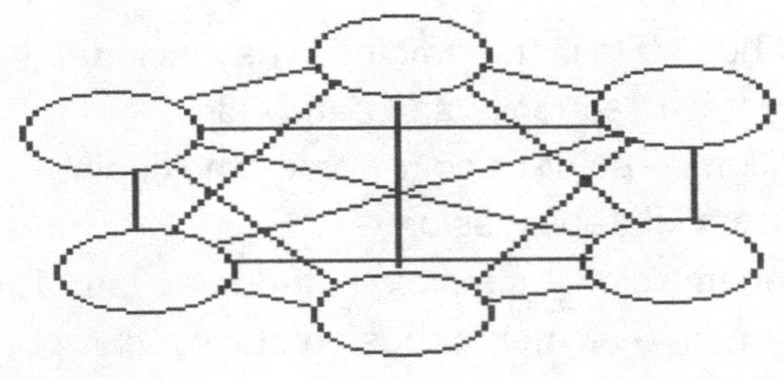

Fig. 13.15 Mesh Topology

Generally mesh topologies used in a hybrid network with just the largest or most important sites interconnected. For example, suppose your organization operates a WAN with 4 or 5 main sites and a large number of remote offices. Each main site has a mainframe and all or the mainframes must communicate to maintain a distributed main site to ensure continuous communications between the mainframes.

Advantages and Disadvantages of the Mesh Topology:

Advantages

Units Affected by Media Failure: Mesh topologies resist media failure better than other topologies Implementations that include more than two devices will always have multiple paths to send signals from one device to another. If one path fails, the transmission signals can be routed around the failed link.

Ease of Troubleshooting: Mesh topologies are easy to troubleshoot because each medium link is independent of all others. You can easily identify faults and can isolate the affected link.

Disadvantages

Ease to installation: Mesh networks are relatively difficult to install because each device must be linked directly to all other devices. As the number of devices increase, the difficulty of installation increases geometrically.

Ease of Reconfiguration: Mesh topologies are difficult to reconfigure for the same reasons that they are difficult to install.

13.6   Factors Affecting Communications among Devices

Factors affecting how data is transmitted include the transmission rate (frequency and bandwidth), the line configuration (point-to-point or multipoint), serial versus parallel transmission, the direction of transmission flow (Simplex, half-duplex, or full-duplex),

Several factors affect how data is transmitted. They include:
- Transmission rate – frequency and bandwidth
- Line configurations – point-to-point verses multipoint
- Serial versus parallel transmission
- Direction of transmission – simplex, half-duplex, and full-duplex
- Transmission mode – asynchronous versus synchronous
- switching
- Multiplexing
- Protocols

Transmission Rate: Transmission Rate is a function of two variables : frequency and bandwidth.

- **Frequency:** The amount of data that can be transmitted on a channel depends on the wave frequency the cycles of waves per second. frequency is expressed in hertz: one cycle per second equals one hertz. The more cycles per second, the more data that can be sent through that channel.

- **Bandwidth:** The amount of data that can be transmitted in a unit of time. For digital devices, the bandwidth is usually expressed in bits per second (bps) or bytes per second. For analog devices, the bandwidth is expressed in cycles per second, or Hertz (Hz).

The bandwidth is particularly important for I/O devices. For example, a bus with a low bandwidth can hamper a fast disk drive. This is the main reason that new buses, such as AGP, have been developed for the PC.

A twisted-pair telephone wire of 4000 hertz might send only 1 kilobyte of data in a second. A coaxial cable of 100 megahertz might send 10 megabytes/s. And a fiber-optic cable of 200 trillion hertz might send 1 gigabyte/s.

Line Configurations: There are two principal line configurations, or ways of connecting communications lines: point-to-point and multipoint.

- **Point-to-point:** A point-to-point line directly connects the sending and receiving devices, such as a terminal with a central computer. This arrangement is appropriate for a private line whose sole purpose is to keep data secure by transmitting it from one device to another.

- **Multipoint:** A multipoint line is a single line that interconnects several communications devices to one computer. Often on a multipoint line only one communications device, such as a terminal, can transmit at any given time.

Serial & Parallel Transmission: Data is transmitted in two ways – serial and in parallel. Serial data transfer refers to transmitting data one bit a time. The opposite of serial is parallel, in which several bits are transmitted concurrently.

Printers and other devices are said to be either parallel or serial. Parallel means the device is capable of receiving more than one bit at a time (that is, it receives several bit in parallel). Most modern printers are parallel.

13.7   Direction of Transmission Flow

When two devices are in communication, data can be flow in three ways – simplex, half duplex, or full duplex. These are describe as follows:

Simplex data transmission: This refers to transmission in only one direction. Note the difference between simplex and half-duplex. Simplex refers to one-way communications where one party is the transmitter and the other is the receiver. An example of simplex communications is a simple radio, which you can receive data from stations but can't transmit data.

Half duplex data transmission: It refers to the transmission of data in just one direction at a time. For example, a walkie-talkie is a half-duplex device because only one party can talk at a time. In contrast, a telephone is a full-duplex device because both parties can talk simultaneously.

Most modems contain a switch that lets you select between half-duplex and full-duplex modes. The correct choice depends on which program is using to transmit data through the modem.

In half-duplex mode, each character transmitted is immediately displayed on your screen. (For this reason, it is sometimes called local echo—the local device echoes characters). In full-duplex mode, transmitted data is not displayed on your monitor until it has been received and returned (remotely echoed) by the other device. If you are running a communications program and every character appears twice, it probably means that your modem is in half-duplex mode when it should be in full-duplex mode, and every character is being both locally and remotely echoed.

Full duplex data transmission: This refers to the transmission of data in two directions simultaneously. For example, a telephone is a full-duplex device because both parties can talk at once.

Most modems have a switch that lets choose between full-duplex and half-duplex modes. The choice depends on which communications program you are running.

In full-duplex mode, data transmit does not appear on screen until it has been received and sent back by the other party. This enables you to validate that the data has been accurately transmitted. If your display screen shows two of each character, it probably means that modem is set to half-duplex mode when it should be in full-duplex mode.

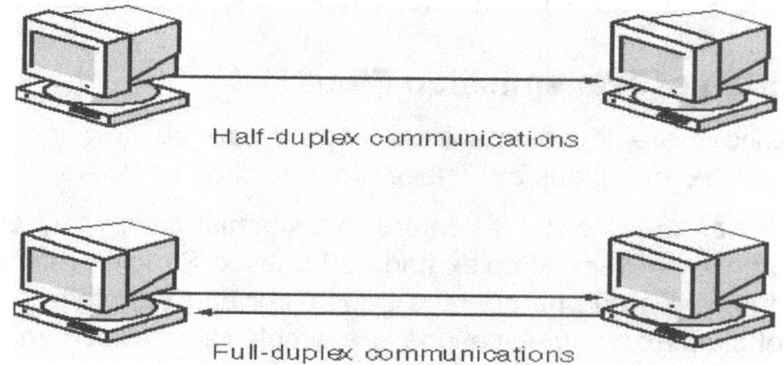

Fig. 13.16 Simplex data transmission

13.8 Transmission Modes

Asynchronous mode: Asynchronous mode means not synchronized mode; that is, the transmission not occurring at predetermined or regular intervals. The term asynchronous is usually used to describe communications in which data can be transmitted intermittently rather than in a steady stream. For example, a telephone conversation is asynchronous because both parties can talk whenever they like. If the communication were synchronous, each party would be required to wait a specified interval before speaking.

The difficulty with asynchronous communications is that the receiver must have a way to distinguish between valid data and noise. In computer communications, this is usually accomplished through a special start bit and stop bit at the beginning and end of each piece of data. For this reason, asynchronous communication is sometimes called start-stop transmission. Most communications between computers and devices are asynchronous.

Synchronous mode: In this mode transmission occurring at regular intervals. The opposite of synchronous is asynchronous. Most communication between computers and devices is asynchronous – it can occur at any time and at irregular intervals. Communication within a computer, however, is usually synchronous and is governed by the microprocessor clock. Signals along the bus, for example, can occur only at specific points in the clock cycle.

13.9   Switching

13.9.1 Circuit Switching

Circuit switching is the transmission technology that has been used since the first communication networks in the nineteenth century. In circuit switching, a caller must first establish a connection to a callee before any communication is possible. During the connection establishment, resources are allocated between the caller and the callee.

Circuit switching is commonly used technique in telephony, where the caller sends a special message with the address of the callee (i.e. by dialing a number) to state its destination.

Circuit Establishment: To establish an end-to-end connection before any transfer of data. Some segments of the circuit may be a dedicated link, while some other segments may be shared.

13.9.2   Message Switching

A Message is a logical unit of information and can be of any length. In this method, if a station or a switching office wishes to send a message to another, it first attaches the destination address to message. When the sender has a block of data to be sent, it is stored in the first switching office and then forwarded later. This method is known as store-and-forward. Each block is received entirely, checked for errors and then retransmitted.

In message switching, no physical connection is required between the source and destination.

But one disadvantage is that the message length is unlimited i.e. each switching node must have sufficient storage to buffer message and another one is that a message is delay at each node because of time required to receive the message plus a queuing delay waiting for a chance to retransmit message to next node.

13.9.3 Packet Switching

This is refers to protocols in which messages are divided into packets before they are sent. Each packet is then transmitted individually and can even follow different routes to its destination. Once all the packets forming a message arrive at the destination, they are recompiled into the original message.

Most modern Wide Area Network (WAN) protocols, including TCP/IP, X.25, and Frame Relay, are based on packet-switching technologies. In contrast, normal telephone service is based on a circuit-switching technology, in which a dedicated line is allocated for transmission between two parties. Circuit switching is ideal when data must be with most real-time data, such as live audio and video. Packet switching is more efficient and robust for data that can withstand some delays in transmission, such as e-mail messages and Web pages.

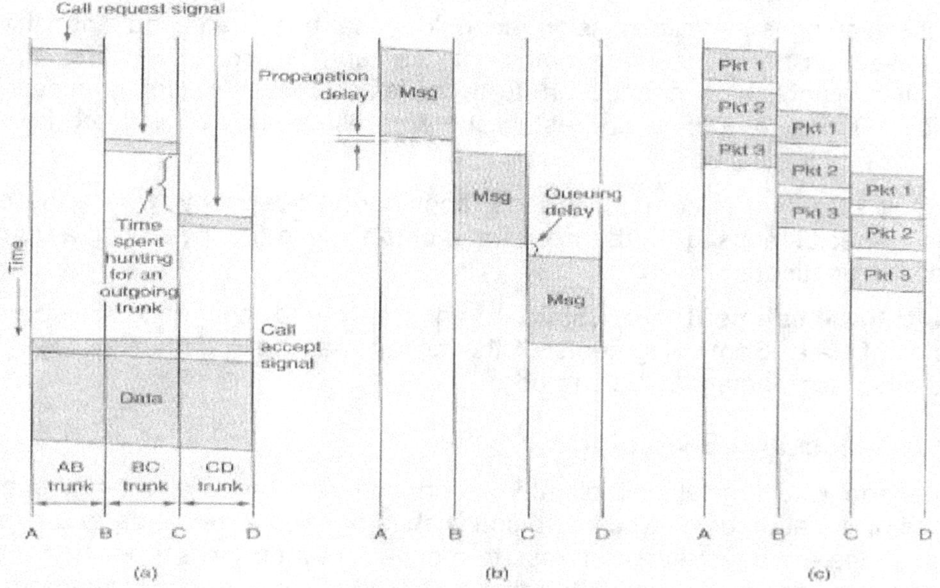

(a) Circuit switching (b) Message switching (c) Packet switching

13.10 ATM

Short for asynchronous transfer mode, a network technology based on transferring data in cells or packets of fixed size. The cell used with ATM is relatively small compared to units used with older technologies. The small, constant cell size allows ATM equipment to transmit video, audio, and computer data over the same network, and assure that no single type of data hogs the line.

Current implementations of ATM support data transfer rates of from 25 to 622 Mbps. This compares to a maximum of 100 Mbps for Ethernet, the current technology used for most LANs.

Some people think that ATM holds the answer to the Internet bandwidth problem, but others are skeptical. ATM creates a fixed channel, or route, between two points whenever data transfer begins. This differs from TCP/IP, in which messages are divided into packets and each packet can take a different route from source to destination. This difference makes it easier to track and bill data usage across an ATM network, but it makes it less adaptable to sudden surges in network traffic.

13.11 Wide Area Network

As the name suggest, WAN spread across countries and continents, satellite being our of the transmission media. A wide area network is a network that links separate geographical locations. A WAN can be public system or can also use most other types of circuit including satellite networks, value added networks (VANS/VADS).

The network can be a private system made up from a network of circuits leased from the local telephone company or setup public system as virtual private networks. A virtual private network is one which operates in the same way as a private network but which uses public switched services for the transmission of information. The main distinguishing feature between a WAN and LAN is that the LAN is under the complete control of the owner, where as the WAN needs the involvement of another authority. LAN are also able to handle very high data transfer rates at low cost because of the limited area covered, LAN's have a lower error rate than WAN's.

13.11.1 Type of Wide Area Networks

The essential purpose of WAN, regardless of the size or technology used is to link separate locations in order to move data around. A WAN allows these locations the access shared computer resources and provides the essential infrastructure for developing widespread distributed computing systems. The different types of WAN are:

Public Networks: Public networks are those networks, which are installed and run by the telecommunications authorities and are made available to any organisation or individual who subscribe it. The main feature of public network services is:

Public Switched Telephone Network (PSTN): The feature of the PSTN are its low speed, the analog nature of transmission, a restricted bandwidth and its widespread availability. The PSTN is most useful in wide area data communication systems as an adjusted to other mechanism.

Public Switched Data Network's (PSDN): The term PSDN course a number of technologies, although currently it is limited to public packet switched network available to the public. The main feature of all PSDNs are their high level of reliability and the high quality of the connections provided. PSDN is very popular for connecting public and private mail system to implement electronic mail services with other companies.

Value Added Services (VANS/VADS): In value added services the provider of such services must process, store and manipulate the data is carried on the network, that is, add value to it. The technique can be used in specific type of business in which it is advantageous to be able to share information with other companies in the secure line. Electronic data interchange (EDI) is one area for value added services in which two trading partners exchange trading documents.

Integrated Service Digital Network (ISDN): The ISDN is a networking concept providing for integration of voice, video and data services using digital transmission media and combining both circuit and packet switching techniques. The motivating force behind ISDN is that telephone networks around the world have been making a transition towards utilizing digital transmission facilities for many years.

Private Network: The basic technique used in all forms of private WAN is to use private circuits to link the locations to be served by the network. Between these fixed points the owner of the network has complete freedom to use the circuits in anyway they want. They can use the circuits to carry large quantities of data or high-speed transmission.

13.12 Transmission Media

13.12.1 Magnetic Media

One of the most common way to transport data from one computer to another is to write them onto magnetic tape or floppy disks, physically transport the tape or disks to the destination machine, and read the back in again. While this methods is not as sophisticated as using a geo synchroms communication satellite it is after much more cost affective, especially for applications in which high bandwidth or cast per bit transported is the key factor.

A simple calculation makes this point clear. An industry slandered 6250 bpi magnetic tape can hold 180 megabytes. A station wagon or light truck can easily transport 200 tapes at one time. Suppose the source and destination machines are an hour's due apart. The effective data rate between these two machines is then 288000 megabits in 3600 sec or 80 Mbps. No wide area network transfer in this order of magnitude of this bandwidth. Few local networks can even match it for a bank with gigabytes of data to be backed up daily an a second machine it is likely that no other transmission technology can even begin to approach magnetic tape for performance or cost effectiveness.

13.12.2 Twisted Pair

Although the bandwidth characteristics of magnetic tape are excellent the delay characteristics are poor. Transmission time is measured in minutes or hours not milliseconds. For many application an online connection is needed; the oldest and still most common transmission medium is twisted pair.

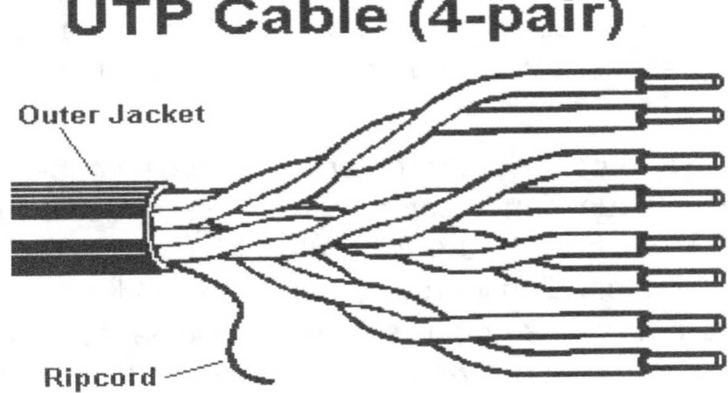

Fig. 13.17 Twisted Pair

A twisted pair consists of two insulated copper wires, typically about 1 mm thick. The wires are twisted together in a helical form, just as a DNA molecule, the twisted from is used to reduce electrical interference to similar pairs close by. The most commonly used application of twisted pair is telephone system.

13.12.3 Coaxial Cable

Another common transmission medium is the co-axial cable (known to its many funds as just "Core") two kinds of coaxial cable are widely used. One kind 50-ohm cable is used for analog transmission and will be described in the novel part.

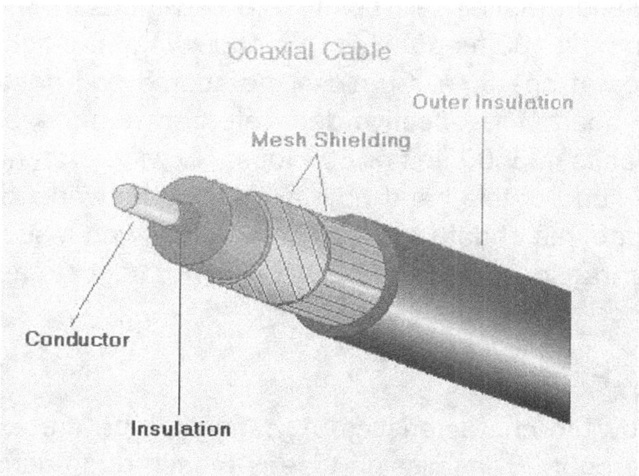

Fig. 13.18 Coaxial Cable

The construction of the coaxial cable gives it a good combination of high bandwidth and excellent noise immunity. The band width possible depends on the cable length. For 1 km cables a data rate 10 Mbps is feasible. Coaxial cables are used for local area networks and for long distance transmission within the telephone system.

There are two ways to connect computers to a coaxial cable. The first is to the cable cleanly insert a T junction a connector that reconnects the cable but also provide a third wire leading off to the computer. The second is to use a vampire tap, which is a hole of exceedingly precise depth and width drilled into due cable, terminating in the core. Into this hole is secured a special connector that achieves the same goal as a T-junction, but without the need to cut the cable in two.

Inserting a T-junction requires cutting the cable; if the hole is drilled too deep it may break the core into unconnected pieces. If it is not deep enough the connection may give inter milder errors.

The cable used for empire tops are thickest and more expensive than the cable used width T-junctions.

The other kind of coaxial cable system uses analog transmission, a slandered cable television cabling. It is called broadband. Through the term broad comes from the telephone world, where it refers to anything wider than 4 Khz in the computer networking used "broadband" means any cable network using analog transmission.

Since broadband network used slandered cable television technology, the cables can be used up to 300 MHz and can run for nearly 100 km due to the analog signaling which is much critical than digital signaling. The transmit digits signals and analog network, each interface must certain electronics to convert the outgoing bit stream to an analog signal, and the incoming analog signal to a bit stream.

Broadband systems are normally divided into multiple channels frequently the 6-MHz channels used for television broadcasting. Each channel can be used for analog televisions high quality audio, or a digital bit stream at, say 3 Mbps, independent of other channels. Television and data can be mixed on the same cable.

One key difference between base band and broadband is that broadband systems need analog amplifiers to strengthen the signal periodically. This amplifier only transits signals in one direction so a computer outputting a packet will not be able to reach computer upstuam from it if an amplifier lies between them. To get around these problem two types of broadband systems have been developed – cable and single cable systems.

13.12.4 Fiber Optics

Recent developments in optical technology have made it possible to transmit data by pulse of light. A light pulse can be used to signal a 1 bit the absence of a pulse signals a 0 bit. Visible light has a frequency of about 10 MHz, so the bandwidth of an optical transmission system is potentially enormous.

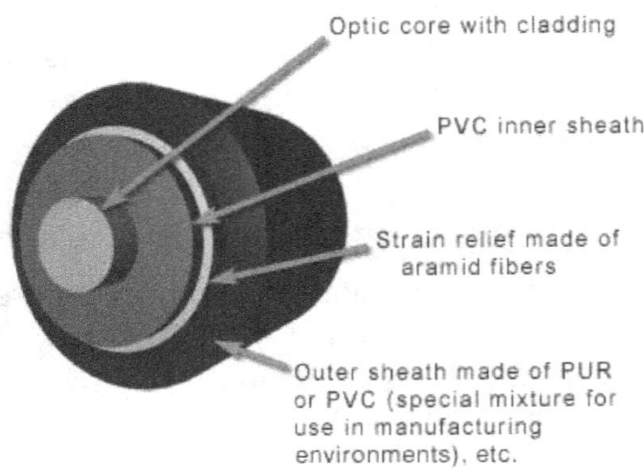

Fig. 13.19 Fiber Optics

An optical transmission system has three components – the transmission medium, the light source, and the detector. The transmission medium is an ultra thin fiber of glass or fused silica. The light source is either an LED (Light Emitting Diode) or a laser diode, which unit light pulses when an electrical current is applied. The detector is a photodiode, which generates an electrical pulse when light falls on it. By attaching an LED or laser diode to one and of an optical fiber and a photodiode to the other, we have a unidirectional data transmission system that accepts an electrical signal, converts and transmits it by light pulses and then reconverts the output to an electrical signal at the receiving ends.

This transmission system based uninteresting principle of physics. When a light way passes from one medium to another, for example from fused silica to air, is refracted at the silica air boundary. Here we see a light ray incident on the boundary at an angle $\alpha 1$ emerging at one angle $\beta 1$. The amount of refraction depends endure properties of the two media. For angles of incidence above a certain critical value the light is reflected back into the silica. Thus a light ray incident at or above the critical angle is trapped inside the fiber and can propagate for many kilometers with virtually no loss.

Fiber optics links are being installed for long distance telephone lines in many countries. Fibers can also form the basis for lanes although the technology is more complex. The basic problem is that which ampire taps can be made on fiber LAN's by fusing the incoming fiber from the computer with the LAN fiber, the process of making a tap is very tricky and substantially light is lost.

Two types of interfaces are used. A passive interface consists of two fused onto the main fiber. One tap has an LED or laser diode at the end of it and other has a photodiode. The tap itself is completely passive and is thus extremely reliable because a broken LED or photodiode does not break the ring. If one computer does not break the ring. It just takes one computer offline.

Other interface type is the active repeater. The incoming light in corrected to an electrical signal, regenerated to full strength if it has been weakened, and retransmitted as light. The interface with the computer is an ordinary copper wire that comes into the signal regenerator.

In this design each interface has a fiber running from its transmitter to a silica cylinder, with due incoming fibers fused to one end of the cylinder.

Similarly fibers fused to the other end of the cylinder are run to each of the receivers whenever an interface a light pulse, it is diffused inside the passive to start illuminate all the receivers, thus achieving broad cost. In effect the passive start performs a Boolean OR of all the incoming signals and transmits the result out on all lines.

Since the incoming energy is decided among all the outgoing lines, the number of nodes in the network is limited by the sensitivity of the photodiodes.

It is instructive to compare coaxial cable to fiber optics. Fiber provides extremely high bandwidth with little power loss; it can run for long distances without repeaters.

13.13 ISDN

For last more than a century, the primary international communication infrastructure has been the telephone system. This system was designed for analog voice transmission and is providing inadequate for modem communication needs such as data transmission facsimile and video. User demands for these and other services have led to an international undertaking to replace a major portion of the world wide telephone system with an allowanced digital system by the early part of the twenty first century. This new system, called ISDN (Integrated services digital network), has its primary goal – the integration of voice and non voice services.

Services: The key service will continue to be voice although many enhanced will be added, for example many corporate managers have an intercom button on their telephone that rings their recreations instantly. One ISDN feature is telephones with multiple buttons for instant called setup to arbitrary telephones anywhere in world. Another feature is telephones that display the caller's telephone no., name and address or a display while singing. A more sophisticated feature allows the telephone to be connected to a computer, so that the caller's database record is displayed on the screen as the call comes in.

They allow users to connect their ISDN terminal or computer to any other one in the world. At present such connections are frequently impossible internationally due to incomputable national telephone systems. Connections may also involve three or more parties, along with the possibility of a broadcast may also involve three or more Multinational Corporation sends an electronic message about changes in the retirement policy to all employers over the age of 60.

Some other feature makes it possible for a computer to use the telephone system as a private network.

13.14   OSI Reference Model

Computer network also called NETWORK. Besides physically connecting computer and communication devices, network system serves the important functions of establishing a cohesive architecture that allows a variety of equipment type of transfer information in a near-seamless fashion. A popular architecture is Open System Interconnection (OSI). It is a standard description for new messages should be transmitted between any two points in a telecommunication network.

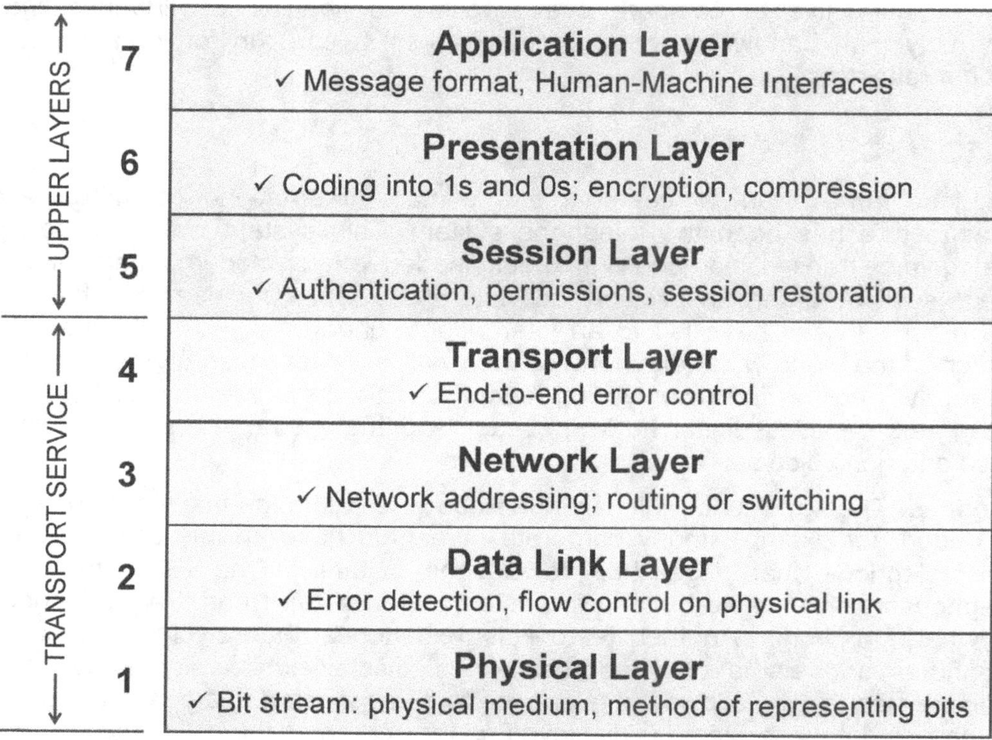

Fig. 13.20 OSI Reference Model

The main idea in OSI is that the process of communication between two and users in a telecommunication network can be divided into layers, with each layer adding its own set of special, related functions. Each communicating user is at a computer equipped with these seven layers of functions. So, in a given message between users, there will be a flow of data through each layer at one end down through the layers in that computer and at the other hand when the messages arrives another flow of data up through the layers in the receiving computer and ultimately to the end user. The actual programming and hardware that furnishes these seven layers of function is usually a combination of the computer operating system, applications.

Physical Layer (Layer-1): The Physical layer is responsible for passing bits onto and receiving them from the connecting medium. This layer conveys the bit stream through the network at the electrical and mechanical level. It provides the hardware means of sending and receiving data on a carrier. Physical layer includes hardware, wires, plugs and sockets, signal generators etc. This layer has no understanding of the meaning of the bits, but deals with the electrical and mechanical characteristic of the signals and signaling methods.

Data Link Layer (Layer-2): Also called line layer of media access. Controls access to the physical network hardware. This layer provides error control and synchronization for the physical level and does bit-stuffing for strings of is in access of 5. It furnishes transmission protocol knowledge and management. The data link is responsible for node-to-node validity and integrity of the transmission. The transmitted bits are divided into frames. The data link layer, which packages the data units into frames, is divided into two sub layers:

- LLC (Local Link Control) Top Sub layer; establishes and maintains links between communicating devices. It also responsible for frame error connection and hardware address.

- MAC (Media Access Control) Bottom sub layer; Controls how devices share a media channel. There are two main methods.

  (i) With connection, all devices attached to the network can transmit whenever they have something to communicate.

  (ii) With token passing, computers on the network cannot transmit on to the network cable until they are given a frame or token.

Network Layer (Layer-3): Network layer from individual packets from data supplied by the transport layer. The network layer establishes the route between the sending and receiving stations. The node-to-node function of the data link layer is extended across the entire internet-work, because the routable protocol contains a network address in an addition to a station addresses. This layer handles the routing of the data. This layer is the switching function of the dial-up telephone system as well as the functions performed by routable protocol such as IP. If all stations are contained within a single network segment, then the routing capability in this layer is not required.

Transport Layer (Layer–4): It is responsible for constructing streams of data packets, sending and checking for correct delivery. This layer manages the end-to-end control and error checking. It ensure complete data transfer. The transfer layer is responsible for overall end-to-end validity and integrity of the transmission. The lower data link layer is only responsible for delivering packets from one made to another. Thus, if a packet gets lost in a router somewhere in the enterprise internet, the transport layer will detect it.

Session Layer (Layer 5): This layer sets up, coordinates, and terminates conversations, exchanges and dialogs between the applications at each end. It deals with session and connection coordination. This layer manages network connections on behalf of the high-level layers.

It is responsible for 'logging in' and users authentications. It provides coordination's of the communications in an orderly manner. It determines one way or two-way communications and manages the dialogue between both parties. For example, making sure that the previous request has been fulfilled before the next one is sent. It also marks significant parts of the transmitted data with checkpoints to allow for fast recovery in the event of a connection failure.

Presentation Layer (Layer – 6): This layer defines how the system provides files and services in a uniform way to applications. This layer can in some ways be considered the function of the operating system. When data is transmitted between different types of computer system, the presentation layer negotiates and manages the way data is represented and encoded. For example, it provides a common denominator between ASCII and EBCDIC machines as well as between different floating point and binary formats. This layer is also used for encryption and decryption.

Application Layer (Layer – 7): This is largely by applications software. Applications software is that which carries out useful functions on behalf of the user. This software may well need access to network services. This top layer defines the language and syntax that program use to communicate with other programs. This application layer represents the purpose of communicating in the first place. At this layer, the communication partners are identified, quality of service is identified, user authentication and privacy are considered, and many constraints on data syntax are identified.

13.15 TCP/IP Protocol

The Internet protocol model is the networking model and a set of communications protocols. It is used for the Internet and similar networks. It is commonly known as TCP/IP, because its most important protocols are Transmission Control Protocol (TCP) and Internet Protocol (IP) were the first networking protocols defined in this standard. It is also known as the DoD model.

TCP/IP provides end-to-end connectivity specifying how data should be formatted, addressed, transmitted, routed and received at the destination. This functionality has been organized into four layers which are used to sort all related protocols according to the scope of networking involved.

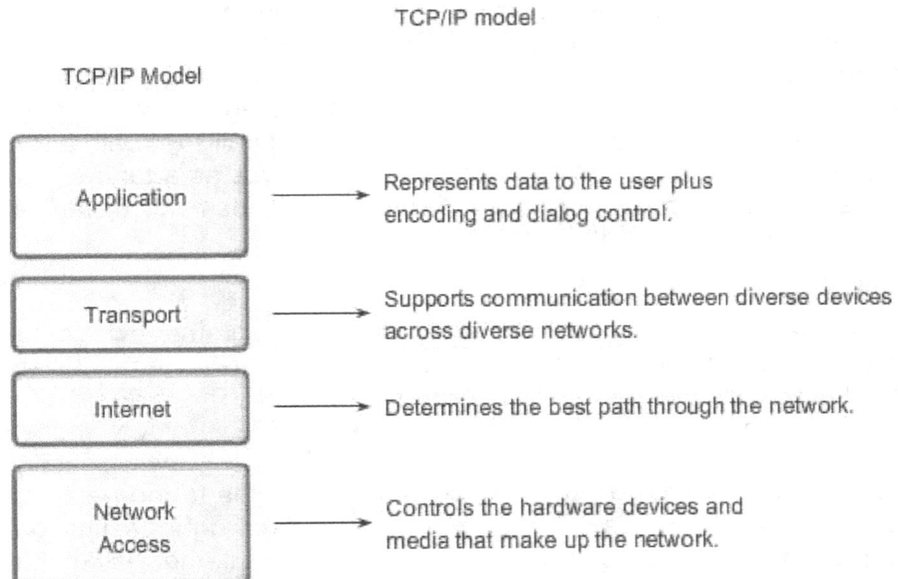

Network access

Network access, containing communication technologies for a single network segment (link), This layer defines the networking methods within the scope of the local network link on which hosts communicate without intervening routers. This layer describes the protocols used to describe the local network topology and the interfaces needed to effect transmission of Internet layer datagrams to next-neighbor hosts. This layer corresponds to the bottom two layers of the OSI model.

This layer is the networking scope of the local network. As a result TCP/IP may be implemented on top of virtually any hardware networking technology.

The Network access layer is used to move packets between the Internet layer interfaces of two different hosts on the same link. The processes of transmitting and receiving packets on a given link can be controlled both in the software device driver for the network card, as well as on firmware or specialized chipsets. These perform data link functions such as adding a packet header to prepare it for transmission, and then actually transmit the frame over a physical medium. The TCP/IP model includes specifications of translating the network addressing methods used in the Internet Protocol to data link addressing, such as Media Access Control (MAC), however all other aspects below that level are implicitly assumed to exist in the link layer, but are not explicitly defined.

This is also the layer where packets may be selected to be sent over a virtual private network or other networking tunnel. In this scenario, the network access layer data may be considered application data which traverses another instantiation of the IP stack for transmission or reception over another IP connection. Such a connection, or virtual link, may be established with a transport protocol or even an application scope protocol that serves as a tunnel in the link layer of the protocol stack. Thus, the TCP/IP model does not dictate a strict hierarchical encapsulation sequence.

Internet layer

The internet layer has the task of exchanging datagrams across network boundaries. It is therefore also referred to as the layer that establishes internetworking; it defines and establishes the Internet. This layer defines the addressing and routing structures used for the TCP/IP protocol model. The primary protocol in this scope is the Internet Protocol, which defines IP addresses. Its function in routing is to transport datagrams to the next IP router that has the connectivity to a network closer to the final data destination. This layer corresponds to the OSI Network layer. The internet layer has the responsibility of sending packets across potentially multiple networks. Internetworking requires sending data from the source network to the destination network. This process is called routing.

In the Internet protocol model, the Internet Protocol performs two basic functions:

- Host addressing and identification
- Packet routing: This is the basic task of sending packets of data (datagrams) from source to destination by forwarding them to the next network router closer to the final destination.

The internet layer is not only agnostic of application data structures at the transport layer, but it also does not distinguish between operation of the various transport layer protocols. IP can carry data for a variety of different upper layer protocols. These protocols are each identified by a unique protocol number: for example, Internet Control Message Protocol (ICMP) and Internet Group Management Protocol (IGMP) are protocols 1 and 2, respectively.

Some of the protocols carried by IP, such as ICMP which is used to transmit diagnostic information, and IGMP which is used to manage IP Multicast data, are layered on top of IP but perform internetworking functions. This illustrates the differences in the architecture of the TCP/IP stack of the Internet and the OSI model.

The internet layer provides only an unreliable datagram transmission facility between hosts located on potentially different IP networks by forwarding the transport layer datagrams to an appropriate next-hop router for further relaying to its destination. With this functionality, the internet layer makes possible internetworking, the interworking of different IP networks, and it essentially establishes the Internet. The Internet Protocol is the principal component of the internet layer, and it defines two addressing systems to identify network hosts computers, and to locate them on the network. The original address system of the ARPANET and its successor is Internet Protocol version 4 (IPv4). It uses a 32-bit IP address and is therefore capable of identifying approximately four billion hosts. This limitation was eliminated by the standardization of Internet Protocol version 6 (IPv6).

Transport layer

The transport layer constitutes the networking regime between two network hosts, either on the local network or on remote networks separated by routers. The transport layer provides a uniform networking interface that hides the actual topology (layout) of the underlying network connections. This is where flow-control, error-correction, and correction protocols exist, such as TCP. This layer deals with opening and maintaining connections between Internet hosts. This is also called Host-to-host layer. This layer corresponds to transport layer of OSI model.

The transport layer establishes a basic data channel that an application uses in its task-specific data exchange. The layer establishes host-to-host connectivity, meaning it handles the details of data transmission that are independent of the structure of user data and the logistics of exchanging information for any particular specific purpose. Its responsibility includes end-to-end message transfer independent of the underlying network, along with error control, segmentation, flow control, congestion control, and application addressing. End to end message transmission or connecting applications at the transport layer can be categorized as TCP or UDP.

Because IP provides only a best effort delivery, the transport layer is the first layer of the TCP/IP stack to offer reliability. However, IP can run over a reliable data link protocol such as the High-Level Data Link Control (HDLC).

For example, the TCP is a connection-oriented protocol that addresses numerous reliability issues in providing a reliable byte stream:

- data arrives in-order
- data has minimal error (i.e. correctness)
- duplicate data is discarded
- lost or discarded packets are resent
- includes traffic congestion control

The newer Stream Control Transmission Protocol (SCTP) is also a reliable, connection-oriented transport mechanism. It is message-stream-oriented while TCP byte-stream-oriented and provides multiple streams multiplexed over a single connection. It also provides multi-homing support, in which a connection end can be represented by multiple IP addresses (representing multiple physical interfaces), such that if one fails, the connection is not interrupted. It was developed initially for telephony applications), but can also be used for other applications.

The User Datagram Protocol is a connectionless datagram protocol. Like IP, it is a best effort, "unreliable" protocol. Reliability is addressed through error detection using a weak checksum algorithm. UDP is typically used for applications such as streaming media (audio, video, voice over IP etc.) where on-time arrival is more important than reliability.

Application layer

Application layer, which contains all protocols for specific data communications services on a process-to-process level. This is the scope within which applications create user data and communicate this data to other processes or applications on another or the same host. The communications partners are often called peers. This is where the higher level protocols such as SMTP, FTP, SSH, HTTP, etc. operate.

The application layer contains the higher-level protocols used by most applications for network communication. Examples of application layer protocols include the File Transfer Protocol (FTP) and the Simple Mail Transfer Protocol (SMTP). Data coded according to application layer protocols are then encapsulated into one or more transport layer protocols (such as TCP or UDP), which in turn use lower layer protocols to effect actual data transfer.

As the IP model does not consider the specifics of formatting and presenting data, it defines no layers between the application and transport layers as in the OSI model (presentation and session layers). Such functions are combine with the applications which often implement such functions in libraries and application programming interfaces.

Application layer protocols generally treat the transport layer protocols as black boxes which provide a stable network connection across which to communicate, although the applications are usually aware of key qualities of the transport layer connection such as the end point IP addresses and port numbers. As noted above, layers are not necessarily clearly defined in the Internet protocol suite

13.16 Web Browser

A Web browser is a software application which enables a user to display and interact with text, images, videos, music, games and other information typically located on a Web page at a Web site on the World Wide Web or a local area network. Text and images on a Web page can contain hyperlinks to other Web pages at the same or different Web site. Web browsers allow a user to quickly and easily access information provided on many Web pages at many Web sites by traversing these links. Web browsers format HTML information for display, so the appearance of a Web page may differ between browsers.

Web browsers are the most-commonly-used type of HTTP user agent. Although browsers are typically used to access the World Wide Web, they can also be used to access information provided by Web servers in private networks or content in file systems.

Web browser dates back to late 1980s, when a variety of technologies laid the foundation for the first Web browser, the WorldWideWeb, by Tim Berners-Lee in 1991. That browser brought together a variety of existing and new software and hardware technologies.

Over the following years, companies like Mozilla, Netscape, Microsoft, Apple, and Opera introduced Web browsers. More recently, Google entered in the browser market.

Some of the Web browsers currently available for personal computers include Internet Explorer, Mozilla Firefox, Safari, Opera, Avant Browser, Google Chrome, Flock, Arachne.

13.17 Internet Services

13.17.1 E-mail

Electronic Mail is a method of sending a message from a user computer to a recipient on another computer. An e-mail message consists of a header and the body of the message The first part, the header, contains the information about where the message has to be sent, and the path that has followed to reach its destination, as well as other information like date, return path, etc. The body is the actual message that is being sent. An e-mail address has the form user@subdomain. domain, e.g. ntsc@rediffmail.com

13.17.2 FTP

This facility is a method of gaining limited access to another machine in the Internet, and obtaining files from it. It need full Internet connectivity, to do FTP interactively. FTP has many advantages, for example, it allows to get new free software, or updated versions of old programs, as well as useful data for research. Technically, do not have to worry about things like machines with different operating systems (a LINUX machine can retrieve files from a SUN-OS machine with no problems), we can get and send files as big as want and binary files too.

13.17.3 Telnet

Telnet is the Internet facility that allows to execute commands on a remote host (another computer, most likely one to which do not have physical access). It need to know the name of the machine to which we want to connect, and to have a valid user name in it. There is no such thing as "anonymous" telnet. The commands for telnet are:

- Telnet hostname: it will open a connection to the host you name. For example, "telnet bce.ac.in" will connect you to the machine named bce.ac.in

- Telnet "address": it opens a connection to the host at "address".

13.17.4   WWW

The official description describes the World-Wide Web as a "wide-area *hypermedia* information retrieval initiative aiming to give universal access to a large universe of documents". The operation of the Web relies on hypertext as its means of interacting with users. Hypertext is basically the same as regular text - it can be stored, read, searched, or edited - with an important exception: hypertext contains connections within the text to other documents.

13.17.5   E-commerce

E- commerce is generally considered to be the sales aspect of e-business. It also consists of the exchange of data to facilitate the financing and payment aspects of business transactions. This is an effective and efficient way of communicating within an organization and one of the most effective and useful ways of conducting business.

E-commerce can be divided into:

Business to business (B to B)

Business to customer (B to C)

Government to government (G to G)

Government to customer (G to C)

CHAPTER 14

Computer Security

14.1 Computer Virus

A computer virus is a computer program that can copy itself and infect a computer without the permission or knowledge of the user. The term "virus" is also commonly but erroneously used to refer to other types of malware, adware and spyware programs that do not have the reproductive ability. A true virus can only spread from one computer to another (in some form of executable code) when its host is taken to the target computer; for instance because a user sent it over a network or the Internet, or carried it on a removable medium such as a floppy disk, CD, or USB drive. Viruses can increase their chances of spreading to other computers by infecting files on a network file system or a file system that is accessed by another computer.

Viruses are sometimes confused with computer worms and Trojan horses, which are technically different. A worm can spread itself to other computers without needing to be transferred as part of a host, and a Trojan horse is a program that appears harmless but has a hidden agenda. Worms and Trojans, like viruses, may cause harm to a computer system's hosted data,

Most personal computers are now connected to the Internet and to local area networks, facilitating the spread of malicious code. Today's viruses may also spread through network services such as the World Wide Web, e-mail, Instant Messaging and file sharing systems to spread, blurring the line between viruses and worms. Furthermore, some sources use an alternative terminology in which a virus is any form of self-replicating malware.

14.1.1 Classification of Viruses

Resident Viruses

This type of virus is a permanent, which dwells in the RAM memory. From there it can overcome and interrupt all of the operations executed by the system: corrupting files and programs that are opened, closed, copied, renamed etc.

Examples include: Radix, CMJ, Meve, and MrKlunky.

Direct Action Viruses

The main purpose of this virus is to replicate and take action when it is executed. When a specific condition is met, the virus will go into action and infects files in the directory or folder that it is in and in directories that are specified in the AUTOEXEC.BAT file PATH. This batch file is always located in the root directory of the hard disk and carries out certain operations when the computer is booted.

Overwrite Viruses

Virus of this kind is characterized by the fact that it deletes the information contained in the files that it infects, rendering them partially or totally useless once they have been infected. The only way to clean a file infected by an overwrite virus is to delete the file completely, thus losing the original content. Examples of this virus include: Way, Trj.Reboot, Trivial.88.D.

Boot Virus

This type of virus affects the boot sector of a floppy or hard disk. This is a crucial part of a disk, in which information on the disk itself is stored together with a program that makes it possible to boot (start) the computer from the disk. The best way of avoiding boot viruses is to ensure that floppy disks are write-protected and never start your computer with an unknown floppy disk in the disk drive. Examples of boot viruses include: Polyboot.B, AntiEXE.

Macro Virus

Macro viruses infect files that are created using certain applications or programs that contain macros. These mini-programs make it possible to automate series of operations so that they are performed as a single action, thereby saving the user from having to carry them out one by one. Examples of macro viruses: Relax, Melissa.A, Bablas, and O97M/Y2K.

Directory Virus

Directory viruses change the paths that indicate the location of a file. By executing a program (file with the extension .EXE or .COM), which has been infected by a virus, you are unknowingly running the virus program, while the virus has previously moved the original file and program. Once infected it, becomes impossible to locate the original files.

Polymorphic Virus

Polymorphic viruses encrypt or encode themselves in a different way (using different algorithms and encryption keys) every time they infect a system. This makes it impossible for anti-viruses to find them using string or signature searches (because they are different in each encryption) and also enables them to create a large number of copies of themselves. Examples include: Elkern, Marburg, Satan Bug, and Tuareg.

File Infectors

This type of virus infects programs or executable files (files with an .EXE or .COM extension). When one of these programs is run, directly or indirectly, the virus is activated, producing the damaging effects it is programmed to carry out. The majority of existing viruses belongs to this category, and can be classified depending on the actions that they carry out.

Companion Viruses

Companion viruses can be considered file infector viruses like resident or direct action types. They are known as companion viruses because once they get into the system they "accompany" the other files that already exist. In other words, in order to carry out their infection routines, companion viruses can wait in memory until a program is run (resident viruses) or act immediately by making copies of themselves (direct action viruses). Some examples include: Stator, Asimov.1439, and Terrax.1069

FAT Virus

The file allocation table or FAT is the part of a disk used to connect information and is a vital part of the normal functioning of the computer. This type of virus attack can be especially dangerous, by preventing access to certain sections of the disk where important files are stored. Damage caused can result in information losses from individual files or even entire directories.

14.1.2   Effects of Viruses

We are always afraid that viruses do something harmful to files when they get active, but not all the viruses activate. Some viruses just spread out, but when viruses activate they do very different things. Might play a part of melody or play music in the background, show a picture or animated picture, show text, format hard disk or do changes to files.

An example, in one unnamed company: over a long period of time, the files in a server were corrupted just a bit. So backup copies were taken from the corrupted files. And after they noticed that something was wrong, it was too late to get back the data from the backups. That kind of event is the worst that can happen for the uses.

There is also talk that viruses have done something to hardware like hard disk or monitor. Viruses cannot do any harm to hardware but they can do harm to programs and for example to BIOS so that computer does not start after that.

14.1.3   Detection of Virus

In order to avoid detection by users, some viruses employ different kinds of deception. Some old viruses, especially on the MS-DOS platform, make sure that the last modified date of a host file stays the same when the virus infects the file. This approach does not fool anti-virus software, however, especially those, which maintain and date cyclic redundancy checks on file changes.

Some viruses can infect files without increasing their sizes or damaging the files. They accomplish this by overwriting unused areas of executable files. These are called *cavity viruses*. For example the CIH virus, or Chernobyl Virus, infects Portable Executable files. Because those files have many empty gaps, the virus, which was 1 KB in length, did not add to the size of the file.

Some viruses try to avoid detection by killing the tasks associated with antiviral software before it can detect them. As computers and operating systems grow larger and more complex, old hiding techniques need to be updated or replaced. Defending a computer against viruses may demand that a file system migrate towards detailed and explicit permission for every kind of file access.

14.1.4   Avoiding Bait Files and other Undesirable Hosts

A virus needs to infect hosts in order to spread further. In some cases, it might be a bad idea to infect a host program. For example, many anti-virus programs perform an integrity check of their own code. Infecting such programs will therefore increase the likelihood that the virus is detected. For this reason, some viruses are programmed not to infect programs that are known to be part of anti-virus software. Another type of host that viruses sometimes avoid is *a bait file*. Bait files (or *goat files*) are files that are specially created by anti-virus software, or by anti-virus professionals themselves, to be infected by a virus. These files can be created for various reasons, all of which are related to the detection of the virus:

- Anti-virus professionals can use bait files to take a sample of a virus (i.e. a copy of a program file that is infected by the virus). It is more practical to store and exchange a small, infected bait file, than to exchange a large application program that has been infected by the virus.

- Anti-virus professionals can use bait files to study the behavior of a virus and evaluate detection methods. This is especially useful when the virus is polymorphism. In this case, the virus can be made to infect a large number of bait files. The infected files can be used to test whether a virus scanner detects all versions of the virus.

- Some anti-virus software employs bait files that are accessed regularly. When these files are modified, the anti-virus software warns the user that a virus is probably active on the system.

Since bait files are used to detect the virus, or to make detection possible, a virus can benefit from not infecting them. Viruses typically do this by avoiding suspicious programs, such as small program files or programs that contain certain patterns of 'garbage instructions'.

A related strategy to make baiting difficult is *sparse infection*. Sometimes, sparse infectors do not infect a host file that would be a suitable candidate for infection in other circumstances. For example, a virus can decide on a random basis whether to infect a file or not, or a virus can only infect host files on particular days of the week.

1. **Stealth:** Some viruses try to trick anti-virus software by intercepting its requests to the operating system. A virus can hide itself by intercepting the anti-virus software's request to read the file and passing the request to the virus, instead of the OS. The virus can then return an uninfected version of the file to the anti-virus software, so that it seems that the file is clean. Modern anti-virus software employs various techniques to counter stealth mechanisms of viruses. The only completely reliable method to avoid stealth is to boot from a medium that is known to be clean.

2. **Self-modification:** Most modern antiviral programs try to find virus-patterns inside ordinary programs by scanning them for so-called *virus signatures*. A signature is a characteristic byte-pattern that is part of a certain virus or family of viruses. If a virus scanner finds such a pattern in a file, it notifies the user that the file is infected. The user can then delete, or (in some cases) clean or heal the infected file. Some viruses employ techniques that make detection by means of signatures difficult but probably not impossible. These viruses modify their code on each infection. That is, each infected file contains a different variant of the virus.

3. **Encryption with a variable key:** A more advanced method is the use of simple encryption to encipher the virus. In this case, the virus consists of a small decrypting module and an encrypted copy of the virus code. If the virus is encrypted with a different key for each infected file, the only part of the virus that remains constant is the decrypting module, which would (for example) be appended to the end. In this case, a virus scanner cannot directly detect the virus using signatures, but it can still detect the decrypting module, which still makes indirect detection of the virus possible. Since these would be symmetric keys, stored on the infected host, it is in fact entirely possible to decrypt the final virus, but that probably isn't required, since self-modifying code is such a rarity that it may be reason for virus scanners to at least flag the file as suspicious.

An old, but compact, encryption involves <u>XORing</u> each byte in a virus with a constant, so that the exclusive-OR operation had only to be repeated for decryption. It is suspicious code that modifies itself, so the code to do the encryption/decryption may be part of the signature in many virus definitions.

1. **Polymorphism code:** Polymorphism code was the first technique that posed a serious threat to virus scanners. Just like regular encrypted viruses, a polymorphism virus infects files with an encrypted copy of it, which is decoded by a decryption module. In the case of polymorphism viruses, however, this decryption module is also modified on each infection. A well-written polymorphism virus therefore has no parts, which remain identical between infections, making it very difficult to detect directly using signatures. Anti-virus software can detect it by decrypting the viruses using an emulator, or by statistical pattern analysis of the encrypted virus body. To enable polymorphism code, the virus has to have a polymorphism engine (also called mutating engine or mutation engine) somewhere in its encrypted body.

   Some viruses employ polymorphism code in a way that constrains the mutation rate of the virus significantly. For example, a virus can be programmed to mutate only slightly over time, or it can be programmed to refrain from mutating when it infects a file on a computer that already contains copies of the virus. The advantage of using such slow polymorphism code is that it makes it more difficult for anti-virus professionals to obtain representative samples of the virus, because bait files that are infected in one run will typically contain identical or similar samples of the virus. This will make it more likely that the detection by the virus scanner will be unreliable, and that some instances of the virus may be able to avoid detection.

2. **Metamorphic code:** To avoid being detected by emulation, some viruses rewrite themselves completely each time they are to infect new executables. Viruses that use this technique are said to be metamorphic. To enable metamorphism, a metamorphic engine is needed. A metamorphic virus is usually very large and complex. For example, W32/Simile consisted of over 14000 lines of Assembly language code, 90% of which is part of the metamorphic engine.

14.2 Anti-virus Software

Many users install anti-virus software that can detect and eliminate known viruses after the computer downloads or runs the executable. There are two common methods that an anti-virus software application uses to detect viruses. The first, and by far the most common method of virus detection are using a list of virus signature definitions. This works by examining the content of the computer's memory (its RAM, and boot sectors) and the files stored on fixed or removable drives (hard drives, floppy drives), and comparing those files against a database of known virus signatures. The disadvantage of this detection method is that users are only protected from viruses that pre-date their last virus definition update. The second method is to use a heuristic algorithm to find viruses based on common behaviors. This method has the ability to detect viruses that anti-virus security firms have yet to create a signature for.

Some anti-virus programs are able to scan opened files in addition to sent and received e-mails on the fly in a similar manner. This practice is known as on-access scanning. Anti-virus software does not change the underlying capability of host software to transmit viruses. Users must update their software regularly to patch security holes. Anti-virus software also needs to be regularly updated in order to prevent the latest threats.

One may also minimize the damage done by viruses by making regular backups of data (and the Operating Systems) on different media, that are either kept unconnected to the system (most of the time), read-only or not accessible for other reasons, such as using different file systems. This way, if data is lost through a virus, one can start again using the backup (which should preferably be recent). A notable exception to this rule is the Gammima virus, which propagates via infected removable media. If a backup session on optical media like CD and DVD is closed, it becomes read-only and can no longer be affected by a virus (so long as a virus or infected file was not copied onto the CD/DVD). Likewise, an Operating System on a bootable can be used to start the computer if the installed Operating Systems become unusable. Another method is to use different Operating Systems on different file systems. A virus is not likely to affect both. Data backups can also be put on different file systems. For example, Linux requires specific software to write to NTFS partitions, so if one does not install such software and uses a separate installation of MS Windows to make the backups on an NTFS partition, the backup should remain safe from any Linux viruses. Likewise, MS Windows cannot read file systems like ext3, so if one normally uses MS Windows, the backups can be made on an ext3 partition using a Linux installation.

Recovery methods

Once a virus has compromised a computer, it is usually unsafe to continue using the same computer without completely reinstalling the operating system. However, there are a number of recovery options that exist after a computer has a virus. These actions depend on severity of the type of virus.

14.3 Virus Removal

One possibility on Windows, Windows XP and Windows Vista is a tool known as System Restore, which restores the registry and critical system files to a previous checkpoint. Often a virus will cause a system to hang, and a subsequent hard reboot will render a system restore point from the same day corrupt. Restore points from previous days should work provided the virus is not designed to corrupt the restore files or also exists in previous restore points. Some viruses, however, disable system restore and other important tools such as Task Manager and Command Prompt. An example of a virus that does this is CIA Door.

Administrators have the option to disable such tools from limited users for various reasons. The virus modifies the registry to do the same, except, when the Administrator is controlling the computer, it blocks *all* users from accessing the tools. When an infected tool activates it gives the message Task Manager has been disabled by your administrator. even if the user trying to open the program is the administrator.

Users running a Microsoft operating system can access Microsoft's website to run a free scan, provided they have their 20-digit registration number.

14.3.1 Operating System Reinstallation

Reinstalling the operating system is another approach to virus removal. It involves simply reformatting the OS partition and installing the OS from its original media, or imaging the partition with a clean backup image This method has the benefits of being simple to do, being faster than running multiple antiviral scans, and is guaranteed to remove any malware. Downsides include having to reinstall all other software (And reconfiguring them to user preference) as well as the operating system. User data can be backed up by booting off of a Live CD or putting the hard drive into another computer and booting from the other computer's operating system.

14.4 Trojan

A Trojan horse is a program that does something else that the user thought it would do. It is mostly done to someone on purpose. The Trojan Horses are usually masked so that they look interesting, for example a saxophone.wav file that interests a person collecting sound samples of instruments. A Trojan horse differs from a destructive virus in that it doesn't reproduce. There has been a password Trojan out in AOL land (the American on Line). Password30 and Pasword50, which some people thought, were wav. Files, but they were disguised and people did not know that they had the Trojan in their systems until they tried to change their passwords.

According to an administrator of AOL, the Trojan steals passwords and sends E-mail to the hacker's fake name and then the hacker has your account in his hands.

14.5 Worms

A worm is a program, which spreads usually over network connections. Unlike a virus, which attaches itself to a host program, worms always need a host program to spread. In practice, worms are not normally associated with one-person computer systems. They are mostly found in multi-user systems such as UNIX environments. A classic example of a worm is Robert Morris's Internet-worm 1988.

14.6 Macro Virus

Macro viruses spread from applications, which use macros. The macro viruses, which are receiving attention currently, are specific to Word 6, WordBasic and Excel. However, many applications, not all of them Windows applications, have potentially damaging and infective macro capabilities too.

A CAP macro virus, now widespread, infects macros attached to Word 6.0 for Windows, Word 6.0.1 for Macintosh, Word 6.0 for Windows NT, and Word for Windows 95 documents. What makes such a virus possible is that the macros are created by Word BASIC and even allows DOS commands to be run. Word BASIC in a program language, which links features used in Word to macros.

A virus, named Concept, has no destructive payload; it merely spreads, after a document containing the virus is opened. Concept copies itself to other documents when they are saved, without affecting the contents of documents. Since then, however, other macro viruses have been discovered, and some of them contain destructive routines. Microsoft suggests opening files without macros to prevent macro viruses from spreading, unless the user can verify that the macros contained in the document will not cause damage. This does NOT work for all macro viruses.

14.7 Difference between a Virus and a Worm

A virus is parasitic code that attaches to another programmed, such a visual basic (vbs files) or an executable (.exe). A worm does not attach itself to other programmes and spreads without any user interaction. It is a technical distinction that does not really matter to the average computer user.

14.8 Spyware

It is software that aids in gathering information about a person or organization without their knowledge and that may send such information to another entity without the consumer's consent, or that asserts control over a computer without the consumer's knowledge."Spyware" is mostly classified into four types: system monitors, trojans, adware, and tracking cookies. Spyware is mostly used for the purposes such as; tracking and storing internet users' movements on the web; serving up pop-up ads to internet users.

Whenever spyware is used for malicious purposes, its presence is typically hidden from the user and can be difficult to detect. Some spyware, such as keyloggers, may be installed by the owner of a shared, corporate, or public computer intentionally in order to monitor users.

While the term *spyware* suggests software that monitors a user's computing, the functions of spyware can extend beyond simple monitoring. Spyware can collect almost any type of data, including personal information like Internet surfing habits, user logins, and bank or credit account information. Spyware can also interfere with user control of a computer by installing additional software or redirecting Web browsers. Some spyware can change computer settings, which can result in slow Internet connection speeds, un-authorized changes in browser settings, or changes to software settings. Sometimes, spyware is included along with genuine software, and may come from a malicious website.

14.8.1 Antispyware Software

Antispyware software helps protect your computer against pop-ups, slow performance, and security threats caused by spyware and other unwanted software. To keep up with the latest forms of spyware, must keep our antispyware software updated. In response to the emergence of spyware, a small industry has sprung up dealing in anti-spyware software. Running anti-spyware software has become a widely recognized element of computer security practices for computers, especially those running Microsoft Windows. A number of jurisdictions have passed anti-spyware laws, which usually target any software that is surreptitiously installed to control a user's computer.

- Many kinds of unwanted software, including spyware, are designed to be difficult to remove. If we try to uninstall this software like any other program, might find that the program reappears as soon as restart the computer.

- Windows 7 and Windows Vista include antispyware software called Windows Defender. To help fight both viruses and spyware, you can download Microsoft Security Essentials at no cost. If download Microsoft

Security Essentials, Windows Defender will be disabled automatically. Make sure to uninstall any other antivirus software on computer first.

- Windows 8 includes antivirus and antispyware software called Windows Defender. Windows Defender for Windows 8 replaces Microsoft Security Essentials. It runs in the background and notifies you when you need to take specific action. If install a different antivirus program, Windows Defender will be disabled automatically

14.9   Information Theft

There have been a growing number of cases of information theft over the past few years. While more and more electronic security measures have been going up to protect people's possessions and information, these new technologies have bugs and design flaws that are opening up whole new worlds for the technologically advanced criminal.

14.9.1 Credit Card Number Theft

People are using credit cards for more and more of their purchases as time goes on. This is opening up a larger and larger arena for credit card fraud. Credit cards are especially easy to use fraudulently, because they require no extra identification number to use. All that a thief needs is pure information – they don't need the card, but just the number on the card. Recently, with people spending more on purchases transacted over the internet, credit card fraud is becoming easier. Now thieves never have to get within 5,000 miles of the people they are stealing from. All they would need is a quick and dirty web site (which could be hosted for free, and anonymously) advertising some fictional product, and including a form for buying online. Instantly the perpetrators would have a list of credit card numbers linked with names and mailing addresses, ready to use for anything they want.

14.9.2   ATM Spoofing

These crooks have pulled some impressively intricate heists. One group of criminals set up a complete fake ATM machine inside a mall in Connecticut. It looked and worked just like a real one, except that after giving it your card and typing in your pin, it would refuse service saying it was out of order. It then had a record of the card and PIN numbers of all the people who tried to use the machine. The thieves then used legitimate ATM machines all over town to withdraw the amounts.

14.9.3   PIN Capturing

Another group of criminals scoured the area across the street from a busy ATM, looking for the perfect spot to hide a video camera aimed at the keys on the ATM machine. They found such a spot and set up their camera. After each successful PIN number identification that they recorded, one of the group members would go check for a discarded receipt at the ATM. If they found one, the group had the card number and the PIN number.

14.9.4   Database Theft

The previous criminal activities are all aimed at compiling databases of information obtained fraudulently from people one by one. This takes time, and these people only have limited amounts of time before their operations will be recognized and shut down. This limits the number of people whose information these criminals can obtain. There are, however, large databases of this kind of information that have been built up slowly and legally by mild-mannered, legitimate internet companies. For example, BMG Music Service lets customers give their credit card numbers when they sign up, so they don't need to bother each time they make a purchase. There are thousands of users of this service, many of whom likely use this feature. Combine this with the fact that hundreds of computer systems are hacked into every day, and we have a situation where hackers could steal an industrial-sized database of this kind of information, and run wild.

14.9.5   Electronic Cash

We are already well on the way to a cash-free society. People now use ATM cards, credit cards, and check-cards for a large percentage of their purchasing. As we move further from a paper-money society, to a purely electronic economy, new types of crime will emerge. What types exactly will depend on what new forms of security tomorrow's criminals will need to break. Will people be synthesizing voice authorizations? Or running replay attacks on retinal scanners? Or even learning to imitate a victim's typing style. All we can be sure of, is that criminals of tomorrow, like those of last century and those of today, will keep on innovating.

14.10 Spoofing

Spoofing is also an illegal online activity which involves intrusion masquerading a genuine user. In this activity a hacker enters in to a distant computer illegally without any authorization, using a different identity than his original one. This is possible when hacker has already obtained actual password somehow. The hacker then creates a new user by misguiding computer to think that the hacker is a genuine person to do that. Thus after that, the hacker over takes the control of the system and can perform a number frauds using the fake identity the hacker created.

For Ex: You can get a mail on the name your bank saying that due to security reasons required to change your password for net banking account. Mostly, these mails warn you for negative consequences if ignored.

Spoof websites and e mails are also a form online fraud and are resulted by technical expertise. In this, a fake website is created which looks like an authentic website, but actually that's a spoof. The purpose of creating such website is to make the user enter personal information and details of his account. Then this information is used to login business and bank accounts of that user. They get traffic to their spoof by shooting spam e mails which misleads them to enter their username and passwords which gets updated to the hacker's server. And thus commit illegal financial transaction making the owner go bankrupt. Be careful to keep ourself away from any such fraud or scam.

14.11 Hacking

Hacking not many of us must be aware that what the word hacker initially meant. Hacker was used for an exceptionally talented programmer. However, these days it is largely used for people practicing unauthorized and unethical use of internet and other network resources. Hacking is considered a crime in most of the countries. It is a punishable offence. However, there are times when the police or investigation teams require the help of hackers to solve a case. Hacking done for such a purpose is not regarded as unauthorized. These hackers are given authorization to look into the details of the person in question.

Hacking is done via network programming. Hackers prepare programs to break network codes and passwords. If you would have tried breaking these codes until a few years ago, you wouldn't have been successful in doing so if you didn't possess enough programming knowledge. However, the hacking methods have evolved over the years and no longer required to have extensive knowledge about network programming in order to accomplish this task. With the hacking methods becoming easier and tools getting cheaper, cyber crime is on the rise.

It has been noted that hackers have hacked millions of computers across the globe and the number is increasing with every passing day. While some hackings are done just for fun others are done for stealing information yet others are done for personal reasons such as taking revenge from someone and so on. The latest Twitter attack is said to be a political battle to hush the critics. The motive of such hackers has never been noble. Stealing someone's personal data for own use, breaking through into a company's account and making changes in their database, accessing someone's network and hacking for several other similar reasons is a punishable offence but this does not stop these notorious hackers from indulging into such activities.

Many hackers practicing unauthorized hacking have been caught and given severe punishments while many of them have also been able to escape leaving the victims even more distressed.

There are certain things that a person must keep in mind in order to reduce the chances of hacking. One thing that a computer user should do is to set a good firewall. It helps in protecting the PC from hackers to a great extent. It is also recommended to check the various software programs for updates from time to time as you may come across security updates which are helpful in protecting PC. It is also said that Java Support has some loopholes and gives easy access to the hackers. Therefore, it is recommended to turn it off the Java Support in browser.

Unauthorised hacking is a threat for the society ethical hacking helps in various ways. The ethical hackers are hired for assistance in investigations. They are also hired to cover up online fraud. For instance there are times when banks need to hire them in order to hide the activities of notorious hackers from the customers. These activities may include stealing someone's ATM or net banking pin. Till the time the bankers sort out the issues they take help from hackers to hide this fact from the customers so as to avoid any kind of panic amongst them. Thus, hacking can be helpful if done for a noble cause.

14.12 Pornography

Pornography is illegal in India but there is no particular definition of it. Indian government has made many attempts to combat pornography and limit the obscene content on the internet. Law governing body all across the globe has not got any success. Pornography has different formats and all formats are openly available on internet. Though, the constitution of India grants the permission of speech and expression as per the fundamental rights of Indian citizens, but a new law prohibits the obscenity and states that it is against the law.

14.12.1 Child Pornography

It is a very inhuman and serious cyber crime offence. Internet is the most frequently used tool for such criminals to reach children and practice child sex abuse. The spreading use internet and its easy accessibility to children has made them viable victim to cyber crime. There is a type of humans called Pedophiles who usually allure the children by obscene pornographic contents and then they approach them for sex. Then they take their naked photographs while having sex. Such people sometime misguide children telling them that they are of the same age and win their confidence. Then they exploit the children either by forcing them to have sex or selling their pictures over internet.

14.12.2 Caution

- Never share any personal information such as your address, contact number or location of your school or college.
- Inform your guardian if you come across any strange situation or activity
- Never send any photograph to any unknown person and without parent's permission
- Never respond to any dirty or threatening messages.
- Do not open website they have any warning message on browser while opening
- Never agree to meet someone while chatting on internet whom you do not know in real
- Do not share you internet or Wi-Fi password with anyone

14.13 Firewall

A **firewall** is software or hardware-based network security system that controls the incoming and outgoing network traffic by analyzing the data packets and determining whether they should be allowed through or not, based on a rule set. A firewall establishes a barrier between a trusted, secure internal network and another network that is not assumed to be secure and trusted.

Many personal computer operating systems include software-based firewalls to protect against threats from the public Internet. Many routers that pass data between networks contain firewall components and, conversely, many firewalls can perform basic routing functions.

14.13.1 Types

There are different types of firewalls depending on where the communication is taking place, where the communication is intercepted and the state that is being traced.

Network layer or packet filters

Network layer firewalls, also called packet filters, operate at a relatively low level of the TCP/IP protocol stack, not allowing packets to pass through the firewall unless they match the established rule set. The firewall administrator may define the rules; or default rules may apply.

Network layer firewalls generally fall into two sub-categories, stateful and stateless. Stateful firewalls maintain context about active sessions, and use that "state information" to speed packet processing. Any existing network connection can be described by several properties, including source and destination IP address, UDP or TCP ports, and the current stage of the connection's lifetime (including session initiation, handshaking, data transfer, or completion connection). If a packet does not match an existing connection, it will be evaluated according to the rule set for new connections. If a packet matches an existing connection based on comparison with the firewall's state table, it will be allowed to pass without further processing.

Stateless firewalls require less memory, and can be faster for simple filters that require less time to filter than to look up a session. They may also be necessary for filtering stateless network protocols that have no concept of a session. However, they cannot make more complex decisions based on what stage communications between hosts have reached.

Modern firewalls can filter traffic based on many packet attributes like source IP address, source port, destination IP address or port, destination service like WWW or FTP. They can filter based on protocols, TTL values, net block of originator, of the source, and many other attributes.

Application-layer

Application-layer firewalls work on the application level of the TCP/IP stack (i.e., all browser traffic, or telnet or ftp), and may intercept all packets traveling to or from an application. They block other packets (usually dropping them without acknowledgment to the sender).

On inspecting all packets for improper content, firewalls can restrict or prevent outright the spread of networked computer worms and Trojans. The additional inspection criteria can add extra latency to the forwarding of packets to their destination.

Application firewalls function by determining whether a process should accept any given connection. Application firewalls accomplish their function by hooking into socket calls to filter the connections between the application layer and the lower layers of the OSI model. Application firewalls that hook into socket calls are also referred to as socket filters. Application firewalls work much like a packet filter but application filters apply filtering rules on a per process basis instead of filtering connections on a per port basis. Generally, prompts are used to define rules for processes that have not yet received a connection. It is rare to find application firewalls not combined or used in conjunction with a packet filter.

Also, application firewalls further filter connections by examining the process ID of data packets against a rule set for the local process involved in the data transmission. The extent of the filtering that occurs is defined by the provided rule set. Given the variety of software that exists, application firewalls only have more complex rule sets for the standard services, such as sharing services. These per process rule sets have limited efficacy in filtering every possible association that may occur with other processes. Also, these per process rule sets cannot defend against modification of the process via exploitation, such as memory corruption exploits

Proxies

A proxy may act as a firewall by responding to input packets in the manner of an application, while blocking other packets. A proxy server is a gateway from one network to another for a specific network application, in the sense that it functions as a proxy on behalf of the network user.

Proxies make tampering with an internal system from the external network more difficult and misuse of one internal system would not necessarily cause a security breach exploitable from outside the firewall. Conversely, intruders may hijack a publicly reachable system and use it as a proxy for their own purposes; the proxy then masquerades as that system to other internal machines. While use of internal address spaces enhances security, crackers may still employ methods such as IP spoofing to attempt to pass packets to a target network.

Network address translation

Firewalls often have network address translation (NAT) functionality, and the hosts protected behind a firewall commonly have addresses in the "private address range", as defined in RFC 1918. Firewalls often have such functionality to hide the true address of protected hosts. Originally, the NAT function was developed to address the limited number of IPv4 routable addresses that could be used or assigned to companies or individuals as well as reduce both the amount and therefore cost of obtaining enough public addresses for every computer in an organization. Hiding the addresses of protected devices has become an increasingly important defense against network reconnaissance.

14.14 Cyber Law in India

Provides legal recognition to electronic documents and a framework to support e-filing and e-commerce transactions and also provides a legal framework to mitigate, check cyber crimes.

- IT Act 2000

- IT(Amendment) Act, 2008

14.15 Computer Ethics

Ethics deals with placing a "**value**" on acts according to whether they are "**good**" or "**bad**". Every society has its rules about whether certain acts are ethical or not. These rules have been established as a result of consensus in society and are often written into laws.

When computers first began to be used in society at large, the absence of ethical standards about their use and related issues caused some problems. However, as their use became widespread in every facet of our lives, discussions in **computer ethics** resulted in some kind of a consensus. Today, many of these rules have been formulated as laws, either national or international. **Computer crimes** and **computer fraud** are now common terms. There are laws against them, and everyone is responsible for knowing what constitutes computer crime and computer fraud.

Computer Ethics Institute has defined **Ten Commandments of computer ethics**

1. **Computer should not use to harm other people:** If it is unethical to harm people by making a bomb, for example, it is equally bad to write a

program that handles the timing of the bomb. Or, to put it more simply, if it is bad to steal and destroy other people's books and notebooks, it is equally bad to access and destroy their files.

2. **Should not interfere with other people's computer work:** Computer **viruses** are small programs that disrupt other people's computer work by destroying their files, taking huge amounts of computer time or memory, or by simply displaying annoying messages. Generating and consciously spreading computer viruses is unethical.

3. **Should not snoop around in other people's files:** Reading other people's e-mail messages is as bad as opening and reading their letters: This is invading their privacy. Obtaining other people's non-public files should be judged the same way as breaking into their rooms and stealing their documents. Text documents on the Internet may be protected by **encryption**.

4. **Should not use a computer to steal:** Using a computer to break into the accounts of a company or a bank and transferring money should be judged the same way as robbery. It is illegal and there are strict laws against it.

5. **Should not use a computer to bear false witness:** The Internet can spread untruth as fast as it can spread truth. Putting out false "information" to the world is bad. For instance, spreading false rumors about a person or false propaganda about historical events is wrong.

6. **Should not use or copy software for which you have not paid:** Software is an intellectual product. In that way, it is like a book: Obtaining illegal copies of copyrighted software is as bad as photocopying a copyrighted book. There are laws against both. Information about the copyright owner can be embedded by a process called **watermarking** into pictures in the digital format.

7. **Should not use other people's computer resources without authorization:** Multiuser systems use **user id's** and **passwords** to enforce their memory and time allocations, and to safeguard information. You should not try to bypass this authorization system. **Hacking** a system to break and bypass the authorization is unethical.

8. **Should not appropriate other people's intellectual output:** For example, the programs you write for the projects assigned in this course are your own intellectual output. Copying somebody else's program

without proper authorization is **software piracy** and is unethical. **Intellectual property** is a form of ownership, and may be protected by copyright laws.

9. **Should think about the social consequences of the program you write:** You have to think about computer issues in a more general social framework: Can the program you write be used in a way that is harmful to society? For example, if you are working for an animation house, and are producing animated films for children, you are responsible for their contents. Do the animations include scenes that can be harmful to children? In the United States, the **Communications Decency Act** was an attempt by lawmakers to ban certain types of content from Internet websites to protect young children from harmful material. That law was struck down because it violated the free speech principles in that country's constitution. The discussion, of course, is going on.

10. **Should use a computer in ways that show consideration and respect:** Just like public buses or banks, people using computer communications systems may find themselves in situations where there is some form of queuing and you have to wait for your turn and generally be nice to other people in the environment. The fact that you cannot see the people you are interacting with does not mean that you can be rude to them.

CHAPTER 15

Data Base Management System

15.1 Introduction

We start learning programming with small programs where all effort is put in developing logic. In initial learning programs, data is very small. Every time program is run just enter the data through key board and see the output on computer Monitor. When start writing serious programs, input data size starts increasing. Sometimes, even output may become so large that to store output in a file in a secondary storage to be browsed later.

Most high level programming languages provide file handling capability. One can store input data in a file and program can read input data from this file available on secondary storage. The advantage is, input data can be stored on to a file once for all. Program when executed can read data from file, there is no need to feed data through keyboard every time, while executing program. If program output is large, the output can be sent to a file. This output file can be opened in a suitable editor and browsed as and when required.

Most of the application programs involve huge data handling. Consider, University Result Processing Application and imagine how much data handling is required. Large number of student's record is to be handled while storing data into a secondary storage. There are many things to be taken care besides manipulating data. There are requirements of keeping data to be secured. It should never be lost or corrupted.

Try to relate this with an online banking application. Can afford if banker says, "Sir, we don't have details of your deposits, our data is lost due to x, y or z reason". You disapprove any logic given by the banker; you want your money and deposit details. Similarly, unauthorized access to the database is to be prevented at any cost. There are many such challenges that DBMS handles reliably.

It is not that the programming languages cannot handle above situations. We know logic is powerful and a computer program can accomplice this task. But if all these features are implemented through a conventional programming language using file system, each time a lot of programming effort is needed.

343

Work of the programmers have been eased by partitioning applications software into two broad layers, namely application programe layer and data base layer.

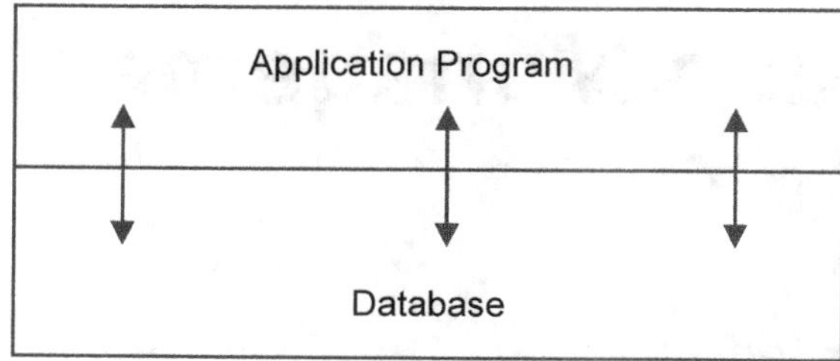

Programmer has the responsibility of developing application programs. Database layer is implemented using DBMS software. DBMS software takes all responsibilities of handling huge data with ease.

15.2 Limitations of File System to Handle Database

Initially, database applications were built on top of file systems. High level programming language COBOL was well suited to develop business applications that involved large databases. However there were many issues that limited the application development to a wider range. Modern applications make use of data in multi user environment across locations. These applications pose appalling challenges maintaining databases. Following are the main areas where DBMS provides explicit support where as files systems do not. These issues are summarised below.

1. **Data redundancy and inconsistency:** Data redundancy relates to data duplication. Duplication of data may give rise to data inconsistency. If some data is stored at multiple locations there are chances that data values differ due to updates over the time and data inconsistency may arise. Data inconsistency if it occurs shall make the data unreliable.

2. **Difficulty in accessing data:** File system poses the need to write a new program to carry out each new task. Need for storing separately for different programs should be minimized. Different programs should have easy access to common data.

3. **Data isolation:** Isolation requires that multiple transactions occurring at the same time do not impact each other's execution.

4. **Integrity problems:** Putting integrity constraints on data like account balance > 0 or a roll number has to be numeric, become part of program code. On us lies as programmer to impose integrity constraints to maintain the integrity of database. In dynamic environment it is difficult for the programmer to add new constraints or change existing ones.

the integrity of database. In dynamic environment it is difficult for the programmer to add new constraints or change existing ones.

5. **Atomicity of transactions:** While executing transaction, a midterm failures may leave database in an inconsistent state with partial updates carried out. For example transfer of funds from one account to another should either be complete or should not happen at all. Otherwise there is a possibility that payers account debits and receiver do not get the money. DBMS provides the facility of rolling back or undo incomplete transactions.

6. **Concurrent access by multiple users:** Concurrent access is a big challenge to handle in modern applications. In a rail reservation scenario, if one seat is left and many people see this across the globe through rail reservation software, the allocation is to be handled carefully. To these type of situations of concurrent access of data, file systems do not provide support.

7. **Security problems:** Data should be safe and secure. It should be safe against technical faults and even natural calamity should not destroy the data.

8. **Data Privacy:** Preventing data from unauthorized access.

15.3 Need of Data Modeling

For better understanding of the concepts of data models, we next present a scenario in an example, which we will refer in all future discussions

Example: Let us consider database requirements for an online shopping web application. Information is to be stored regarding **Products** being sold. There are **customers** who place the **Orders**. A **Shipment** is dispatched for each **Order**. Of course, **stock** position of Products is to be maintained.

There are relationships between these real world entities or objects shown in bold. For example, each **customer** can purchase one or more **Products**. Each **Product** can be sold to one or more **customers**. For each **Product** a **stock** entry is maintained. For each **Order** a **Shipment** is sent and Shipment is tracked for its delivery. Each **Order** is for one or more Products. Each **Order** is related with one specific **customer**.

In a real world scenario there will be many more entities and numerous such relationships.

Additionally, there will be requirements of putting constraints or restrictions on data. For example, while maintaining stock position of '**Products**', the available quantity should never become less than zero.

If the above scenario is, for a business which is not online and operates for home delivery, and people place order on phone or personally. All the information to run this business shall be on typical physical files and registers to maintain records. There will be a file of Orders that have been received from vendors. There will be some stock register to maintain stock position. When we think of developing web based application software for this scenario, we need a database. Information about the entities, their relationships and business rules about data are required to be known for creation of a good reliable database. When a house is constructed, a map is prepared by the architect and material requirements are calculated. Similarly, a data model is needed for creation of a database.

In summary, we need data models because Data models

- provide a collection of tools for representing data relationships, data semantics and data constraints

- represent real world data in conceptual form

- provide relatively simple representations, usually graphical, of complex real-world data

- facilitate interaction among the designer, the programmer, and the end user

- facilitate different end-users views and needs for data

- facilitate to organize data for various users

15.4 Data Models

Building up a database requires a frame work or tools for describing data, data relationships, data semantics, and data constraints. Data models provide a collection of tools for representing data relationships, data semantics and data constraints.

History of DBMS begins in late 1960s. Since then many data models have been proposed and on top of these models DBMS software have been developed. These important data models have been listed below.

- Hierarchical Model.
- Network Model.
- Relational Model.
- E-R Model.
- Object Oriented Model.

While discussing data models some terms will be used in different models. A summary presented in a table 15.1 shall be helpful. Terms appearing on the same row are synonymous.

Table 15.1

Relational Model	E-R Model	Hierarchical & Network Model	Object Oriented Model
Table	Entity set	File	Class
Tuple or row	Entity	Record	Object
Attribute or Column name	Attribute	Field	Property

15.4.1 Hierarchical Model

In hierarchical model Data was structured hierarchically in form of forests of trees of records. Hierarchical model came into existence in 1960s. IBM's Product IMS, based on this model, came in 1971.

Features

- Basic logical structure is hierarchical and resembles an over turned tree

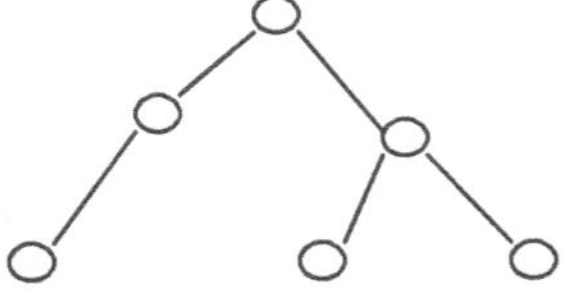

- The hierarchical structure contains levels.
- In hierarchical relationships each parent node can have many child node but each child can have one parent.
- This depicts a set of one-to-many (1:M) relationships between data.
- Data objects are records which are collection of fields. For example, **Product** record is represented by fields such as its name, specifications, unit price etc.
- In implementation, hierarchical database consists of a collection of records which are connected to another records through links

Advantages

- Many of the hierarchical data model's features formed the foundation for current data models
- Its database application advantages are replicated, albeit in a different form, in current database environments
- Generated a large installed (mainframe) base, created a pool of programmers who developed numerous tried-and-true business applications

Disadvantages

- Complex to implement
- Difficulty in implementing many to many relationships, where as in real world there are plenty of such relationships
- Lacks structural independence
- Implementation limitations
- Lack of standards or strong theoretical background

Example: Following relationships can be modeled by a hierarchical model

- A **shop** can supply one or many **Orders**
- A **shop** can supply one or many **customers**
- Each **Order** can contain one or more **Products**

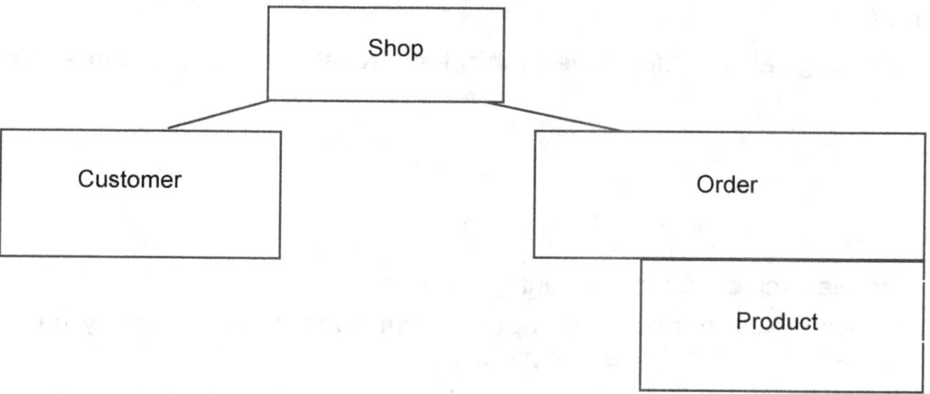

15.4.2 Network Model

A consortium of industry and government people, Codasyl-DBTG(Database Task Group) introduced a network database model in 1969. In this model data was structured as graphs of records, implemented through linked lists. This model had advantages over earlier hierarchical model

Features

- Network model based database consists of a collection of records which were related to one another by links
- In this model too, many-to many link was not allowed due to implementation problems but same was managed through intermediate nodes and all one to many relationships

Advantages

- Network databases modeled many to many relationship better than the way Hierarchical model handled

- Improved database performance
- Contributed towards database standardization
- Provided Data Definition Language(DDL) and Data Management Language(DML) support

Disadvantages

- Ad hoc query capability is not there
- Structural independence not there, changes in database structure forced major changes in application programs
- System implementation is complex

Example

We show by modeling following relationships in network model

- Each entry in **Order** belongs to exactly one **Product** and exactly one **Customer** i.e Order has one to many relationship with Product and Customer.
- A **Product** like pen-drive can be procured from more than one **Manufacturer** again a one to many relationship.
- A **Manufacturer** can have multiple **Depots** for supplying the Products, again an example of one to many relationship

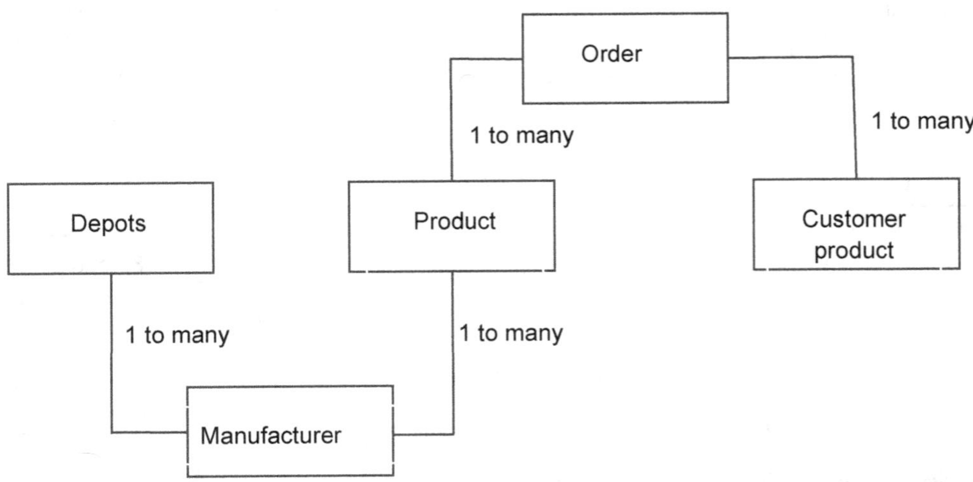

A Network Data Model representation

Lets further see, what fields are required for storing information in records for Order, Product, Manufacturer and Depot in the Table 15.2.

Table 15.2

File	Fields in the record
Customer	C_id, name, address, email, cell_number
Product	P-id, M_id, name, category, specifications, price
Order	C_id, P_id, quantity, date
Manufacturer	M_id, name, address, email, cell_number
Depot	M_id, D_id, address

Following diagram shows record level relationship in network model for simplicity we consider relationships among Order, Customer and Product only. Records in the diagram contain sample values for fields

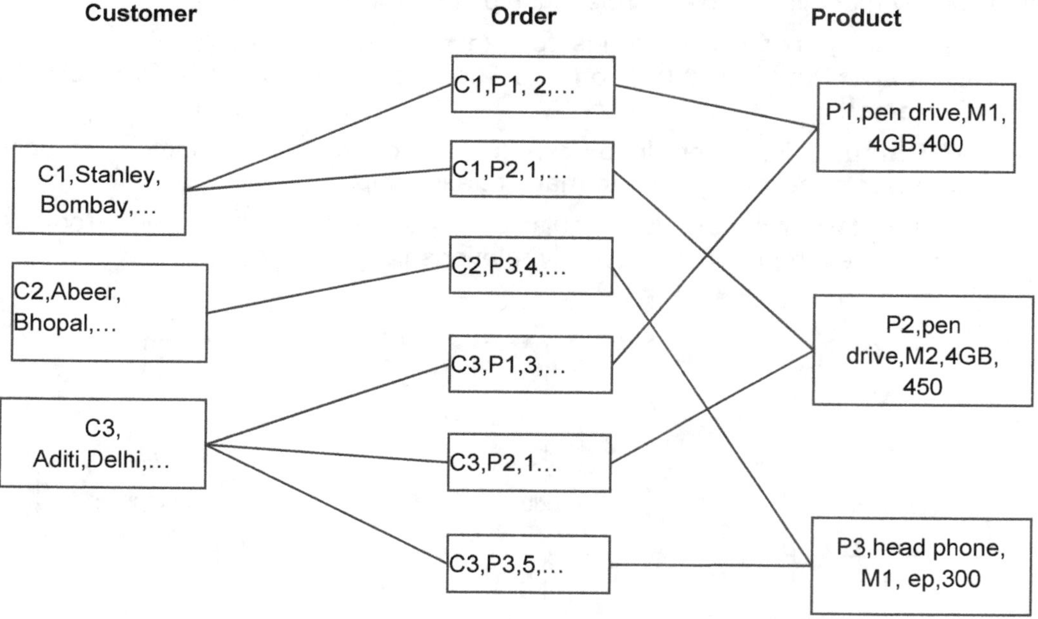

Representing record level relationship among records

15.4.3 Relational Model

Relational model is the most popular model amongst all. Based on relational model very popular Relational Database Management Systems (RDBMS) are developed. Development of RDBMS took place between 1970 and 1980. E. F. Codd's contributions are the foundations of RDBMS.

IBM has produced System R, SQL/DS and DB2 as their RDBMS products. ORACLE is market leader in RDBMS software in contemporary world. Some other popular RDBMS products are INGRESS, MS SQL Server, MS Access, MySQL,

RDBMS (Relational Database Management Systems):

Relational Model of DBMS became very popular and is used widely. There are two main reasons attributed to its success.

1. SQL being common in all RDBMS software.
2. Being based on strong foundation of Relational Algebra.

15.4.4 Entity-Relationship (E-R) Model

E-R model is a conceptual Model to describe a database. It greatly contributes to popular RDBMS systems. Database design in E-R model can be easily converted to design in the relational model. Automated tools like Rational ROSE can convert an E_R model to a database schema in a number of RDBMS software. Most RDBMS provide graphical E-R Model design facility; designed E-R Model can lead to tables in relational database in automatic manner.

In E-R Model, Entities and their Relationships are the central concept. Entities are real world objects like Customer, Product, Manufacturer, stock, and Shipment etc. There are relationships between entities. A Customer can buy one or more Products. A Product can be sold to one or more Customers. This is a many to many relationship between Customer and Product. Relationships between entities can be of one to one, one to many and many to many types.

E-R Model is a graphical representation of database. There are many ER modeling approaches that suggest different set of symbols for drawing ER Diagrams. Some popular ER Models are Chen's mode, Crow's foot model, Rein85 model and IDEFIX model. Here we use symbols commonly used for E-R Modeling. Symbols are given in following figure to draw an E-R diagram.

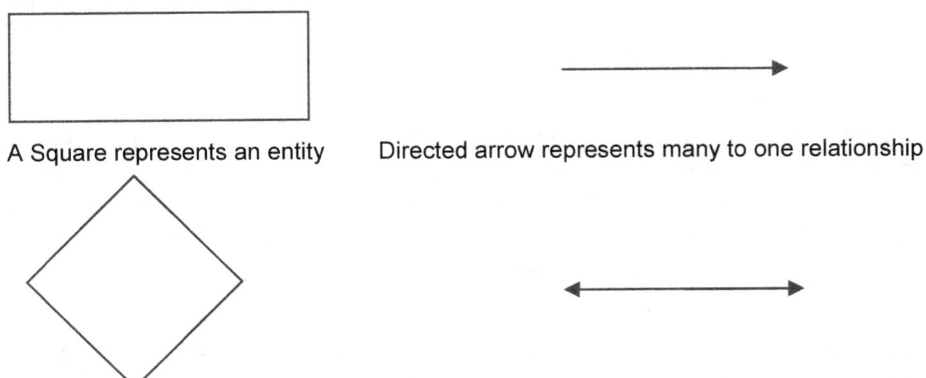

A Square represents an entity   Directed arrow represents many to one relationship

A diamond represents a relationship By-directional arrow represents one to one relationship

Example: E-R Model in the following figure presents relationship between Customer and Product.

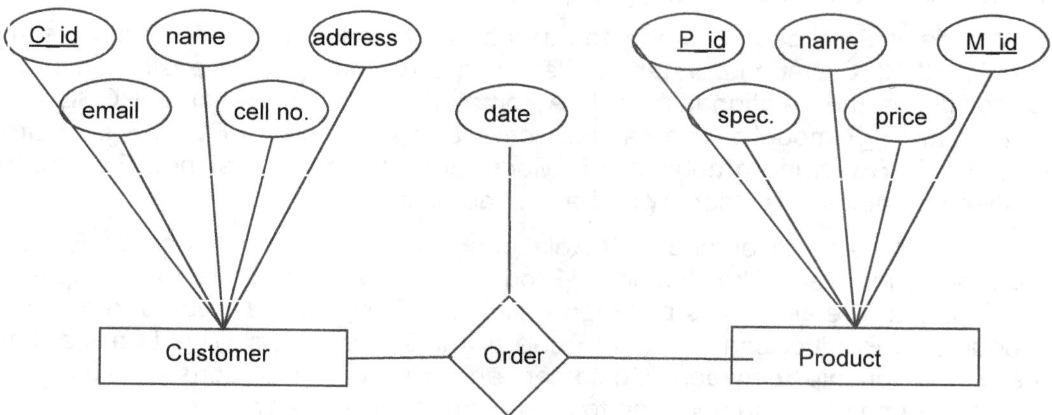

Observation/explanation

In above E-R diagram, entities are mentioned within rectangles and attributes of entities are within ovals. Here relationship between Customer and Product entities are many to many hence un-directional line has been drawn between these two. In one to many or many to one relationship we draw directional lines or arrows. In case of an arrow drawn, arrow points to 'one' and other end points to 'many' in one to many and many to one relationship.

Observe underlining of some attributes. It is a convention to underline the attributes that form the primary key of an entity. Primary key is capable of unique identification of an entity. Observe, we have also named the relationship as **Order**, moreover the relationship also have an attribute. Not all relationships have attributes. Entities in E-R model are transformed to tables when a corresponding database is created in a RDBMS. Tables are given same attributes as that of entities.

Sometimes relationships are also transformed to tables, such as 'Order' relationship in this case. To be specific, while converting many to many entities into database tables, it is a requirement that a table is also created for the relationship that essentially contains primary keys of both participating entities. While creating database tables to map one to many or many to one relationships, no separate table is required for relationship. This is accomplished by adding primary key attribute of an entity which is on 'one' side of relationship to the entity which is on 'many' side of the relationship.

There are more symbols in E-R modeling for modeling more complex data relationships. Some of these symbols are shown in the following figure

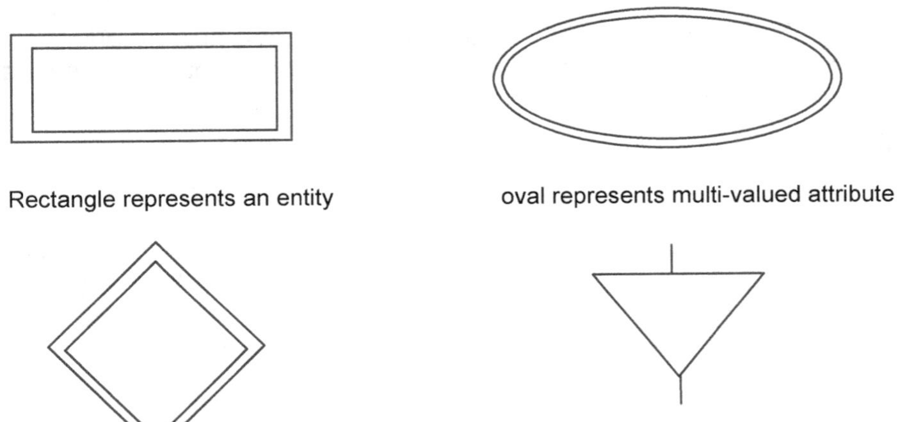

Rectangle represents an entity

oval represents multi-valued attribute

Diamond represents weak entity relationship   this shape represents is (specialization)

Strong and Weak Entities

Normal entities like student, vehicle, teacher, customer etc. are called strong entities as their uniqueness is ensured by one or a combination of some attributes. For example, entity student can be uniquely distinguished by its roll number. Student name cannot ensure uniqueness, as there can be more students with the same name.

There are some entities which need support of some strong entity for their existence. Such entities are called weak entities. Uniqueness of weak entities is ensured by adding to it, the primary key of its associated entity. Consider a scenario, where an organization extends medical benefits to the dependents of its employee; now as long as employee is working in the organization, company would like to maintain its dependents information in the database. In this scenario, employee is a strong entity whereas, dependent is a weak entity. E-R model has double outlined rectangle for representing weak entities and double outlined diamond shape to represent relationships with them.

Multi-valued attribute

An attribute of an entity which can take more than one values is called a muti-valued attribute. *Roll_number* attribute of entity *student* is single valued because every student has only one roll number. What about *hobby* attribute? A student may have zero, one or more hobbies. Hence it is a multi-valued attribute. While creating a database this information is to be conveyed. E-R model conveys this information by using a double outlined oval for multi-valued attribute representation.

We present one more E_R diagram example. For brevity and paucity of space, we have omitted mentioning of attributes in this example. However an E-R model does contain attributes too.

Example

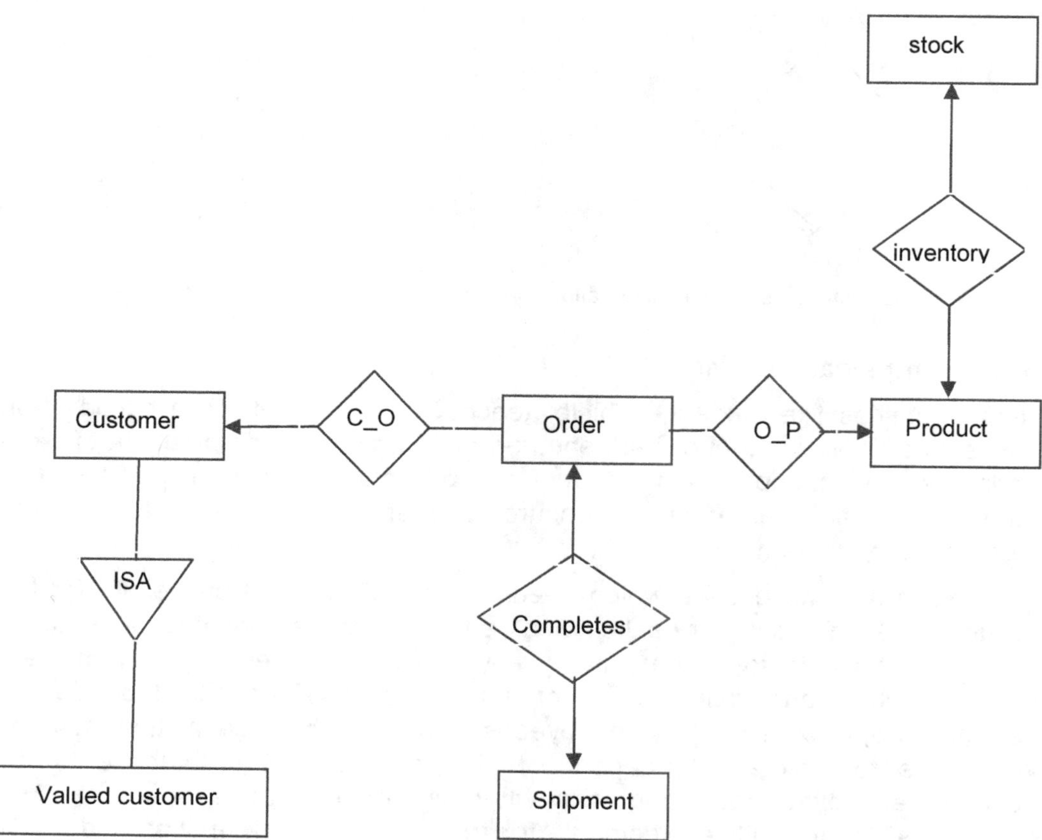

Advantages

- A picture says thousand words. An E-R model is graphical representation hence is not verbose. Its pictorial representation conveys a lot of information about database design requirements.

- It is simple to build.

- It is highly suitable to relational database design hence there are tools that convert E-R model to database table in an RDBMS. E_R modeling is integrated in many RDBMS software.

Observations and Explanation

In the above E-R model an entity **valued_customer** is related to **Customer** entity by 'is a' relationship. This is a specialization relationship modeling. Valued customers are special cases of Customers who purchase more frequently or they are old Customers. If a company wants to give them some special advantages, it would like to maintain their records. Valued_customer entity shall have attributes of Customer entity and will have more attributes like special_discount.

Relationship between Product and stock has one to one relationship shown as an arrow on both sides. Precisely, there will be one record in stock table for each one of the Product. There is one to one relation between Order and Shipment. Now, since each Customer can place any number of Orders but a particular Order shall belong to exactly one Customer. Similarly, one product can appear in many Orders but a record or tuple in an Order table shall point to a specific product. Hence these relationships are one to many as shown in E-R model by arrows.

15.4.5 Object Oriented Models

Object is the buzz word today. Object orientation is the core of modern software concepts.

While modeling real world objects, relational model needs its representation in two dimensional tables. In order to extend database technology to more complex domains object orientation concepts were applied to database. For database modeling of domains like multimedia, it is difficult to map objects in tables. Mapping of such objects and their relationships is easier using object oriented concepts. Thus object oriented models are capable of handling text, image, audio, and video and of course traditional data. Object oriented databases have features of object oriented technology, like polymorphism, dynamic binding etc.

However owing to the popularity and deep penetration of relational data base management systems, a hybrid approach called object relational model, is developed. Most of the commercially available RDBMS are enriched with object relational capabilities.

15.5 DBMS (Database Management Systems)

A few years back services like banking, rail reservation and alike were not computerized, offices used to have large number of pages of information. Every interaction with such services involved handling of physical files, registers and pages to record information. Every decision making required support of the information. This large collection of data to support information needed to operate is called database. That is, database was there even when computerization was not there. As data used grew it was a nightmare to handle data stored into cabinets in large offices.

A DBMS involves data, hardware, software and users that manage and use database.

A DBMS is software that defines a database, stores the data and provides set of programs to access data with ease.

With the advent of computers and automation of services 'database' has become important component of all vital application software. With efficient Database Management System it has become easy to handle large databases.

Sitting at home, with a few clicks of mouse you can book your rail reservation ticket from any source to any destination. Rail Reservation Website Software is supported by a database, managed by a DBMS software to book rail tickets.

Human life has been made easy by automation of common services like:

- Banking.
- Airline.
- Online Shopping.
- Rail Reservation.
- Electricity, Phone bill payment.
- Online Result.

You can add many more examples to this list.

All these software application development require support of database and in turn a Database Management System software.

15.5.1 Database

A database is a repository of data. Simply database is a place where large data is safely stored. Database is a collection of interrelated data stored in a standardized format to be shared by multiple users.

Database Examples are: Club member database, University database of student's information, database of products information for a company, Human resource database of a company.

Some databases used in more sophisticated applications are: Finger print database, Genome database, spatial database etc.

15.5.2 Primary Key

Primary key is used to implement uniqueness of the tuples in a table.

As a student you have a unique Enrollment Number, as a bank customer you have a unique Account Number. Even nowadays, Aadhar Cards are being made for each citizen of India that assigns a unique identification number to every citizen of India.

To ensure uniqueness of identity, some key attribute is required. In fact all above mentioned attributes are the primary keys in their own contexts.

With your unique roll number, it is ensured that you get your own result, even if there any many students that share your name or even your father's initials.

Let's consider following Customer table with some records in it.

Customer

C_id	name	city	email	Cell_phone
C1	stanley	mumbai	stanley@xy.com	9891234567
C2	Abeer	bhopal	abeer@xy.com	9987656544
C3	Aditi	delhi	aditi@xy.com	9987656543
C4	stanley	mumbai	Stanley2@xy.in	8891234445

Observe the attributes of Customer table and answer the question. Can 'Name' attribute uniquely identify Customer? Answer is 'no' as names are not unique. There can be more Customers with the same name. Here itself there are two stanleys, they share even their cities.

What is the primary key of above customer table? Answer is obviously, C_id. C_id is customer identification code which has been assigned to this table to ensure uniqueness of customers; in a manner same as students are alotted roll numbers.

In some tables there can be two attributes which can uniquely identify tuples in a table. For example roll_number and enroll_number in case of students.

Are both of these Primary Keys?

Answer is 'no', both are the candidate keys to be selected as Primary Key. Any of these can be chosen by database designer to become the primary key.

15.5.3 Foreign Key

A foreign key is an attribute in a relational database table that provides a reference to the primary key of another table. It establishes a link between data in two tables. It acts as a cross-reference between tables because it references the primary key of another table, thereby establishing a link between them.

Foreign key is used to implement referential integrity constraint.

To understand the concept let's consider tables **Manufacturer** and **Product**. Both these tables with some records are presented below

Product

P_id	M_id	Name	Categoty	Specification	Price
P1	M1	Pen drive	media	4 GB	400
P2	M2	Pen drive	media	4 GB	450
P3	M1	Head phone	speaker	ep	300

Manufacturer

M_id	name	city	emai	Cell_number
M1	HP	mumbai	sales@hp.com	9874321451
M2	Kingston	bhopal	sales@kingston.com	8765544321
M3	Creative	delhi	care@xy.com	9997776564

Observe that primary key of *Manufacturer* table, M_id is appearing in *Product* table. Database designer can declare M_id, as a **foreign** key of *Product* table. P_id is the primary key of *Product* table ensuring uniqueness of each Product. Foreign key, M_id in *Product* table is ensuring that you maintain only those records whose manufacturers are present in your *Manufacturer* table. Thus it is being ensured that you should have only those Products in your record which are produced by your associated manufacturers. If we try to enter a product's details in *Product* table where M_ id value is not present in Manufacturer table, it will not allow us. Here foreign key puts a constraint that all manufacturers in Product table should have a reference in Manufacturer *table*. Thus, foreign key implements referential integrity constraint. A table can have only one primary key but more than one foreign keys are possible.

15.5.4 Data Definition Language (DDL)

Creating database objects, altering and deleting them are known as data definition tasks. Database objects are like table, view, and index etc. For example, for automating a library a database would be needed. Creating a table for storing information of books is an example of data definition. DBMS supports these operations by providing a Data definition language (DDL). DDL commands are mainly CREATE, ALTER and DROP in SQL. Altering a database object design is like adding a column in a table which we did not define while creating the table. Using ALTER command Primary key or a Foreign key specifications can be added or removed, if required. If a table is not required any more in a database, it can be deleted using DROP command.

15.5.5 Data Manipulation Language (DML)

Data manipulation involves insertion, deletion and modification of data in database tables. Once database is designed, using DML commands data manipulation can be done. SQL provides commands synonymous to their operations, known as INSERT, DELETE and UPDATE. Here it can be pointed that, DELETE command can delete one or more records in a table whereas DDL command DROP can delete the structure of the table.

Performing queries for retrieval of data is referred as Data query operation. Sometimes it is also referred as a part of DML. Query operation is read only; it only fetches the desired data from data base but doesn't make changes in data. Usually querying means obtaining data from database that satisfies certain conditions specified in user query, such as obtaining the address of a specific student from a student table.

SQL provides versatile SELECT command for writing queries.

15.5.6 DBMS Architecture

Logical architecture of DBMS describes various levels of data abstraction.

Data Abstraction

In broad sense, abstraction means showing up necessary details and deferring complexity until they are required to be revealed. The complexity of data should not be seen at every level. By abstraction we need to present a useful view of data and expose limited amount of complexity.

Abstraction simply means, hiding unnecessary details and presenting a convenient useful view. For example when you want to learn Car driving, you are told that a car starts by switching the ignition, the internal mechanism is not explained because you don't need to learn it. To a car mechanic, more internal details are revealed because mechanic has to repair the machine if there is a fault. For different levels of users different levels of abstraction will be required.

Three Views of Data

DBMS design is based upon basically three views of data abstraction.

- External view
- Conceptual view
- Internal or Physical view

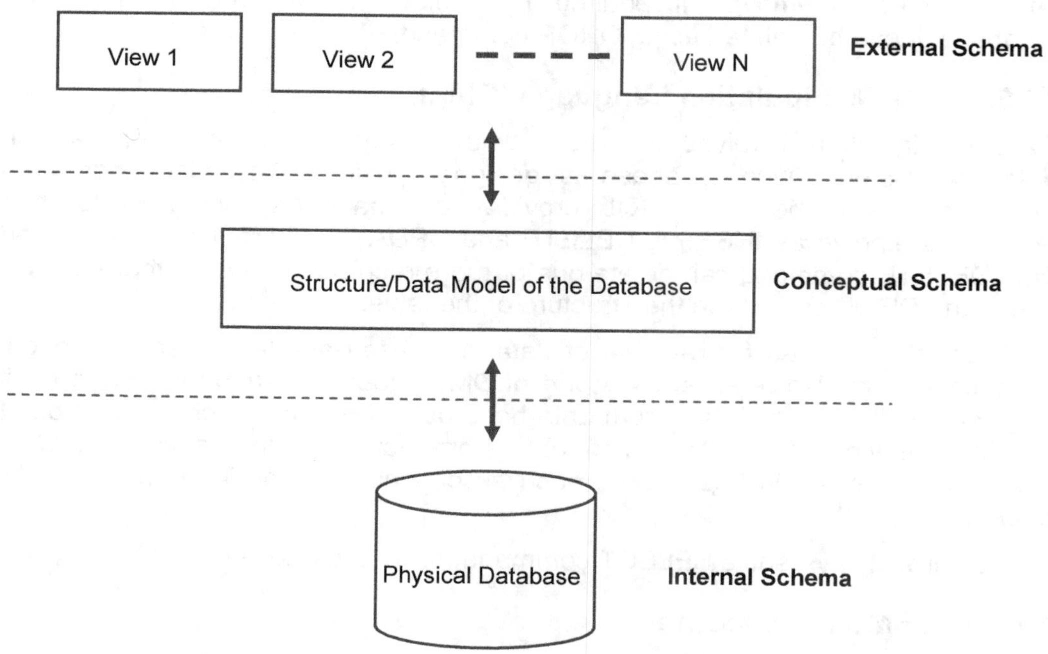

Three views of data

1. **External view:** External view is a view of data environment that is a simple and convenient view for the end user. The end user comprises of application developers and ad hoc users of a database.

    Advantages:

    - Application program development becomes simpler
    - Helps to increase security constraints in the database design
    - Easy to identify specific data required to support different business requirement

- Facilitates designer's job by providing feedback about the model's adequacy

2. **Conceptual view:** This intermediate view provides a relatively easily understood macro level view of data environment. This view explains the conceptual schema of database environment. Independent of software implementation details, this conceptual view is modeled using data models like E-R models. At this level of modeling, internals or physical details of data storage are completely abstracted.

   Advantages

   - Hardware level changes do not affect conceptual schema. For example if data moves to some faster storage media, your table structures do not get impacted
   - Database designers are free from the intricacies of physical data design

3. **Physical or Internal view:** This view deals with the physical level, describing the data storage at hardware level. Knowledge of storage medium and hardware level knowledge is needed by the designers of physical schema. This level maps the conceptual model to the DBMS

15.5.7 Data Independence

Data independence is the property which ensures that if changes are made at some level the schema at its immediately above levels is least affected.

For example if changes are made at conceptual level, application programmes running on top of the database keep executing.

Data independence is classified into physical data independence and logical data independence

1. **Physical Data Independence:** This means that for any change made in the physical schema, the need to change the logical schema is minimal. If database is to be ported to some faster storage medium, a momentary halt may take place for database users; after database is ported normal functioning resumes. There is no effect on program execution and hence on end users. Physical data independence is less difficult to implement as compared to that of logical data independence.

2. **Logical Data Independence:** If the users of database are not affected with the changes in conceptual schema we say logical data independence has been achieved. If schema designers are forced to make changes in the structure then it is to be done in a manner that programmers and end users do not feel that changes have occurred. Though RDBMS supports to achieve logical data independence, it is skillful to achieve this.

15.5.8 Data Dictionary

Data dictionary in a DBMS is centrally located repository of data descriptions maintained by Data base administrator using data definition language. Data dictionary contains Meta data. Meta data means data about data. To put it simply data dictionary contains data definitions/information about tables, views, attributes, keys etc along with descriptive text for the user.

Data dictionary may be referenced during database system design, can be referred during program design and during program execution. It is a catalogue of data. Data dictionary can be maintained separately or as an integral part of database. But, Data dictionary is an integral part in most RDMBS and it is active too. Active data dictionary means that it automatically updated as and when changes are made in data base design. Since data base is designed for a large number of users one can refer data dictionary to understand a database. Data dictionary also helps to maintain data integrity.

In RDBMS, data dictionary is maintained in the form of a database table. Data dictionary is also maintained using Excel tables, xml files etc.

15.5.9 Users of a DBMS

A variety of individuals interact with DBMS for different purposes. Following are the typical users of DBMS.

- End user
- Application Programmers
- Sophisticated users

1. **End users:** End users are Naïve users, they are common man. These users interact with an already developed application for their needs. They do not require any knowledge about Database technology. Some examples of such users are:

    - Student accessing their exam results.

    - A bank account holder making an online payment.

2. **Application Programmers:** Application programmers develop application software using high level languages and query languages. They need to access DBMS for their data needs. DBMS should offer a view of database to suit their data requirements.

3. **Sophisticated users:** Sophisticated users have requirements which sometimes standard application software may not address. Such users have knowledge of query languages and they write queries using query language to access database to suit their data requirements.

15.5.10 Database Administrator (DBA)

DBMS is complex software that requires a team of people to manage database of enterprise. This team installs, runs, maintains and upgrades DBMS. Database Administrator or DBA is a person who plays a key role in making an efficient use of Database.

His/her roles are summarized below:

- **Creation of Database:** DBA conceptualize the requirements. DBA designs database scheme using data models. Implements database scheme by creating database, then loads the database with actual data.

- **Interface between Users and Database:** DBA works as a liaison between user community and database. DBA understands user requirements and facilitates them with efficient use of database.

- **Maintaining privacy of Data:** DBA restricts the uses of data by granting limited rights to user by giving passwords. Different users at different level are given access rights of using data only as per their needs, thus protecting unauthorized access to database.

- **Ensuring data Integrity:** DBA puts constraints to database to ensure data integrity. As an example, in an education system a student cannot get marks less than zero. DBA shall implement this constraint/restriction so that marks are never less than zero even if somebody deliberately tries to do so.

- **Keeping Data Secure:** DBA is in-charge of security of database. DBA takes frequent backups of databases and protects the database from accidental damages or even from natural calamities.

- **Responding to the Changes in requirements:** Operation in enterprise is dynamic and changes take place. This forces changes in Application Software that subsequently needs changes in database. DBA has to support to this function.

- **Monitoring Performance of Database:** Over the period of time if database becomes slow due to increased size or any other reason, DBA has to fine tune it to improve its performance. DBA may shift database to a faster storage system or make internal changes to improve its performance.

15.6 An Introduction to SQL

SQL is common to most RDBMS with minor variations. For better understanding of DBMS it would be relevant to present here, some important DDL and DML commands of SQL with suitable examples.

We consider an online shop database with two tables as given below

Table	Column names
Product	P_id, M_id, name, Category, Specifications, Price
Manufacturer	M_id, Name, city, cell_number

Product table has P_id as its primary key. Manufacturer table has M_id as its primary key. M_id also appears in Product table to ensure that only those products are entered in Product table, for which we have a manufacturer detail available in Manufacturer table. Hence we will declare M_id as a foreign key in Product table referencing Manufacturer table.

We will write DDL commands and DML commands to accomplish following tasks. SQL queries/commands have been executed in MS Access 2007.

1. Create table Manufacturer and declare M_id as its primary key.

```
CREATE TABLE Manufacturer
    (M_id Text(10) PRIMARY KEY,
    Name TEXT(30),
        city TEXT(30),
        cell_number number);
```

CREATE TABLE command creates Manufacturer table with column names M_id, Name, city and cell_number. TEXT is a data type that makes the variable capable of storing text type data. Here we have sealing of 30 characters for storage in our TEXT variables; it can be made more or less depending on requirements. Similarly, NUMBER data type declares the variable of numeric type.

2. Insert a few records in Manufacturer table

```
INSERT INTO Manufacturer (M_id, Name, city, cell_number)
    VALUES('M1', 'HP', 'Mumbai', 9874321451);


INSERT INTO Manufacturer (M_id, Name, city, cell_number)
    VALUES('M2', 'Kingston', 'Bhopal', 8765544321);


INSERT INTO Manufacturer
    VALUES('M3', 'Creative', 'Delhi', 9997776564);
```

Syntax of INSERT INTO command requires table name, attribute names and values. Observe that text values are to be included within quotes. Also observe third statement where attribute names have been omitted. In fact if we are assigning values to all the attributes of the table, attribute names can be omitted from the syntax.

3. List all Manufacturers

SELECT *

FROM Manufacturer;

Output

M_id	Name	city	cell_number
M1	HP	Mumbai	9874321451
M2	Kingston	Bhopal	8765544321
M3	Creative	Delhi	9997776564

4. Try to insert a record with already used PRIMARY KEY value

INSERT INTO Manufacturer

VALUES('M3', 'Dell', 'Delhi', 9996667771);

It should not be allowed, as M3 value is already assigned to an existing record. Hence Microsoft Access is not happy and scolds us through a message box. Message box says many things including .....*it did not add a record to the table due to key violations..* Thus Primary Key ensures uniqueness of records.

5. Create table Product and declare P_id as its primary key.

CREATE TABLE Product

(P_id Text(10) PRIMARY KEY,

M_id TEXT(10),

Name TEXT(30),

Category TEXT(30),

Specifications TEXT(30),

Price CURRENCY)

Here a new data type CURRENCY is assigned to Price. This data type is basically numeric but associates some currency with it. Default currency assigned is $.

6. Insert a few records in Product

```
INSERT INTO Product
    VALUES ('P1','M1', 'Pen drive', 'media','4 GB',400);
INSERT INTO Product
    VALUES ('P2','M2', 'Pen drive', 'media','4 GB',450);
INSERT INTO Product
    VALUES ('P3','M1', 'Head Phone', 'speaker','ep',300);
```

7. Display all products, whose category is 'media'

```
SELECT *
    FROM  Product
    WHERE Category='media';
```

Output

P_id	M_id	Name	Category	Specifications	Price
P1	M1	Pen drive	media	4 GB	$400.00
P2	M2	Pen drive	media	4 GB	$450.00

Select is a most frequently used command in SQL. This does not alter any values in the table but simply retrieves data from the database.

SELECT specifies the attributes to be displayed. If all attributes are to be displayed then * does the job. Instead of writing names of all attributes simply * can be used. Clause FROM specifies the name of the table from which data is to be retrieved. Clause WHERE filters the record set using the mentioned condition; only those records are displayed that match the condition specified in this clause. In Price column "$" has been inserted as it is default setting for CURRENCY data types.

8. Declare M_id as foreign key in Product table

```
ALTER TABLE Product
    ADD CONSTRAINT
    Fk1 FOREIGN KEY (M_id) REFERENCES Manufacturer (M_id);
```

9. Try to insert a record in Product table with M_id not present in Manufacturer table

INSERT INTO Product

VALUES ('P4', 'M10', 'Head set', 'speaker', 'ep',600);

It should not be allowed as M10 value is not there in Manufacturer table.

Microsoft beeps and displays a message box. Message box says .....*it did not add a record to the table due to key violations* and blah-blah–blah. Ponit is that declaration of Foreign key stops violation of referential integrity.

10. List Product name and Manufacturer name by joining the two tables

SELECT Product.Name, Manufacturer.Name

FROM Product, Manufacturer

WHERE Product.M_id=Manufacturer.M_id;

Output

Product. Name	Manufacturer. Name
Pen drive	HP
Pen drive	Kingston
Head Phone	HP

This query was more demanding as the result was to be procured from two different tables having common attribute M_id. Clause FROM contains names of two tables, the Product and the Manufacturer tables. This leads to **cartesian product of these two data sets. It means that each row of first table is paired with eve**ry other row of second table specified in the FROM clause. Resultant output contains m x n rows, if there are m rows in first table and n rows in second table. Similarly, there are p + q attributes including p attributes of first table and q attributes of second table. Before displaying this meaningless result, it is filtered with the condition specified in the WHERE clause and only those attributes are displayed which are available on SELECT clause. Observe that, M_id appears in both the tables, hence it is required to be preceded with a dot and their table names to avoid confusion.

11. Increase price of all Products by 10%

UPDATE Product

SET Price = Price * 1.1;

UPDATE command modifies the values based on the statement after SET clause. In this case Price value of all the records is multiplied by 110% as there is no WHERE clause. If required WHERE clause can be included, as it is an optional part of UPDATE clause.

12. Delete all Products where price is less than 400

    DELETE FROM Product

        WHERE Price < 400;

    SELECT *

        FROM product;

Output

P_id	M_id	Name	Category	Specifications	Price
P1	M1	Pen drive	media	4 GB	$440.00
P2	M2	Pen drive	media	4 GB	$495.00

Here DELETE statement has been used with a where condition. In current instance of Product table only one record satisfies the condition and hence it is deleted. SELECT statement displays the output.

13. Remove Products table from the database

    DROP TABLE Product;

This command is to be used with utmost care, it is a DDL command that deletes the table itself.

Above mentioned SQL- DDL and DML examples present fairly good idea of simplicity and power of SQL. However, it is only the tip of the iceberg. Each of the statements used in the queries have lot more features. For the sake of avoiding complexity the detailed syntax is not given here.

CHAPTER 16

Cloud Computing

The term cloud as appears to have its origins in network diagrams that represented the internet, or various parts of it, as schematic clouds. "Cloud computing" was coined for what happens when applications and services are moved into the internet "cloud." Cloud computing is not something that suddenly appeared overnight; in some form it may trace back to a time when computer systems remotely time-shared computing resources and applications. More currently though, cloud computing refers to the many different types of services and applications being delivered in the internet cloud, and the fact that, in many cases, the devices used to access these services and applications do not require any special applications.

Many companies are delivering services from the cloud. Such as:

- **Google:** Has a private cloud that it uses for delivering many different services to its users, including email access, document applications, text translations, maps, web analytics, and much more.

- **Microsoft:** Has Microsoft Share point online service that allows for content and business intelligence tools to be moved into the cloud, and Microsoft currently makes its office applications available in a cloud.

- **Salesforce.com:** Runs its application set for its customers in a cloud, and its Force.com and Vmforce.com products provide developers with platforms to build customized cloud services.

16.1 Features

Cloud computing has a variety of Features such as

- **Shared Infrastructure:** Uses a virtualised software model, enabling the sharing of physical services, storage, and networking capabilities. The cloud infrastructure, regardless of deployment model, seeks to make the most of the available infrastructure across a number of users.

- **Dynamic Provisioning:** Allows for the provision of services based on current demand requirements. This is done automatically using software automation, enabling the expansion and contraction of service capability, as needed. This dynamic scaling needs to be done while maintaining high levels of reliability and security.

- **Network Access:** Needs to be accessed across the internet from a broad range of devices such as PCs, laptops, and mobile devices, using standards-based APIs (for example, ones based on HTTP). Deployments of services in the cloud include everything from using business applications to the latest application on the newest smart phones.

- **Managed Metering:** uses metering for managing and optimizing the service and to provide reporting and billing information. In this way, consumers are billed for services according to how much they have actually used during the billing period.

In short, cloud computing allows for the sharing and scalable deployment of services, as needed, from almost any location, and for which the customer can be billed based on actual usage.

16.2 Service Models

Once a cloud is established, how its cloud computing services are deployed in terms of business models can differ depending on requirements. The primary service models being deployed are commonly known as:

- **Software as a Service (SaaS):** Consumers purchase the ability to access and use an application or service that is hosted in the cloud. A benchmark example of this is Salesforce.com, where necessary information for the interaction between the consumer and the service is hosted as part of the service in the cloud.

    Also, Microsoft is expanding its involvement in this area, and as part of the cloud computing option for Microsoft Office 2010, its Office Web Apps are available to Office volume licensing customers and Office Web App subscriptions through its cloud-based Online Services.

- **Platform as a Service (PaaS):** Consumers purchase access to the platforms, enabling them to deploy their own software and applications in the cloud. The operating systems and network access are not managed by the consumer, and there might be constraints as to which applications can be deployed.

- **Infrastructure as a Service (IaaS):** Consumers control and manage the systems in terms of the operating systems, applications, storage, and network connectivity, but do not themselves control the cloud infrastructure.

Also known are the various subsets of these models that may be related to a particular industry or market.

Communications as a Service (CaaS): is one such subset model used to describe hosted IP telephony services. Along with the move to CaaS is a shift to more IP-centric communications and more SIP trucking deployments. With IP and SIP in place, it can be as easy to have the PBX in the cloud as it is to have it on the premise. In this context, CaaS could be seen as a subset of SaaS.

16.3 Deployment Models

Deploying cloud computing can differ depending on requirements, and the following four deployment models have been identified, each with specific characteristics that support the needs of the services and users of the clouds in particular ways

- **Private Cloud:** The cloud infrastructure has been deployed, and is maintained and operated for a specific organization. The operation may be in-house or with a third party on the premises.

- **Community Cloud:** The cloud infrastructure is shared among a number of organizations with similar interests and requirements. This may help limit the capital expenditure costs for its establishment as the costs are shared among the organizations. The operation may be in-house or with a third party on the premises.

- **Public Cloud:** The cloud infrastructure is available to the public on a commercial basis by a cloud service provider. This enables a consumer to develop and deploy a service in the cloud with very little financial outlay compared to the capital expenditure requirements normally associated with other deployment options.

- **Hybrid Cloud:** The cloud infrastructure consists of a number of clouds of any type, but the clouds have the ability through their interfaces to allow data and/or applications to be moved from one cloud to another. This can be a combination of private and public clouds that support the requirement to retain some data in an organisation, and also the need to offer services in the cloud.

16.4 Pros and Cons

16.4.1 Pros

The following are some of the possible Pro for those who offer cloud computing-based services and applications:

- **Cost Savings:** Companies can reduce their capital expenditures and use operational expenditures for increasing their computing capabilities. This is a lower barrier to entry and also requires fewer in-house IT resources to provide system support.

- **Scalability/Flexibility:** Companies can start with a small deployment and grow to a large deployment fairly, rapidly, and then scale back if necessary. Also, the flexibility of cloud computing allows companies to use extra resources at peak times, enabling them to satisfy consumer demands.

- **Reliability:** Services using multiple redundant sites can support business continuity and disaster recovery.

- **Maintenance:** Cloud service providers do the system maintenance, and access is through APIs that do not require application installations onto PCs, thus further reducing maintenance requirements.

- **Mobile Accessible:** Mobile workers have increased productivity due to systems accessible in an infrastructure available from anywhere.

16.4.2 Cons

The following are some of the notable Cons associated with cloud computing, and although some of these may cause a slowdown when delivering more services in the cloud, most also can provide opportunities, if resolved with due care and attention in the planning stages.

- **Security and Privacy:** Perhaps two of the more hot button issues surrounding cloud computing relate to storing and securing data, and monitoring the use of the cloud by the service providers. These issues are generally attributed to slowing the deployment of cloud services. These challenges can be addressed, for example, by storing the information internal to the organisation, but allowing it to be used in the cloud. For this to occur, though, the security mechanisms between organisation and the cloud need to be robust and a Hybrid cloud could support such a deployment.

- **Lack of Standards:** Clouds have documented interfaces; however, no standards are associated with these, and thus it is unlikely that most clouds will be interoperable. The Open Grid Forum is developing an Open Cloud Computing Interface to resolve this issue and the Open Cloud Consortium is working on cloud computing standards and practices. The findings of these groups will need to mature, but it is not known whether they will address the needs of the people deploying the services and the specific interfaces these services need. However, keeping up to date on the latest standards as they evolve will allow them to be leveraged, if applicable.

- **Continuously Evolving:** User requirements are continuously evolving, as are the requirements for interfaces, networking, and storage. This means that a cloud, especially a public one, does not remain static and is also continuously evolving.

- **Compliance Concerns:** The Sarbanes-Oxley Act (SOX) in the US and Data Protection directives in the EU are just two among many compliance issues affecting cloud computing, based on the type of data and application for which the cloud is being used. The EU has a legislative backing for data protection across all member states, but in the US data protection is different and can vary from state to state. As with security and privacy mentioned previously, these typically result in Hybrid cloud deployment with one cloud storing the data.

Index

L

Laptop, 50

Leibnitz's machine, 29

Light pen, 57

Linear structure, 239

Linked list, 257

LISP, 162

Lists, 255

Local Area Network (LAN), 285

Logic errors or logical errors, 175

Logical operator, 189

LOGO, 163

M

Machine language, 155

Macro virus, 331

Magnetic Ink
Character Readers (MICR), 60

Magnetic media, 308

Magnetic tape, 81

Main frame computers, 46

MAN, 287

Media, 291

Medical transcription, 20

Memory management, 100

Memory, 8

Merge sort, 277

Mesh topology, 301

Message passing, 213

Message switching, 305

Meteorology and climatology, 12

Metropolitan Area Network (MAN), 285

Micro computers, 46

Microprocessors, 40

Microsoft word, 102

Mini computers, 46

MODULA-2, 163

Monitor, 6

Mouse, 57

Multimedia and animation, 12

Multi-processing, 85

Multi-programming, 84

Multi-valued attribute, 354

M-Way search trees, 273

N

Napier's bones, 29

Natural languages, 164

Network access, 317

Network layer, 315

Network model, 346

Network Operating System (NOS), 293

Network, 283

O

Object language, 165

Object oriented model, 346

Object oriented, 181

Objects, 213

OOPs, 181

Operating system, 83

Optical bar code readers, 60

Optical Character Reader (OCR), 60

Optical Mark Readers (OMR), 60

Optical scanners, 60

OS, 83

OSI reference model, 313

W

Web browser, 321
while Loop, 191
Wide Area Network (WAN), 285
Wireless network, 285, 287

Workstation, 50
Worms, 323
WWW, 322

X

XGA, 66